GERMAN
FEMINIST
WRITINGS

GERMAN FEMINIST WRITINGS

Edited by Patricia A. Herminghouse
and Magda Mueller

CONTINUUM

NEW YORK · LONDON

2001

The Continuum International Publishing Group Inc
370 Lexington Avenue, New York, NY 10017

The Continuum International Publishing Group Ltd
The Tower Building, 11 York Road, London SE1 7NX

The German Library is published in cooperation with
Deutsches Haus, New York University.
This volume has been supported by Inter Nationes,
and a grant from the funds of
Stifterverband für die Deutsche Wissenschaft.

Printed in the United States of America

Library of Congress Cataloging-in-Publication Data

German feminist writings / edited by Patricia Herminghouse and Magda Mueller.
p.   cm. — (The German library ; v. 95)
Includes bibliographical references.
ISBN 0-8264-1280-7 (alk. paper) — ISBN 0-8264-1281-5 (pbk. : alk. paper)
1. Women—Germany—History.   2. Women—Germany—Social conditions.   3.
Feminism—Germany.   I. Herminghouse, Patricia.   II. Mueller, Magda.   III. Series.

HQ1623 .G468   2001
305.42′0943′—dc21
00-057007

Contents

Contents · vii

Contents · ix

ISSUES OF GENDER

Contents · xiii

Contents · xv

Introduction

The desire to offer, in one volume, a spectrum of German feminist thought from a period of more than two hundred fifty years posed a challenge that we have tried to meet with several principles of selectivity: first, by identifying five topical clusters of central cultural and historical importance (Education for Girls and Women, Women and Work, Women and Politics, Issues of Gender, and Women in Art and Literature); second, by seeking a balance between more and less familiar representatives of various strands of feminist thinking; and, finally, by deciding—not without misgivings—to excerpt key portions of many longer texts. Nonetheless, more than a few that an individual reader or editor might expect to find had to be left out— and others appear which may not correspond to contemporary understandings of feminism, our own included. We have sought to offer an interdisciplinary point of view and to reflect, historically and thematically, the diversity of feminist thought in German-speaking societies.

The present collection of texts dealing with "women's issues" needs to be read against the historical backdrop of arguments that emphasize the inferiority of women and defines this as their God-given nature. Through the centuries, the debate on the human equality of women has often been carried out in theological and philosophical terms, including at times the question of whether women even have a soul. It is well to recall that the last witch trials in Germany took place in 1755, more or less contemporaneously with the appearance of the earliest texts in this volume. And since these oppressive concepts of women's nature have endured, in a variety of guises, so women have likewise persisted in attempts to represent their own interests.

Education for Girls and Women

Although there had always been individual women (or groups of women, such as nuns) who were able to achieve a certain amount of learning, the move to improve women's access to education—which emerged in the wake of the Enlightenment and continued until the admission of women to the German university at the end of the nineteenth century—was viewed as the necessary first step toward the human emancipation of women. Since their duty had been defined for centuries in terms of keeping house and bearing children, women's pursuit of literacy was often perceived as frivolous or even disruptive. The advancement of women's education in Germany was behind the progressive developments in England, Switzerland, and the United States, where, at Oberlin College for instance, women were already allowed to study together with men in 1833; and several first-rate colleges for women were also founded in the 1830s. That demands for equal education of women were expressed more belatedly in Germany was in part due to the late arrival of industrialization and to the fact that Germany was not a unified nation until 1871.

Before the impact of the early feminists, in bourgeois circles a girl's education had been seen as complete when she was adequately prepared to manage whatever household funds might be allocated to her as wife, to supervise servants and organize the preparation and seasonal preservation of food, and to oversee the production of household goods, including domestic linens and clothing. Furthermore, she was to be educated in the arts of entertainment: playing the piano, reading poetry, and exercising conversational skills. With the development of technology and industrialization, as well as women's own changing self-perceptions, the content of education for girls and women underwent enormous changes, although attitudes toward education continued to reflect class differences. For daughters of the bourgeoisie, the question was often framed in terms of the return that an investment in education would bring to the family and society. Whereas the bourgeois women's movement was also concerned with the education of working-class women, for women of the emerging proletariat, many of whom had barely learned to read, it remained a secondary question.

Early on, some women refused to accept that access to knowledge depended on gender. An early example of a woman's desire to open her intellectual horizons beyond the domestic sphere is the 1777 poem by Nantchen Göckingk (1743–81), who rebels against the idea that a woman's life should be limited to conventional household chores. In "A Letter from Dorothea Schlözer to Luise Michaelis" (1785), an early form of individual consciousness-raising is evident in the young writer's declaration that since women and men are both human beings, a woman's goal in life should not be focused on amusing the man, but on attaining a higher level of cultivation that would enable their mutual happiness.

Even before the middle of the eighteenth century, a few women had begun to pursue the right to university study. The first German woman physician, Dorothea Christiane Leporin (1715–62), takes up the issue in her "Thorough Investigation of the Causes That Prevent the Female Sex from Attending the University" (1742). After establishing that the exclusion of women from education leads to a contempt for learning, however, Leporin emphasizes that she has no intent of "persuading the entire female sex to pursue their studies as a career" but merely wants to assert the unfairness of excluding women because of their domestic duties.

Addressing "Woman's Obligation toward the Higher Cultivation of the Mind" in 1802, Amalie Holst (1758–1829) demands an end to educational discrimination of "one entire half of the human race" and rejects misogynist arguments regarding both the "physical and mental predispositions" that undermine women's fitness for knowledge and the incompatibility of the intellectual life with their womanly obligations. A few years later, Betty Gleim (1781–1827), too, takes up the question of "Education and Instruction of the Female Sex" (1810). In her detailed analysis of the ambiguities of the term *femininity,* she counters prejudices that exclude women from education by insisting on their inclusion in the category of human being.

In the mid-nineteenth century, Louise Otto-Peters (1819–95) also challenged the custom of considering female education completed at the age of fourteen. In "Participation of the Feminine Sphere in Affairs of the State" (1847), she emphasizes the importance of improvements in their further education for the good of society, suggesting reforms, for example, in the teaching of history. True femininity, she argues, is promoted by an education that would enable women to live independently with dignity, without the need to sell themselves as wives to men. A few years later, in "Instruction for Women" (1856), Luise Büchner (1821–77) appeals to parents to demand the most rigorous intellectual education, including the natural sciences, for their daughters rather than the "purely mechanical learning" to which they were being subjected.

This line of argumentation is continued by Fanny Lewald (1811–89) in "Treat Us like Men so That We Can Become Competent Women" (1870), where she maintains that before one can think about such privileges as university studies, the state must provide appropriate secondary education for all. She holds that women's schooling has been extremely superficial and demands the development of equal competence in girls and boys. While praising the opening of the Victoria Lyceum for women, which was under the special protection of Empress Victoria of Prussia, Lewald also adds that such education should not remain a luxury for only the privileged.

The always provocative Hedwig Dohm (1833–1919) was one of the first nineteenth-century feminists to argue for women's admission to university study. In her essay "Are Women Allowed to Study? Can They Do It? Should They?" (1874), she points out that in the United States women are already allowed to study and argues—as did other feminists before her—that women are human beings and therefore entitled to equal educational opportunities.

Another aspect of Louise Otto-Peters's concern with education for women emerges in "Hopes for the Future" (1876). Here she recounts technological developments in the domestic sphere, such as matches, running water, oil and gas heat, as well as innovations in women's education that lead her to hope for broader access to higher education. By the time she wrote "On the Domestic Education of Girls" (1876), kindergarten, elementary schools, and boarding schools for women had already been successfully established; but, she notes, the shift of education to institutional settings also increases the importance of experiences within the family, including play activities. She condemns, for example, the overemphasis on elegant dolls and dollhouses, equipped with every imaginable domestic utensil, as opposed to playthings that activate young imaginations, or pets and gardens that promote responsibility.

The increasing number of unmarried women in Germany, who were turning to teaching and nursing to support themselves, also led to a call for higher education for women by Helene Lange (1848–1930). In dealing with Germany in *Higher Education of Women in Europe* (1889), she addresses the supposed moral threats posed by coeducation by referring to the constructive measures instituted in England and even suggesting the possibility of women as administrators.

In the first decade of a new century, Hedwig Dohm's comments on "The Reform of Girl's Schools" (1908) draws attention to the persistence of gender prejudice in the education system from early childhood through secondary school. Looking back at her own experience, she criticizes "the physical and intellectual inhibition that crippled every gifted female soul," a point that is reiterated by Alice Salomon (1872–1948) in "Twenty Years Ago" (1913). Salomon— who herself had a university degree in economics—stresses, however, the fulfillment that middle-class women could find in social service.

After emigrating to the United States from Nazi Germany in 1937, she found it difficult to continue her activities.

Gertrud Bäumer (1873–1954), the life companion of Helene Lange, recounts the difficulties she encountered as one of the first women admitted to university studies in her memoir "In the Light of Memory" (1953). Despite a pervasive male-fraternity culture and professors who were able to limit women's participation in seminars, she recalls individuals who were supportive of them. Often identified as the "Anna O" of Freudian theory, Bertha Pappenheim (1859–1936) reviews in "The Jewish Girl" (1934) the severe limitations of the upbringing that Viennese girls of her class received, aimed as it was at preparation for marriage. A cofounder of the Jüdischer Frauenbund (League of Jewish Women) in 1904, she died a natural death before the worst of the Nazi genocide began.

The postwar years in Germany have been marked by an increased presence of racially mixed Germans, who now number over five hundred thousand and, particularly since the 1980s, have begun to speak out about their treatment. In "At Home en Route: A German Life" (1998), Ika Hügel-Marshall (1947–) describes her comfortable upbringing as a black "occupation child" in her white German family until—for her benefit and her personal as well as career development, as she was told—she is sent in the 1950s to a girls' home under fundamentalist auspices. The education she endures there, by women who profess "Christian morals," entails the double humiliation of the cruel discipline inflicted on the girls and insidious racial prejudice.

Women and Work

Whereas there was no question of whether women of the lower classes could work—it was a matter of fact that they had to work for a living—it was a different matter for middle- and upper-class women. With the development of technology and industrialization, a pauperization of the bourgeoisie and the lower-middle class occurred that—as a direct result—had even more women looking for work. "Women's work," of course, always included housework. While in the centuries before mechanization and industrialization women produced most of what households needed, the nineteenth century reflects a move away from this role. Masses of women began working outside the home in jobs other than the "feminine" professions of teaching and nursing—at first in factories and later, as advances in business and industry required more administration, as white-collar workers. Even before the "double burden" was publicly addressed, women spent most of the time when they were not working outside the home on household tasks. In the debate about housekeeping reforms, suggested improvements ranged from the organization of communal households to the efficient single-family kitchen.

Although women's labor always has been perceived as cheap labor, the struggle for fair treatment has gone on for more than a century. Examples in this section extend from the fight for unionization of working women to the still-unsatisfactory attempt to implement gender equality at the level of communal administration. Two texts by Louise Otto-Peters center around "women's work" in the mid-nineteenth century. "The Lace-Makers" (1851), a poem, reflects the harsh working and living conditions of homeworkers who produce delicate laces for the rich at great cost to their well-being. To change these conditions required the kind of organization she suggests in "For the Female Workers" (1849), where she also elaborates on the exploitative working conditions and fierce competition faced by the (often old) women and children who, for example, knit stockings or embroider linens. Louise Dittmar (1807–84), picking up on earlier critiques of the drudgery that confines women to the home, offers in "Domestic Life" (1848) some radical solutions, well in advance of later nineteenth-century feminists, who also suggested moving these activities out of the home into communal establishments. In this way, she argues, the work could be accomplished more scientifically, while enabling women to gain economic independence by engaging in it professionally. The necessity of independent income for genuine emancipation is again asserted by Louise Otto-Peters in "The Right of Women to Earn a Living" (1866), where she turns her attention to the situation in the middle classes.

With the intent of initiating public debate on bleak social conditions, Fanny Lewald (1811–89) chose the genre of fictitious letters, of which the three following texts are examples. In the "Third Easter Letter for Women: Training for Domestic Servants" (1863), she points out the harsh working conditions under which fourteen- and fifteen-year-old working-class girls enter employment as domestic servants. Even when they are living in households, they remain strangers to the members of the family. Poor education, the lack of appropriate training in their position, and frequent changes of employers make adjustment even more difficult for them. Reporting on the social circumstances of girls from small towns and villages arriving in Berlin to seek factory work, the "Ninth Easter Letter" (1863) promotes the idea of developing hostels to provide temporary shelter for such new arrivals. In her "Tenth Political Letter: Work and Family Values" (1869), Lewald censures affluent women who, while themselves enjoying life's luxuries and the help of housekeepers, nursemaids, and governesses, talk of "femininity" and "family values" in their opposition to employment for professional women. Lewald argues that men, too, benefit from marriage to "intellectually developed and independent women" who are capable of contributing to the welfare of the family. In "Are Motherhood and Domesticity Compatible with a Profession?" (1903), Hedwig Dohm argues that the decision to work must be left to the individual, but society must eliminate the barriers to her free choice.

The long and difficult fight for women workers' rights is documented in two texts by Austrians. In "Autobiography of a Working Woman" (1903), Adelheid Popp (1869–1939) recalls the circumstances that gave her the courage to make her first public speech, despite her lack of formal education. Popp's fellow activist, Amalie Seidl, describes the harsh working conditions and meager pay that led to "The First Female Workers' Strike in Vienna" (1912).

The organization of work in the bourgeois household, especially the kitchen, depended on having several women attend to domestic tasks, since the preparation and preservation of food, for example, was a long and labor-intensive process. With changes in society that also affected the middle and upper classes, such as women working outside the home and smaller households, the organization of housework became an important issue. In "Women's Work and Housekeeping" (1901), Lily Braun (1865–1916) suggests that, contrary to popular belief, the kitchen is not the heart of family life but an obstacle to family relations. She offers one possible solution: a reconceptualization of living spaces in household cooperatives with communal kitchens, where the time-consuming preparation and serving of meals can be rationalized. That such solutions did not catch on is evident in another model with more lasting impact offered by the architect Grete Lihotzky (1897–2000) in "Rationalization in the Household" (ca. 1927): the efficient Frankfurt kitchen, a mass-produced design that was both attractive and functional.

In "The Social Condition of Female White-Collar Workers" (1930), the journalist Susanne Suhr traces the dramatic increase in the number of urban working women to a combination of factors, especially the impoverishment of the middle class and young women's desire for new opportunities. She raises concerns, however, about the potential for exploitative wages and the pitting of male and female workers against one another.

The largest group of women in the "free professions," Gertrud Bäumer informs us, are the "Female Teachers" (1930). She recalls the evolution of this middle-class profession from women's older roles as governesses, chaperones, and teachers of reading, writing, and arithmetic to young children. Alluding to their long struggle for professionalization (including the 1890 founding of the General Association of German Female Teachers), Bäumer sees the female teacher as the "true pioneer" of the women's movement.

One consequence of the women's movement in the late twentieth century has been the establishment of offices for *Frauenbeauftragte,* who are supposed to promote gender equality in the context of local government. In "Community Commissioners for [Gender] Equality: Possibilities and Problems" (1992), Katharina Gröning reviews their brief history and discusses factors that have contributed to their mixed success.

Women and Politics

Ten years after the repeal of the *"Vereinsgesetz"* finally gave German women the right to assemble and participate in political activities, the new Weimar constitution of 1919 (adopted as a consequence of Germany's defeat in World War I in 1918) gave women the right to vote—a right that was not granted to American women until a constitutional amendment one year later. Women's pursuit of enfranchisement encountered much the same set of prejudices as had been raised against their further education. Their struggles for education and for rights as workers also have, of course, a political dimension, but entail less direct involvement in the "male" realm of politics itself than do the positions represented in this section.

Well before the nineteenth century, women had questioned the privileges of males who "flaunt [their] rights with much ado," as Christiana Mariana von Ziegler (1695–1760) expresses it with considerable wit in her 1739 poem. In comparison, however, to the relative harmlessness of an occasional poem, an avowedly "feminist" journal, such as the *Frauen-Zeitung,* published by Louise Otto (later Otto-Peters), claimed for women "the right to cultivate in ourselves the purely human [. . .] and the right to self-representation and autonomy in the state." The paper lasted only two years before a new law restricted editorial management of a newspaper to *male* persons, effectively forcing her to take leave of her readers in her "Farewell" editorial of 1850.

Nor was Otto the only woman to engage in journalism on women's behalf. Mathilde Franziska Anneke (1817–84), who had entered the battles of 1848 at the side of her husband, started the first women's newspaper in Germany, the *Frauen-Zeitung*. Upon her husband's release from prison in 1849, the couple emmigrated to the United States, where she established a school for girls in Milwaukee and functioned as a liaison between American suffragists and German immigrant women. For a brief period, she also published the first feminist paper in the United States, the *Deutsche Frauen-Zeitung*, of which only a single copy now exists. One of the few German immigrant women to become involved in American politics, Anneke offers a spirited defense of Susan B. Anthony, who was convicted in 1873 for having voted in Rochester, New York, in defiance of the Fourteenth Amendment to the Constitution, which had enfranchised only *male* citizens.

The wariness that the French Revolution had occasioned toward the "specter of the 'emancipated woman' " in public life is evident in Fanny Lewald's "Ninth Political Letter," analyzing the contradictory notions of "feminine virtue" that led German women to acquiescence to men's opposition to their emancipation. Noting the gradual liberalization of manners and mores that had circumscribed the lives of middle- and upper-class girls and women, Lewald criticizes their lack of concern for the "feminine virtues of poor and uneducated women." Since society felt a need for the services of these women, artificial constraints were not imposed on their freedom of movement or chance to earn their living. In a similar vein, Louise Otto-Peters points out in "The Woman Question" (1876) how women's response to the exigencies of war had demonstrated their capacity for patriotism and service to the "fatherland," but with no lasting effect, either in terms of their readiness to engage in politics on their own behalf or of the state's willingness to grant them the rights of citizenship.

Foremost among these rights, as Hedwig Dohm asserts in her bold essay, "The Right of Woman's Suffrage" (1876), is the right to vote. Approvingly citing British and American women's refusal to pay taxes as long as they were not allowed to vote, Dohm argues that, in contrast to the natural right of women to vote, men do not have any right to deny women their rights. Finally, in contrast to our contemporary image of Switzerland as the last European country to enfranchise women, Marie Goegg (1829–89), who was elected the first president of the Women's International Association in 1868, describes some of the more progressive developments, such as granting women admission to university study, control of their own finances, and the right to divorce.

Women's attempts to organize on their own behalf were, then as now, also hampered by tensions between various factions. Looking back near the end of their lives together, Lida Gustava Heymann (1868–1943) and Anita Augspurg (1857–1943) contrast tendencies in "The Conservative and the Radical Women's Movement" in Germany (1941), clearly preferring the confrontational tactics of the radicals to those of the conservatives—especially the Bund Deutscher Frauenvereine (BDF)—which they criticize not only for clinging to what today might be called an "essentialist" view of "women's nature," but also for claiming credit for the achievements of the radical women. The position that they criticize can be clearly seen in Helene Lange's insistence that "There Were No Social-Democratic Women's Organizations" (1921), where she rejects the accusation that Socialist women were excluded from the BDF on the grounds that a Socialist women's *organization* would have been illegal and result in the demise of the BDF under the *"Vereinsgesetz."* In the 1893 statement of goals published in the first issue of *Die Frau,* the journal of the BDF edited by Lange, one encounters the familiar rhetoric of the ennobling influence of woman as first and foremost wife and mother, and as professional only before or in the absence of the opportunity to realize this true calling.

A very useful summary of the obstacles to the progress of women's rights in Germany, as well as of certain achievements pushed through by the more radical women of the movement, is offered in a chapter on "Germany" in the survey of *The Modern Women's Rights Movement in Europe* (1912) by Käthe Schirmacher (1865–1930). The article does not reflect, however, Schirmacher's increasing attraction to reactionary nationalism, which eventually led her to advocate roles for women that anticipated later developments in Nazi Germany.

The Austrian Adelheid Popp came to the Social-Democratic Party (SPD) in 1885 from a working-class background. After three years of schooling, she started working at the age of ten-and-a-half, but continued in the attempt to educate herself. Introduced to the SPD at the age of seventeen, she soon became active in party journalism for women and participated in the first strike of women workers in Vienna in 1893. After women in Austria achieved the right to vote, she served in the Austrian Parliament from 1919 to 1934 and succeeded Clara Zetkin as chairperson of the International Women's Committee. In "The New Woman" (1893), Popp argues that Social Democracy can only succeed if women attain equality in education, economic independence, and citizenship.

Whereas Popp was deeply rooted in the working class, Lily Braun (1865–1916) belonged by birth to the nobility. However, a financial disaster in her family, her charitable visits to poor working-class families, as well as her reading of socially critical literature sharpened her consciousness. A member of the left-bourgeois women's organization *Frauenwohl* and cofounder in 1895 of the journal *Die Frauenbewegung,* she was attacked by various factions of the Socialists as well as by feminists because of her attempts to mediate between the predominantly bourgeois women's movement and the working class. Some of these tensions can be seen in "The Transformation of Women from Workers to Citizens" (1903). Late in life she became an apologist for Germany's role in World War I, insisting that it also brought about cooperation of women across class lines.

A quite different Socialist voice is that of Rosa Luxemburg (1870–1919), one of the most influential women politicians and theorists of women's liberation and German Marxism. With two doctorates from the University of Zurich, she edited several Marxist journals, taught Marxist economics, and played a leading role in the extreme-left wing of the German Marxist movement. Known for her sharp mind and her rhetorical skill, she was imprisoned several times, both in her native Poland and in Berlin, because of her radical political activities. A coauthor of the 1918–19 program of the Communist Party, Luxemburg, together with Karl Liebknecht (1871–1919), was murdered by right-wingers in Berlin. In "Women's Suffrage and Class Struggle" (1912), she asserts that, despite their increasing unionization and their newly gained freedom to take part in political activities, women's lack of suffrage remains a "vile injustice."

Particularly in the twentieth century, women's involvement in politics has often been in the cause of pacifism, although the demand for peace came from feminists of different political persuasions. Unlike Lily Braun, Clara Zetkin (1857–1933), the Socialist editor of *Die Arbeiterin* and *Die Gleichheit,* opposed the Social Democratic Party's voting of war credits in 1914. In 1917 she became a member of the German Communist Party but, unlike her friend Rosa Luxemburg, focused her energies primarily on women's issues. "Women of the Working People" (1915) documents her passionate commitment to peace and internationalism while addressing the specific situation of proletarian women.

An early bourgeois voice in the chorus of European peace activists is Bertha von Suttner (1843–1914), who became world-famous with her novel *Lay Down Your Arms!* (1889) and in 1905 herself received the Peace Prize that she had persuaded Alfred Nobel to establish in 1892. Her international commitment to peace is reflected in her "Speech in San Francisco" (1912), given at the invitation of American women two years before the outbreak of World War I.

Lida Gustava Heymann, a founder and leader of the Women's International League for Peace and Freedom, belonged to the radical wing of the bourgeois women's movement. Together with Anita Augspurg, she fought both for peace and women's suffrage. Her remarks in "Female Pacifism" (1917/1922), however, are grounded in an essentialist position that opposes the "female, constructive principle" to the "male, destructive principle," leading her to assert the fundamental identity of pacifism with "female nature and instinct," an argument that has been recycled throughout the twentieth century.

In "Love and the Right to Vote" (1914) Gabriele Reuter (1859–1941), a journalist who also wrote novels thematizing the constraints imposed on women's self-fulfillment by the social order of Wilhelminian Germany, stresses the need for suffrage as crucial for the realization of women's full human potential.

When, in 1919, women finally achieved the right to vote, they had to be educated in the exercise of this right. Known as the founder of the profession of social work for women, Alice Salomon outlines in "The German Woman and Her Tasks in the New Republic" (1919) women's new responsibility in shaping the social ideals of the new postwar republic. Here, too, one finds faith in a notion of the "essential nature of woman," which will promote their civilizing mission beyond the barriers of class.

The constructive role of German women in politics in the World War I era and its aftermath ended with the advent of National Socialism; the immediate post–World War II years were marked by working women's return to domesticity and abstinence from the political sphere. In the wake of the 1960s-student movement, based in large measure on opposition to the Vietnam War, a new women's movement emerged. In 1968, women in the SDS (Socialist German Students, which had initiated the protest movements of the 1960s) began to separate themselves from men's political battles and to organize on their own behalf. Their decision to search for their own way is documented in the "Speech of the Action Council for the Liberation of Women," delivered by pioneer feminist filmmaker Helke Sander (1937–). In her essay of the same year, "Women in the SDS,"

Ulrike Maria Meinhof (1934–76), a journalist for the leftist journal *Konkret,* who later gained notoriety for her involvement in terrorist activities, analyzes the necessity of the separate way the women had chosen to pursue.

Beyond the often-colorful feminist demonstrations and street actions of the 1970s and 1980s, a range of theoretical approaches emerged along a continuum from naive essentialism to sophisticated dialectics. Among the more challenging theorizations of woman's oppression is the ground-breaking 1987 essay by Christina Thürmer-Rohr (1936–), "Cross-Thinking/Counter-Questioning/Protest," which deconstructs the victim status of woman and examines woman's consciousness of her own complicity.

The fall of the Berlin Wall and the suddenness of German unification in 1990 produced a variety of feminist examinations of the implications for women, especially in East Germany, where women had not been able to develop an autonomous movement as did feminists in the West. In "The End of Socialism in Europe: A New Challenge for Socialist Feminism?" (1992), Frigga Haug (1937–) analyzes, from the viewpoint of Western materialist feminism, the differing effects of a capitalist-market economy on women in Eastern and Western Germany.

Issues of Gender

Although in some ways all our selections deal with "issues of gender," we have here attempted to group those that, in one way or another, specifically address the situation of women in the context of gender ideologies. Unsurprisingly, marriage and motherhood, female sexuality, prostitution, abortion, and violence toward women are among the topics taken up here. But there are also less commonly considered issues, including a return to the topos of woman as witch, now regarded as a symbol of resistance; arguments on behalf of women's pleasures in old age; critiques of feminist film censorship and of feminist aggression; feminist theology; an analysis of gender bias in language; and a report on migrant women in contemporary Germany.

In contrast to the lively defense of Sidonie Hedwig Zäunemann (1714–40) of her life as an unmarried woman in her poem "A Maid's Fortune" (1739), the following texts address the obstacles women faced when they refused to follow the path that their parents (and society) had established for them; for example, in arranged marriages. In "A Marriage Proposal" (1862), Fanny Lewald describes her successful refusal to accept her father's choice of a husband for her. The lack of agency and the emotional and moral reproaches women had to overcome when they did not conform to gender expectations are evident in the case of Louise Aston (1814–71), whose "emancipated" behavior was denounced as a danger to state and society. An atheist and believer in free love, Aston also wore men's clothing, smoked cigars, and engaged in intellectual discourse with men. In "Banishment" (1846), Aston exposes how Prussian authorities reacted to the threat that they perceived in her nonconformity. Mathilde Franziska Anneke responds in "Woman in Conflict with Social Relations" (1847) to Aston's report with a perceptive analysis of the state's fear of the subversive power of women. Like Aston, a free-thinking atheist, Anneke also experienced the heavy hand of the state when her newspaper was shut down and her husband imprisoned in 1848 for his revolutionary activities. In equally passionate language, Anneke's contemporary, Louise Dittmar, criticizes the so-called marriage of convenience, "The Rational Marriage" (1848), as the "pinnacle of irrationality." Although she is not always thought of as a feminist, the well-known Austrian writer Marie von Ebner-Eschenbach (1830–1916) reveals her sharp wit in "Aphorisms," which capture the absurdities of gender relations. Far less well-known, her fellow Austrian Irma von Troll-Borostyáni (1848–1912) satirizes in "Shame" (1896) the absurd cultural contradictions of wedding customs.

Although feminists have generally agreed on the exploitative nature of prostitution, they do not necessarily agree on the remedies. In "Prostitution" (1896), Troll-Borostyáni reflects the position of many feminists of her time, who opposed any state supervision of prostitution that enforced health controls for the prostitute but not for the customer. The socialist Lily Braun approaches the issue from a quite different point of view in "A Manifesto to Germany's Women" (1908), holding that prostitution is tied to poverty and appealing to all women to help change the living conditions of these women. Since the 1970s, on the other hand, some feminists have called for the liberation of prostitutes by allowing them to take charge of the business themselves and engaging in it as a profession that would entitle them to a state pension and similar benefits.

The female body is identified as the locus of many prejudices against women by one of the most radical advocates for women's rights, Hedwig Dohm. In "Three Doctors as Knights of the *Mater Dolorosa*" she accuses male physicians of reducing women to their reproductive organs and denounces the medicalization of menstruation, pregnancy, and childbirth as a way of deterring women from achieving a productive position in society. "The Old Woman" (1903) was written when Dohm herself was almost seventy. Here she takes on prejudices against old age, asserting the right of women to enjoy life fully and to be active in their old age.

In an essay that is almost contemporary with Dohm's piece on "The Old Woman," Anna Rueling, who had ties to Magnus Hirschfeld's Scientific Humanitarian Committee in Berlin, answers the question, "What Interest Does the Women's Movement Have in the Homosexual Question?" (1904), by pointing out that lesbians (whom she calls *Uranian,* or *homosexual women)* are not found in any particular social class or family, but exist in all strata of society, in the forefront of the women's movement as well as among the prostitutes of the street. Alluding to the social injustices that Uranian women have suffered, Rueling calls on her sisters in the women's movement to respect and understand their "differences."

Among the first German women to enjoy a university education, Adele Schreiber (1872–1957) devoted her energies to the causes of suffrage and the protection of mothers. In "Unwed Mothers" (1912), she attacks the double standard regarding motherhood when it occurs outside of established social parameters, drawing on her own extensive research to illustrate the plight of unwed mothers in a variety of social situations. After moving politically from the left wing of the bourgeois women's movement to the Socialist Party, as whose delegate she sat in the Reichstag from 1928 to 1933, Schreiber fled Germany in 1933 and spent the rest of her days as an activist in England and Switzerland.

Another academically trained feminist and early adherent of Nietzschean philosophy, Helene Stöcker (1869–1943) gained notoriety beyond the women's movement as an advocate for the reform of sexual ethics and the end of the double standard. As a founder of the League for the Protection of Motherhood and Sexual Reform in 1905, she insisted on women's right to control their own reproductive functions, a position that can be readily identified in "Marriage and Sexual Reform" (1916). Also active in the cause of pacifism, Stöcker, like Schreiber, emigrated from Nazi Germany to Switzerland and then to the United States.

The issue of control of the female body is also at the heart of the fight for legalized abortion, which can be traced in literature, film, and the visual arts as well as in more typical modes of political discourse. A 1924 lithograph by Käthe Kollwitz (1867–1945)—part of a campaign for repeal of Paragraph 218 of the German penal code, which had criminalized abortion since 1871—serves as an example of her artistic engagement in this cause. In the wake of the second women's movement during the 1970s, this struggle for woman-friendly abortion laws was taken up again. In "How It All Began: I Have Had an Abortion" (1981), Alice Schwarzer (1942–), the founder and editor of the popular feminist journal *Emma,* emphasizes the unifying momentum of that campaign, which featured testimonies from women, many of them well-known, who had undergone the procedure. A hotly debated text from this same era was Schwarzer's "The Function of Sexuality in the Oppression of Women" (1975), in which she bluntly argued that penises and vaginas stand for power and powerlessness, and that the male sexual monopoly derives from the myth of vaginal orgasm. The separatism that often characterized German feminism in the 1970s is defended in "The Future of Feminism" (1976) by Marielouise Janssen-Jurreit (1941–), who early on draws attention to the danger of female tokenism and adduces arguments for separate or independent feminist organizations.

Silvia Bovenschen's "The Contemporary Witch, the Historical Witch, and the Witch Myth" (1981) typifies a strand of research that was pursued in a variety of fields during the 1970s and 1980s. The essay demonstrates the fashionable transformation that the word *witch* has undergone in the course of feminist reappropriations of collective myths. In the 1970s, attention was drawn to the issue of violence against women through feminists' organization of "Take Back the Night" marches. Public discussion of the battering of women in intimate relationships also led to the establishment of autonomous safe houses for women. In "For the Dignity of Women" (1981), a speech delivered in support of such a shelter, the architect and political activist Karola Bloch (1905–94) defines individual acts of violence against women as a reflection of a society that is fundamentally misogynous.

Certain aspects of the women's movement have also elicited strong criticism from feminists themselves. Such criticism is expressed by the filmmaker Monika Treut in "The Ceremony of the Bleeding Rose: Preliminary Reflections on a Film Project" (1984). She accuses the women's movement of censoring sexual, sensual, and erotic transgressions and argues that it is time to break with such prescribed taboos.

The psychoanalyst Margarete Mitscherlich (1917–) first gained prominence as coauthor, with her husband Alexander Mitscherlich, of a landmark analysis of Germans' unfinished attempt to come to terms with the Nazi Holocaust (*The Inability to Mourn,* 1967). In "Aggression and Gender" (1985), she traces fears of female aggression to male psychoanalysts' misperceptions of female sexuality. Although German universities have been the home of many important theologians, feminist theology had a hard time gaining institutional recognition. Elisabeth Moltmann-Wendel (1926–), one of first feminist theologians in Germany, documents in "Feminist Theology" (1985) the transformative power of the link between liberation theology and feminism.

In a sophisticated but humorous way, the linguist Luise Pusch (1944–) takes a critical look at the gendered relationship of "fatherland and mother tongue." In "Language Is Publicity for Men—but Enough Is Enough!" (1995), she puts her finger on ways that this feature of the German language fosters the continued marginalization of women. With the influx of migrant workers, asylum-seekers, and ethnic Germans, German society in recent years has become complexly multicultural. Thus this section closes with "Forty Years of Women Migrants in Germany," Chong-Sook Kang's 1996 description of the difficult socialization process faced by this growing component of the population in Germany.

Women in Art and Literature

German women artists and writers often faced a long struggle before they were granted a place within artistic and literary circles. At first, many felt compelled to write under a pseudonym, often male, because work that appeared under a woman's name was evaluated through a gendered lens and usually perceived as aesthetically inferior. Some women artists were stigmatized as morally lax and, in the case of actresses, even regarded as prostitutes.

With the new women's movement of the 1970s, a flood of publications dealing with women's issues began to appear, but the term *women's literature* continued to be tainted by a long history of negative associations. The search for "lost" literary and artistic achievements of women began, often with very fruitful results, and was soon reinforced by extensive discussions of the nature of a specifically feminine aesthetic, not only in literature but also in the visual and performing arts, especially film.

In the absence of women's studies programs, which have been part of American colleges and universities since the 1970s, German feminist culture was primarily produced in autonomous women's centers outside of established institutions. However, questions regarding feminist aesthetics and the artistic canon were usually addressed within the universities and took place in the context of international debates on gender issues.

The rigid societal constraints on the life of an upper-class woman artist can be glimpsed in the poem that opens this section, "On the Tower" (1842) by Annette von Droste-Hülshoff (1797–1848), the most important German woman poet of the nineteenth century. The obstacles with which she had to contend, including her own ill health and the care of sick and dying relatives, are not as evident here, however, as in the "The Daily Routine of an Eighteenth-Century Woman Writer (1783)." Although Sophie von La Roche (1730–1807) does not complain about the little time she is able to devote to her own reading and writing after caring for her husband, children, and household, the same litany of obstacles to literary pursuits will be repeated by women writers, although not with the same degree of acceptance, for another two centuries.

The social pressures—and consequences for the reception of their work—that often led women to publish anonymously or under a male pseudonym are addressed in "Women Writers" (1862). Fanny Lewald defends her initial decision to publish under a man's name, since she "wanted to be treated fairly." Notions of "women's nature" also affected the quality of literature directed at women as consumers, as Rosa Mayreder (1858–1938) explains in her 1905 essay "Family Literature." Mayreder, a left-bourgeois Austrian artist and writer, is particularly sharp in her criticism of the sort of romance fiction directed at young women in the popular family journals of her day. While Mayreder condemns the deceptiveness of the illusions created by such stories, the 1906 "Fable" of Lou Andreas-Salomé (1861–1937) alludes positively to some of Henrik Ibsen's (1828–1906) famous female protagonists through her little allegory of a wild duckling trapped in an attic room. Although more often thought of as a muse to famous men (Friedrich Nietzsche, Rainer Maria Rilke, and Sigmund Freud among others) than as a feminist, Andreas-Salomé's analysis reveals her own contradictory blend of essentialist and emancipatory thought.

In "Backstage" (1894), the socialist Lily Braun turns our attention to the gendered perception of stage actresses, who are thought to be available for all men and, at the same time, envied by virtuous housewives for the apparent luxury in which they lived. However, Braun claims, closer acquaintance with the social condition and multifaceted exploitation of the actresses, who are forced to compete against one another and submit to the "patronage" of affluent men, will reveal that they are in fact caught up in the "worst kind of slavery." Although by the 1930s dramatic production by women had increased significantly, we still know little about their contributions as playwrights beyond the success of a few, such as Marieluise Fleißer (1901–74). In "Women's Dramatic Sensibility" (1930), Fleißer concludes in her critical analysis that even though a woman's "fine sensitivity for human idiosyncrasies" enables her to observe closely and write superb individual scenes, she will not enjoy real success as a playwright until she masters the ability to integrate them into a well-balanced construction.

The subsequent years of National Socialism (1933–45) and the immediate postwar era were not conducive to feminist artistic discourse in the public sphere. Not until the rise of a new feminist movement in the 1970s did awareness of significant differences in women's postwar experiences, particularly between East and West Germany, develop. The different meanings that "emancipation" had taken on for women in divided Germany becomes evident in a 1975 interview with the East German author Irmtraud Morgner (1933–90). Writing in a society that did not have a women's movement and where equal rights for women were simply declared by the state, Morgner frames her argument within the parameters of socialist discourse, however unconventional her comments on human sexuality as a "productive force" may be. Her belief—that the differences in the ways men and women live their lives must be reflected in literary forms—is the premise that underlay her own ground-breaking novels of the 1970s and 1980s.

Concurrent with the emergence of a feminist public sphere and its own cultural production apparatus (publishing houses, journals, and bookstores) in West Germany, arose the question of what might constitute a feminist aesthetics. In an important 1976 essay asking "Is There a Feminine Aesthetic?," the literary scholar Silvia Bovenschen (1946–) not only calls for rediscovering the many forgotten women artists, but also holds that differences between men and women should no longer lead to a sense of "deficiency, loss, self-effacement, and deprivation, but rather [. . .] opportunity." Like Morgner, Bovenschen proposes that women's experience shapes feminine aesthetic perceptions and that artistic originality can be found in the "pre-aesthetic" realm of women's daily creative activities, such as weaving, decorative handicrafts, and literary forms such as diary- and letter-writing.

The continued absence of women from the elite ranks of the writing profession is the focus of the 1977 essay by writer Angelika Mechtel (1943–), "The White Raven Has Learned to Fly." In her experience, female authors remain the exception in mainstream publishing houses. Taken together, a tacit "quota system" and the sexist attitudes of editors and reviewers make women writers the "white ravens" of the literary system, at least until women began to take matters into their own hands and establish their own publishing venues.

In her 1980 essay "Overcoming Speechlessness," the Germanist and journalist Gabriele Dietze (1951–) points to the "special structures of communication" that have developed in women's groups. But she also cautions about certain new tendencies in thinking about female creativity, which run the danger of reinforcing age-old male– female stereotypes: culture versus nature, reason versus feeling, spirit versus body. Such dualistic thinking together with a deep-seated fear of criticism, she warns, only serve to hamper the emergence of a women's voice in culture.

Unlike their American colleagues, independent filmmakers in the Federal Republic of Germany have benefitted from monies channeled through state-owned television stations and public foundations, enabling them to gain visibility and transform the male-dominated film scene in Germany. Herself a renown feminist filmmaker, Jutta Brückner (1941–) claims in "The Spot of Blood in the Eye of the Camera" (1981) that women's cinematic pleasure is less tied to the visible surface of concrete film images and more open to fantasy images. Brückner argues that the mechanistic and anonymous sexuality of the "pornographic cinema is the most obvious consequence of a culture in which the women had delegated their gaze to the men. In that sense, the gaze that they directed toward themselves was always a pornographic one." Rather than run away from it, however, she suggests that women discover in pornography a demystifying function that could enable them to liberate their relationship to their own bodies.

In "Indiscretions of the Literary Beast: Pariah Consciousness of Women Writers since Romanticism" (1981), literary scholar Elisabeth Lenk compares the exclusion of women from the literary canon to the societal exclusion of certain ethnic groups who, as a result, develop a kind of "pariah consciousness." For such individuals, the alternatives of a futile pursuit of homogeneity within the dominant group or a self-absorbed flaunting of their heterogeneity entail acquiescence to a cultural and societal caste system that reduces them to caricatures of their genuine selves. An especially influential contribution to the aesthetic discourse of the 1970s was "Double Focus: On the History of Women's Writing" (1983) by literary scholar Sigrid Weigel (1950–). Moving beyond an essentialist reconstruction of the cultural history of women, she advocates examinating the "rediscovered" texts of women writers through a lens that allows us to refract "the writers' relation to the dominant image of woman, the strategies that they developed within the context of the mirror-image, and how they related to their existence as the 'second sex' in the male order." A focus on the ambiguities of their double existence, Bovenschen argues, reveals how women are simultaneously involved in, and excluded from, in the male order.

Ginka Steinwachs (1942–) is one of a number of feminist artists who—like the performance artist and filmmaker Valie Export—use the body as material or who—like Elfriede Jelinek—transform language into an experience of the body. In her provocative text, "the palatheater of the mouth," Steinwachs demonstrates the "language music" [*Sprachmusik*] that she brings to life in her performances. In her aesthetic practice, the oral cavity is a site of performance in which the language of the body and the body of language become interrelated. Her often surrealistic writing employs metaphors, wordplay, and a variety of sources from cultural history, including slightly altered quotations from famous German literary figures such as Goethe and Brecht.

Libuše Moníková (1945–98), who was born in Prague and moved to Germany in 1971, is included here as only one representative of a new ethnically diverse generation of writers who have chosen to write in German. In "Some Theses Regarding Women's Writing" (1997) she does not ask for special consideration for women writers, but rather demands that their writing reflect the fact that they "also have a head." Refusing to apply lesser standards to women's writing, she looks for literature by women that is "funny, humorous, biting, satirical." As her comments regarding "pumpkin-breasts and bellies" make clear, however, she is highly critical of some feminist texts, such as Verena Stefan's 1975 *Shedding*. Stefan (1947–), a political activist who enjoyed stunning success with this, her first book, became a key figure in the emerging feminist publishing scene in Germany. In "Cacophony" (1994), she reflects on her status as the first author of the contemporary women's movement in Germany, her resulting identity crisis, and the struggle to overcome it.

Finally, the Austrian writer Anna Mitgutsch (1948–) returns in 1996 to the question "What Is 'Women's Literature'?," claiming that the increased number of women writers poses a threat to male authors, which has in turn fueled the tendency to trivialize and marginalize "feminine experience, feminine narrative perspective, and feminine perception." She asserts that "women's literature" must not be defined by its content but by the search for a feminine aesthetic perspective "that takes into account that which cannot be narrated and refuses unambiguous solutions, for how else should that which cannot be expressed become visible?" In the few years since Mitgutsch wrote these words, it remains evident that both the practice of women's literature and art, including film, as well as theoretical approaches to its study, continue to flourish and, what is more important for the future, to participate in changing understandings of "feminism."

In our own process of selecting texts for this anthology, we owe a great debt to the editors of previous anthologies of German-language feminist texts, including Hansjürgen Blinn, *Emanzipation und Literatur* (1984); Andrea van Dülmen, *Frauen: Ein historisches Lesebuch* (1988); Elke Frederiksen, *Die Frauenfrage in Deutschland 1865–1915* (1981); Renate Möhrmann, *Frauenemanzipation im deutschen Vormärz* (1978); Margit Twellmann, *Die deutsche Frauenbewegung 1843–1889* (1972); and to the useful thematic series compiled by Gisela Brinker-Gabler. In our search for appropriate texts, friends and colleagues too numerous to mention supported our efforts and pointed us in fruitful directions.

Furthermore, we are grateful to the Department of Foreign Languages and Literatures at California State University, Chico, for providing travel funds and the Susan B. Anthony Institute for Gender and Women's Studies at the University of Rochester for supporting some of the final manuscript preparation. We also wish to thank the Interlibrary Loan divisions of both our universities' libraries for the efficiency and inventiveness with which they assisted us in obtaining difficult-to-find materials.

P. A. H.
M. M.

EDUCATION
FOR GIRLS
AND WOMEN

Nantchen Göckingk

Für einen Mann zu kochen und zu spinnen—
Unwürdiger Beruf!
Wenns der nur ist, wozu mit diesen Sinnen
Und diesem Geist mich die Natur erschuf!

Hat sie nur bloß die wundervollen Zonen
Für Männer ausgespannt?
Und darf ich gleich dem Stier sie nur bewohnen,
Der, wenn er stirbt, sein Futter nur gekannt?

Soll ich nicht auch in jenem Leben leben?
Wer wird ein Wunder thun?
Und meinem Geist dort Sapphos Denkkraft geben,
Ließ ich ihn hier bei Töpf' und Spindel ruhn?

Ist's nicht genug, die Hälfte meines Lebens
Geschäft'ge Martha sein?
Ist's Hochverrat, ist's Thorheit, ist's vergebens,
Der Weisheit kaum die andere Hälfte weihn?

O Männer! Männer! So uns zu erziehen!—
Wenn Nesseln an dem Bach
Des Lebens unter Euren Veilchen blühen:
Wer soll sie jäten? Eure Gattin? Ach!

Was sind schon mir die Mädchen nicht für Dinger,
Gilts für mein Herz und Geist!
Was sind sie? Ha! Gesellschaft für die Finger,
Wenn mich der Zwang Quadrille spielen heißt.

Nantchen Göckingk[1]

To Cook and Spin for a Man *(1777)*

To cook and spin for a man—
An unworthy profession!
Be it the one for which Nature made me
With these senses and with this spirit!

Has nature opened up her marvels
Just for men alone?
And shall I dwell here just like the steer
That when it dies, has only known to eat?

Should I not also live in that life?
Who will perform the miracle
And impart to my spirit the intellect of Sappho
If here by pot and spindle I let it idly rest?

Is it not enough to spend half my life
As the dutiful Martha?
Is it treason, is it folly, is it all in vain
To pledge the second half to wisdom?

Oh men, men! How do you raise us!
If nettles bloom among your violets
Along the streams of life:
Who shall weed them? Your wife? Alas!

What sort of creatures these girls are,
Not the sort for my mind and heart!
Company for my fingers
When I have to play a quadrille.

---

1. Sophie Ferdinande Maria Philippine (Nantchen) Göckingk, née Vopel, exchanged many letters with her fiance, Leopold Friedrich Günther von Göckingk, who "edited" them into poems.—Trans.

O, daß ich doch nur eine Babet hätte!
Wie wollt ich mit ihr thun!
Wir liebten uns einander um die Wette,
Wir wollten Nachts auf einem Kissen ruhn;

Umfaßt zusammen durch das Leben eilen,
Die Bürden leicht und schwer,
Die Freuden groß und klein zusammen teilen—
O weißt Du, Freund! denn keine Babet mehr.

Oh, if only I had a Babet![2]
What I would do with her!
Intensely would we love each other
And each night upon one pillow rest.

Hastening through life arm in arm,
Sharing burdens light and heavy,
Sharing joys great and small—
Oh my friend, know you not another Babet?

Translated by Melanie Archangeli and
Patricia A. Herminghouse

---

2. Babet, fictional author of Edme Boursault's *Lettres de Babet* (1669), popular in eighteenth-century Germany.—Trans.

Dorothea von Schlözer

Letter from Dorothea von Schlözer
to Luise Michaelis

Göttingen, June 19, 1785

Dearest Luise,

I understand your question perfectly well now. Do you think, then, that I enjoy cooking and spinning more than I would enjoy listening to my father's history lectures? I admit that at times I no doubt lose my patience when I have to prepare Latin or a difficult theorem in Euclid, but then I think that if I understand this theorem and the Latin well, I then know how a pair of spectacles must be fashioned, and that is certainly more pleasant than standing in the kitchen through heat and frost. And if I sometimes find it a bit tiresome, I am repaid more than enough because my father allows me so much extra amusement in return.

You must not delude yourself, however, that I understand nothing of women's work: I am probably your match in cooking, and my mother often flatters me about my nimble knitting. I can spin, sew, and take care of the wine, for I see to the cellar mostly by myself; only in making hats do I still have much to learn, whereas you are probably already an expert at this, and I will never be able to compete with my mother in this area in all my days. Not just once, but probably ten times my father has left it up to me to decide whether I should have no more lessons but instead engage in feminine pursuits, but I still consider it advisable, and in truth, not just because I am afraid of making my father cross.

Dear girl, I will confess much to you that we fifteen-year-olds would never otherwise learn at such an early age and that cannot be found in any book, but something told to me in private that I have known for many years thanks to a reliable source: women are not in the world simply to amuse men. Women are human beings just as men are: one should make the other happy. Whoever simply wants to be amused is a rascal, or deserves a wife who is but a pretty face, of which he will have had enough in four weeks.

Well then, does a wife make a husband happy simply by being his cook and seamstress and spinning the yarn? Ha. Then I would rather hire myself out as cook, seamstress, and spinner, so that I could free myself from the devil if that's what he is. Or don't you think that a young lady can amuse a man using what I am learning? Do you believe that through my studies I completely escape the estate to which I am devoted? What if I were to marry a businessman or a manufacturer who conducts business with Spain, France, Holland, Italy, England, Sweden, etc., and I would understand the language of these lands and could conduct his correspondence? How many wives of businessmen are there who understand a half dozen languages? And would my future husband (God willing) then not be a boor, if he did not hire a cook for me because I saved him the cost of a bookkeeper?

Of course we girls cannot choose, neither you nor I; if I were to marry a scholar, my bit of learning would be lost, but still it would not hurt me either. Assuming I would have to set aside playing the piano, singing, math, and Latin for the sake of running the household, I would still continue to speak my languages, and my husband would take pleasure in it, and I would always be reading something of Rome on the side. To stand forever at the stove would not be my cup of tea, for I will not wed some poor wretch, and my father will not force me to, either. I do not lie in wait for a man with an income as large as your father's and mine. But neither will I hunger and suffer want; in that case I prefer to remain alone. If my temperament remains as it is now, then I will marry for no other reason than good sense.

Here the weather is now quite miserable. It is raining again today, and I will stay at home. On the fifteenth of this week we were eating at your house,[1] and now I have written you such a long letter that my fingers hurt quite awfully.

Translated by Melanie Archangeli

---

1. The families of these girls were united through the friendship of their famous fathers, Göttingen University professors August Ludwing von Schlözer (1735–1809) and Johann David Michaelis (1717–91). Dorothea Schlözer (von Rodde) became the first German woman to earn a doctorate.—Eds.

Dorothea Christiane Leporin

A Thorough Investigation of the Causes That Prevent the Female Sex from Attending the University *(1742)*

Paragraph 3

If learning is such a precious treasure, then one has just cause to marvel that it is, nevertheless, held in contempt by so many. Does one not hold gold in high esteem and set great store by precious gems just because they are regarded as noble treasures: How, then, is it possible to look down upon learning, which is such a precious treasure? And yet we see also in our time that learning is still considered of very little worth by the masses.

[...]

Paragraph 6

My intention does not require me to address all types of contempt for learning. Only this must I add in accordance with my purpose: that learning cannot be despised more markedly than when it is seen as something that is not appropriate for the female sex, with the consequence that women are completely excluded from university study.

Paragraph 7

Neither fondness for my sex nor an all-too-high esteem for the same stirs my pen. The reason for my thesis, why I am tracing a contempt for learning, is significant, and concerns erudition as well as our sex. A reverence for learning, not self-love, has forced my essay.

Paragraph 8

Something that is not necessary and useful for all human beings, but rather is said to be detrimental to the majority (in short, the sex of the greatest number), this thing by far does not earn such high praise as something else whose necessity and usefulness is said to be universal. And for this reason I am entitled to say that the attempt to exclude our sex from university study must lead to a contempt for learning. And just as this growing injustice to learning is almost as great as that under which our sex suffers, those who would rob women of such a magnificent and precious treasure neglect their own business, so that both are justified in a common grievance.

Paragraph 9
People may now seek support for their suspicion that I write these pages more in the service of our sex than of erudition; I can accept this as well. It is sufficient that, on the one hand, the more one is convinced of the grand, magnificent, and countless benefits of erudition, the more we find, on the other hand, the magnitude of the injustice because one endeavors to rob our sex of this magnificent and precious treasure.
[...]
Paragraph 12
The roots from which this evil flows are manifold: I will do then no injustice within these pages if I not only identify the various reasons for which the female sex is prevented from pursuing studies, but also expose the irrelevance of these reasons.
[...]
Paragraph 13
I do this in no way, however, with the intention of persuading the entire female sex to pursue their studies as a career. This would cause much disorder, and I realize full well that this demand would probably not be feasible, either; on the contrary, I assert only that it is extremely unfair to want to dedicate almost each and every one of our sex to domestic duties exclusively without taking into consideration the abilities of their minds as well as their bodies, and not to want or permit most of these women to develop their minds so that they could use them even in everyday life. No excuse is sufficient for this intent, and not one human being should be found who ought not be permitted to pursue learning. When the question is however: Should the female sex study more seriously and perhaps as a career? Then the objections that are raised here are of two types. The one type is so constituted that the objections can neither be rejected completely, nor considered superfluous, because they hold true for some. Others, however, are fashioned in such a way that a person is to be excused when he, because the first group of obstacles does not stand in his way, neglects his studies because of the latter.[1]
Paragraph 14
I count among the first type of obstacles the heavy domestic chores that must be executed by manual labor. It is true that people are needed to do this work; and as this work demands much time, it appears to be almost impossible for someone who wants to pursue studies seriously to wait until the time can be found. One should

---

1. Objections to making a career of studying.—Eds.

understand me correctly, however. I do not say that a woman cannot study and also be in charge of a household, because this may well be possible, and afterward will be explained in depth. Rather, I assert that a woman who is supposed to achieve something significant in her studies is not able to execute those activities that constitute neither the concept nor the practice of the domestic sciences, but appertain nonetheless most often to the female sex, and that are still necessary. I admit then, that certain people must devote all their time to these activities, consequently they cannot pursue an education.

Translated by Melanie Archangeli with
Patricia A. Herminghouse

Amalie Holst

On Woman's Obligation toward the Higher Cultivation of the Mind *(1802)*

Does the Higher Cultivation of the Mind Conflict
with the More Immediate Occupation of the Woman
as Wife, Mother, and Housewife?

Recently much has been written about the female vocation. Men dared to draw the line which our minds would not be permitted to cross in the field of knowledge; they believe that a higher cultivation of our intellect would conflict with our individual duties.

[. . .]

In the name of our entire sex I challenge the men to prove to us the rights they claim in discriminating against one entire half of the human race, denying it access to the source of the sciences, willing at most to allow it to skim the surface.

Will we acknowledge this presumptuous claim? Will they be able to justify it? Have they been able to thus far?

Those authors state two reasons as the main factors against the higher cultivation of the woman. Our physical and mental predispositions make us unfit to achieve an equally high flight into the regions of knowledge, and secondly, this high degree of intellectual cultivation would completely conflict with our individual duties.

[. . .]

If only I could truly convince my sex that the duty of the human race is to cultivate all its faculties, and that without this higher cultivation we cannot assert the honor of humankind; then we would achieve more in this splendid proposition than the men. Because in our case so many selfish aims, of which the men have more regarding their cultivation than we do, fall away. Aside from the duty to humanity nothing could spur us on to cultivate our minds other than the pathetic quest to shine, and how pitiable this aim would be. By contrast men have selfish aims far more than we do; for them, the sciences are a means to earning a living and rising to honors and offices. To us, and indeed to our benefit, such motives are denied; thus, to a much greater extent, we can be human beings in the more noble sense of the word. We wish and ask for nothing else; the honor of humankind suffices.

As long as we are permitted our education only under certain conditions, as long as we are still limited as to how far we are allowed to go, and, whenever we are driven by our genius to cross this line, we are forced to do so surreptitiously without the authority of the law, finally, as long as functions of secondary importance are dictated to us: so long will the state of our education and the education of the human race in general be precarious.

[. . .]

The Woman Considered as Wife: Does the Higher Civilization of Her Mind Make Her Incapable of Fulfilling the Duties of This Station?

Do we exist simply for the sake of men? This question seems laughable when one brings it before the court of common sense. Common sense tells us that both sexes exist to promote the happiness of one another, so that, united in the most splendid union, they are able to cultivate in themselves the highest ideal of humanity and act for the best of the whole.

[. . .]

If [. . .] marriage is a contract that is entered into by two equally free beings in order to enjoy the advantages of sociability in its most intimate form, and, through the careful formation of the children, to educate members of society who do credit to mankind and are of service to the state, so must we seek first to develop the duties of the spouses to each other; for here must everything be reciprocal, the duties of one are also the duties of the other. The insignificant modifications of the more or less, the when or how, will not be considered here.

Should any union, any association among human beings exist for the happiness of the opposite part, so must the individuals first strive toward one aim, they must be in agreement. To be so, they owe each other reciprocally a just appreciation of their worth, forbearance and tolerance of their deficiencies and weaknesses, help and support in danger and suffering, willing accommodation in the ordinary needs of life, and happy, sincere participation in the joys of that life.

Marriage, as the most intimate and enduring union because it is entered into for life, requires the fulfillment of all these duties more strictly than in any other union. It demands moreover from both spouses a common striving toward ever greater improvement and perfection, since they should affirm moral teachings by example to their children.

Should it really then be possible that learning, or the higher education of the woman, could distort her outlook so that she would fail to recognize her duties? On the contrary, will this and must this not enlighten and correct her outlook? The educated woman will not simply sense it, she will see with conviction that only by fulfilling all her duties, only by making her husband, with whom she is so intimately joined, happy, can she herself have a claim to happiness. No selfishness, no exaggerated claims will blind her and disturb this splendid union, for true education or learning makes one modest and tolerant. She rightly expects, however, the same understanding from her husband; for I repeat once again, unilaterally no happiness can exist for one or the other.

And here is where I would so gladly convince men that, in this tender union, they could win everything and lose nothing through the highest cultivation of the woman.

[. . .]

The most important reproach that is made against the higher cultivation of the woman as to why she could not be as good a wife is this: women then put on more airs and are no longer gentle, obliging, conforming, compliant creatures; they sense their own abilities more vigorously and those of the men less; in short, they lose what one is accustomed to calling their femininity.

From these words one could easily draw the conclusion that such men fear that by acquiring a higher cultivation, it may occur to women to hold men accountable for the various injustices that women must tolerate. Because a creature who knows the source of its duties and the complete extent of them will, of course, at the same time also attain to its rights, the one cannot be separated from the other.

Yet even then these men have nothing to fear from truly enlightened women. These know too well that in such a case, intimate union, stubborn insistence upon rights is not the means to achieve them.

[. . .]

The woman of knowledge, the woman educated in humanity, will never succumb to the charm of luxury, vanity, or a mania for fashion; on the contrary, there will be no need for battle here. Her noble soul, her educated mind lifts her above this nonsense; she strives for no other fame than for the applause of the noble and the reasonable; her contentment flows from the sweet inner consciousness of having fulfilled her duties. The lively interest she takes in all that is important to mankind fills her hours of leisure; she would hardly be able to imagine the concept of boredom if her circumstances did not occasionally necessitate that she attend large social gatherings, where head and heart often find so little amusement. And fortunate is the man whose wife finds boredom only at these gatherings; his gain cannot be measured, for boredom is the mother of most follies from which weak mortals suffer.

Oh you men! When will you learn to see that you could only win, never lose, by the proper cultivation of our intellect. I have often reflected that marriage is the greatest masterpiece in nature. There is an infinite amount involved in melting two beings, each of whom must have and maintain their personality, into one in such a way that only one beautiful whole becomes of it. The marriage must be the true unity of two. Only inner friendship, true respect, unbreachable trust, and unhypocritical openness can bring about this greatest of all natural wonders.

Fortunate is the man who has a wife in harmony with him, fortunate is the woman who meets a husband who stands with her at the same level of cultivation. And the higher they both stand, that much greater will be their happiness; they attain earthly bliss beyond measure.

Translated by Melanie Archangeli

Betty Gleim

Education and Instruction of the Female Sex: A Book for Parents and Educators *(1810)*

Every child who is a girl should become first: a human being; second: a woman; third: a citizen of the world.

The Human Being

To this end is required the development and exercise of all the faculties, or, in other words, intellectual, aesthetic, moral, and religious education.

No one will have any objections to moral and religious education, but all the more voices will be raised against the intellectual and the aesthetic. The objections that one hears are:

First: Through cultivation, especially intellectual cultivation, the woman loses her femininity.

Second: Intellectual and aesthetic education prevent the woman from any faithful fulfillment of duty because her inclinations are not taken into account.

Third: Such education especially prevents the fulfillment of her duties as wife, mother, and housewife.

All these objections could quickly be dismissed for the following two reasons:

First: All human beings (as I hope has been demonstrated) should be educated intellectually, aesthetically, morally, and religiously; all women are human beings; therefore they must also be educated intellectually, aesthetically, morally, and religiously.

Second: The woman is granted a moral and a religious education, but it is impossible to complete this process without intellectual and aesthetic education; therefore also the woman cannot do without intellectual and aesthetic cultivation.

[. . .]

The first thing that one fears from the cultivation of women, especially in the case of intellectual education, is that the woman could lose her femininity. The word femininity is an ambiguous term, a word with which one associates many things. One usually understands by this word nothing other than soft, pampered weakness; vanity; a craving for admiration; triviality; on the whole a character-less, insignificant being. One can, however, also understand by "fem-ininity," and understand correctly, the sum of those characteristics that comprise and create the individuality of the woman.

[...]

Where femininity is lost, one should not conclude that intellectual ability is too fully developed, but only that the other talents are too stunted. Wherever one talent subjugates all the others, a dispropor-tionate and unharmonious cultivation has surely taken place. The rule: Suppress one strength because it might become the ruin of the rest! is fundamentally wrong. Contrary to that this rule is recom-mended: Do not develop any talent at the cost of the others; develop and elevate each to the highest possible level of perfection of which it is capable; but cultivate all talents in agreeable proportion and to a harmonious whole!

The second reason that is given for the non-education of women is that intellectual and aesthetic cultivation prevent her from any loyal fulfillment of duty because those inclinations are not taken into ac-count. One can answer that this reproach would apply to an unbal-anced cultivation, but it would not apply to any woman who is also educated in morals and religion.

[...]

Education is further reproached for preventing the woman from ful-filling her occupational duties as wife; it can be shown, however, that education promotes these duties. Let us imagine an educated woman as the wife of either an uneducated or an educated man. ... Precisely because of her cultivation, the educated woman possesses a thousand more points of contact with other human beings, hence also her husband, than she would without an education; and the more this is the case, the less one will be able to complain about the boredom and monotony of conversation. Because of her cultivation she pos-sesses more tact in interacting with others, more delicacy in her entire behavior, a more accurate sense of the needs of others, and more skill is satisfying those needs. All misfortune in the relations of human beings with one another arises most often from the power of egotism and unbridled passions. Cultivation, however, which directs one's gaze and longing toward the totality and the universal, leads to the kingdom of ideas, weakens the claims of self-love, kills base instincts, and allows a greater degree of concern for that which belongs to others by turning the narrow gaze away from the self.

[...]

Regarding the Institutions through which the Idea of
Education Can Become Reality

Whether or not men want to hear it, women rule the world. The well-being and the woe, the ennobling or the corruption of the whole depends on their qualities; as they are, so will be the human race. If this is true, then it is oh so necessary to take care that this important half of the human race, and with it the other half, no longer perishes intellectually. Thus, it is extremely urgent to improve this half so that its descendents improve; to redeem it from the moral paralysis of vanity, shallowness, and intellectual poverty; and to create in it self-knowledge instead of vanity, depth instead of insignificance, and emotional fullness instead of emptiness. Therefore the call is issued in true earnestness: Educate women more seriously, worthily, nobly! Alas, in so many the mind lies dormant in a dead sleep, unaware of the power that it could have. Oh, awaken the mind! Call it into being with a mighty voice so it can perceive the higher life, recognize its great destiny, and henceforth wish no more to be grounded with base desire in the lower depths of the earth, but rather with its most noble impulses aspire to the heights!

But who should educate women, since most human beings are themselves not educated? Of course the best thing would be to follow Fichte's advice to separate children from their parents and have them educated in special institutions by some carefully selected people. The parents, however, will not want to make this great sacrifice of parental love, and the state has no right to compel the sacrifice with force.

The state can, however, do something which is, of course, a less effective means, but in the absence of a better method the best that can be done: it should establish institutions so that the notion of education and of a superior existence can be brought to the people, and to women in particular.

The most necessary of these institutions are:

First: Seminaries for women so that we can have female teachers, because for several reasons women are best instructed and educated by other women. However do not make the first priority cramming them full of fragmentary knowledge and the learning of an enormous catechism, but rather educating and training their strength and skill. Let not realism but humanism dominate in these schools. What will the dead mass of knowledge do for us? It fades. Truth, beauty, virtue, and faith remain; the unfading leaves of an unfading flower.

Second: Institutions for the education of nursemaids.

Third: Centers where the children will be cared for. An example of this can be found in Detmold. The poor craftspeople and wage laborers of this city bring their children there every morning and can pursue their work peacefully and worry free. During the day the children are attended to, cared for, and kept busy. The most respected ladies of Detmold supervise the entire operation.

Fourth: Good elementary schools; i.e., schools in which reading is not the only objective of teaching, but rather schools in which all abilities are systematically stimulated.

Fifth: Appropriately structured middle schools for girls.

Sixth: Industrial schools for the poorest class of people. In these schools instruction will be provided to the children free of charge, and in addition, the children will be paid for the work they produce. By this means poor people will have a powerful incentive to send their children to school. In these institutions, in the course of developing and exercising the intellectual ability of female students, refining their thoughts and perceptions and awakening in them more noble desires, their hands will be gainfully employed, and thus the state will gain many a good female citizen, whose sad trade would otherwise have been begging or stealing. On the whole this type of assistance for the poor, which strives to prevent poverty, will accomplish a great deal more than those methods that only try to help those who are poor. This latter method is nothing more than a palliative, the former a radical cure; and industrial schools are precisely the most effective means to that end.

Translated by Melanie Archangeli

Louise Otto-Peters

The Participation of the Feminine Sphere in Affairs of the State *(1847)*

. . . The situation of women with regard to education, cultivation, and position has remained just the same as it always was, and we still have no assurance that the participation of women in current events that is now beginning will not sink back again into its earlier nothingness (as did their participation in 1815) as soon as events are less powerful and earthshaking than they are now. Still nothing has been done for the instruction of female youth, no more autonomous position in society has been ascribed to women. That which was true three years ago is still true: *the education and improvement of women conflicts with our national and social circumstances.*

Perhaps everything that the female mind can grasp up until its fourteenth year is being taught in our schools—but then, at an age when all the intellectual abilities begin to unfold, when we first comprehend the proper love of scientific interests, when we first are able to realize how necessary it is to acquire knowledge, when we first gain the ability not to blindly accept in good faith everything we are told—at just such an age female education is considered complete. [. . .]

If girls would have to cultivate themselves only to become excellent housewives, this might be tolerable! But the design of their education seldom intends to educate them to be housewives, but rather much more to be dolls; they are taught nothing for its own sake, but only so they shine in polite society; they are trained to be *dolls* of men yet are still supposed to be their *companions.* "The desire to be noticed," "heartless judgments about others," "superficial knowledge," "parroting without thinking for oneself"—in her book, "Slavery and Freedom of Women" [1845], Ida Frick justifiably reproaches German women of today for these traits and identifies them as the causes of female "slavery." Indeed, but these four evils are *not* the *causes* of our education and position, they are the sad *consequences* of such. Whoever is decorated as a doll—I cannot say dressed—and as such sent off to the market of life to seek a *buyer,* must indeed aspire to be noticed when exactly this exhibition is the aim. Whoever has been deprived of broader interests in higher and greater things must indeed be interested in trifles and petty things; whoever has had the path toward learning something in depth made a thousand times more difficult must indeed seek refuge in superficial knowledge; and whoever is never taught to think, but instead is constantly denied the chance to do so, can ultimately do nothing else but venture—to parrot what others have said.

Thus one should seek to cure the malady at its origin and begin with a revised education of female youth. *In secondary schools for girls world history should not be taught as a dead encyclopedia with a systematic account of rulers, massacres, and dates, period by period—but rather as a living, organic whole,* in which every part is connected by inner necessity in a history of peoples and the development of the nations.—World history must not be viewed as a dead body, in it must be demonstrated the working of the mind. The spirit of world history must stand full of life before teachers and students. Special care should be taken with regard to the history of the fatherland, German history. It would be advisable if particular class hours would be established for world history and for German history, and in addition a class for *contemporary* history; yet it is not required that the children be politicized! But they should not be left in the dark about that which is taking place around them, and be fascinated by the battles of the Greeks and Romans while it remains unknown to them that in the present their fathers are perhaps fighting for them not with swords but with words. Thus is cultivated already in tender minds a fascination for the affairs of the fatherland.

[. . .]

How disgraceful for a German girl—but even more so for a Germany that says to its daughters: "Take care you that you soon sell yourselves to a husband who can provide for you properly and for whom you can manage his household in return—what your heart says about it is immaterial. You may not, in order to "fulfill your female destiny, take your female feelings too seriously." But nothing futher on this topic! I blush at this abasement of marriage, this ridiculing of all youthful feminine feeling and all chaste custom. But whom should I indict? The mothers who deliver these teachings? The daughters who obey them? No! I indict the circumstances, indict the society that *forces both to this!*

That would not be the case if girls would have the opportunity to acquire knowledge and assume an independent position in life. If they would have the ability as teachers to direct female education (as I outlined above), to work in commercial businesses, of which many are even better suited for women than men, so could it perhaps yet be that marriage in Germany would again come into its own and would not be demeaned as it is now in thousands of cases as a "charitable institution for" the female sex.

German women must become *self-reliant,* only then will they be capable of pursuing always and in the right manner their duty to participate in the interests of the nation. This self-reliance can only be promoted, however, through individual education; because only an independent heart leads to independent action. Throughout their entire lives most women remain—children. First they live under constant, indeed hourly supervision in the parental home and dare to have no other opinions than those that rule in the family; then they become wives, and if they love their husbands, the transformation of their earlier opinions into those held by him easily takes place, regardless of whether they are completely opposite or not. First they formed judgments in the spirit of their parents, now they judge in the spirit of their husbands; first they repeated what the one said, now they repeat what the other says—with such a lack of character, the question of whether a woman has a political opinion or not is quite obvious! The woman must be capable of forming independent judgments or she offends against human dignity and her femininity by becoming a parrot that mindlessly repeats what the master has said to it. The situation with regard to the independent actions of the woman is just as dismal as it is with her judgments: one is the necessary consequence of the other. And yet in noble, freely developed femininity, every woman has the power to regulate her thought and action without outside influence. She has in this femininity a sacred protection against every danger to her true virtue to which she could be exposed in a free independent position. Indeed, she will be able to develop true femininity even more easily and beautifully if she is not perpetually kept on a lead by the hand of another, if she can hear and follow her own inner voice without requiring supervision by which she is not only made a prisoner but also a suspect, and thus instead of her feminine dignity being kept intact, as one pretends, it is actually ground right into the dust.

[. . .]

You, however, German brothers, whose hearts glow the warmest for our people, who have recognized that freedom is a unique good that cannot penetrate one situation and be lacking in the other, to you I plead: fight also for the rights of German women, and as you are no longer able to tolerate any more among yourselves who are dependent, so help the women become of age intellectually.

And you, German sisters, who are awake to the bright day of the present in which all our people fight for their most sacred rights, never forget that the fatherland also makes solemn demands on you, and so call out to your sisters who are still dreaming and educate your daughters to be worthy companions of a free people.

Everything, everything that strives toward freedom must be mutually uplifting and supportive—for there is only *one* freedom, one sun that must penetrate all the limbs and pores of the body of the state with its sacred, life-giving breath—a sun that has not yet dawned!

Translated by Melanie Archangeli
with Patricia A. Herminghouse

Luise Büchner

Instruction for Women *(1856)*

It is gratifying that people in general now place more worth on sound education for women than formerly, and that the present has also opened areas of knowledge to women which otherwise were accessible almost exclusively to the specialist, but the instruction itself is still mostly done in the old, careless manner. Our girls continue to be taught shallowly, superficially, and without real seriousness.
[. . .]
However, we dare say that usually only the appearance of education is found when girls leave most of our secondary-level institutes and schools, and this is often combined with an unpleasant pretentiousness. Even the objection that there are truly educated women everywhere cannot be valid here. The aspiring and thinking women of our own and of earlier times owe their more thorough education only in the rarest cases to the instruction they received in school. Either this education was provided through favorable domestic circumstances, or they acquired it only later on by their own energy and efforts, looking back reproachfully at poorly used school time, and making up what was missed earlier with a good deal of difficulty. These examples provide sufficient proof that the fault should not be sought in feminine nature but in the fact that this nature is not met in the right way.

It is true that the feminine mind on its own tends toward a certain superficiality, but instead of fighting this even more decisively with seriousness and thoroughness, the teaching generally goes along with this tendency and tries to spare the girl as much as possible any reflection of her own and any deeper consideration. However, can a child ever learn to run, if it is continually led about on a leash? In a woman, feeling and an active imagination dominate as a rule, but instead of providing a healthy counterweight to these tendencies by means of a careful and well-ordered intellectual development, which then gives to these tendencies their greatest charm, they are heightened purposefully and diligently by means of one-sided and superficial teaching.
[. . .]

Part of the fault lies with the very short-sighted views which many parents still hold regarding the intellectual education of their daughters, but to a greater extent it lies with the frequent incompetence of the teaching staff itself, both men and women. If the instruction of boys, so it seems, must be led mostly by specialists, then that of girls requires male and female teachers who have themselves been taught thoroughly and conscientiously but at the same time broadly.

[. . .]

In their instruction, which is so very important for their later intellectual development, women are usually only given the result of something, but not its first principles and development. We learn a mass of things, which we forget again in a very short time because they only float, in a manner of speaking, before our intellectual eyes, since we never discover their cause and inner relationship. Our mind is weighed down with secondary things and superficialities but the heart, the essence of a subject is seldom made clear.

Many men will maintain women should be thankful that it is made so easy for them; they actually have little reason to be thankful because intellectual energies are just as strained by purely mechanical learning, if not more so, than if they are accustomed from an early age to think and to learn logically and conscientiously. There can be nothing more useless than teaching higher concepts without an accurate elementary foundation. This way the wall of knowledge of our sex is built without inner stability and connection, without a solid foundation, and therefore it is so often full of holes and unstable from the very beginning. Several years of distraction, of learning nothing, almost destroys it from the ground up, and a woman whose impulse toward intellectual pursuits and activity reawakens in more mature years must begin to build anew, without having the liveliness and elasticity of a youthful mind any longer.

Here we express the pain and suffering of a great many younger and older women, who must conscientiously labor in their later studies to make up what was missed, and who often reach for the schoolbooks of their boys or younger brothers to clarify for themselves even the simplest characteristics of a subject with which they are working. However, not all women are sufficiently conscientious and desirous of the truth to return to this honest point of view, and for many, other duties and circumstances make it impossible later.

The youthful feminine mind is no slower and weaker than the masculine one. It naturally longs for nourishment and growth like the body, but it also needs, like the body, fresh and lively nourishment. There is no better way to dull it than mere mechanical instruction, mere memorization, a catechismlike drumming of things into a person's head, which are neither clear, nor appealing, nor appropriate for developing her abilities. The branch of instruction which is probably the most appropriate for evoking and strengthening a lively mind in a girls' school is surely natural science. It has already been introduced in many institutes and high schools; however, the usually inadequate instruction must be lamented. The natural sciences are still more often viewed as a fashionable field of study, as a concession to the demands of the times, than pursued with the necessary seriousness. Of course, it is enough to introduce a woman to the main outlines of the science, not to its details. However, to understand the main outlines, the same foundation is appropriate which a boy also needs, and which is given to him naturally without objection. It is not the same with girls. More than in any other field of study, there is almost only playing and dallying, with little really learned. As a rule, what we see announced pompously enough as physics, mineralogy, and botany is limited to the display of an electrical machine, a capillary tube, some stones, some dried plants, and a list of Linné's classifications. Only seldom is more achieved. However, it seems that, precisely for the intellectual development of a woman, a thorough, extensive teaching of the laws of nature would be of greater importance. In this field, logical thinking, conscientious thoroughness, and clear comprehension are quite indispensable. Except for grammar, which is always a somewhat dry science, there is certainly nothing so suitable for teaching the female sex, for steadily developing the mind and the ability to comprehend, as becoming well-versed in the laws of the world around us and viewing their harmonious connection. In addition, a woman's small world, in which she is so often called on to work practically, becomes more valued and more interesting to her.

Everything which she has to produce and process in domestic matters is subject to chemical and physical laws, and for every meal which she prepares she needs the various products of the plant or animal world. However, strangely enough, there is nothing we women know so little about as the things with which we have daily contact, and therein lies the best proof of the very abstract nature of our instructional methods and the subjects taught. Certainly we do not mean to say that people can learn how to cook by the study of chemistry alone, and through physics how to keep a dwelling clean, etc., but women would certainly arrange many things in a more thrifty and sensible way if they had a real grasp of these sciences. The mechanical activities of a woman would increase significantly in charm and interest if she could compare them with what she has learned of natural laws and phenomena, and if she could see how they are revealed in the smallest and most insignificant things as well as in the biggest. We women should often be quite ashamed that we can explain neither to ourselves nor to others the normal phenomena which are before our eyes every day. Yet this deficiency is caused as much by the ignorance we are left in by our instruction about the most natural things, as by the inability and lack of desire to investigate a matter thoroughly by ourselves because our intellectual capacity is not sufficiently developed. Precisely for this education on a small scale, for the correct consideration of practical matters, and then on a larger scale for the care of health, for a sensible preparation and combination of foods, for rational care of children and their education—for all these things a woman can become competent in no better way than through a solid teaching of the natural sciences. [. . .]

This way the free and unprejudiced development of the feminine mind is best encouraged to fight against the pettiness and narrow-mindedness which women with a deficient education so easily fall into. At the same time, the ceaseless and harmonious activity of nature sets the finest and most noble example of creation and management before a woman's eyes. Then she will certainly not fall prey to an unpleasant erudition; on the contrary, a truly educated girl will also become the best housewife and mother, provided that she has learned her domestic duties thoroughly as well. A developed intelligence, developed reflection and deliberation are like the sun which delights everything, the greatest to the smallest, equally with its warmth. A person's level of intellectual development is always a gauge of her way of carrying out practical activities. As a woman thinks, speaks, and writes, so she will perform music or any other art; so she will cook, embroider, and sew, so she will run her household and raise her children. The better and more thoroughly our girls learn, the more conscientious and skillful housewives and mothers they will become. Let men realize this especially, and their constant concern about excessive erudition in women will be banished.

Translated by Susan L. Piepke

Fanny Lewald

Seventh Political Letter: Treat Us like Men, so That We Can Become Competent Women *(1870)*

Rahel Varnhagen[1] said once in one of her letters: "Ugly women and Jewesses are always in a fix. The first thing they must always do is prove that they are worthy of love." By and large all women find themselves in the same situation with regard to their intellectual talent. One disputes their ability for this or that branch of knowledge without considering that until now they were denied almost every opportunity to cultivate themselves in the sciences. We are supposed to swim and have not learned how! And now that people are beginning to believe in the possibility that we can make our way in the world as well as men, the same old mistake is being made of treating us as exceptions and adopting or devising separate educational tracks just for us.

I was vividly confronted with an example of this when the Victoria Lyceum for Girls was opened three months ago here in Berlin, and it always strikes me again when there is talk of establishing a university for women.

[...]

If one then asks what this lyceum for girls (where it is planned to increase the subjects of study according to demand and likewise to expand the numbers of lessons for each discipline as needed) can accomplish for the general education of the female sex, then it would seem to me that it is an organization of the type of private instruction that sophisticated and wealthy women occasionally used to acquire for themselves and which in this way can be provided by good teachers to a group and much more cheaply than was possible until now. That is something for which we should be very grateful, a great convenience for many women. It also benefits those who shall earn their bread as teachers and governesses; but such institutes are not a lever or means to improving and elevating the entire level of cultivation, and thus the position, of women in civil society.

---

1. Rahel Varnhagen (1771–1833), Berlin *salonière,* whose letters and diaries often comment cogently on the limitations of being female and Jewish.—Eds.

I must often laugh when I hear it said that there are people who already want to establish universities for women in Germany, because it has not yet occurred to anyone to found universities for male students in their fourth and fifth year of secondary school [*Tertianer*]; and the quality of the work and the truly solid knowledge of the majority of women will hardly compete successfully with a respectable male student in eleventh grade [*Tertianer*], ready for twelfth [*Secunda*].[2] It is always the same pernicious system of being an exception that does not allow women to achieve a more thorough education and thus a complete development of their abilities. However: the complete development of their abilities, which alone makes it possible to use their talents freely, that is true emancipation (in plain German, liberation from the chains of slavery) of the female sex, at least as I understand this often misused expression.

The Victoria Lyceum is, I repeat expressly, a very good institution, but in a certain sense it is an institution of luxury. What we lack, however, is not the top of the tower, but rather a sound foundation. *We need schools, secondary schools* [Realschule] *for women as well as for men. No committee of supportive and highly educated men with their patronage and their good will can help here. Rather, these institutions of learning are owed to us by the cities and the state, to which we women must pay taxes from each dollar that we earn through our own efforts in the same proportion as the men.*

It must be made possible for parents to have their daughters, exactly as their sons, complete from the age of seven to eighteen all levels of an educational establishment that prepares them for further thorough studies, if the daughters have the drive and the ability for this latter possibility. That will not preclude—just as is now done with the boys—taking the girls, depending on the profession that has been designated for them, back into the home, placing them in an apprenticeship for a trade or in a job for which the skills of a secondary school student are sufficient, or employing them in the household of one's own family. I am firmly convinced that the years of strict discipline in a proper school and appropriate employment will do no harm to any woman, that it cannot make her less suited to managing her duties within the house and family. On the contrary.

Indeed, according to the judgment of men, what women are lacking is precisely enduring competence. We are told that our knowl-

---

2. The boys' school is a *Gymnasium,* completion of which is a requirement for university entrance. The new *Lyceum* did not offer the upper levels of classes requisite for completion of the *Abitur.*—Eds.

edge is superficial and that is entirely correct—but the way in which we are instructed in the "secondary schools for young ladies" (the very name is absurd) is set up to make us superficial. In a few years, with moderate effort, we are supposed to master that which one matter-of-factly grants the young man his ten, twelve years to acquire, and in addition from our eighth to our fifteenth year, we should become if possible virtuoso pianists, learn English, French, and Italian, draw from nature, be familiar with and accomplished in needlework and in domestic skills, and have learned to dance. Because that is clearly impossible, we are just taught a little bit of everything, and we leave the schools as one stands up after a dinner of fifteen courses: overfed but in effect not yet satisfied, full of illusions, full of an overestimation of ourselves, and with a true terror about our ignorance when one fine day the hard reality of privation steps up to us and with its pale, serious countenance calls to us: "My elegant young lady! My charming creature of the salon! Kindly find your way now through life and the world."

Whoever really wants to become a liberator of the female sex must therefore above all deliver it from its chronic position of being an exception. The tailor complains: No woman can make a durable button hole. Of course not! A woman learns tailoring in sixteen hours; the tailor's apprentice has an apprenticeship of three years. The critic says: Thoroughness is of no interest to women! Even my own husband has said to me a hundred times: You should not just rely on your dates and facts, but check them carefully! And all who reproach us for these failings, and all of us, who reproach the mass of so-called good housewives for petty prejudices and unresponsiveness to new and improved ideas, and God knows what other weaknesses—all are correct. But the women are not to blame for their superficiality.

The intellectual talents of women are considered less great than those of men, yet we are treated as though we were pure geniuses, and into the bargain as though the genius could find its way without trouble, without effort, and without proper instruction. *Treat us like men, so that we can become competent women!*
[...]
It is not a good deed that one does for us, it is a right that one must and will grant to us; but the rulers, and men are our rulers, are usually more prone to do good deeds than to allow justice. Thus here in Berlin they thought of a shelter for homeless women rather than a solid secondary school (*Realschule*) for us—and of course the shelters are desperately needed.

Translated by Melanie Archangeli

Hedwig Dohm

Are Women Allowed to Study?
Can They Do It? Should They? *(1874)*

I will pose three questions to myself and my readers concerning university study for women:

Are women allowed to study?

Are women capable of study?

Should women study?

To me personally these questions seem as pointless as asking: Is a human being allowed to develop his strengths? Ought he to use his legs for walking? And so forth. But since the majority of my German contemporaries still deny women the right to a learned profession, we in the small minority must not tire of fighting for our convictions, even though we are absolutely certain that shortly, what now seems strange and paradoxical will soon be considered one of the most trivial truths.

[. . .]

Are women allowed to study? Was and is it permitted?

My opponents answer this question in the affirmative, I in the negative. [. . .]

Up to now, one can say that only in America *are women allowed to study*. There, as reported by C. Hippeau,[1] the president of the University of Michigan declared in 1868 that the state legislature had determined that the University of Michigan would achieve the lofty purpose for which it was founded only when women "participated in the rights and privileges of the University."

Thus women are not and have not been allowed to study up until today, or if so, only under conditions so difficult that they amounted to a legal prohibition.

Women, poor things, are and have been allowed to sleep. Educating them would mean waking them up. Can it be that the beautiful fairy tale of Sleeping Beauty is an allegory for womankind? A prick

---

1. The Frenchman Celestin Hippeau (1803–83) reported on developments in higher education around the world. His report, *L'instruction publique aux États-Unis*, had appeared in Paris in 1870.—Eds.

by a spindle plunged Sleeping Beauty into a sleep of many hundreds of years. But the spindle is a symbol of the home and of household work.

Let those thorny hedges keep on growing! The prince (science) will come nonetheless, he will come and awaken her with his kiss of fire.

Are women capable of study?

Obviously, the professors had to answer the question of *whether women are allowed to study* affirmatively. How else could they have denied women's *ability* to study so unconditionally, with such absolute certainty?

[. . .]

It is my opinion that *women should study.*

(1) They should study because every human being has a right to the individual freedom to pursue an occupation according to his inclination. In order to be fulfilling, every activity must be to some extent a performance of a person's inner processes. Freedom to choose one's profession is the most inalienable condition for individual happiness.

(2) They should study because in all probability they possess an internal mental organization that is different from men's (different, but not of lesser quality) and will therefore most likely be in a position to lead the way to new forms of knowledge, new directions for ideas in science. Buckle[2] assumes that women would favor a deductive and ideal method in science, thereby forming a counterweight to men's inductive method, the one-sidedness of which is apt to hold back the progress of knowledge. Here I will refrain from agreeing with him. It is clear that Buckle's view can only be considered an astute hypothesis.

(3) But women should study *medicine,* first in the interest of morality and second, in order to reclaim the lost health of the female sex. A woman knows the physical workings of her own body better than does a man, and never will the latter have the deep compassion that stimulates research or the keen and delicate powers of observation for the sufferings that de-

---

2. Henry Thomas Buckle, English historian (1821–62), applied the law of causality in the sense of materialism to history. Major work: *History of Civilization in England* (1857–61). Hedwig Dohm is probably referring here to Buckle's essay "Women's Influence on Science" (Ger. 1896).—Trans.

stroy a woman's life, the causes and consequences of which he does not comprehend, for reasons I will not go into here.

(4) Women should study for the sake of their subsistence. No one has the right to restrict a class of people with respect to their means of subsistence, unless the state and society assume responsibility for providing appropriately for that class.

(5) Women should study because knowledge and understanding are the highest and most desirable earthly good and because the most suitable sphere for every human being is the highest sphere that humankind has the potential to reach.

[. . .]

We should always turn to "cultural history" to learn about female occupations! The facts of this cultural history are a long story; it holds still so patiently, one can read so much out of and into it! Thus, the masters of science read into it that the home is, was, and forever will be women's sphere.

But I read from cultural history that from the beginning of all time the more powerful one, whether his power was based on his fists, on his soldiers' weapons, or on privileges, oppressed the weaker one, allocating the latter's position in life according to *his will* and for *his benefit,* never inquiring into the natural laws of the oppressed.

I read between the lines how the position of woman in human history changed from century to century, how she gradually wrested her way up from deepest humiliation and disgrace to an existence approximating human dignity. I read from cultural history that before the dawn of civilization, woman was the prey of the lustful male; that she was later raped; then, when the loving father became aware that he possessed, in his daughter, a lucrative consumer good, he sold her and traded her off; that thereupon she was driven into the seraglio like a sheep into the fold. I see her beaten, enslaved, fattened, used as a beast of burden, offered as the prize in a competition like a goose or a calf.

I see her driven out of the temple as "impure"; I see her as a servant at man's side. But that is not all that I learn from cultural history. I also hear the breath of history that drove woman forward from the stultified, vegetative life of a plant to conscious feeling and thinking. And the breath of history and the unconsciously working power of nature will propel her onward, inexorably, until her brow too will be radiant in the glory of the God-man.

You believe, and the majority of men believe with you, that God and the laws of nature have long since decided the woman question;

but *I* believe that the conscious struggle is only beginning and that it will end only when woman has gained the right that is innate to all human beings—the right to be human. With Fichte, I think: "A human being *should* constitute an individual whole, existing on its own. Only under this condition is he a human being."

Translated by Jeanette Clausen

Louise Otto-Peters

Hopes for the Future *(1876)*

Whoever would have said fifty or sixty years ago that every child could create light by means of a little piece of wood would have called forth only laughter.

Whoever upon seeing the first locomotive and the first steamer thirty or forty years ago would have asserted that one would soon be able to travel around the world in eighty or ninety days would have been thought a joker. Pleasure trips by women without male protection were considered the exception.

Whoever would have said that water would be available on every floor of our apartments without the necessity of having the servant girls carry it up, that we could cook without wood and coal, etc., by using oil and gas, would have been thought to be telling fairy tales from never never land.

Ten or twenty years ago whoever set a sewing machine in place of the pretty little sewing table or a washing machine in the washhouse was looked at with a shrug of the shoulders.

These reforms and revolutions in the domestic sphere have countless consequences, some larger, some smaller, and so it continues—on and on.

The changes in our houses and kitchens must lead to changes in the entire lives of women, and the labor that has become superfluous for the family must look for other areas.

Thirty years ago no one would have dreamed that girls would learn gymnastics, swimming, and ice-skating. That was left to boys and men. In general girls had to stay prettily at home and far away from physical activities that were considered unfeminine and injurious to grace and charm. Only dancing was permitted, during dance lessons and at balls the whole night through. There every freedom of interaction between girls and men was also allowed. The girls were permitted, and are still permitted today, to be embraced by the men and spun breathlessly in a passionate whirl, but to meet with men in the course of business or travel without supervision had girls blushing and was thought to be, at least by a certain type of men, a good opportunity, if not a request, to take all liberty with these women. Had anyone said that in stores, offices, etc., young girls and men would work together without associating this with tender interests or physical attraction and without offending, if not morality, at least decorum—there would have been an inquisition into his concept of manners and morality.

Even ten or twelve years ago when we held the first conference of German women, a public meeting led by women was considered a daring enterprise that one would gladly have characterized as comical if it had not turned out to be so worthy of esteem (and more so with every repetition), so that now such an event is no longer extraordinary.

What an event it was about thirty years ago when the first colleges for women teachers were established; again when female teachers, who until then had worked only at private institutions or in families, were also employed by the state and the cities at public schools; yet again when secondary schools for girls (which later included further training until the age of eighteen) were established. Why, then, should it not be likely that some day the number of female teachers will equal that of male teachers, and indeed, in all the schools for females, and that, based on their accomplishments, the female teachers will be considered fully equal to the male teachers? Why should the state not also establish schools for its daughters, similar to the present *Gymnasien* and universities, which are equal to those for its sons (along with other institutions, of course, that meet the needs not just of womanhood, but of future progress in general), because even if we cannot discuss this topic any further here, the reorganization of these secondary schools belongs to the burning issues of the day.

If a *few* women have now succeeded in achieving an academic education and doctorates—why should not some day many succeed and finally everything be arranged so that they can succeed? If there are already some female physicians who wrest respect from their male colleagues—why should there not one day be so many that it would no longer be necessary for any woman to be treated by a man, and no longer required that women overcome their natural feeling of shame? Were this feeling still to occur, it would be characterized as excessive, since it would no longer be called for as it is now. Why then should it not reach the point that even at the highest educational establishments women, like men, would lecture for women so that here, too, every currently unavoidable offense to the feminine sense of delicacy, shame, and propriety would no longer be necessary? Whether in this future these women would be called doctors or professors does not matter. As soon as they have the same opportunity as the men to develop their abilities and the same right to practice them, the goal that hovers before us will be achieved.

Translated by Melanie Archangeli
with Patricia A. Herminghouse

On the Domestic Education of Girls *(1876)*

If we add to our reflections on the present some tips on the domestic education of girls, we mean by this their education at home and for the home, and do not intend to speak here about kindergarten, elementary school, or boarding school; not that we disregard them because we underestimate, also in their educational influence, these establishments devoted to the instruction and cultivation of girls. Yet at this very moment so much is being written and debated about them, that it seems appropriate for once to draw attention to domestic education, because in many families the notion threatens to spread that it is sufficient to send their children to the best kindergarten and the best elementary school for them to become good, useful, and happy human beings, while we are of the opinion that the best education to this end must take place in the home.

(1) Playtime for Girls

In kindergarten, the games are divided into active games—whenever possible outdoors—and games for the imagination and needlework while sitting quietly inside, and this arrangement should be maintained until the end of schooling draws nearer. One should grant the girls this harmless playtime not just because life becomes serious and filled with work and sorrow all too soon anyway, but also for the sake of their physical and psychological growth—only in the proper sequence of work and pleasure, of the free unfolding and thoughtful direction of will and strength, can character attain the harmony that is the law of the world and thus of all human existence and life.

Kindergarten games—those symbolic games of action with their clever songs, those building blocks, colorful balls, and woven baskets—should lay the foundation for this harmonious development and can be carried beyond kindergarten; but neither parents nor children should be satisfied with that.

Then there is, however, the main plaything for girls: the doll.

We do not want to be so cruel as to deprive girls of all dolls, to get rid of entirely all the dolls in the world as was recently suggested by some thinking women and mothers, but we do want to advise caution in the choice of dolls and to make people aware of the influence that precisely dolls have on the development of the female character—as strange as that may sound.

Realism is unfortunately the sign of our time and it has also seized control of toys, and our industry, which has progressed to the level of art, takes pleasure in imitating everything real and thus transferring all the fashions of adults to the world of dolls and reproducing all household gadgets in miniature.

One must in fact be amazed by these dolls, infants that cry, open and close their eyes, wiggle their arms and legs, or say "Papa" and "Mama," crawl around the room, or have such an abundance of hair that one can fix any hairstyle. One can't help but smile about these kitchens with alcohol burners in the appliances and stoves, with all the necessary cooking utensils and supplies in the pantry, with real ham measured in inches, and hampers with bottles of champagne, etc. One finds them charming, these dollhouses with the most elegant parlor that lacks neither the clock on the mantelpiece nor the photo album on the reading table, or the bedroom where neither the toiletries on the washstand nor the wax tapers in their silver box are missing, and everything according to the latest design. And one must be equally amazed by these female dolls who are attired in the latest fashions and own a trunk with a complete wardrobe for every season, but in all this there are two very important considerations:

First: that nothing remains to be done by the imagination, that the imagination is spared all effort and so must atrophy without use.

Second: that by playing with dolls the mind of the young girl is directed only toward the superficial and is forcefully driven to find pleasure in fashion and luxury and to concentrate its own efforts and desires solely in this area.

Actual play and its purpose almost ceases with this imitation of reality. Instead of one's faculty being trained to think for oneself, invent, and create, it is lulled to sleep, and very soon boredom enters in place of lively interest. So it is that exactly those girls who have the most beautiful and fully equipped dolls and playthings are the ones who most quickly grow weary of playing, or who constantly demand more and new toys, and who do not even know where to begin with other more simple material. They consider themselves too refined and intelligent for that, but in truth they are not only too spoiled, but rather too dumb, too lacking in fantasy and thoughts, to imagine something other than what exists in reality, what can be grasped in one's hands and recognized at first sight without effort. Through this stifling of the imagination the foundation is laid for the future world of fine ladies, boring to themselves and others, where interests revolve only around real and material things, which, in the best case, only make sense for one's children as long as they let themselves be considered as dolls, and for the kitchen as long as it only concerns arranging it, and in the worse case for the salon and everything that has to do with clothing, fashion, and luxury.

Some mother will perhaps want to contradict us and say that her little daughter does not waste her time by playing with her elegant doll because all its modern costumes as the lady of the ball and the salon, or at home and in morning dress, are fashioned by her daughter's own little hands. In that case we want precisely this woman to consider how this little girl, who studies the costumes of adults and the fashion journals in order to try them out on the doll, most surely prepares herself to be infatuated by fashion, to become a spendthrift for whom, as was first the case with the dolls and later with herself, nothing is good or elegant enough, a creature who, in a word, knows no higher interest than fashion and luxury, who sacrifices her time and youth, perhaps even herself, in a marriage based on calculation or in some other relationship even more unworthy.

So often girls are accused of their superficiality, of their limited horizon—without considering that the foundation for this is laid in the nursery.

Much less dangerous than these realistic toys are the imaginative ones: puppets and puppet theater. Here the subjective element moves to the background and the objective is forced to the foreground. The girl does not identify with the puppets, she controls them and thus stands above them. In a more romantic time than the present, our classic writers, in the form of the main characters of their works, were represented in the puppets and games of girls. To costume the puppets beautifully and with historical accuracy was a more poetic and selfless pleasure than consulting the fashion journals for the dolls' toilette and this pursuit employed small hands no less.

In contrast to playing with dolls we would like to recommend, whenever possible, activity with flowers and animals as a source of joy. A bit of gardening outdoors or inside promotes one's sense of nature, without which no pure enjoyment of nature is possible later on, and taking on the care of animals, be it hens or rabbits in the yard, be it a dog in the house, a cat, a little bird in the room, provides the opportunity for the unfolding of the most precious instinct of feminine nature: taking care of others, doing for others, protecting them, loving them. Of course this should not degenerate into that excessive affection that only torments the animals instead of benefiting them; rather that love must prevail which hears the wishes of the object of love and seeks to satisfy them.

The girl who takes good care of her little bird, protects the brooding hen, feeds the cat and the dog, will improve her own ability to love and become accustomed to the consideration of others for all time.

Generally speaking, it is in no way necessary to constantly direct the girls at play, only to give them the time and opportunity, to leave them alone and not always observe them, for without freedom and self-determination not only the joy of play is lost, but also the best aspects of its formative and determinative influence on character.

Girls should and must learn much more today, and thus they need more time for recovery and play than did their predecessors. Constant sitting with lessons and needlework or at the piano endangers their physical and mental abilities. Therefore let also girls frisk about as much as possible in the yard and garden, and grant them not just restrained walks on popular promenades, but also seek the opportunity for carefree romps, best of all in the country, in the woods, and in the fields.

Translated by Melanie Archangeli

Helene Lange

From Higher Education of Women in Europe *Why Women Should Be Admitted to Universities (1889)*

Attempts have also been made by women in Germany during the last two decades to obtain admission to the universities, although they were but rare cases. A few professors have looked upon such endeavors with favor, but they did not care to make themselves the leaders of the cause. Here and there permission has been granted to a few auditors—especially to foreign ladies—but of late this has been accompanied by many limitations. No women are admitted to regular enrollment and women are excluded on principle from taking the secondary school examination that would make them eligible for university study. German women are forced to go to foreign countries if they will not forego a higher education.

It can not be asserted, and it certainly is not, that the two great nations of the German tongue have taken a very progressive position in this question, but German Austria stands ahead of Germany, to be sure.

To answer the question, why women insist at present upon admission to the university, is to give all the reasons for the great women's movement. In our time material and intellectual wants urge woman as never before. Material hardship—the replacement of hand labor by machine labor, on the one hand, and the increasing number of unmarried women, on the other—leaves a great number of women without visible means of support. The same circumstances create an intellectual hardship in comfortable circles where there is no material need, and this need is equally hard to bear.

[...]

Complaints are being raised about the crowds of female applicants at teachers' examinations, which is interpreted as an evil sign of the times. *There can be no better sign.* That something happens which in former times would have been thought outrageous, namely, that the daughters of our first families long for work and demand rational, intelligent assistance in and control of their studies, that they elevate the profession upon which they used to look down, is a gain that can not be gauged too highly.

But the teacher's profession is not for all. Let them choose another livelihood. It is equally gratifying to notice that nursing the sick is beginning to be taken up as a profession and that it is deemed important enough to be learned professionally. Likewise it is a sign of better times that the kindergartens are attracting the girls of better situated classes. The realm of arts and crafts and of trades, too, is opening to women. All that, however, is insufficient. If work is to have a redeeming influence, it must be chosen in conformity with one's taste, and according to one's own powers and talents. Hence no area should be closed to women, not even the highest intellectual development. Those who hunger intellectually should be offered the best intellectual food available in Germany. No one in Germany should be denied opportunities to fill that inner desolate void, no one obliged to stifle what we most respect: the longing for serious mental and professional work. Yet this murder of the mind is committed daily in our country.

Should any one be unreceptive to such idealistic arguments for offering academic training and the professions themselves to women, he may be open to practical ones. They are the ever increasing hardships faced by women and the necessity for employing them in certain professions. People still prefer to deny the need among German women. A few figures will prove it. According to the census of December 1, 1885, Germany had 15,181,823 adult women, that is, women of marriageable age, sixteen years and over. Of these, 7,944,445, or 52.3 percent, were married; 5,155,241, or 34 percent, were unmarried; 2,082,137, or 13.7 percent, had been married. Hence, taking the last two numbers together, there were 7,237,378 women, or 47.7 percent, without any "natural supporter," leaving out of consideration the fact that many of those who had this supporter were still without support.

[. . .]

Causes of Failure in Germany

But let us further examine the peculiarly German conditions that are always said to be obstacles in the way of higher education of women. "The conditions that exist at our universities do not allow it." Why not? The examinations are more difficult than elsewhere. Maybe, but who asks that they should be made easier for women? The demand is only that women be admitted under precisely the same conditions applied in the case of men. If the women prove less capable of meeting the requirements, as will probably be the case in the beginning, it could only please those who desire to limit the higher studies of women; but that the difficulty of the examinations should be a cause for nonadmittance of women is incomprehensible to me. Furthermore: "Our students would never tolerate females as fellow-students." Are these students really so far behind other nations in culture? But that leads me to a point that deserves a more extensive treatment.

It is true that the German student still reflects many of the values of the old traditional fraternity, but, I think, he has enough regard for woman to respect her, even if he sees her walking unfamiliar roads, provided she remains a woman. But I do not require him to respect women to whom scholarship is the subordinate, and the life of a student the principal goal. I fear, in this respect, that much mischief has been done by foreign women in Switzerland, who have thus made the life of their successors, who are bent upon pursuing knowledge, a life of many hardships. The cause of unfeminine excesses may be found in the fact that quite young girls at the university often have no choice except to live as male students do without any restraint, to take their meals and to live without intimate association with older educated women. Of course, gradually but surely, the sense for that which is proper gets blunted, and the maxim "Allowed is what is proper" must yield to "Allowed is what pleases." I can suggest only one remedy, namely, the one that was applied in England, of course adapted to existing institutions: the establishment of boarding institutions in which the students associate with older, finely educated women and are subject not to harsh discipline, but to moral influence; homes in which the student enjoys the same liberty that an educated and cultured lady *has,* or better, *takes* in her own home. For the liberty to lead a street or tavern life, which seems to be the highest ambition for a young man after entering the university, is one which a cultured woman will not take even where the circumstances would permit it. Since she cannot find interesting society in taverns and on the street, she needs it all the more at home. A woman must not, during the years of study, lose the instincts which make her seek her happiness at home; she must not lose the standard of measurement for what she may or may not do. In time to come and under the influence of another kind of education she will be enabled to avoid the shoals on which she is likely to experience shipwreck at present.

[. . .]

In short, it does not seem to lie in external circumstances that the women of Germany are not successful. Even pecuniary difficulties cannot be advanced as causes. Germany is not so poor that it could not make arrangements for higher education of women, since the existing institutions for men could mostly be shared.

Is it the men, then, who are the problem? Without doubt they are partly to blame. For many years certain women have tried to interest men of influence in their cause, but it must be confessed, they have not found the cooperation that women found in other countries. The year in which Girton College was founded, and the professors and students of Cambridge observed its growth with increasing interest, is the same year (1872) in which a teachers' congress at Weimar met with scorn and derision the women who sought their support for a plan to found a modest academy for women. The propositions and petitions which subsequently were submitted to the authorities with reference to that plan have been completely ignored. The authorities have engaged men exclusively in the many newly-established secondary schools for girls, although women were available who have through self-instruction gained the necessary requirements and have proved in private schools that they are capable of managing schools as well as teaching the higher levels.

Translated by L. R. Klemm;
revised by Patricia A. Herminghouse

Hedwig Dohm

The Reform of Girls' Schools *(1908)*

Little child-humans know nothing of their gender. They are trained from infancy to be different, even their toys suggesting the nature they should have. A doll for the girl, a toy soldier for the boy.
[...]
Teaching girls to prepare for their future occupation [as wives and mothers] means abandoning the reform of female education. . . . The old identification of gender and occupation, which makes further development of the female impossible in any case, is perpetuated; social

and intellectual progress are halted in favor of an ideal of domesticity that is daily becoming more dubious.

The most serious objection to coeducation is based on female biology, on the view that woman's biological side will necessarily be stunted by emphasizing the intellectual side.

Recently, learned professors (addressing the debates on girls' schools) have again emphasized in writings and lectures that women "lose not only their nobility of heart but also their immediacy of feeling and judgment through too much knowledge." One of the professors even added derisively: "Apparently there is a desire to correct female nature orthopedically."

"The more knowledge one drums into girls, the dumber they get." This pronouncement of male intelligence was delivered in the *Reichstag*.

Thus I—lacking higher education as I do—may perhaps be permitted to try to solve the question of girls' education with the unspoiled immediacy of thought and judgment conferred on me by the grace of the professor. For me it is like the egg of Columbus. Three words will settle the matter: *comprehensive schooling* and *coeducation*.

[. . .]

Germany's postsecondary schools still do not have coeducation. But studying the same curriculum in the high schools is already having a unifying effect on the children. I have many opportunities to observe interaction among these young people. I am surprised and deeply pleased by the nature of this interaction, where emotional and intellectual interests intersect. The boys no longer ignore or disparage the girls; the idea that "you can't talk about anything with girls" no longer exists.

Boys between the ages of fourteen and eighteen are nearly always poets. However, they read the infant progeny of their muses not to their male schoolmates—but to the girls.

No doubt they also help each other with their math and Latin homework, discuss their essay topics, lend each other serious books or poetry, and argue spiritedly over their views of a hero from Schiller or Shakespeare.

Suffice it to say that boys discern the girls' intellectual equality during coeducational instruction, and in sports their comparable dexterity and endurance.

[. . .]

To my astonishment, even progressively-minded women's groups have offered only feeble and lukewarm opposition to that ministerial decree [limiting girls' education],[1] if they did not actually support it. And yet this question is of fundamental significance for all women (and in particular concerning education for suffrage).

It is possible that a politics of opportunism played a role in this lukewarm reaction, a tactic that was adapted to the obduracy of the authorities who make the rules.

Perhaps the women's modesty was also based on a feeling of gratitude for what has already been achieved.

And in fact, when I think back on my youth, I am amazed and delighted by the achievements of the last fifty years.

Alas for the schoolchild of my childhood days! Fifty or sixty years ago it was still believed that keeping still—outwardly and inwardly—was something desired by nature in the female child. As if such a poor little mite must serve out its time for failing to have been born a boy.

Knitting and darning stockings in their free time! The more rounds that were knitted during a specific period of time, the more well-behaved the child (reminiscent of Cinderella picking peas out of the ashes). What an important role stockings played at the time! The knitting machine was not yet universally available, nor had the Kneipp cure[2] yet removed the stigma from going barefoot—though only at certain times.

Going sliding, along the gutter for example, was a boy's prank. Even throwing a snowball had to be done furtively by girls, with a bad conscience.

I think back with inexpressible bitterness on that period of physical and intellectual inhibition, which crippled every gifted female soul who had been born to become a full human being, wearing her down to an automaton-like creature.

Only those who experienced that age as their destiny know how tragic it was.

Translated by Jeanette Clausen

---

1. Dohm is here referring to a proposal by the then minister of education to limit the reformed girls' schools to offering religious and moral education.—Trans.

2. Kneipp cure: a holistic health treatment based on natural foods, exercise in the fresh air, and cold baths, developed by a pastor, Sebastian Kneipp (1821–97)—Trans.

Alice Salomon

Twenty Years Ago *(1913)*

Of the generation of girls growing up twenty years ago, those from the wealthy and educated classes and many from middle class circles no longer had the obligation or even the opportunity to do useful work. Today it is everyday knowledge, discussed already by school-boys and girls in their essays, that industrial development and modern technology have lessened the economic tasks of the household, and that daughters often no longer find a sufficient sphere of activity in the family. Today the daughters of the middle class have followed on the path trodden long ago by the girls of the working classes. They have turned to employment, to paid work. Twenty years ago, this was still seen—by no means only in wealthy circles—as something very extraordinary and usually as something inappropriate. Louise Otto-Peters's dictum that "work is a duty and an honor for the female sex"[1] had not yet passed into the consciousness of the masses. And just as wide circles of society saw employment of their daughters as inappropriate to their social position, the desire for higher education was not thought "girl-like." Those who wanted to learn far more than was taught in old-style secondary schools for girls were labeled bluestockings, which was not a title of honor. People also thought that a lot of learning was not healthy for young girls. But above all, there was no opportunity for it whatsoever. One took some language lessons, heard some lectures in the Victoria Lyceum for girls,[2] which back then offered the *only* advanced educational opportunity in Berlin apart from seminaries for female teachers, which were vocational schools. For girls who left school at the end of the 1880s, there was still no opportunity for a college-preparatory education. In order to achieve what today is possible for girls in any larger provincial town, preparation for the diploma exam *(Abitur),* one would have had to send fifteen or sixteen-year-old chil-

---

1. See, for example, Otto-Peters's essay, "On the Domestic Education of Girls," pp. 33–36 in this section.—Eds.

2. See Fanny Lewald's comments in the Victoria Lyceum, p. 25 in this section. —Eds.

dren abroad. But the thought of something like that was as far from the girls' minds as from their parents'. They did not even know it was possible. Most girls had neither enough imagination nor originality to make of their own accord such demands beyond their ken. If, between my sixteenth and twentieth year, I had heard of a woman with a university education, it would surely not have seemed to me an ideal worth striving for, but rather a kind of natural wonder.

Therefore, girls just stayed home and lay fallow, feeding canaries, watering plants, embroidering doilies, playing piano, and "waiting." What a modern poetess has said about women in general was absolutely true for the girls of that time: that "they are always sitting there and waiting to see if the door opens and someone comes in." It was such an unbearable situation for both active and thoughtful natures that many of them gradually lost faith in the meaningfulness of life. But it was also a situation that could seriously endanger the girls' moral standard. The lack of real tasks easily led to the loss of any sense of duty; their whole existence in the shadows led to superficiality and shallowness; energies focused on externalities led to failure to recognize life's true values, to confusing appearance and essence; and habituation to inactivity led to disinclination toward even the smallest services and acts of kindness. Finally, not being needed by others led to gross egotism. It was the worst preparation conceivable for the life of a woman, which after all tends to bring duties in one form or another. It was a waste of vital energies that meant an injustice to society as well as to those concerned.

The founding of the "girls' and women's groups for social service" pulled us out of this misery. It brought girls the call to work that they needed so desperately; to work for which they were needed, work that was waiting for them and that allowed them to feel needed. It thus brought purpose and meaning to their lives.

Translated by Jörg Esleben

Gertrud Bäumer

In the Light of Memory *(1953)*

Female students were not admitted for enrollment in the university until 1908. Until this date, the decision as to whether and to what extent they could attend lectures and courses had rested with the professor. There were uncompromising opponents, like Weinhold's successor, Roethe,[1] who upon his appointment had even arranged to reserve for himself the right to still exclude matriculated women. There were professors who admitted us, but only from a certain feeling of propriety, with no positive inner attitude toward the new academic type. Erich Schmidt[2] was among them, which I quite understood. This handsome, lively, masculine teacher had his own hearty and strong relationship to his students—his seminar had a definite style in this respect, an old-fashioned atmosphere of male academia prevailed in the group. We did not exactly fit into this, despite all individual demonstrations of colleagueship, which was quite unconditional among the students when they respected one's achievements. A certain elite worked very well and with complete dedication, with a true *amor intellectualis,* in the seminar. The professor's assistant wrote a letter to me after my doctoral defense, in which he remarked, in a fine show of loyalty, on this unconditional common sense of purpose in our work as the basis for the attitude toward women in academe. Nonetheless, we felt strongly how different the academic atmosphere was. This difference, much more than any exterior obstacles, presented an inner, psychological challenge to us. By "us," however, I do not mean all female students. There were those who did not have the nerves for this challenge and also those who saw in it a form of resistance to women in academe, a resistance against which one "ought to go to battle." But after all, we were confronted by a youthful way of life that reflected male nature through the centuries. We certainly shared the characteristics of

---

1. Karl Weinhold (1823–1901), professor of German and folklore; Gustav Roethe (1859–1926), professor of German in Göttingen and Berlin.—Trans.

2. Erich Schmidt (1853–1913), literary historian, professor in Strasbourg, Vienna, and Berlin.—Trans.

youth and spirit, but the organic fusion of male and female nature was still lacking. In a certain sense, this was also true for ways of looking at the objects of humanistic study; one sensed it clearly in some professors from the start, then not at all in others. Harnack[3] and Dilthey,[4] for example, stood above this way of thinking and evaluating in terms of gender. They opened a zone of human wisdom as unconditionally to us as to our male fellow students. By contrast, old Weinhold, whose fine book *German Women in the Middle Ages* reflected his chivalrous attitude, could not overcome the conflict between his benevolence and his sense of style with regard to the atmosphere of the university. He was reluctant to see female students exposed to the robust tone of the men, but he also did not want to bar their access to academe, and so he established a ladies' seminar in addition to the regular German seminar. However, in the long run we could not accept this compromise, especially those who wanted to go further than the exam for female secondary school teachers, the goal which fundamentally determined the requirements and level of the courses. Consequently, the insistent requests of some succeeded in opening up admission into the regular seminar. Not for long, though, since Weinhold died and the "ban on ladies" of his successor Roethe came into effect. The female students of Erich Schmidt, who as such were members of the German seminar, sat in the library next to the seminar room and had to see what they could glean; given Roethe's vocal capacity, it was fairly possible to follow along. Most of the female students were older back then, in their mid-twenties. Thus, they experienced their studies differently than if they had come straight from school. Almost all of them had to endure conflicts with the world in which they lived in order to study. In the fullest, most significant sense, their studies were a matter of vital concern for them, and so they experienced the grandeur and problems of academe more intensively.

Translated by Jörg Esleben

---

3. Adolf von Harnack (1851–1930), Protestant theologian, famous for his lectures about the nature of Christianity (1909).—Trans.

4. Wilhelm Dilthey (1833–1911), founder of the new humanities based on experience and understanding.—Trans.

Bertha Pappenheim

The Jewish Girl *(1934)*

"The Jewish Girl," like "The Jewish Woman," cannot be captured in a modern snapshot so that one sees the background in the picture. For this one has to go back to the vague time of "the Old Jews," in order to get a little perspective on the present situation. Working this way one comes to the strange realization that although the sexual and married life of Jews has received extreme attention, the partners necessary for these are esteemed unequal—as if service to God and service to the world would not be extinguished and exhausted if the differences between man and woman were not complementary in this service.

The unequal estimate of both creatures, absolutely dependent on each other, can only be explained in that male law givers and interpreters had given themselves a preferred position, which in the course of time became a philosophy. If there were strong solidarity among women—which does *not* now exist—there might have been an amusing strike by women to undo this philosophy and demonstrate its absurdity.

Although the "Old Jews" cannot possibly have overlooked that women are necessary, they consider a female child of second rank. This can already be seen in the different reception of a new citizen of the world. If, after the birth, the father or somebody else asked what "it" was, the answer might be either a satisfied report of a boy or, with much pity for the disappointment, "Nothing, a girl," "Only a girl." Thus ended not only months of expectation but many happy hopes that had to be postponed for some other time.

[...]

In the "good old days" there was no trouble about pedogogic problems. The basis of education was Jewish law and its demands on life. An education outside of the Jewish one had little place in the family. In the East boys were sent to *Cheder* (primary school) from the third year on to learn. Girls just picked up the little they were allowed to know or wanted to know. In the somewhat more advanced West, well-to-do families had tutors. In this way *Bachurim,* students, brought a certain spirituality to the families and in return got a little culture.

But for girls' education, very few efforts were made because the goal of their life was seen in the earliest possible marriage. At an age at which we today consider a girl still to be half a child and treat her accordingly, in the ghetto she was married, or at least engaged. These engagements and early marriages were very often arranged by parents without any question of involvement by the young partners. Carefully prepared, discussed in all details and laid down in a contract, they were accepted by all involved without any romantic feelings.

"Enlightenment" of the often completely innocent bride is said often to have been handled after the wedding ceremony by her mother with deep psychological trauma and torrents of tears on both sides. Here, I believe, is to be seen atavistically for our time the beginning (although historically not the deepest origin) of psychological and sexual practices which seem to us today crude mistakes and blunders: white slave trade and pretended marriage. The foolish and myopic way of arranging marriages without any mutual attraction, even without the basis of a marriage of convenience can't hold up in present day conditions—and girls and women are made to bear the consequences. The end of the short girlhood was usually and traditionally the ritual cutting of the hair of the weeping young bride during the wedding ceremony. Her charm was substituted with a bad fitting *"scheitel"* (wig) or a big cap which also covered the forehead. Wearing the cap was naturally not only a Jewish custom. These elaborate creations of colored ribbons and often very valuable lace-work were everywhere the sign of wedded dignity, and to wear a cap was always the dream and goal of all young maidens. In spite of all that strikes us today as strange and antiquated, it seems that careful discussion of all mutual conditions and expectations by future marriage partners, strengthened rather than weakened family life and happiness. It was understood, in those days, that every Jewish girl married. The "gray plait" of the unmarried girl—the spinster—was a nightmare. To collect the dowry and outfit for poor brides was one of the *mitzvahs* of families and congregations.

[. . .]

The life of these childish girls developed exclusively in the narrow confines and under strict supervision of the family. The goal of such existence may be summed up in three words: Children, kitchen, clothes—and the practical skills necessary to acquire and care for them. Because of the dietary laws it was important to be able to cook. It was always important because eating—to counter-balance despised drinking—was a well-accepted, religiously consecrated pleasure of Jews, which to this day holds special importance on Friday evening and on the Sabbath. Girls and young brides had to know how to cook. To be able to cook and to manage a home, however, require different gifts and techniques. Physical labor was not well liked by Jewish girls and if at all possible handed over to somebody else, which was not at all good for the people concerned—even today. It was very important psychologically where one worked: in one's own home or in someone else's for pay. Here is the root of our rejection of domestic service as a despised profession, despite its great importance for the future life of girls. Jewish girls never considered spiritualizing housework. Even today few women and girls think that these are wings which may lift them above the quotidian.

The short apprenticeship of a Jewish girl before her marriage and development into a wife and mother of a large number of children gave her little chance to practice needlework. Preparation of the dowry was considered very important. Big parcels of linen, tablecloths, silk and lace showed off the wealth of the family and were included in the dowry. Preparation of the dowry offered some opportunity to do needlework, but the ability to cut and to sew scarcely extended beyond making a shirt with a neckband of the type a German girl was supposed to finish in one month and which had to be sewn like embroidery. There were no "unmentionables" [lingerie]. Knitting, patching, and mending were considered important. The trousseau was mostly marked in red cross-stitches with the name of the bride, because one began long before one knew the future groom and because—"God forbid—one never knows!" There was very little taste. Technique was undeveloped and design when it was used, primitive.

When the windows and doors of the ghettos slowly opened, girls were the first to sniff the new air. They could do it because nobody was interested in their spiritual development or attached any importance to it, and also, because the age of marriage slowly advanced. A real "girlhood" finally made its appearance. The lasting influence of the new age of emancipation came to the girls less in a purely spiritual way—through the influence of philosophy, art, and romance in literature (which seldom diminished their willingness to marry)—but rather through economic, social, and political upheaval and reorganization, social and political influences. Regardless from which direction the wind came which made the girls wish for spiritual and material independence, there was in the beginning a common tendency to reject the family, which did not prevent financial assistance—so to speak, a flight of a kite, on a longer or shorter cord for each flight.

Nowhere did these changes begin suddenly, but they were very much influenced by the milieu, whether in the East or in the West, according to the tradition and economic situation, the political and religious inclination of the family, and the opinion of what is right and desirable for a girl—there is, fortunately, still no unanimity today. The misery and the repression under which the Jews in Eastern Europe were forced to live and which made out of them pauperized and proletarian masses influenced the Jewish girl as soon as she took wings to leave home and join the ranks of working women and students. In such highly political groups their long-repressed vitality found a hard-won but happy freedom—the breaking of all ties and practices was almost a sacred act for the individual. Many Jewish girls, especially in Russia and Poland, assimilated completely to their gentile, non-religious, political surroundings in a most revolutionary way. These women have been described in literature. For others, Zionism offered an equally valuable release and stimulation, as a movement "national," social and revolutionary in some ways, but without deserting Jewish tradition. On the contrary, to follow it and to revitalize it in culture, history, and language was the highest goal. It looks, at a distance, as if Zionism might give women equality; but the question remains whether the Zionists will, within equality, respect the difference of girls within their own social constellation—or whether these issues will be overridden by political considerations.

In the West the development of girlhood has taken completely different forms from those in the East. There was no proletarian misery, but a relatively secure, bourgeois existence for Jews. Compulsory school attendance was of decisive importance. All types of schools up to the university level were equally accessible to all three denominations. In Germany the struggles which preceded the possibility of professional education for women, sought by the women of the feminist movement, did not exclude Jewish girls. Thus we see them take the path which until the most recent fate of the Jews was available or at least theoretically possible: almost without outside effort—sometimes only with the opposition of families—Jewish girls had for almost two decades a relatively free choice of profession depending on their desires, their gifts, and their economic situation. This was not without influence on the human substance of the flexible nature of girls, but they differed very much from each other; so much so that the different types each went their separate ways. What they had in common was their distance from the family—often they called it *sacro-egoismo*—and a later marriage age. Most important is that we can no more speak of girlhood in the usual way if we mean the transition from childhood to marriage. We see that in this age group the individual borders of girlhood have become very fluid. The unmarried, mature, respected independent woman, welcome in all cultural circles, emerged, who in her entire being can be, and is, fully responsible for shaping her life, shaping her fate, in a sexual way fully responsible only to herself and completely free in the world. If one identifies girlhood with marriage-age, including, practically and psychologically, the possibility, chance, and desire to get married, then one must consider this time one full of spiritual and social development for a Jewish woman in Germany, yet one might also find in it the root of a reproach that the education of girls is handled rather superficially—considered only as a stopgap—while waiting to get married, with no goal of a serious profession. This assumption, like others, may not always be true and depends on individual and social conditions. For the older ones it is less true for than for the younger ones. Therefore, we find that—if we try to see some pattern in the whirl of girlhood—the members of trade and business professions are least serious at the start. I willingly admit exceptions. They have few broader interests because, tired from physical exertion, they naturally accept the easiest and cheapest relaxation; they are willing to be sexually stimulated and happily do not consider that at their age lipstick and powder do not improve their youthful freshness and charm, but only hurt it.

It is different—no, it was once—for university students who through secondary school and college entrance examinations [*Abitur*] have already shown their determination. But even study at the university doesn't always mean maturity, which gives a serious goal to girlhood although it may well be combined with a healthy bubbling gaiety. Many women students in the halls and classrooms of the university, more or less subdued flirts, shaking their permanent curls and taking out of their briefcases (status symbols of their scholarly interests) a surprising number of apples and sandwiches, will not grow out of their "girlhood" by study. Music and other subjects very seldom develop beyond the expectations of girlhood, or let a happy talent develop into a serious achievement and endeavor.

[. . .]

The last decade has touched and enriched the life of Jewish girls in two different ways, by sports and by life in youth groups. I have not been able to watch the girl Jewish athlete closely, but I forsee only a good physical influence from gymnastics, swimming, lawn games, and hiking, if not overdone so that all other activities are excluded. But the influence of youth groups has to be mentioned in a serious study like this one, if only briefly. Girls naturally prefer mixed youth groups to those for girls only, although in the latter there is more chance to deal with special interests and career planning through discussion and lectures. Mixed activities, however, are more acceptable to youth and certainly more amusing because of the way they bring together the sexes. The strict partisan approach seems to me less attractive for girls who are instinctively less narrow. That youth groups are already breeding grounds later partisan divisiveness is very much to be deplored, in view of the desirability of maintaining the generally peaceful atmosphere of the Jewish community but this we cannot discuss. We can unfortunately see that the influence of the youth groups on the girls is very often not a positive one. The youth groups tear the pre-adolescent and adolescent young people out of their families, in which they should remain firmly rooted for the future, because during girlhood religious ties through education and custom should surround the whole religious existence. Outside the home, demands on the strength and time of young people disturb or reduce this continuity.

[. . .]

And now a word concerning the attitude which the whole younger generation, not only the Jewish one, takes toward the feminist movement. In their arrogant judgment of the goals of the "old ladies," university women in particular look down on the times that they have outgrown and on the women who fought for them with indulgent pity. But the mills of time sometimes grind uncannily fast. What yesterday was acquired and won, is now disappearing. Therefore, we old ones should not speak of "ingratitude" but should try to understand the law of historical development. Whatever form the development of the Jewish people may take in any place, the Jewish girl must obviously be considered a living part of it and her determination and ability will be decisive for the possibility and durability of the edifice of Jewish life, as a preparation for the important duty of a "mother in Israel," the last and highest goal of Jewish woman's essence.

Translator unknown

Ika Hügel-Marshall

At Home en Route: A German Life *(1998)*

In the same little Bavarian town where I was born, my mother had come into the world, she in 1925, I in 1947. She was tall and slim then, with medium-brown hair and blue eyes, the youngest child of a respectable working-class family of eleven. When she was ten years old, her father died. At age fourteen she was already earning money; continuing her schooling or pursuing higher education was unthinkable, despite good grades. She worked as a domestic in an exclusive Munich residential area.

When the so-called ban on fraternization was proclaimed on September 12, 1944, my mother was a girl of nineteen. According to this ban, members of the Allied Forces were forbidden to visit Germans in their homes, to accompany them to dances, sports events, public functions or on walks, or to marry German women. A strict check was kept on the Allies' contacts with Germans. The reason for these rigid measures was a desire to ensure the safety of the military personnel. After all, the German Reich had instigated a frightful war and thus every contact with the population of this country was considered dangerous and suspected of espionage. Germans must have no opportunity to attack members of the Allied Forces. The media warned the soldiers over and over against contact with Germans, especially against keeping company with German women and girls. The prohibition on friendly contact was further intended to force the Germans to face their culpability for their fascist crimes.

However, the ban on fraternization had a completely different effect on the African-American soldiers in the U.S. Army. The racism within the Army converged with the racism they faced from Germans. They would have been forbidden to enter into any kind of contact with the white population even without a ban on fraternization. Thus, this ban applied doubly to them. As far as black soldiers were concerned, the Allies and the Germans were apparently in agreement. Nonetheless, white and black soldiers alike paid little heed to the order. They proved to be extremely fond of children and were generous in handing out food, chocolate, and cigarettes.

In May 1945—after the end of the war in Europe—the bans related to fraternization were relaxed: members of the Army could now be seen in public with Germans, and all restrictions were finally lifted on October 1, 1945, except for two regulations. Visiting Germans in their homes or marrying Germans was still forbidden. German women who had contact with American soldiers were reviled as "Yankee-whores," "Yankee-lovers," and—in the case of African-American soldiers, as "Nigger-whores."

My parents met in the summer of 1946; my mother was almost twenty-one years old. They met secretly, for their relationship was immoral in the eyes of Germans and counted as treason against the German people, as *Rassenschande,* desecration of the race—as it always had. Once in a while, when they got up the courage, my father and mother went for walks in the park. Yankee-lover, Nigger-whore: who wanted to be called that in public? For eight months their meetings took place in secret at the home of a woman friend—always at the same place, always in the same house. Hidden from the outside world, hidden from the family, a place from which happiness and desire were never allowed to make their way outside. My father was twenty-eight years old at the time, a noncommissioned officer. In November 1946, after an illness, an Army promptly sent him back to the United States. Both of them were aware of the pregnancy; not until later did my mother find out about his sudden return home.

I was born in March 1947. My arrival was celebrated quietly and anxiously within the immediate family, while the outside world had long since determined my and our expulsion from society. When I was a year old, my mother married a white German; my sister was born a year later. For the first five years we grew up relatively untroubled, like most other children. There was enough to eat—although it was very simple fare; we slept in our parents' bedroom. We felt that we were a family, even though I knew from early on that my father was not my real father. People whispered and talked behind our backs when I went shopping with my mother. Something about me had to be "different" from other children. There was only one world, the white world that I had been born into; a black world did not exist, and there was only one reality, only one truth. There was no black father, no black grandmother; there were no black brothers and sisters, no other black children or black neighbors in my surroundings. Everyone was white, and since children look like their parents, I was white too: how else could it be? Only much later did I look into a mirror. I did not yet divide the world into black and white, but perhaps into good and bad, friendly and unfriendly. For me, there was absolutely no reason to doubt that I would grow up and be happy with my white mother and in my white family in my white homeland.

[...]

I was five years old and had no idea that to most people in my country, I would never grow up, but would always be an "occupation child."

[...]

I was five years old and had no idea that the name my mother had given me had no meaning for others. They called me *Negermischling*, "Negro half-breed."

[...]

I was five years old and had no idea that I presented a human and racial problem for other people.

[...]

I was five years old and had no idea that it was less I myself than the others who would present the real problem for me.

After eight months in elementary school I am sent to a Christian Home, far away from my family. The Home was run by the Pentecostal Congregation and the Free Evangelical Congregation. The reason given for my institutionalization by the youth welfare office was that my personal and career development would be at risk if I grew up with my family in this small town.

[...]

I am the only black child in the home. For that reason alone the other children are not especially fond of me and like to order me around.

[...]

Together we all sing the song "Ten little Negroes"[1] and we play "Who's Afraid of the Big Black Man?"—with one difference, that I am to learn something about myself from the so-called truths.

Although I liked going to school during my first years at the Home, I now begin to hate school. Everything that I succeed in, that I achieve and that I am proud of, including my academic achievements, is in my teachers' eyes a result of my skin color. If I do well,

---

1. A German version of the song "One little, two little, three little Indians" once sung by American children. Each verse describes the demise of one more "little Negro" in the German environment. For example: "Five little Negroes, liked to drink beer. One got dead drunk, then there were four."—Eds.

perhaps am the best in the class, it goes unnoticed, or they confuse me with another child, who is then praised instead of me. Or they say, "You cheated, didn't you? We wouldn't put it past you." My insatiable curiosity and joy in learning are also ruined by the fact that I have no opportunity to show what I know and can do. Speaking or asking questions without being called on is not allowed. Every question the teacher asks, on the other hand, must be answered immediately and directly. We are never allowed to digress from the topic, no matter what ideas occur to us. Imagination is punishable and you get rapped on the hand if you talk loudly with your neighbor or stop paying attention. I feel dead, always having to just sit there and listen.

Neither my knowledge and ability nor my actions are the decisive factors for the behavior of most of the teachers; it is my skin color that they don't want to deal with, and that I cannot change. Thus it is not surprising that my transgressions are not punished the same way as the other children's. Even if we all break the rules together, for example, by climbing trees, chewing gum in class, or talking out loud with each other in defiance of the rules, in the end it always comes down to: "You should really be ashamed of yourself, we'll beat that wildness out of you, we're not in the jungle with the Hottentots, fix your hair, you look just like them."

[. . .]

When it's time for a beating, we sit on chairs in a row and have to wait for our turn to get our "deserved" thrashing. One of these times, I resolved, I must manage not to cry. I try to suppress my tears and pain, warding off the blows with one hand before they land violently on my bottom. I grit my teeth. My hand reaches behind me every time that Sister Hildegard raises her arm to strike. I don't cry. She strikes my hand ten times or even more: "What's the matter with you, doesn't it hurt as much today, or what are you trying to prove?" Her blows keep coming, harder and faster, she seems not to want to stop at all. I can't take any more, fall down before her on my knees, and beg her to stop. "Get up, did you think you were something special, do you think you can fool us all, playing hero? You over there, you'll be next, think good and hard about whether you want to be able to sit on your bottoms afterward." The lower knuckle of my index finger is swollen and I'm nauseated from pain. "You don't need a doctor, not you, you think you're so strong and anyway, that's the way you wanted it," she says to me. I go back to my seat.

It is always the same words: "Next, pants down, bend over, so it's you again, we'll thrash the devil out of you yet!" Every time I resolve anew not to show how humiliated I feel. Not because I am beaten, but because, half naked and doubled over, I am robbed of any kind of privacy.

Worse than the beatings are the lies, which I take to be truths: blacks are dumb, underdeveloped, primitive, uncivilized; blacks are unpredictable, instinctive, dangerous, and pitiable.

When Sister Hildegard comes after me with the stick in her hand and says: "In reality I'm not beating you, but the devils that are in you," she does not want to deal with my pain and certainly does not want to let me hope that I too might be strong and brave. Since all learning begins in childhood, I am absorbing moral concepts with respect to myself that define my thoughts and actions. I learn that a lie becomes truth if someone wants to believe it. Whites teach me to mistrust them.

Even more disastrous are the lessons that lead me to hate myself. In the home, they try systematically to destroy my personality and I help them by despising myself in order to become more acceptable to them.

In the middle of the week, the air is heavy and muggy, I lie down on my bed and wallow in the delightful feeling that a much-longed-for dream is coming true: a classmate has actually invited me to her birthday party. I lie on my bed, clap my hands for joy, not knowing what to do with my happiness. The door is yanked open and Sister Hildegard rushes into the room: "What are you doing here, we'll get these filthy habits out of you, see if we don't." Like a flash I am up, running out of the room in fear and panic. "Don't think you can get away so easily," she calls after me. That evening and every evening for six months, my hands are tied tightly together with a narrow white cloth when I go to bed. "You want to go to a birthday party, they invited you of all people? Learn to behave properly first, then maybe you can visit other children. What are their parents going to think of us? You make us ashamed of you. I forbid you to go. Do you understand me?" I am silent. "Do you understand me? Or did you forget how to talk? But acting like a pig, that you can do. We'll find out if you can open your mouth. There's always tomorrow."

The next day, while all the others are doing their homework, I am sent into the yard. I have to take off my shoes and hop on one foot around an apple tree for half an hour. I am not allowed to rest or to change from one leg to the other. Just stick it out, I tell myself over and over, just don't fall down.

"You're done, you can put your shoes back on, let's go, hurry up, when it's anything else you're not so slow."

For the first time I am truly furious. I refuse to put my shoes and stockings back on, nor do I sit down with the others later at the supper table. When someone asks me a question, I give no answer. I have done something forbidden again, as so often. And as so often, I don't know what, nor did I ever find out.

With bound hands, how can I still be ready to approach people with open arms, extend to them my hands in solidarity, in greeting, or in reconciliation?

How can I hop on one foot and yet learn to stand on my own two feet in life?

How can I manage not to become hard, not even when the price of surviving amounts to a balancing act?

Translated by Jeanette Clausen

WOMEN
AND WORK

Louise Otto-Peters

Klöpplerinnen

Seht ihr sie sitzen am Klöppelkissen
    Die Wangen bleich und die Augen rot—
Sie mühen sich all' für einen Bissen,
    Für einen Bissen schwarzes Brot!

Großmutter hat sich die Augen erblindet,
    Sie wartet bis sie der Tod befreit—
Im stillen Gebet sie die Hände windet:
    Gott schütz' uns in der schweren Zeit!

Die Kinder regen die kleinen Hände,
    Die Klöppel fliegen herab, hinauf,
Der Müh' und Sorge kein Ende, kein Ende!
    Das ist ihr künftger Lebenslauf.

Die Jungfrauen all', daß Gott sich erbarme,
    Sie ahnen nimmer der Jugend Lust,
Es schließt sie das Elend in seine Arme,
    Der Mangel schmiegt sich an ihre Brust!

Seht ihr sie sitzen am Klöppelkissen,
    Sehr ihr die Spitzen, die sie gewebt:
Ihr Reichen, Großen—hat das Gewissen
    Euch nie in der innersten Seele gebebt?

Ihr schwelgt und prasset, wo sie verderben,
    Genießt das Leben in Saus und Braus,
Indessen sie vor Hunger sterben,
    Gott dankend, daß die Qual nun aus!

Seht ihr sie sitzen am Klöppelkissen
    Und redet noch schön von Gottvertrau'n?
Ihr habt es aus unserer Seele gerissen:
    Weil wir euch selber gottlos schaun.

Louise Otto-Peters

The Lace-Makers *(1851)*

See the lace-makers sitting at their pillows
    Their cheeks pale and their eyes red—
All toiling for a bite,
    A bite of black bread.

Grandmother has lost her sight,
    And waits for death to set her free,
In silent prayer she wrings her hands:
    God protect us in these difficult times!

The children move their little hands,
    The bobbins flying up and down
To the toil and sorrow there is no end, no end!
    Here is their future course of life.

All the maidens, God grant them mercy,
    They know not the pleasure of life's youth,
Misery holds them in its arms,
    Privation nestles in their breast!

See them sitting at their pillows,
    See the lace that they have made:
Rich men, great men—has your conscience
    Never trembled in your soul?

You live in luxury and debauchery while they perish,
    You enjoy life carousing and feasting,
Meantime they will die of hunger,
    Thanking God the torture is over.

You see them sitting at their pillows
    And still speak of faith in God?
You have torn it from our souls:
    We only see your godlessness.

Seht ihr sie sitzen am Klöppelkissen
    Und fühlt kein Erbarmen in solcher Zeit:
Dann werde euer Sterbekissen
    Der Armut Fluch und all ihr Leid!

You see them sitting at their pillows
    And feel no mercy in such a time:
Then shall your own death-pillow be
    The curse of poverty and all its pain!

Translated by Melanie Archangeli and
Patricia A. Herminghouse

Louise Otto-Peters

For the Female Workers *(1849)*

The right of association is won; the ministry of Saxony has even ordered its general application, and thus the right has quickly become a duty.

[...]

Already the men, the male workers, have also taken these steps. In some factories, where the interests of the female workers go hand in hand with the interests of the male workers, the women have been represented at the same time by the men, but where these interests part, where the women and girls themselves form a separate body among the workers, where the interests of the men are in no way connected to theirs, it is also necessary that the women themselves represent their concerns and bring them up for discussion.

The female domestic servants in Leipzig have already recognized this and led other classes of female workers with their good example. They have held a meeting and brought their requests and complaints to the attention of the public. One must acknowledge the modesty of their claims, but one must also remember that the lot of female domestic servants is in no way the most wretched among the female working population: those girls who must earn their living by means of female handiwork have a much more deplorable fate. These poor girls are oppressed by the burden of excessive competition, competition that of course arises from the fact that girls and women always and everywhere remain neglected, are taught little, and are cut off from or hindered in their access to all ways and means of getting ahead in the world.

There has almost never been an advocate to represent the concerns of German women. Only a few poets have considered them, but songs die away so easily in the wind or find again and again only a silent echo in the hearts of women.

[...]

For knitting a pair of stockings a female knitter normally receives five neugroschen—if she does nothing else at the same time, she must knit for two to three days. Because it is the easiest work, knitting stockings is usually done by girls and old women who are unable to do other work. But what competition! Whoever knits continuously can earn 15 to 18 pfennig—but who has so many customers? Because knitting is an easy sideline for every woman, there are hundreds of women who knit just to avoid idleness and then sell their work. This is not to blame those who are not in extreme need for wanting to earn a little, but by doing so, since many are not in need and consider the payment of secondary importance, they also allow the work to be paid more poorly, and thus the more prosperous women unknowingly and cheerfully force down the earnings of the poor people who must live from such work, who then must work as cheaply as those who only work for their amusement. Thus the poor knitters consider themselves lucky if they can knit for the "hosiers" who deal in hosiery; then they can always count on work, even if they are *paid even less* for it.

The same reason drives the embroiderers to work in factories. They are paid very poorly for embroidering linens, but at least they have no outlays because the material, thread, and patterns are supplied to them, and, except in a time of economic crisis, they are guaranteed employment. Such an embroiderer—and certainly everyone is familiar with the artistic work on fashionable linens—earns two to three neugroschen per day, if she works from early morning until late in the evening. Do not believe that more is paid for these things in the cities or privately. I have seen wonderful monograms on handkerchiefs for which only 10 neugroschen were paid (and the embroiderer pays for the thread); it is not possible to complete such a handkerchief in fewer than two days of continuous work. If the embroiderer is not practiced in sketching, then she must first pay two to five neugroschen for the design—how little is left to her then? The female workers in the large cities, too, consider themselves lucky if they can work for a store, a milliner, or something similar, because then they always have work, but if they work from six in the morning until nine at night with a short break at lunchtime they can earn, depending on the work, about three to five neugroschen—*definitely no more!*—except perhaps around Christmas time, when the work is pressing and many of these workers stay awake the entire night, certainly *never* daring *before midnight* to lay the work aside. And what eye-straining work, half of which must be done in artificial light besides—and probably in a cold room as well—since light and wood must also be paid for! These are the women with *the best jobs*.

What should I say then about the lace-makers in the Erzgebirge [a mountainous region in Saxony]? Here the going wage per day is three to five pfennig! Once I came across a lace-maker working on an extremely arduous lace of black silk, and she told me that her eyes can hardly endure winding the thin, dark threads around the shiny needles. In the evening she is in no state to work on it, but she considers herself lucky to have this work, because the black lace is better paid: she can make a half a yard per day and thus earn *one neugroschen* without having to continue in the evening, when she can do coarser work. For her one neugroschen per day was a *good* wage! Thus, the buyer paid her two neugroschen per yard, the satin thread to make it cost about as much, and on the market one pays for a yard of similar black satin lace *twenty neugroschen.* Just draw your own conclusion!

The quill trembles in my hand whenever I think of the entire abominable system of commerce, manufacturing, and its victims! If only you had seen the girls and women of the upper Erzgebirge! The children who grew up in gloomy rooms, looking ghostly and pale, with arms and legs wasted away and bodies distended from the only nourishment that they have, the potato. The father has got himself an early death at the dye works or peddles tubs of nuts or wooden kitchen utensils across the countryside—at home woman and child must work since he cannot provide for them. The little girls must make lace as soon as they can control their little hands. Then they waste away at the pillow for making lace, where their mother, who could only give birth to *feeble* children, has already atrophied, at the pillow for making lace where their grandmother went blind! For the constant staring at the fine threads and pins soon steals the ability to see, and the easy movement of the small bobbins makes their fingers delicate and their arms weak and thin, incapable of any other work. And now the clever people come and say that the women could do something other than make lace—it is crazy that they insist on doing it! No, they cannot do something else, because they were never able to build up their strength and have grown weak and completely incapable of performing any heavy work—even if you could procure it for them. You can assume responsibility for the children so they can learn something else—but you cannot take them away from their mother, for no one has that right.

No, you will reply to me: in the mountains the misery is twice as bad—but in the other cities, large and small, everyone who wants to work, including women and girls, finds sufficient and rewarding employment; indeed they find it, but often only—in the brothels.

Translated by Melanie Archangeli
with Patricia A. Herminghouse

Louise Dittmar

Domestic Life *(1848)*

The overcooked, washed-out, and ironed-out life of women would lead one to doubt, as Jean Paul says, whether women had a soul, if they did not love. But does this love not also have an overcooked, washed-out, and ironed-out soul, or worse still, one diluted by novels and tea? Should one believe in the thoughts and inventions of the nineteenth century, in view of all the domestic toils, this spinning around one's own axis, confined to the narrowest of circles. And "as today, so tomorrow." Can, in this monotonous killing of time, any uplifting thought permeate the soul; does any time, inclination, and opportunity remain for the larger interests of the collectivity, for attaining higher goals, for the cultivation of the heart, for the development of the soul's powers; does not all energy exhaust itself in the satisfaction of the constant demands and needs of the moment?

A woman would have to be a genius to meet even halfway the demands posed to her by her peculiar situation. Her position is defined by a combination of medieval spinning-wheels and modern whatnots. She is supposed to be economical and play the amicable hostess, supervise the help and make social calls, wash the children and entertain the husband, educate the children and give birth to the children, in short, she must be the ideal wife, mother, housewife, and society lady, be capable of everything and want nothing, be able to do everything and need nothing; be virtuous, amiable, educated, modest, simple, etc., a genius in performance and an automaton in will. For if she is lacking in one of these characteristics, it is a sore fault which necessarily must lead to discord and grievances. Her dependent situation and the equally constrained and oppressed position of the man indeed demand all these characteristics imperiously. And now one can judge what can be expected from the kind of domestic bliss, from the family life, that stipulates these conditions.

We want to advance moral nature and we condemn one half of humanity to be the handmaid of sensual nature. What is this domesticity other than a constant exertion for the most base needs.

In times past, flour was ground on a hand-mill, and there was a time when clothes were spun, woven, and finished in the home, when everyone also made their own shoes. Cooking and everything that goes with it in every family makes as much sense today as having a pharmacy in every household. Every shoemaker shows us what a gain of time and resources is achieved by uniting what belongs together, and every pharmacy teaches us what a gain in the matter at hand, e.g., for the perfection of the culinary art—as one of the crucial means to health—would be achieved by bringing resources together. A chemical laboratory is the intellectual kitchen of humanity, but if everyone had to pursue chemistry in their house and with their private means, chemistry would still be classed with alchemy and the alchemists. Of course, we say that chemistry belongs among the sciences, while the art of cooking and housekeeping belongs among private affairs. But what is science for, if it is not meant to liberate and ease life, what is chemistry and all its crucibles for, if not to serve that cause which it by its nature is closest to: the fortification and establishment of health, i.e., its application to cookery and medicine. But is this possible as long as everyone cooks in their own pot on their own stove?

Limiting female activity to the household hinders the development of life to the highest degree. What knowledge women could acquire in all fields, if instead of boiling and frying food—as today, so tomorrow—on their own stoves, they participated in large communal establishments, where everything is done skillfully and scientifically. And would not the most varied talents be able to participate in this and to secure their economic independence at the same time? Necessity and cultural resources will bring about such establishments in the near future. But their indispensability and their profitability will not be generally recognized before chance, i.e., necessity, will have called them forth. And the current system of housekeeping will not be condemned, the destiny of women will not be released from this treadmill, no true domesticity—a comfortable existence at home and a genial family life—will be achieved, until this female galley-slave institution is banned as a consequence of flexible, cooperative establishments.

Translated by Jörg Esleben

Louise Otto-Peters

The Right of Women to Earn a Living *(1866)*

Especially among the educated classes, there are complaints that the number of marriages is declining, and that with today's heightened pretensions it is hardly possible to marry a woman who does not have a fortune. It would make more sense if it were said: without the capacity to contribute and earn. Because a rather large amount of capital is needed if the interest earned is to provide a considerable contribution to the new household, especially if one considers that a girl of means is usually raised with pretensions that exceed this wealth. In addition, in ninety cases out of a hundred, this wealth is greatly depleted in a short time if indeed it does not just vanish without a trace. With it, the man pays his debts, and, with the knowledge of having a financial cushion, one is not so particular about accumulating new debts or consuming more than one's income permits or aspiring to increase the wealth through stocks and other forms of speculation that often fail. In short, when the man dies, the woman finds herself just as poor as those who never possessed a fortune, and more helpless than they.

Is it not then more advantageous to marry a woman who possesses a fortune in her capacity to work, which she is prepared to dedicate to her husband? Prepared not to burden him alone with the pressure of providing for a family, but to work toward this in union with him? Indeed, one such activity is also the management of a large household: for example, when the husband has a large business whose employees are boarded or pensioners provided for (which however is evermore seldom the case today), and caring for the children. In this way the wife *supports* the household and saves money for the husband without specifically earning it, but these are the exceptions to the rule. In most marriages the wife assumes an idle or completely subordinate role, the latter when she herself performs the work of the housemaid, the former when she employs one, because then she has, if not the whole day, then still half a day to occupy herself usefully in other ways.

Do not say that a woman neglects her husband if she helps make a living by giving lessons, for example, or by doing some other work that brings in money. Of course then the husband cannot dispose of his wife's time arbitrarily, as little as she does of his, but he will also hear no complaints from her about boredom or neglect and a thousand other things that occur to every person whose daily hours are not filled with useful activity. A thousand occasions for making life more difficult for each other through trivialities disappear when the woman has her own income and can dispose of it freely. This puts an end to the idea that the woman is merely the foremost servant of the husband—a servant whose needs the husband often fails to satisfy to the same extent that he does those of a housekeeper. The wife pays for these needs through her service to the household, yet must *beg* the husband for every little thing she requires. This would be another significant step for upholding the *dignity* of women, which thus far has been taken into account more in German *poems* than in the German way of life. Marriages will become more numerous and happier when women achieve economic independence.

[. . .]

We have shown already in the first section that the girl who has a profession and a purpose in life, who can support herself and be of use to others, will marry only for love. When she realizes that she can relieve her husband of some of his worries about their life together, or, where this is not necessary, still possesses the ability to do so, she feels more secure against all the twists of fate than she would without this realization. To give this awareness to all girls and women is the purpose of our entire effort, for only in this way can they be truly liberated. Every attempt at emancipation that rests upon another basis is—fraud.

[. . .]

The man who *wants* to work finds always and everywhere an opportunity to work and earn a living—only the lazy, the frivolous, the arrogant, and the wicked become unemployed and thus sink into shame and misery, defeated by "the battle for survival." And no one goes up to them and says: "Come, you do not need to work. You shall have it better and earn more than if you work and spend your life sacrificing and doing without!" No one says this to the man, but to the girl it is said a thousand times in both refined and harsh ways; it is said by men who are subject only to the rule of their sensuality; it is said by old women, who themselves a long time ago sank into and became hardened in the abyss of shame; by young women who merrily exist in the intoxication of sin; and it may be said by one's own parents.

And so thousands upon thousands heed this voice and seize the means that are oh so easily grasped! Some give themselves to the man who lures them with presents and promises and who transports them from their forsaken situation to a pleasant one; others throw themselves into the arms of the most horrible profession because it is the only one that is open to them. In the latter case people are then scandalized by the degeneracy of the female sex and hold it responsible for a criminal life that treads upon the most holy laws of nature, undermines the sanctity of the family, and becomes for the lawmakers a problem for which no satisfactory solution has been found.

And who is to blame for this crime? "The immorality of men and women!" one answers quickly and believes thereby to pronounce a just verdict, because men are not entirely acquitted.

And who is to blame for this immorality? Not only those who succumb to it. All men and women, even the most morally pure, have this guilt on their conscience when they hold fast to the maxim that woman is there only for the sake of man—all *those* men and women who do not raise their daughters so they can provide for themselves, all *those* men, who dispute women's *right to make a living through their own work,* all those who condemn women to idleness, who do not grant them the means to education, employment, to an autonomous position in life! The state is also to blame when it permits the right of women to earn a living to be curtailed—and in order to eliminate a tiny particle of *this* great wrong of the times, I have written this text.

Translated by Melanie Archangeli

Fanny Lewald

Third Easter Letter for Women: Training for Domestic Servants *(1863)*

In the home of a poor craftsman's family, a day-laborer's family—the majority of the female workers in our homes come from these social classes—a baby girl is born. There are older children in the home, there will be younger ones. In the cramped apartment the father and frequently also the mother pursue their craft; sometimes one of the parents, often enough both of them are occupied outside the house for the greater part of the day; thus, the children grow up without proper supervision, without attention. Only rarely is this the parents' fault. It is difficult for a family to earn enough for life's bare necessities; the effort requires the entire day, and all their energy. So, the children of such families are left mostly to their own devices during their first six or seven years of life; indeed when the little girl is barely capable of looking out for herself, she must become the caregiver of younger siblings.

At age six or seven the children start school and make their first acquaintance with discipline; at age fourteen or fifteen they are confirmed and then the boy's apprenticeship period begins. But the girl has no such thing. If she is not needed or put to work in her parents' home, she must begin earning her living, going into service among strangers, and entering into a contractual relationship in which she is expected to perform duties in exchange for payment. What capital does the girl have for assuming this responsibility?

As a rule, she has a poorly trained and inadequately nourished body. She has attended school, where she learned reading, writing, arithmetic, the rudiments of geography, a modicum of knitting, perhaps a little sewing, and had the benefit of confirmation classes. If you add up the years, she has had seven or eight years of schooling, the same as the daughters of the well-to-do. But the lessons in the crowded schools were insufficiently reinforced at home, and it is amazing and deplorable how little the daughters of the poor usually bring with them into life.

In the fifteen years that I have lived in Berlin, I have had five girls in our home. Three of them attended city schools, two attended country schools. All regretted that they had not made good use of their school days and that their parents "didn't think much of school." In my entire circle of acquaintances I have found, among the servant girls between the ages of about twenty to twenty-eight, only one girl who could write with facility and with correct spelling.

Even the ability to read with facility, reading for pleasure, is not common among these girls. It is possible that they know a certain amount, that they can read easily enough when they have just finished school and confirmation classes. But for those girls, and their number is very large, who are placed into service at age fifteen, any opportunity, any instruction, any impetus for learning and reading abruptly ceases. They rarely come into contact with books and if later on it does happen, they find that it no longer "goes so smoothly," they find it irksome, and since they have more than enough irksomeness anyway, they forego the need to be irked at themselves and "give reading a miss," concluding in the end that it is an arduous task, that it gives them no pleasure, that they have "better things" to do instead.

[. . .]

Upon leaving school they know a little about North, South, East, and West; about the residences and countries of various rulers; and a lot about the Hittites and the Amalekites, about Potiphar's wife, Judith and Holofernes, Samson and Delilah, King David and Absalom, and all the myths and horrors that fill the poetic but wild and bloody history and literature of the Jews known as the Old Testament. The girl can make no use whatsoever of all these things for her immediate purposes, and the gentle lessons of Christian morality that she received in confirmation class are little enough heeded by those who will become her role models during her first years of service.

The boy who enters an apprenticehip is expected to learn that which he does not understand. The girl who goes to work for strangers is expected to know and understand that which she has not learned and which no one properly teaches her. As a rule, it is the families of small craftsmen, the lowest subordinate civil servants, poor people for whom the girl performs her first service, and it is almost always harsh. The roughest work, the work that is too difficult for an adult woman, is expected from the barely full-grown child. She hauls and runs herself ragged in the house, and runs through town in snow and rain, in heat and cold, to deliver her employers' finished work. If she suffers from the weather, if she gets wet, that is secondary; the box she is carrying and its contents are the main thing. The customer who is not satisfied with the work directs his first reproaches to the messenger; the producer of the goods, to whom she must convey the criticism, also vents his anger on her. All this happens to the boy apprentice too, but, as mentioned before, he knows that it will cease as soon as he has learned something, and he knows what he has to learn.

But for the girl that too is different. For her there is no end in sight. She has no specific task. She is expected to cook, do laundry, mind the children; sometimes the mistress herself understands these things only minimally, often not at all, and above all she does not understand that one must teach that which is to be learned; for she too has "gradually picked up" what she knows, and she remembers how bitter that was for her, how hard others made it for her, remembers it, precisely because she is less educated than her husband, as a rule only to insist that she had it far worse than she is making it for her subordinate.

Much work, great effort, bad treatment, little relaxation, and even less pay, these are the first fruits of life for women among strangers, and they would not be human if they did not find this bitter. After six months, a year if they are very persistent, they leave their first service and enter a new one. Now they are "experienced," they have a good record, now they turn to more well-to-do families; in the end, when it costs her nothing, the first mistress has sympathy and does not want to "stand in the way of the girl's advancement." She calls her "willing and able." This recommendation is trusted, and in fact the girls usually are willing and able enough, but that which their new mistress in the more well-to-do household requires of them, they once again do not understand. They are let go, because "teaching everything to such a girl is not what I'm here for." One new service position comes after another, the short stays in various homes do not tempt well-organized families to take in girls "who don't settle down anywhere," who have occasionally shown themselves to be "contrary." And while the male apprentice progresses steadily toward his future at one place, the girl is shoved around among three, four, six or more homes and situations, whatever way it turns out. She receives better or worse treatment, she is required to do one thing and then another, and in this way, by the time she is eighteen or twenty, in the course of being shoved around and thanks to the fortunate human instinct for imitating others, she has learned just about enough to justify hiring herself out for the tasks that are required of her.

Now the girls receive better, though still relatively low wages; their lives become easier, their work more regular, if they "fit in well." But that supportive community between apprentice, journeyman, and master is still missing. The girls do not become links in a chain. The relationship between work and pay, between employee and employer, the strictly contractual relationship does not prevail at all times between servants and families; instead, the spiritual and moral relationship comes to the fore. We are compelled to integrate these girls, who are total strangers to us, into our most intimate family life, and what we demand of our servants, to some extent must demand of them if our families are to thrive and be kept clean, is not insignificant.

The girls are expected to understand various tasks, to be hardworking, honest, and moral. We demand obedience from them, willing and modest subordination to us and all adult members of the family; we demand a polite demeanor, good manners, and above all a constant awareness of our superiority, a devotion to us and ours without exception, even during illness, during danger of infection, in performing inconvenient or unpleasant tasks. We expect them to sacrifice their rest, their pleasure whenever it seems necessary or even simply convenient to us. Indeed, in order to satisfy many of their mistresses, servants would have to be truly perfect creatures; and in this respect I often think involuntarily of a woman who, when asked by a friend to find and hire the perfect private tutor, exclaimed upon hearing all the qualities her friend demanded: "If I can find a man like that, I'll marry him!" It is easy to draw the parallel!

But now the other side of the coin! We are all more or less in agreement as to what we demand. But what has happened to a young girl of the working class before she enters a so-called cultured family at age eighteen or twenty? And what happens to her within such a family to prepare her for her responsibilities?

It is necessary to summarize this briefly once again in order to have a clear picture.

As children, the girls played unsupervised on doorsteps, in court-yards, in the hallways and stairways of the less elegantly and exclusively kept homes. Everyone they came in contact with yelled at them; the children of the well-to-do avoided them, as they had been told to do, or even worse, often treated them imperiously when joining them for games. In this way they learned to submit grudgingly and to sulk in silence, whenever it was to their advantage. Idle and bored, they became good observers early on. Sooner than one would think, they knew everything that the house servants hide from their employer, the love affairs and intrigues that go on in the hallways and on the back stairs, and soon enough, against their parents' wishes, they were led by the bad example of the poorly brought-up older girls to view the relationship between masters and servants as a hostile one, to view the mistress as the enemy, as a tyrant over the servants. Hearing servants speak with respect and deference about their mistresses behind their backs is certainly a great rarity.

What the girls of the working classes experience during their first years of service does not contribute to improvement of their character or morals. They are inevitably forced into a position of warding off unreasonable demands; what they have been told from childhood on they find confirmed in themselves; they try to compensate as their role models did. Meager fare leaves them constantly nibbling, unforgiving attitudes force them to tell lies, severe and violent treatment makes them defiant. The extent to which these social evils develop in them during early youth depends on each individual life course as well as on the individual girls' characters. When they enter our homes and our service, the seeds of their first experiences and encounters are almost always present and have germinated. They are usually dishonest, insincere down to their innermost being, irresponsible, thoughtless, and inclined toward disrespectful contrariness; they are in fact, given the way they are, often a trial and a trouble for the mistress. They are so especially because of the uncomprehending, hostile distrust they harbor toward us, because of their belief that we have no fondness for them, that we think only of ourselves, of our superiority, and our convenience, and that we forget that they "are human beings too!"

Translated by Jeanette Clausen

Ninth Easter Letter for Women: Shelters for Working-Class Women *(1863)*

According to a statistical estimate, when all the factories in Berlin are operating at full capacity, they employ approximately ten-thousand girls, while approximately twenty-thousand young women are needed for service in families. The majority of the latter group, however, are not native to this city, for the young women of Berlin generally prefer factory work to service in families.

Their reasons are easily explained. In factories, the girls do only one thing, they have to perform one specific task that is taught to them there; they soon receive the daily wage of an adult, thus becoming independent early on, and able to help out their parents with their earnings, which are paid weekly in cash. Indeed, they are often in a position of having to contribute substantively to the support of the family. That makes them free and independent of their parents too; and the latter cannot, even with good intentions, prevent their daughters from wanting to "kick up their heels" after a hard week's work. And that would be perfectly all right, except that the only entertainment and distraction available to the girls are dance halls with high-sounding names, where they make the acquaintance of dissolute young men and where in most cases they take their first steps toward moral decline.

There are, if we look one or two steps higher up, daughters of relatively well-to-do citizens who perform in their parents' homes tasks requiring skill and neatness for linen services, for producers of mantles and mantillas, and for similar lines of business. They are not badly paid, frequently save money despite their love of finery, and marry honorably within the parental sphere. The children of the poor on the other hand, the less skillful girls who go to work for tailors or other tradesmen, whether they hire themselves out on "piecework" or for day wages, rarely manage to earn more than two taler per week, even if they also work the early morning and evening hours. So they earn, if their work is paid at the same rate all year, just over one-hundred taler annually. Therefore, after paying for rent, food, and laundry, they could hardly save to spend on themselves the thirty-six taler that an even halfway well-situated servant girl invariably has; quite apart from the fact that female factory workers live and eat far less well than servant girls. They go to work early in the morning, getting by with a sandwich brought from home and a cup of coffee until late in the evening because they frequently work too far from their apartments to be able to go home at noon. When they finally get supper, it too is rarely equivalent to that of a maidservant. If the girls are honorable, which unfortunately is seldom enough the case, this arduous life at best continues year in and year out, with no increase in their daily wage. If the factories shut down, poverty is at the door immediately, and then all too frequently and too quickly, need consumates what thoughtlessness began: the female workers' complete moral downfall. How could it be otherwise when essentially nothing has been done for them?

It is precisely the local girls' preference for factory work and for a precarious freedom that stimulates the influx of out-of-town girls for service in families. Every year, and especially at Easter and Michaelmas, considerable numbers of young women come to the capital city from small and middle-sized towns, from villages and farms; and the same is doubtless true in all our various German states, even though the sizes of the provinces and their capitals create substantial differences in the circumstances of the new arrivals. The big city, the higher wages, the dream of "making their fortune" somewhere else, these factors hold the same attraction for inexperience everywhere. [. . .]

But how do young women arriving as strangers here fare?

Confused, dazed by the unaccustomed journey and by new impressions, they find themselves at a loss on the platform and in the halls of the train stations. Everything that confronts them is alien: the buildings, the people, the sound of the language. They stand there, their hands full of all their personal belongings, worried that these will be taken from them, even more worried about how to find their way with their luggage receipt to their trunk or their suitcase, and totally ignorant of where to go with themselves and their belongings. In that situation it must seem a true stroke of luck if someone takes them under his wing, and unfortunately there is no lack of such seemingly helpful souls.

[...]

What should be done to provide temporary accommodations and a foothold for the girls newly arriving here, as well as for those who are unemployed and without support, is readily apparent and has already been accomplished in certain quarters: hostels for the women of the working classes must be constructed.

I have mentioned elsewhere that *one* such hostel, Martha's Hof on Schwedter Strasse, was established eight years ago. The hostel is run by thirteen deaconesses from Königswerth under the supervision of a clergyman, and it is done in a strictly religious spirit: the institution's motto is "Pray and Work."

The hostel currently has eighty-two clean beds, but this number has proven to be insufficient at Easter and Michaelmas. From October 1861 to October 1862, it sheltered 523 girls, among them only 54 native to Berlin. The average daily number runs between 60 and 70, according to a report from the committee that presides over the facility. This figure could not be reconciled with a total of 523 if Martha's Hof were only a hostel. But it is also an institute for the training of servants; thus, individual girls have stayed in the hostel for a longer period. Only 21 girls stayed there for only one night, 84 for up to a week, 93 for two weeks, 161 up to four weeks, 58 for three months, 25 for six months and five for a whole year.

The institute provides as far as possible for the girls' ongoing need for lodgings; it also shelters girls whose employers are away until the latter return. That is certainly a good deed, for there is no question that many girls come to ruin during our travels abroad for health or pleasure.

Martha's Hof has, in addition to the hostel, a girls' school and a facility for the care of small children, in which the pupils of the maidservants' training school receive instruction in caring for children; similarly, Martha's Hof also does laundry and sewing for outside clients, in order to instruct the girls in these tasks and to use their time purposefully.

[...]

To be sure, it is impossible to undo injustices or evils that have befallen a group or individuals; indeed, only rarely can these even be effectively offset. But one can prevent new evils or new injustices from being done; one can make late remorse fruitful for the future.

Without in any way criticizing the achievements of Martha's Hof, of whose contributions as a whole my visit has given me a favorable impression, I have become convinced that the power of charitable works will always be insufficient in the long run, given the material dimensions of the assistance that is needed. It is also quite unnecessary, indeed, in my opinion it is a mistake and an injustice to turn people who are capable of helping themselves into charity cases; and if it is possible to construct hostels and inns for people with modest requirements who can support themselves from their earnings and who thereby afford the provider a comparative advantage, then it must be possible to accomplish this for women just as well as for men.

[. . .]

But *one* hostel maintained by charity, miles away from most train stations, is not sufficient for large cities—Berlin, for example. What then should be done? How can we help?

It seems to me that, without an association of the well-educated and well-intentioned that takes as its lofty task the elevation of female workers' moral condition, no assistance is possible.

So, come together, you women and girls, you who have a heart for your sisters' misery and who understand the greatness and dignity of the nation into which you were born! Help the women of the poor classes, that you may be helped. Protect their children in order to save yours. Come together, you who have time that you often enough know not how to fill, come together, organize, for only organization can help.

[. . .]

Believe resolutely and faithfully: The working classes do not experience their daughters' disgrace as a stroke of luck or as a matter of pleasure! They only endure, who knows how painfully, what they have not been able to change. They, and we too, are doing penance for the sins of our fathers; but how many fathers and how many mothers who now part tearfully from their daughters would watch them leave with greater peace of mind if they knew that their daughters, upon arriving in the strange city, were not so helplessly exposed to all the unforeseen events of life, that they were not so much worse off, infinitely worse off than their sons. And how minor are the dangers that threaten young men compared with those to which girls are exposed!

Translated by Jeanette Clausen

Tenth Political Letter:
Work and Family Values *(1869)*

In virtually no other important matter have people so thoughtlessly succumbed to prejudice, so mindlessly accepted prevailing clichés as in their assessment of the social and political position of women; and even worse than the thoughtless prejudice of men is the arrogant rigidity of prejudice against women's emancipation on the part of those affluent women who have never encountered the seriousness or the deprivations of life and all the oppressive worries that go along with them.

It has often filled my heart with indignation to hear women of those social classes singing the praises of home and hearth when they never in their lives tended one; to hear those vain and pleasure-obsessed women, who only too frequently shirk nearly all their domestic responsibilities, preaching unctuously and emotionally about the vocation of wife and mother while a paid housekeeper did their housework, a paid dishonored woman nursed their children, and a paid governess supervised and taught their children. Meanwhile they themselves spent their mornings promenading with their entourage and their evenings at the dressing table with the hairdresser, then at the theater or a party with or without their husbands because they did not know what to do with themselves and had no idea how to fill their husbands' lonely evenings in their own home.
[. . .]
It is ludicrous and offensive to hear those affluent and idle women continually repeating "that the true feminine aura is stripped away from women by professional and gainful employment;" and it is equally offensive to hear men asserting that women who learned a respectable vocation, who made something of themselves, would lose the capacity for true devotion to their husband.

I have often asked those women: "What constitutes that so-called special aura that women supposedly lose by working?" And they have never been able to explain this mysterious something to me. To be sure, weakness and affectation must be sacrificed when a woman is not in a position to have others working for her. Someone who must work cannot spend the morning wondering whether the faint cloud about her brow might turn into a migraine and cannot wait in a soft, curtained bed of leisure for the migraine to arrive. With those crystal-clear, clawlike pointed fingernails she can do nothing for herself or in the home; nails that take a half hour each morning and are obviously useless for making anything but filet-work and tapestries—not even a respectable baby gown with a proper French seam can be stitched with these Chinese nails; and those costumes with flawless pleats and bows that demand attention all day long are something that we other working women must also do without. But what does the handkerchief that cost twenty-five Taler, what does the dress for which the tailor's bill was perhaps even more, what do all the endless buckles and phials and fans and flower stands and goldfish and lap dogs with which the affluent upper-class female self-indulgently surrounds herself have to do with sincere respect for the man she belongs to? What do they have in common with love for him, with devoted care and sacrifice for the family of which the woman is mother and co-founder?

[. . .]

Women of the old nobility, scholars' wives, women from families of lesser means in the smaller cities, in the provinces, in the parsonages are for the most part far superior to those other women with regard to their true worth. But still the influence of the wealthy middle class is great; the men of that class still derive their honor from profitable work. And for the women of this same class work is supposedly demeaning? What marvelous logic! It is just as false as the previously mentioned assertion by many men that intellectually developed and independent women are not capable of true devotion.

I would like to ask the opposite question: What does a woman with no intellectual life of her own, who has not learned a real trade and has no real skills, what can she devote to you except her body? And do you want nothing from marriage but to satisfy your sensual desires? Do you not need a serious teacher for your sons, a conscientious advisor for your daughters, an intelligent manager of your income?—Did you never face the hour of discouragement in which you wanted more from your wife than a helpless being capable only of lamenting your sorrow and care and whose powerless grief only burdened your heart even more? Did an illness never come over you, bringing you face to face with death, and did you not then yearn to say to yourself: My wife is there, the mother is there! She will know what to do, she can work and earn money if need be; she will lead and guide and educate and earn a living if I am no longer able.

But let us turn away from those fathers toward the men who despite all their diligence, circumstances in our country being what they are, often cannot even think of establishing their own household because their income is not adequate to support a family. I am sure that among the readers of this newspaper there are hundreds and hundreds of men—young teachers, civil servants, docents, and so forth—who at one time or another have said to themselves: "This girl would be the woman for you, with this girl you would lead a happy life; but you are poor and so is she; a family of our class cannot exist on your three, four, or five hundred taler income, and this fine girl knows only how to keep house and save money—but keeping house and saving money won't do the trick." What is the consequence? The girl, "brought up to rear a family," does not get the opportunity to become the co-founder of a family, she remains unmarried despite all her good qualities, she misses out on her true feminine vocation because she was not emancipated in a timely fashion for employment and earning.

Bear this firmly in mind: The emancipation of women for employment and earning is the surest means to promote marriage and to raise the standard and morals of family life in general.

Translated by Jeanette Clausen

Hedwig Dohm

Are Motherhood and Domesticity Compatible with a Profession? *(1903)*

A very energetic person writes to me: "There is only one either/or. Either a profession or marriage and motherhood. Both together—preposterous."

A pronouncement as foolish and arrogant as its opposite: that a woman *must* pursue a profession along with marriage and motherhood.

Whether she wants to or not, whether she can do it or not—that is her business, not mine. Mine is to eliminate barriers, to the extent possible.

[. . .]

Some people give no money to the poor because they would just buy schnapps with it. Similarly, they deny women the means to intellectual advancement, for fear that cultivation of their intelligence would function as a kind of schnapps to deaden their emotions.

What? A woman's emotions, above all her motherly love, would necessarily break down if she practiced an art or held an office? Where are the people—including men—who are so absorbed in their professions that they race past all emotions as if they had blinders on? A woman can love her children, love them to distraction— there's no trick to that—and neglect them nonetheless. Love and fulfilling one's responsibilities are not at all the same thing.

What? Because I am a writer or a doctor or a painter, I must love my children less or not at all?! But that is nonsense, purest nonsense! Men cannot speak to this—since in their own judgment they feel differently than women—and women who hold the same opinion, which does happen, can only be childless women!

Even if I worked ever so diligently in a profession, would I not still delight in the love and affection of my husband? My senses would remain receptive to music, theater, to all the finer and cruder joys and pleasures, and only my inclination for motherliness would expire? Women will cheat themselves of the greatest happiness, the most intimate bliss? But that is the farthest thing from their minds! No woman is that stupid—not one!

By the way, I certainly do not deny that a professionally employed woman's heart and soul will be less fully occupied by her children than may possibly be the case for an unemployed mother. (Possibly, I say, for in fact there are a great many mothers—professionally innocent as they may be—who have mind- and time-consuming areas of interest—rarely of an elevated nature—beyond motherhood.) I believe, however, that the one and only important consideration is whether it is useful and necessary for children that their mother be totally absorbed by them.

It seems to me that the decisive factor is not the amount of emotions and time that a mother devotes to her children, not constant togetherness or a single-minded preoccupation with their welfare— which is the universal meaning of motherhood after all—but a goodness of character that precludes neglect of duty and the intelligent insight of the woman who is a mother, insight that teaches her to recognize and understand what the children's psychic and physical development requires and that enables her to find the means to realize these ends.

Without the foundation of these qualities, maternal feelings are like the beautiful facade of a house that is unhealthy to live in.

Good and intelligent women who become mothers will shape their lives in such a way (assuming that external circumstances do not exert pressure on them) that their maternal duties need suffer no harm, regardless of whether the child is the entire content of their existence or whether they know how to combine motherhood and profession. Motherly love is only a secondary requirement. One could possibly even get along without it, though meeting the responsibilities would then be incomparably more difficult.

Translated by Jeanette Clausen

Adelheid Popp

Autobiography of a Working Woman *(1903)*

[After May 1,] I made my first public speech.[1] It was on a Sunday morning at a meeting of the union local. I told no one where I was going, and as I often went alone on a Sunday morning to visit a gallery or a museum my departure created no sensation. The meeting was attended by three hundred men and nine women, as I later learned from the union paper. As women's work was beginning to play an important part in this union, and the men were already feeling the effect of the supply of cheaper women workers, at this meeting the meaning of trade organization was to be discussed. There had been a special endeavour to make the meeting known to working women and although hundreds were working in a single factory only nine women came. When the convenor of the meeting announced this and the speaker referred to it, I felt great shame at the indifference of members of my own sex. I took everything that was said personally and felt myself attacked by the speakers. The speaker described the conditions of women's labor and called the backwardness, the meekness, and the contentedness of women workers crimes

---

1. In 1891, the Social Democratic Party succeeded in having May 1 declared a holiday for working people. Popp's speech appeared in the first issue of the Viennese *Arbeiterinnen-Zeitung* (January 1, 1892). See the following text by Amelie Seidl for a description of the 1893 strike by women workers.—Eds.

which drew all other evils after them in their train. He also spoke generally on the woman question, and I heard for the first time from him of August Bebel's book *Woman and Socialism*.

When the speaker had finished the chairman announced that those present should express their opinions on this important question. I had the feeling that I must speak. I fancied that all eyes were directed toward me, that all were wanting to hear what I could say in defense of my sex. I lifted my hand and requested permission to speak. They cried "Bravo" before I opened my mouth; merely because a working woman wanted to speak. As I mounted the steps to the platform my eyes swam and my throat was parched—I felt as though I were choking. But I conquered my excitement and made my first speech. I spoke of the sufferings, the exploitation, and the psychic neglect of working women. I laid special emphasis on the last, for it seemed to me the foundation of all the other backwardness and traits harmful for working women. I spoke of all that I had experienced and observed among my fellow workers. I demanded enlightenment, culture, and knowledge for my sex, and I begged the men to help us attain them.

The applause in the meeting was boundless; they surrounded me and wanted to know who I was; they took me at first for a member of the union local and requested me to write an article addressed to working women for the union paper along the lines of my speech.

That was certainly an awkward task. I had only gone to school for three years, I had no notion of spelling nor of composition, and my writing was like that of a child as I had never had the opportunity of practicing it. Yet I promised to try to get the article written.

I felt as though I were in an ecstasy of delight as I went home. An unspeakable feeling of happiness inspired me, it seemed to me as though I had conquered the world. No sleep visited my eyes that night. I wrote the article for the Union paper. It was short, and not well expressed, and ran as follows:

On the Position of Women Occupied as Workers in Factories

"Working Women! Have you ever once considered your position? Do you not all suffer from the brutality and exploitation of your so-called masters? Many slaves for wages work from early morning until late at night, while thousands of their sisters, out of work, besiege the doors of factories and workshops because it is not possible for them to obtain work to protect themselves from hunger and to procure the bare minimum of clothing for their bodies. But how far does the wage for such long, continuous work go?

"Is it possible for an unmarried working woman to lead a life fit for a human being? And especially a married working woman? Is it possible for her in spite of strenuous work to care properly for her children? Must she not hunger and starve in order to procure what is absolutely necessary for them? That is the situation of women workers, and if we look on idly it will never be improved; on the contrary, we shall continually be more trodden down and trampled upon.

"Working Women! Show that you are not completely debased and mentally stunted. Rise up and recognize that men and women workers must join hands in a common bond. Do not close your ears to the cry which goes out to you. Stand by the organization which will also train women for the social and political struggle.

"Attend meetings, read workers' papers, become goal- and class-conscious workers in the ranks of the Social Democratic Party."
[. . .]
I had become an object of general attention. My speeches were written about in the papers, the police served me with notices to learn about the charges which I had raised at meetings over cases of exploitation of working women and ill treatment of domestic servants. The agitation engrossed me more and more. I had become a member of the managing committee of an organization of working women, and had to take part in many meetings. I was quite engrossed with my public work and ready for any sacrifice. I had often to give up my dinner to pay for the fee for opening the door to the building after hours when I came home late in the evening. Then for three cents I bought some soup and bread for dinner. But it would not have done for my mother to know that my public work cost money. So I had actually to go without things secretly in order to deceive her, for had she known that it cost money when I made a speech at a meeting it would have been worse for me.

Translated by E. C. Harvey;
revised by Patricia A. Herminghouse

Amalie Seidl

The First Female Workers' Strike in Vienna *(1912)*

About twenty years ago, conditions in the textile factories of Vienna
were far worse than now, which is not to say that female workers
today have reason to be satisfied. But back in the year 1892, when I
was hired by a finishing-plant at the age of sixteen, working hours
from six o'clock in the morning to seven o'clock in the evening were
the rule. Female workers were not organized at all and put up with
wages from one to 1.5 crowns. You can imagine their standard of
living. In 1893 I worked in a factory where about 300 men and
women were employed, most of whom did not earn more than seven
crowns. Hence one of the demands of the strike that ensued was
payment of a weekly wage of eight crowns. As a packer in the warehouse, however, I got the stellar wage of ten crowns weekly and was
among the best-paid female workers. Although there was no mention
of an organization, I still managed to make the value of the May
celebrations clear to my women colleagues, and we did succeed in
getting May Day off. Naturally, the May celebrations were the only
topic of conversation in the factory the next day, and during the
lunch break in a large factory hall I endeavored to prove that with
the right organization we in the factory could also improve our conditions. In the course of the speech and in the eagerness to listen none
of us noticed that the boss had also been listening for several minutes. Needless to say, punishment or rather dismissal followed. I had
hardly returned to my warehouse when I found out that my papers
were already in the office. Since I had to work overtime, I did not
leave the factory at the same time as the other women, who, by the
way, must have heard of my dismissal already. For when I came into
the narrow street where my parents lived, I was more than a little
astonished to see police in front of the door to the building and the
door itself closed. But the rather large yard was filled with the female
workers from the factory, who were awaiting me and called to me
tumultuously that they would not accept my dismissal quietly. I then
gave a "speech," standing on the chopping block, telling my colleagues that, of course, it was very nice that they did not want to
keep quiet, but that if they did want to strike, they should demand

more than just my re-employment. None of us knew what to demand, but we did want to strike! We only agreed that I should come to the factory the next day (May 3); by then, the women should have agreed on their demands, and perhaps also on the colleagues who would present the wishes of the workers to the firm. I was supposed to wait for the result outside the windows. All this took place; but the demands—reduction of working hours from twelve to ten daily and my reemployment—were rejected by the firm. In an instant, all the women left the factory just as they were, barefoot due to the great heat in some of the work rooms, only half-dressed, with clothes over their arms and baskets with their meager lunch or coffee thermos in hand. The women got dressed in the garden of a nearby inn, while I hastened to comrade Dworschak (Popp)[1] to deliver the news of the strike to her. The first assembly took place already that afternoon, on a meadow in Meidling, and was soon followed by others. The female workers from three other factories also joined in, so that within a few days about seven hundred women and girls were on strike. Naturally, since this was the first women's strike, it attracted attention; the bourgeois press also covered it, in order to complain, of course, that now female workers are also being "stirred up." There were also exceptions. For example, the correspondent of an English bourgeois paper wrote that "the strikers, who were using the fourteen days mainly for recuperation in fresh air, looked far better at the end of the strike than before." No wonder! After working twelve to thirteen hours daily in rooms where the heat sometimes reached fifty-four degrees centigrade, or in the bleaching plant, which was filled by the stench of chlorine, or in the dye-works, where "lovely" aromas also made breathing a torture, women had no way to look good. Thanks to the solidarity of the workers, the strikers could be adequately supported, so that they did not have much less to live on than they normally earned in the factory. It goes without saying that the strikers did not want to give in but rather hold out. And so after a fourteen-day-long strike the demands were pushed through. These demands were: a ten-hour working day, payment of a minimum wage of eight crowns weekly, a holiday on May Day, and in addition my reemployment at Heller, the firm where I had been fired. A large number of women and girls had joined the organization, but only to turn their backs on it soon after I left the factory. The *Arbeiterinnenzeitung* [Female workers' newspaper] was also read much and diligently for a while.

---

1. See also the account by Adelheid Popp in this volume.—Eds.

Of course I had to make speeches during the strike, as well as I then could, and thus I came into the worker's movement. I had already been a member of the Workers' Educational Association VI in the fall of 1892, and had also visited a women's assembly, where I had heard comrade Anna Boschek[2] speak. The fact that a young girl dared to give a speech impressed me greatly and stirred up my own wish to be able to speak; only I did not dare to. But on May Day 1893, I tried after all, and that right off at a large gathering of dyers in the Mariensaal hall in Rudolfsheim. Then the strike came, and I had to speak. At some assemblies in the summer and fall of 1893, a few of my speeches also got me indicted for several violations of the law and sentenced to three weeks' imprisonment, which I "served" in the district court in February of 1894. I still remember today how pleasantly surprised I was when I entered the "cell." The room, which, depending on circumstances, I had to share with twelve to seventeen prisoners, was large, bright, and pleasant. Since they were not prepared for "political women" at the Viennese district court, I did not get an individual cell. I also did not know that I could have demanded one, and I probably would not have dared to. Other than that, detention was not bad, and I was not spoiled to begin with. Surely I was better off in the district court than I had been as a maid with a monthly wage of six crowns.

But back then I must have been a "person dangerous for the state." My lawyer, Dr. Ornstein, had to intervene when the police wanted to deport me to my father's home town in Bohemia, even though I was living with my parents. And after my release from prison I had to sign a declaration in police headquarters giving the police the right to remove me from Vienna in case of a new conviction.

Since that time, conditions in Austria have changed enough for us to enjoy much more freedom of speech today, and so this remained my only "punishment," although it had of course no deterrent effect. I have given speeches at hundreds of assemblies since then without coming into conflict with the law. I was active in the party to the extent that my family situation allowed; mostly in the last few years, during which my children have needed me less, and when I have been particularly interested in the movement for co-operatives, which, like the union and political movements, is necessary for the rise and final victory of the working class.

Translated by Jörg Esleben

---

2. Anna Boschek (1874–1957), first woman union member to hold a seat in the Austrian parliament.—Eds.

Lily Braun

Women's Work and Housekeeping *(1901)*

The Household Cooperative

We have seen that the married white- and blue-collar woman worker aches under the load of double duties. She is unable to carry either of them out fully and satisfactorily. Neither existing nor desired workers' protection laws can fully relieve her of her burden. And if she is not independently wealthy, the bourgeois woman cannot pursue her profession either. The task thus is to create institutions that make this possible for both of them.

Such an institution is the household cooperative. I imagine it to look about as follows: A housing complex enclosing a large and prettily laid out garden of about fifty or sixty apartments, none of which contains a kitchen. There is only a small gas cooker in a little room, which can be used in case of sickness or to take care of infants. In lieu of the fifty to sixty kitchens in which an equal number of women usually are busy, there is a central kitchen on the ground floor which is equipped with all kinds of modern labor-saving machines. Among the things that exist already are even automatic dishwashers in which twenty-dozen plates or bowls can be washed and dried in three minutes! A pantry and a laundry room with automatic washing machines are located nearby, also a large dining room that can also function as a meeting hall and, during the day, as a playroom for the children. A smaller reading room adjoins it. The management of the entire household is in the hands of an experienced housekeeper who is a specialist in home economics; she has one or two kitchen maids under her supervision. The quarters of these household employees are on the same floor as the housekeeping premises. They also include the room of the woman who takes care of the children; like all others she is employed by all inhabitants jointly. Depending on wish and inclination, meals are either taken in the common dining room or are carried to all the floors by special food elevators. Heat is provided to the apartments by a central heating system, so that here, too, one furnace replaces fifty stoves. While the mothers are at work, the children play under adult supervision, be it in the dining room or in the garden, where playground equipment and sand boxes give

children of all ages something to do. In the evening, when their mothers have put them to bed and the parents want to chat with friends or to read, they go down to the common rooms, where they need not purchase their entertainment with the consumption of alcohol if they do not feel the need for it.

This plan could be modified or elaborated in all possible directions. In order to simplify it, one could omit, say, the elevators and the reading room; the women would then have to go to the food-dispensing counter to get their meals. It could be expanded by centralizing, say, the cleaning of the apartments. For that a crew of chambermaids would have to be employed. By introducing electric light, setting aside tastefully furnished rooms for social occasions, putting in bowling alleys, and other such things, the plan could be elaborated even more. All this would more or less automatically conform to the needs of the inhabitants who—and this is an essential precondition—would all have to be on more or less the same income level. Absolute equality of income would not be necessary, if only because it would not create difficulties if those less well-off wanted, say, a smaller apartment or a meal lacking one particular dish.

This entire plan is by no means as new as it may appear. The beginnings of it can be found in many places. Thus, because of the lack of servants, many families in America live in boarding houses or hotels where they get their meals furnished. In a suburb of Chicago a number of families have gotten together to run their household communally; in England similar steps have been advocated quite a bit: in Manchester a society was founded recently which wants to set up food kitchens in various parts of the city, from which all families could obtain good hot meals. Here, too, it is the scarcity of domestic cooks that provided the occasion for this initiative. There are houses in which single working women live and get fed in common; they exist in large numbers especially in England, but even in Berlin something like this is being started right now. All these institutions, however, with hardly any exception, are begun by, and designated for, bourgeois circles.

Indeed, at first sight it seems virtually impossible for workers with their limited means to establish and maintain household cooperatives. They have never been able to hire any kind of help, and now all of a sudden they are supposed to have the means to pay a housekeeper, nursemaids, and the like? And yet this is in no way outside the realm of possibilities, for not only would these expenditures be distributed over fifty to eighty families, but they would be amply recovered by the advantages of quantity buying of groceries, by sav-

ings in fuel, and by a rational household economy in general. Let us assume for instance that fifty families hire three persons for a salary of 125 marks a month; let us budget one hundred fifty-six marks for their room and board (board 1.40 marks, room ten marks per person). Then every family would have to set aside 5.62 marks per month, which could very easily be recovered by the savings. Moreover, since the individual apartments would need no kitchen, the rent for the central kitchen and the other common rooms could also be made avilable without difficulty.

All that is the least difficult part. The greater difficulty is posed by the question about the practical methods for realizing the household cooperative for the working class. The existing tenement houses are not suitable for this. They usually are designated for tenants from a wide variety of income and property strata, where the worker is assigned any old wretched, dark rooms in the back, and often he cannot afford to pay rent even for those. Many very important features would be impossible here, and their lack could easily mean failure for the whole scheme. But is it too much to hope that those who make speculative investments in the construction industry might take up the practical idea and build houses for housekeeping cooperatives at the latter's risk? . . . Such a route is indicated in building cooperatives whose purpose it is to build houses, not for individual ownership but on the basis of cooperative property and joint administration. In new houses built to the proper specification the desired reform in housekeeping could be accomplished, and in addition building cooperatives would offer all those workers who are capable of helping in their formation the advantage of escaping from the housing shortage.

[. . .]

Effects of Reforms in Housekeeping

The reform in housekeeping I have in mind would have very important results, since the work of the housewife or the cook to which we cling with so much expenditure of sentimentality is nothing else than pernicious dilettantism. The dilettantism would be eliminated so that it can no longer wreak havoc in an area as important as human nutrition. For the children, including even the youngest ones, communal life would be of incalculable advantage. Not only would they be protected against the influence of the street and the deplorable precocity of city children, but they would at the same time learn to develop the spirit of brotherliness in themselves. For the women, however, the housekeeping cooperative constitutes one of the foundations of their

liberation. As Peter Kropotkin[1] writes,"To liberate women means not only to open the doors to the university, the court of law, and parliament for them; rather it means to free them from cooking stove and washtub, it means creating institutions that will permit them to raise their children and to participate in public life." Women will never win the fight for emancipation they are waging today if they do not first win time and leisure and bring their lives into harmony with their aims. The woman's aptitude for productive work is something one will be able to evaluate only when she has ceased to groan under double obligations which ruin her physically and intellectually. As things are today, the married working woman will always have to be inferior to the man because, unlike him, she does not have any opportunity to gather new strength during hours of rest. The very same thing is true for the woman who does intellectual work. Filled with a thousand petty household worries, her head cannot at the same time develop clear ideas that go beyond the narrowest range of interests.

Moreover, a restructuring of housekeeping would promote a whole number of additional important reforms. For instance, it seems to me that a solution to the problems of domestic servants cannot be expected as long as today's private households continue to exist. A solution will be in sight only when domestic servants quit the now prevalent personal relationship to their employer and come closer to the status of the factory worker; and that is possible only in housekeeping cooperatives where higher wages can be paid, better quarters can be provided, the work hours can be regulated more equitably, and the housewife's control over everything her servants do at all times is eliminated.

There is another problem, discussions of which have barely begun until now, that might also receive a powerful push toward its solution, although only as a result of a large-scale spread of household cooperatives. I am speaking about the problem of cottage industry. We will be able to combat this cancerous sore with all the necessary decisiveness only when the worry over her children and her household no longer chain the woman to her home permanently, and when this pretext can no longer be used even by those who regard any legal interference in the home as sacrilege.

---

1. Pyotr Alekseyevitsch Kropotkin (1842–1921), Russian revolutionary and anarchist who, like Lily Braun, broke with his aristocratic background to work for social justice.—Eds.

Does all this spell "revolutions," "dissolution of the family," or whatever those nice slogans may be that send shivers down the philistines' spines?

We have seen how changing economic circumstances and technological progress subjected housekeeping to continual changes until today it has shrunk to near-insignificance. In the depth of our hearts we are aware that the nuclear household already is a thing of the past; if it is now replaced by the communal household, then this is part of the inevitable pattern of development. To declare the kitchen to be the foundation of family life, as it were, to declare that the family stands or falls with the kitchen means to descecrate the concept of the family. If it were indeed only the cooking stove which keeps it together, it would deserve to perish. In reality matters are as follows. The outer form of the family has undergone perpetual change. What remains firm in this continual transformation is the relationship between man, woman, and child. The relationship becomes deeper and more loving, the more it can free itself from external conditions. In ancient times the woman was the man's submissive slave, the first administrix of his property. In modern times he esteemed her primarily as his housekeeper who, after he had sown his wild oats in his youth, created a comfortable home for him. In the future she will be both his lover and his friend, with whom she shares his joys and his sorrows and in whom he finds full understanding. But for the children, to whom in their infancy she was only a nursemaid, she shall turn into their educator and their friend.

Is that the dissolution of the family? Is this not rather the dissolution of today's circumstances which force the wage-earning woman to ruin her health and her mind, while driving the man into the saloon and the children into the street?

But it is not only the enemies of women's liberation who are against us. Even some of our friends voice all kinds of reservations. They argue that the wives in the cooperative will not get along with each other; wrangling, bickering, and gossiping will write a miserable finish to the venture. I do not wish to deny the justification for this objection. Poorly educated and overburdened, women simply have not had the chance to become interested in the more serious questions of life; and it is no wonder that, as a consequence, they have been sticking their noses into their neighbors' affairs. No household commune will be able to change them from one day to the next. But it certainly will eliminate a great deal of the cause for gossip and bickering by preventing the one from finding fault with the other's method of housekeeping and from poking their noses into their pots and pans. In time, moreover, it will exercise an important educational influence precisely in this direction.

[. . .]

Of course, many a man will ask, "But what is the woman to do if she does not do the cooking?" and many a woman herself will cling to her kitchen with genuine affection. That leads me to point out that, after all, the household commune is designed to unite primarily those families whose female members are pursuing independent professions. Nobody who is unwilling to part with the individual family kitchen can be forced to do so.

[. . .]

In his book *Women and Socialism,* August Bebel writes: "Like the workshop of the petty master craftsman, the small private kitchen is a thing of the past, an institution which senselessly squanders and wastes time, energy, and material." He then depicts a kitchen which was exhibited at the Chicago World's Fair in 1893, and in which the heating, cooking, frying, and dishwashing was done electrically; "our women," he suggests, "will grab on to this kitchen of the future with both hands when it can be had in lieu of today's kitchen"; but he places the communal arrangement of food preparation into the "society of the future," as Bellamy, among others, has also done. I do share the view that the definitive victory of the household commune over the private household is possible only when the socialist economic system has replaced the capitalist one; but just as the one will not disappear all of a sudden, the other one will not suddenly come into being; instead, like a butterfly within the pupa, the society of the future will develop gradually until, having matured, it will slip out of the dying husk. Just so the replacement of the individual household by the housekeeping commune will be able to occur only gradually. The first step taken will not conquer the entire country all at once, but it must be taken if the country is to be conquered at all.

More than before the male workers ought to remember that winning the women over to their ideals can be a life-or-death matter for them. The number of women workers is growing rapidly, as we have seen; the moment might come when the men will sense this mass of women with all their intellectual backwardness as a chain that fetters their feet. In order to prevent this, in order to wake the women from the leaden sleep weighing on them, they must be liberated also from the slavery of the household.

Translated by Alfred G. Meyer

Grete Lihotzky[1]

Rationalization in the Household *(ca. 1927)*

Every thinking woman must see how backward housekeeping practices have been up to this day, and must recognize in this the most
severe retardation of her own development and hence also that of
her family. The woman, of whom hectic contemporary urban life
demands far more than the contemplative life of eighty years ago, is
still condemned to keep her house as in grandmother's time, some
conveniences notwithstanding.

The problem of organizing the housewife's work more rationally
is of equal importance for almost all classes of the population. Middle-class women, who frequently manage the house without any
help, as well as working-class women, who frequently have to work
in additional jobs, are so overstrained that in the long run their overworked condition cannot remain without consequences for general
public health.

More than ten years ago, leading women had already recognized
the importance of relieving housewives of the unnecessary burden of
their work and had championed central management of houses, i.e.,
the building of houses with centralized kitchens.[2] They asked, Why
should twenty women go shopping, when one can do it for all of
them? Why should twenty women light twenty stoves, when one
stove suffices to cook on for everyone? Why should twenty women
cook for twenty families, when with the right organization four or
five persons can do the same work for twenty families? These considerations, obvious to any thinking person, were seductive. One-
kitchen houses were built, but it soon became evident that one cannot unite twenty families into one household without problems.
Apart from personal squabbling and qarreling, strong fluctuations in
the material situation of the various inhabitants are unavoidable, and
so the combination of several families must necessarily lead to conflict. Moreover, for workers and employees in the private sector, who

---

1. For most of her professional life as an architect, the author was known as
Margarete Schütte-Lihotzky.—Eds.

2. See, for example, the preceding essay by Lily Braun.—Eds.

can become unemployed on relatively short notice, the one-kitchen house is ruled out from the start, since the unemployed are not able to lower their standard of living as far as they would need to. Hence, the problem of rationalizing the household can not be solved in isolation, but must be pursued hand in hand with necessary social considerations.

In light of our experience thus far, we recognize that we have to stay with the single household, but must design it as rationally as humanly possible. But how can we improve the usual energy- and time-wasting housekeeping procedures? We can apply to housework the principles of labor-saving, economical business management, which through their implementation in factories and offices have led to undreamed-of increases in productivity. We must realize that for each task there must be a best and most simple way, which therefore is the least tiring, as well. It is important that three working groups, namely housewives, manufacturers, and architects, assume responsibility for cooperating in order to determine and make possible the simplest procedure for each job in the house.

Among housewives, the intellectually trained woman will also work ever more efficiently. With proper organization of the living space and the assistance of appropriate appliances and machines, she will soon recognize the most expedient way of doing her work.

Among manufacturers (with the exception of furniture-makers) there are many today who adjust to the new demands of our times and introduce useful, labor-saving appliances and machines to the market. By far the greatest backwardness, however, persists in ways of furnishing living spaces. When will the general population finally realize which kind of furnishings are most appropriate and best for them? Years of efforts by the German Craft Federation [*Werkbund*] and by individual architects, countless writings and lectures demanding clarity, simplicity, and functionality in furnishings and abandonment of the handed-down kitsch of the last fifty years, have been of almost no use.

When we enter dwellings, we still find the old knickknacks and usual useless decoration. The lack of practical success of all these efforts is mainly due to women, who are strangely unreceptive to the new ideas. Furniture dealers say that customers always demand the old things again. Women prefer to endure all the extra work in order to have a "snug and cozy" home. *Even today, the majority still takes simplicity and functionality to be synonymous with austerity.* The Building and Construction Office of the city of Frankfurt am Main has attempted to convince people of the opposite by erecting a fully furnished model house in the exhibition "The New Dwelling and Its Interior Design" at the Frankfurt trade fair. They want to prove that simplicity and functionality do not only mean reduction of labor, but clarity and beauty, if they are combined with good materials and appropriate design and color.

In this exhibition, the section organized by the Frankfurt Association of Housewives illustrated the importance of rationalization in the household particularly well. This part of the exhibition, entitled "The Modern Household," was chiefly concerned with the problem of the labor-saving kitchen. The first exhibit was a completely furnished galley-style kitchen and sideboard, as a particularly instructive example for the reduction of steps and manual operations. Three more furnished kitchens with built-in cabinetry, of which three thousand units of the first two types are being manufactured in Frankfurt, showed how work can be made easier by the correct arrangement and distribution of furnishings. The three different kinds of kitchen utilization were taken into consideration in this:

(1) The household without a maid (with a yearly income of up to approx. five thousand marks)
(2) The household with one maid (with a yearly income of approx. ten thousand marks)
(3) The household with two maids (with a yearly income over ten thousand marks)

In addition to these kitchen designs in wood, a small metal kitchenette for bachelor apartments and a kitchen of washable tile were also shown; these two kitchens represent attempts to find serviceable new materials that are less susceptible to external influences than wood. All kitchens are small for the sake of reducing labor, and completely separable from the living space. The old form of the live-in kitchen seems obsolete. Good examples of freestanding kitchen furnishings, which are available in retail and which contribute significantly to facilitating housework, were also presented. Good and bad domestic and kitchen appliances, those that waste or save labor, and those that can be cleaned easily or with difficulty are designated by signs in different colors. Dish racks for bowls, plates, and cups, which make drying dishes unnecessary, flour dispensers from which one can let a determined, measurable amount flow into the bowl, showed housewives equipment that has long proven itself abroad.

Special attention was also devoted to an exhibition of electrical machines and appliances. Although not yet practicable today for those with low income, we do know that the foreseeable future belongs to the electric kitchen.

Translated by Jörg Esleben

Susanne Suhr

The Social Condition of
Female White-Collar Workers *(1930)*

During the [economic] crises of recent years, questions concerning female employment have again entered public discussion. With the growth in *unemployment* has come a search for its causes and possible solutions. It has been suggested that unemployment is linked to the presence of women in the workplace, one of the most notable phenomena of modern economic development. This large *surplus of women* has determined the labor market for the last five years. At the same time, the *process of rationalization* has caused new shifts in the job market for men and women. No class of working women has been so affected by this process of adjustment as female white collar workers.

In recent times, the extraordinary *increase in white collar workers* has attracted public interest. In relation to rapid growth in this area, the increase in all remaining branches of employment has lagged considerably. The greatest growth has occurred among female white collar workers. While the numbers of male white collar workers doubled during the years between the surveys of 1907 and 1925, the number of female white collar workers tripled, and continues to grow. *The economic significance of white collar workers is based in large part on the role of these female white collar workers.*

Walking through the commercial centers of large cities shortly before eight o'clock in the morning or after office or business hours in the evening, one characteristically encounters an army of young girls and women, who are rushing to their jobs in large office buildings or coming from work in a tired state—these are the masses of white collar workers. The sight of them predominates in the streets of the metropolis, and department stores and corporate secretarial offices as well are marked by their presence. What is more, they have now become the prototype of the modern working woman: *the female white collar worker is the typical working woman of the masses.*

It is a seeming contradiction that female white collar workers are not at all the leading group in terms of numbers among all working women. Of the 11.5 million women that the 1925 survey counted as employed, the largest number were helping out in family businesses; they were followed by very large numbers of female workers and domestic servants. In fourth place were female white collar workers at 1.2 million. But while all other groups only grew in proportion to the increase in population, or—as in the case of domestic servants— even decreased, the number of female white collar workers increased in far greater measure. [. . .] It is quite evident that today young women are moving away from formerly typical jobs, such as housekeeping and the garment industry, and that they are entering white collar jobs in large numbers. But the shift to white collar jobs also includes many women from trade industries, as can be seen in our statistics. These *clear changes in the structure of women's occupations* call for close observation of the condition of female white collar workers. Just as in former years, when the movement of women's work was from housekeeping to factory work, today the movement is from factory work to white collar work. This particular development may be explained by the fact that the former women's jobs— such as housekeeping and the garment industry with its poor working conditions, often in unregulated small businesses with backward ways of operation—are less appealing than the seemingly better paid and less restrictive white collar jobs. In the factory work of women for which statistics are available, rationalization seems to affect women's jobs to the same degree as men's, releasing workers who then hope to find jobs in the white collar sector.

In addition, there has been an influx of white collar workers from two different sources: the first group derives from women of the middle class, who have been impoverished by inflation and thus forced by necessity to work; the second group consists of young women of the bourgeoisie, a generation looking for a job by choice. With both groups providing a supply of new workers, the female white collar labor force has grown from a handful into a typically female professional class. [. . .]

This influx is cause for serious concern, since it not only threatens the subsistence of these white collar workers, but also exceeds the capacity of the present economy. In the past year, the extent of unemployment—which has been even more prevalent among female white collar workers than among their male colleagues—demonstrates that the ability of the economy to absorb them is limited. As a result, the economic insecurity of female white collar workers has increased and the struggle to improve their social condition is exacerbated. Although the economy of today can no longer dispense with female white collar workers, their pay remains subject to [discriminatory] special terms. Antiquated notions and subconscious wishes regarding the *inferiority of women* still limit opportunities for women on the job. Ruthless wage policies operate to play off the sexes against one another and to stir up men against their "female rivals." There is no justification for such undervaluation of women, especially for female white collar workers. No longer should such "special" terms dictate their economic and social situation—which is already made two and three times more difficult by the double process of change in society at large and in women's work in particular.

Translated by Patricia A. Herminghouse
and Magda Mueller

Gertrud Bäumer

Female Teachers *(1930)*

Female teachers form the largest group of women in the free professions. In contrast to the male teaching profession with its double and strictly differentiated origins in the academic school system and the elementary school, the female teaching profession has developed from a single origin, and its uniformity, the intermingling of the various groups, their linking through intermediate levels between academy and teachers' college, still shapes the character of this profession decisively today.

The female branch of the teaching profession is perhaps most characteristic of the modern developments in the professional life of women, the new exterior shape and inner nature of that life. As the first and, for almost a century, only higher profession for women, it still allows us today—in analogy, as it were, to the growth circles of a tree trunk—to recognize the various stages in which women's work in the schools was consolidated, expanded, and organized. And no-where can one observe the transformation of a professional type within the same profession as clearly as here.

From the beginning we have three types, all treated more or less harshly by fate: first, the governess, who was a poor unmarried woman from a good family and who with her limited knowledge from finishing-school followed the path of renunciation through other people's houses; second, a kind of chaperone in advanced educational establishments for girls, who only cautiously was permitted to instruct and whose essential obligation was to supervise her charges; and finally: a robust, harmless auntie, a widow, or an old maid, who taught, often with natural talents for mothering, the beginnings of reading, writing, and arithmetic to the small children, until they were released into the more competent and regulated care of the school. Candidates for all three positions came in droves from the educated middle class, from among the daughters of teachers, rural pastors, and impoverished nobles. All of them were governed by the feeling of having to be grateful from the bottom of their heart that fate and noble human beings permitted them to serve in a modest way, after their life's hopes had foundered. They all felt more or less the stigma attached to earning their living, and were intent upon maintaining outward delicacy and modesty in money matters.

The first institutions for educating female teachers were oriented towards all three types: the governess, the pedagogical chaperones, and the elementary teacher. In any case, these institutions were pervaded by the idea that the women should never be anything other than a supplementary link in the school system. The program of one such early seminar for female teachers, the Institute for Protestant Governesses in Droyssig, explicitly countered any possible lofty desires of its pupils by declaring "all transcending thoughts and hopes as illusory."

Nonetheless, the range of activity for women in the schools expanded quickly despite this general wariness. On the one hand, the persuasiveness of the savings one could achieve with female teachers conquered all hesitation. The protocol of the Prussian ministerial conference of 1872, during which the elementary school system was reorganized, states that "female teachers will accept a lower wage." On the other hand, the insight often expressed by more sensitive pedagogues that female teachers are necessary for the education of girls, gained some more ground after all. Above all, it was the development of secondary education for girls that could not do without female teachers. [. . .] Women's insight into the incongruity between girls' education and the new social situation of women developed gradually out of their professional experience—the female teacher became the true pioneer of the women's movement. That strengthened her professional consciousness and gave her a sense of a higher duty transcending the narrow circle of her position. Unlike any other experience, it also gave her courage and confidence—the confidence that one gains in the service of a cause transcending the person, and the confidence that is provided by understanding a great development, in which one learns to understand oneself together with one's inhibitions and ambitions. Thus the load that had weighed on the self-confidence of female teachers began to grow lighter. One bold strike was the last thing needed to finally break down the false timidity with which traditional judgment and autosuggestion had surrounded the professional destiny of female teachers. The founding in 1890 of their own professional organization, the General Association of German Female Teachers, amounted to such a stroke. This organization set itself a double goal of raising the education of girls and of broadening the influence of women on elementary education. The metamorphosis of the typical female teacher from lady ashamed to be working to professional person took place under the confident leadership of the professional organization; for the elementary school teacher, it was above all the social conception of the profession that expanded her horizon from narrow to wide; for female teachers at secondary schools, it was the new possibilities for academic training that brought hundreds of women into the schools with completely new energy, as new human beings, so to speak. It lies in the nature of things, that among female professions, female teachers display the most developed professional consciousness.

Translated by Jörg Esleben

Katharina Gröning

Community Commissioners for [Gender] Equality: Possibilities and Problems *(1992)*

More than a thousand community commissioners for [gender] equality are presently working in the old and new federal states of Germany. Public interest is often focused on concrete results, reforms, innovations, and changes that these commissioners for equality are expected to bring about. Those who occupy these positions are judged by their effectiveness and the results they produce, but it remains unclear under which structural and institutional conditions these positions are implemented in the various political-administrative systems and which overt or covert interests are involved when someone is chosen for the position of community commissioner for equality. [. . .]

Organizational Problems

Already the 1980 report of the Exploratory Committee on Women and Society attached major political significance to the organizational placement and structure of the institution proposed for assuring gender equality. It therefore called for an organizational study to determine the optimal situation of such an office and its proper range of authority.

In the realities of political life, however, there has only been an inadequate response to this call for systematic reflection about the aims and procedures of these offices and thus little attention has been given to their organizational positioning within local administrations and policy-making bodies. According to various publications by the women who hold these positions, the question of how they fit into the organizational structure brings with it its own set of problems. As a rule, advocates of such community offices argue as follows:

- An office for [gender] equality that is headed by a commissioner for women's affairs who just runs it in addition to her regular work load or on a volunteer basis is in principle just a token. Such an office—according to the critics—is ineffective in terms of policies for women.
- In order to escape public pressure, conservative communities in particular tend to choose volunteer commissioners for women's affairs, preferably from among like-minded candidates.

In their own analysis, commissioners for women's affairs in large West German cities [. . .] have favored an organizational model with a staff-level position for a full-time commissioner, who answers only to the top administrative officer. As Otti Stein, Marianne Vollmer, and Marianne Weg stated in 1988: "Assignment to the top administrator facilitates quick unbureaucratic action and cooperation with other special departments and offices in order to effectively address the concerns of women and to communicate local policies affecting women to the public."

Commissioners for women's affairs regard the following kinds of authority as necessary and conducive to doing their job effectively: power to endorse proposals to legislative and administrative bodies; the right to participate and speak in legislative committees and council meetings, access to information and files, public relations work, and involvement in personnel decisions.

All in all, the Federal Association of Community Commissioners for Women's Affairs demands the same legal status for the offices of equality that, for example, audit departments have. The latter are liable only to general oversight by the chief administrator and not to detailed supervision.

Within the organization of commissioners for women's affairs as well as within feminist groups that support the offices for equality there is agreement about the tasks and aims of such offices. But even if those who support these policies tend to outdo one another in their demands for power and influence for these commissioners, there remain questions regarding the need for explicit organizational arrangements for the equality offices.

"Power Makes Women Powerful"?

Strategically located at the nexus of the political and administrative systems, vested with high moral, political, and gender-related authority, the commissioners for women's affairs themselves conceive of their office as a staff-level position with power to influence the political-administrative system. They want to emphasize the extent of their responsibilities even if it entails being given a highly diverse and complex range of duties. Gaining political power seems to them a desirable goal. As Stein, Vollmer, and Weg explain, "Those who hold ministerial offices, such as city managers, department heads, bureau chiefs—whether elected, appointed, or hired—have the authority and tools to achieve their ideas and plans even against the will of others, if necessary."

The female advocates of governmental policies for equality want to share in such institutional power in order to establish a society in accordance with the interests of women. They have decided that it is necessary to have political power, which they promise to deploy in a thoughtful, self-critical, and careful manner. Those who take these positions now openly seek to be considered as representatives of the political will of the people. Nonetheless they question the desirability of women's participation in patriarchal power via government positions and functions and they invite debate about such power and critical reflection on "how far we have come." Again and again, they allude to special female qualities such as flexibility and adroitness, the ability to sustain conflict and to negotiate, or willingness to compromise—to a female culture of social interaction which is more likely to bring about innovations in the political realm than the male workplace culture that characterizes the political-administrative system.

It is obvious that hardly any attention is being paid to important aspects of democratic control—including specifying how a strategy of women's emancipation can be combined with the development of democracy or elaborating problems inherent in the autonomy of political-administrative systems and of those who assume the role the commissioners for equality envision for themselves. Rather, their demand to participate in power is made quite openly at a time when complaints are being heard about the breakdown of the political system and the reduced influence and importance of democratic decision-making, and when technocratic constraints on opportunities to influence policy present the greatest challenges to democracy today. [. . .]

The principle of autonomy in local government is being used to justify placing policy-making for women under the control and hegemonic interests of the "powers that be." The dilemma can be adequately described as "commissioner without commission," since the areas of activity that are outlined in the job descriptions of the community commissioners for women are not binding within the political-administrative system. This must be remedied in comprehensive legislation on gender equality, especially since there is a curious discrepancy between the existence of offices for equality on all levels and their lack of authorization. The meaning of legal protection for equal opportunity and other consequences for the state, the economy, public policy, and so forth must be spelled out more clearly.

Translated by Patricia A. Herminghouse
and Magda Mueller

WOMEN
AND POLITICS

Christiana Mariana von Ziegler

Das männliche Geschlechte, im Namen einiger Frauenzimmer besungen

Du Weltgepriesenes Geschlechte,
Du in dich selbst verliebte Schaar,
Prahlst allzusehr mit deinem Rechte,
Das Adams erster Vorzug war.
Doch soll ich deinen Werth besingen,
Der dir auch wirklich zugehört;
So wird mein Lied ganz anders klingen,
Als das, womit man dich verehrt.

Ihr rühmt das günstige Geschicke,
Das euch zu ganzen Menschen macht;
Und wißt in einem Augenblicke
Worauf wir nimmermehr gedacht.
Allein; wenn wir euch recht betrachten,
So seyd ihr schwächer als ein Weib.
Ihr müßt oft unsre Klugheit pachten,
Noch weiter als zum Zeitvertreib.

Kommt her, und tretet vor den Spiegel:
Und sprechet selbst, wie seht ihr aus?
Der Bär, der Löwe, Luchs, und Igel
Sieht bey euch überall heraus.
Vergebt, ich muß die Namen nennen,
Wodurch man eure Sitten zeigt.
Ihr mögt euch selber wohl nicht kennen,
Weil man von euren Fehlern schweigt.

Seht doch wie ihr vor Eifer schäumet,
Wenns nicht nach eurem Kopfe geht.
O Himmel, was ist da versäumet,
Wenn man nicht gleich zu Diensten steht?
Ihr flucht mit fürchterlicher Stimme,
Als kämt ihr aus des Pluto Kluft.

Christiana Mariana von Ziegler

In Praise of the Male Sex
as Seen by Certain Females *(1739)*

You males, praised the whole world through,
You charming, narcissistic crowd,
You flaunt your rights with much ado,
Rights with which Adam was endowed.
But should I laud your accomplishments
With words you are entitled to,
Then you'd certainly note a difference
From other songs that praise you.

You say that fortune's favored you
By making you someone complete;
And in a wink you can construe
Thoughts with which we can't compete.
Yet if we'd investigate your privilege
You'd be found weaker by a measure;
You often borrow from our knowledge
More than is needed for your pleasure.

Come here, go to the mirror, stare:
And say yourself, what do you see?
The lion, lynx, the hedgehog, bear?
All those appear in there to me.
Excuse me, if such names I use—
To describe your manners as I must—
You probably have different views
Since your faults are ne'er discussed.

But look at how you rant and rave,
If things fail to go your way.
O Heavens, how you misbehave,
If one incurs a slight delay.
You utter dreadful imprecations
As if you'd just escaped from Hell,

Und wer entgehet Eurem Grimme,
Wenn ihr das Haus zusammen ruft?

Die, welche sich nur selbst erheben,
Die gerne groß und vornehm sind,
Nach allen Ehrenämtern streben,
Da doch den Kopf nichts füllt als Wind:
Die keine Wissenschaften kennen,
Und dringen sich in Würden ein,
Die kann man wohl mit Namen nennen,
Daß sie der Thorheit Kinder seyn.

Die Männer müssen doch gestehen,
Daß sie wie wir, auch Menschen sind.
Daß sie auch auf zwey Beinen gehen;
Und daß sich manche Schwachheit findt.
Sie trinken, schlafen, essen, wachen.
Nur dieses ist der Unterscheid,
Sie bleiben Herr in allen Sachen,
Und was wir thun, heißt Schuldigkeit.

Der Mann muß seine Frau ernähren,
Die Kinder, und das Hausgesind.
Er dient der Welt mit weisen Lehren,
So, wie sie vorgeschrieben sind.
Das Weib darf seinen Witz nicht zeigen:
Die Vorsicht hat es ausgedacht,
Es soll in der Gemeine schweigen,
Sonst würdet ihr oft ausgelacht.

Ihr klugen Männer schweigt nur stille:
Endecket unsre Fehler nicht.
Denn es ist selbst nicht unser Wille,
Daß euch die Schwachheit wiederspricht.
Trag eines nur des andern Mängel,
So habt ihr schon genug gethan,
Denn Menschen sind fürwahr nicht Engel,
An denen man nichts tadeln kann.

And who has escaped your indignation
At the domestic personnel?

Those who claim to be superior,
Who think they're important and refined,
Who strive for titulary honor,
Though idle matters fill their mind:
They don't know any science
But still get titles and degrees;
One must admit with all due deference:
They are fools with pedigrees.

Yet one day men too must confess,
That they are flesh and blood as we.
That they, as we, two legs possess
And are not free of infirmity.
They also eat, drink, sleep, and wake,
There only is one difference:
They are masters of their fate
While we serve in obedience.

The man must indeed support his wife,
The children, and domestic servants.
He teaches what he's learned in life
As is prescribed by ordinance.
The woman dare not show her intellect:
Providence decrees this too,
Our public silence you expect
Else we'd be making fun of you.

You clever men, now just be still
And overlook what we can't do.
For indeed it's not our will,
That the weak sex speaks up to you.
If we each other's faults would bear,
Then you would have done enough:
For people are not angels fair
And are made from weaker stuff.

Translated by Susan L. Cocalis and
Gerlind M. Geiger

Louise Otto-Peters

Editor's Farewell *(1850)*

It was about two years ago when I established this newspaper and wrote in the prospectus for it: "The history of all time and especially that of today teaches: *Those were forgotten who forgot to remember themselves.*"

"Come, my sisters, unite with me so that we do not stay behind while everyone and everything around us and beside us forges ahead and fights. We, too, want to demand our due and benefit from the great world deliverance that must finally come to the entire human race, of which we are half.

"*We want to demand our due:* the right to cultivate in ourselves the purely human through the unrestrained development of all our abilities and the right to self-representation and autonomy in the state.

"*We want to do our share:* we want to make every effort to promote the work of saving the world, above all by endeavoring to disseminate the two great ideas of the future—freedom and humanity (two words that basically mean the same thing)—in all circles that are accessible to us: in the broader areas of life in general through the press, and in the narrower circles of the family by example, instruction, and education. However, we also want to do our share, not by striving in isolation, each for herself, but rather each for everyone, and above all by looking after those who languish forgotten and neglected in poverty, misery, and ignorance."

Two years of this newspaper lie before the public for review. The public must testify that the paper has remained true to its prospectus, and the ever increasing interest that it found through subscribers and co-workers, and, what is more, found under the most unfavorable circumstances that only a democratic newspaper could have (the Saxon paper began in April 1849; the third issue appeared during occupation), will obviously confirm that this prospectus was not written in vain.

It is not vanity and self-praise, but the inspiration of the experience of two years that allows me to say that the *Frauen-Zeitung*

[Women's Newspaper] has stuck to what it promised: what it wanted and intended, it aimed for and achieved.

[. . .]

Far removed from the usual language of other laws, Paragraph twelve of the press law emphasized especially that only *"male persons"* are permitted to head the editorial management of periodicals. Thus there is no doubt that women were not forgotten this time. In this respect our efforts in recent years have brought things so far that attention is paid to women as never before. When we distributed our prospectus for the paper two years ago, of course we only thought in each point on the distribution of *rights* to all citizens, and we did not want to be forgotten. As matters now stand, it is, on the contrary, a matter of the withdrawal of rights, and from our standpoint no less respectful to us, i.e., not to have been forgotten. The opposite case would have been the same as before.

Now I come to the reason why I am giving up the *Frauen-Zeitung* and must write this farewell today.

Paragraph twelve of the draft of the press law states: "In the kingdom of Saxony the responsible editorial management of a newspaper may be led only by resident *male* persons"—etc. It is not necessary to repeat the remaining conditions of assuming editorial leadership; this provision *alone* explains the impossibility of the further existence of a "women's newspaper," since also "persons participating in the editorial management must have the same characteristics." I *could* have satisfied all the other conditions for continuing as editor, even putting up the deposit would not have been an impediment for us, but women are once and for all forbidden as editors, and so nothing remains for me but, together with the *Frauen-Zeitung,* to bid farewell to its readers, male and female.

Translated by Melanie Archangeli

Mathilde Franziska Anneke

The Conviction of Susan B. Anthony *(1873)*

Equality of rights will raise the female sex up from feelings of degradation and dependence to awareness of equal status and self-determination, and elevate it to human dignity. This participation in legislation will make woman a responsible party in the regulation of political and social questions of the time, authorizing her to root out injustices and abolish the absence of rights that everywhere prevails against her in the laws. The right to vote will authorize her to be included in all public affairs and to have a definitive say in questions that are her own immediate interests, such as marriage and marriage law, education, and children's rights. Her right to vote will offer protection for the reawakened concern for rights in public life and a shield against all forms of corruption. It will arouse enthusiasm and interest for the highest values in human life and, through activity that is linked to public interests, release woman from the vain and childish trivia in which idleness and false life goals had hitherto trapped her. It will also free her from the bonds in which she was still restrained to some extent by church and clergy, and from the dark powers to which she was consigned in obstinate egotism by the powerful of this earth despite ongoing progress of the scientific enlightenment. It will lead her from blind faith and prejudice to mental activity that gives her practical support and zest for life as well as triumphant awareness of an ability to achieve, through her own energy, her own education, and her own intellectual inclination, a life of human dignity that can no longer be postponed until heaven and the hereafter.

The women of this country have struggled for more than a quarter-century for equal status and its manifestation in the right to vote, for this palladium of a free people. They have been unshakable in forcing attention to and closer investigation of the question, through unrelenting demands, through most impassioned propaganda, and by presenting their opponents with the most adroit arguments that vanquish all doubt; they have personally demonstrated to Congress that the principles upon which the proud edifice of the Union is based are falsehoods, and their institutions vain boasts as long as the greater half of their citizens is excluded from participation in legislation and kept in subjection to the other half; they have induced insightful statesmen to examine their demands and have enabled Congress as well as state legislatures to attempt to amend the respective constitutions, possibly even to revise them by striking the word "male," which refers to the privileged citizens, from their pages altogether. Finally, they have convinced the greatest philosophers and men of science of all countries to acknowledge the truth and to propound the indisputable realization that women too are human beings.

[. . .]

Susan B. Anthony, that bright, courageous, unselfish and always prepared champion of radical principles of every kind . . . cast her vote in trust and good faith in her native city of Rochester [New York]. She cast it in awareness of an obligation as a female citizen of the United States, as a representative of a great humanitarian principle. She placed it into the ballot box with the approval of local election officials, who had become convinced of women's right to vote. She cast it, encouraged by the opinion of an incumbent legislator who, when asked, had stated that the right was irrefutable. She had grounds for hoping that, if she were brought before the court to answer for her glorious deed, the truth of the principle for which she and the best women of our country had fought, sanctioned by the better and best minds of our people and of other peoples, would also have penetrated the hearts of the judges and would be raised to the level of a test, through their solemn verdict. She was mistaken. The better and best minds had erred with her. She was convicted because she voted—and is only a woman!

Translated by Jeanette Clausen

Fanny Lewald

Ninth Political Letter: Emancipation and Feminine Virtue *(1869)*

Humankind has made great strides in justice since the beginning of this century, and we have marched vigorously forward along the path that Rousseau trod in his *Contrat social.* Serfdom and bondage have been abolished in all of Europe and even in that half–Asian land, Russia; in Germany the Jews, in Ireland the Catholics, and across the ocean the Negroes have been emancipated, and all these advancements of oppressed human beings were effected by those who in fact still held the power of continued oppression in their hands. Thus, these were truly acts of independent understanding toward the liberation of the oppressed; and one can scarcely doubt that a similar feat of liberation will be performed on behalf of women in the not too distant future, because one can predict that every rational idea will progress consistently, even if it cannot always be determined in advance when and in what form it will develop. Yet wherever such liberation has taken place, the desire on the part of the downtrodden for this advancement has been present and expressed beforehand, for good deeds are seldom forced upon them, and I believe it is worth the effort of taking a look at the extent to which women themselves desire to be emancipated here in Germany and in what ways they have prepared themselves for equality with men.

When speaking in this context of "women" in general, of course I do not mean that still relatively small number of women who, by means of intellectual maturity, moral seriousness, steadfastness, and the courage of their convictions, as well as diligent hard work, have risen above the great mass of their sisters and taken their place beside men. It is self-evident that this minority desires the necessary freedom of movement for their intelligence and energy. But in our country the great masses of women are still almost universally opposed to women's emancipation and, it must be admitted, they often side in word and deed with those men who describe women's emancipation, for the time being or in general, as foolishness, as a verdict, or as an impossibility.

[. . .]

It was shortly after the July Revolution that discussion of women's emancipation first began within our educated middle-class society. The concept and the name came to our country from France, primarily from French novels, and coincided with the theory of the so-called emancipation of the flesh that was advocated, thoughtlessly enough, in various German novels at the time. One novel after the other was immoral to the core, and while the charm of description and isolated traces of truth in the French and German literary works could blind us younger readers and delude us as to their conceptual confusion, the more mature minds of our nation were absolutely right in delivering a damning verdict upon this poetic glorification of women's emancipation and the emancipation of the flesh for which Saint-Simonism[1] had prepared the way, since both essentially preached nothing less than total lack of restraint in sensual pleasure between men and women.

[. . .]

Those not exactly promising female pioneers of women's emancipation vanished in short order from the scene of our public life; only the specter of the "emancipated woman" hovers eerily among us as their legacy, casting its shadow to this day on all women who take the liberty of cultivating their talents, developing their abilities, and moving about fearlessly and self-assuredly through life and the world, supporting and taking responsibility for themselves—when no one else is there to spare them of the effort.

Now that almost a generation has passed since those days, I often think back with amusement and regret on how arduously we have had to work against that prejudice to regain, step by step, the ground on which all women now stand unselfconsciously and how we have had to recapture for ourselves that which everyone now enjoys in carefree security. How many things were considered offensive in earlier times! How many things were unseemly for a woman and even more so for a girl! A girl was not allowed to look at a statue of a naked person and had to turn her eyes away from a picture with nude figures, blushing and trembling if at all possible; a girl was not allowed to take the briefest of journeys alone, but had to be escorted on even a four-hour drive; it was not proper for a girl to enter a stranger's house to place an order with a craftsman; even a no longer young unmarried female was not allowed to care for a substantially

---

1. Socialist-religious movement founded by Henri de Saint-Simon (1760–1825), noted for alleged emphasis of sexual freedom.—Eds.

older ill friend of her family, could not visit him alone at his sickbed if he happened to be unmarried; and to utter an independent opinion or express interest in matters of general concern was altogether un-maidenly and also unwomanly. We were not supposed to have any opinion of our own, and it was practically a law of femininity to begin each sentence expressly with "I think" or "they say" in order to deflect any appearance of independence, which in and of itself was seen as presumptuous.

At the same time, however, it was obvious enough that all these requirements for a particular kind of femininity applied only to the daughters and wives of the prosperous and more or less well-edu-cated classes. The feminine virtues of poor and uneducated women were thereby forfeited without further ado, which was not especially Christian but rather, cruel; or it was assumed that poor and unedu-cated women were better able than the educated ones to assert their femininity in contact with life. For our poorer sisters were allowed and obliged to follow us unescorted at our command if we were in need of their services on a journey somewhere; they had to go out on the street day or night without protection if we bade them do so; they had to enter the houses to which we sent them; they had to perform the needed assistance at the sickbeds of men. The women of the working classes were always and without exception capable of earning their living; because necessity demanded it, no substantial obstacles or prejudices stood in their way. They were seamstresses, laundresses, milliners, nurses, midwives; they pursued commerce and all kinds of odd jobs, peddled groceries and other goods, and nobody paid attention, nobody saw any harm in it, nobody considered the fact that these women were almost on equal footing with men with respect to freedom of movement and earning a living. This part of their emancipation seemed perfectly natural because necessity de-manded it. For these women, everything that happened was seemly because it had to happen. It was and still is interesting to detect that fine borderline of beginning prosperity beyond which working for a living and freedom of movement is designated as something not fit-ting for women, as contrary to true femininity, as improper for women.

Translated by Jeanette Clausen

Louise Otto-Peters

The Woman Question *(1876)*

. . . When the war[1] came and the call to battle in defense of the fatherland was issued to all able-bodied men, much was demanded of women, too. A dreadful martyrdom was imposed upon the women when their fathers, husbands, sons, lovers, and brothers were claimed, because to endure, silent and idle at home, the fear for far-away loved ones, was much more difficult than to plunge boldly into danger. Yet it was demanded that women joyfully make this sacrifice for the fatherland. There were appeals to their patriotism because there was need of it, although prior to that little or nothing had been done to nurture that patriotism. Women—held at a distance from all public and communal affairs, left out of the laws, or, where included, only to their disadvantage, excluded from all educational institutions that the state established only for its sons, and so excluded from all civil rights except the right to pay taxes, often deliberately left in ignorance about political matters by their own husbands, and still more often by teachers at school and at home—had little reason to be patriotic and to make all the sacrifices that were now demanded of them. That they *were* patriotic, however (including those who had always loved their fatherland and did not first require the urging of their husbands and the knowledge that patriotism was fashionable), demonstrates best their warmth of feeling and their capacity for inspiration, which stood the test in that important time. It says even more about their unselfishness, their selflessness, and their generosity.

That women, as already mentioned, proved so splendidly their capacity for sacrifice, and did everything they could to alleviate the misery of the war and to offer their feminine assistance—that should also have earned them greater freedom than they were granted. It would not have been necessary to reward this service with medals and honors, but indeed with the recognition that would be pleased to make use of these abilities in the service of the fatherland and humanity also in peacetime. Instead, the women were sent home and

---

1. Franco-Prussian War, 1870–71—Eds.

confined within the old limits. The ever more powerful rule of militarism, and the brutality and moral degeneration nurtured by the war, were not very favorable to the emergence and consideration of the female element. In fact, it was a time of new businesses and a certain smug national arrogance as mentioned before.

If women do in fact display the blossoms and fruits of patriotic inspiration, women, and again the state, have only German literature and the cult of Schiller at school and in the home to thank, not the state and social considerations of women. The participation of German women in politics is slight; often they have no interest in or understanding of it. In this respect they lag behind the women of almost all other civilized countries. The reason for this lack of interest is, perhaps, the notion that a woman's femininity is suspect if she concerns herself with politics, and perhaps also (although "unknowingly"), the commonplace maxim that sounds quite trivial and yet is justified to a certain extent: What do I care about the state that considers me only as a subordinate creature? How do I benefit when my "people" stand tall and receive new rights when I do not count under the idea of "people," but rather only the men, when only the male and not the female citizens are recognized, and women remain without rights?

And for that reason—although for the most part unknowingly—women also plunged into the torrent of politics in times of political agitation and exaltation, as, for example, in 1813, 1830, 1848, and 1870. If men were permitted to anticipate becoming German and free and helping to lead up to a better time, could not the women also demand their due and aspire to earn a living? Already thirty years ago I wrote along these lines: "The times never stand still and history happens every day!" Already then and also today it is sad to realize that women who become committed newspaper readers during such times afterwards revert to the old apathy. If in the German Empire it is now happening again that the greatest number of men by far are satisfied by German unity and the more respected position of Germany internationally, and leave everything else to the imperial chancellor in Berlin and pursue only material interests, it is hardly surprising, but certainly sad enough.

Translated by Melanie Archangeli

Hedwig Dohm

The Right of Woman's Suffrage *(1876)*

Women demand the Suffrage as a natural right.
They demand it as a means of raising the human race.
[. . .]
They demand it as a right. Why should I prove that I have a right to suffrage? I am a human being, a citizen; I do not belong to the criminal class, I do not live on alms. These are the proofs which I have to bring in favour of my claim. A man requires to pay a certain rent, to be a certain age, and possess a certain sum, in order to be able to vote, why should a woman need more? Why is a woman classed with criminals and imbeciles? No, not with criminals, for they are only prevented from voting for certain periods of time. It is only the idiot and the woman who belong to the same category.

No one has the right to rob me of my natural political right. But supposing this right is proved to be irreconcilable with the welfare of the State? We demand proofs of the enmity between the welfare of the State and women's rights. We shall have to wait for these proofs till Doomsday, and in the meantime our opponents appeal to that judgment of God and Nature that has characterized woman as unpolitical—she has no beard!

The presumption that a class of persons should have laws imposed upon them, in the making of which they have had no share; the presumption that a class of persons who bear the burdens of citizenship has no right to bring any influence to bear on these burdens, is, in the main, only possible in a despotic State. The admission of such a principle is tyranny, in every language of the world and for both sexes.

The claim to political equality of the sexes, the idea of a woman speaking in Parliament, is to most men the acme of absurdity! Only one sort of political equality do they admit—that of the scaffold. Why did they not laugh when Marie Antoinette's and Madame Roland's heads fell under the guillotine? Madame de Stael wrote, "In a State where men cut off women's heads in its interest, the women should at least know the reason why." But men never answer such impertinent questions.

Men derive their rights over women from their power over them. But the fact of power is not a right. They arrange all the rules, customs and orders which serve to suppress women, and call these arrangements legal power. An injustice is not less unjust because it is sanctioned by the law, an act of oppression is all the more objectionable when universal. There is no right of injustice or at least there ought not be. As long as it is—man *will* and woman *shall,* we live in a State governed by *might* and not by *right.*

[. . .]

Men, they say, represent women. When did women give men the right to represent them? When did men ever give women an account of their resolutions? Never. [. . .] An absolute monarch can say with just as much right that he represents his people, or the slave-holder declare that he represents his slaves. It is an old argument that the workers can be represented by their employer, but it has not convinced the workers, and they have refused such representation with the greatest energy. And then they say that women should accept such an arrangement? Never!

[. . .]

Tear off the bandage with which your eyes have been blinded, so that you might pursue the treadmill of your narrow lives without restiveness and giddiness. Fling from you the conventional character that has been forced upon you, break through the Chinese wall which has limited your sphere.

Arise and demand the suffrage!

[. . .]

And do not forget one thing: demands *minus* the power to enforce them mean nothing. Despotism knows only one limit, the limit set by the growing power of the oppressed. The masses care nothing for judgment, opinions, and principles—they want results. How may you attain power? By the concentration of the strength of every woman who is ready to demand her political rights, and by the organization and energetic leadership of women's associations.

In every large town in England and the United States, there are Women's Suffrage societies. [. . .] But not in Germany. Will German women sleep forever, like the Sleeping Beauty of the fairy story?

Awake, women of Germany, if you have a heart to feel for your sisters' wrongs and tears to shed for their misery, even if you yourselves are contented and happy in your lives. Awake, if you have spirit enough to feel your degradation, and intellect enough to see the source of your misery.

Demand the suffrage because it is the only road to independence and equality, to freedom and happiness for women. Without political rights—no matter how much your spirits overflow with compassion, kindness, and noble intentions regarding the terrible crimes committed against your sex—you are powerless.

Get going! Organize! Show that you are capable of enthusiastic devotion, and awaken the consciences of men. Appeal through word and deed to their hearts and convince their intelligence! Do not rely entirely on the help of German men.

[. . .]

Be courageous, help yourselves and God will help you. Think of Emerson's bold words "Do that which you are afraid to do."

You poor women and victims of gender despotism, you have until now navigated the sea of life without rudder or sail, and seldom reached the shore, while the ship of your happiness has been wrecked in calm and storm alike. Let, in the future, suffrage be your rudder, your own strength your sail, and then trust yourselves fearlessly on the ocean of life, with its storms and its rocks! Sometime you will see land, the land your souls have sought for centuries, aye for thousands of years—the land where women belong to themselves and not to men alone.

[. . .]

The rights of mankind have no sex.

Translated by Constance Campbell;
revised by Patricia A. Herminghouse

Marie Goegg

The Woman Question in Switzerland *(1884)*

. . . Switzerland, taken as a whole, has been one of the least disposed of European countries to accept the idea of the civil emancipation of women, and much less the conferring upon them of political rights. From 1848 to 1868 the claims of American women were looked upon here as the height of extravagance. Yet Switzerland has given to the world so large a number of distinguished women that it is unnecessary to defend before public opinion the proposition of female intelligence. But belief is one thing, and practice is another. Between the admission of women's intellectual capacity and the logical application of rights which naturally result therefrom, yawns a vast abyss of prejudice and injustice. The echo of the demands of which we have just spoken rarely crossed the ocean to trouble the minds of our thinkers, and the general public was completely ignorant of them. From time to time some newspaper, for lack of other material or for the amusement of its readers, would tell how the women had assembled in the United States, at New York or elsewhere, to demand "emancipation." This word emancipation, thrown out on the public without any limitation of its meaning, gave a wrong impression as to the aims of these women, and created an unfortunate prejudice against them and their claims. But ideas are like flowers whose seeds are scattered far and wide. The germ deposited in America in 1848, although its growth was difficult, finally took root in Europe. English women, supported by the celebrated economist [John Stuart] Mill, who had just given to the world his grand book, *The Subjection of Women,* began to see and understand all the evils produced by the legal subjugation of their sex, and established a National Society for Women's Suffrage. Germany also had its awakening in 1865, at almost the same time as England; but German women, in also forming a National Society, overlooked their civil and political rights, and began with the improvement of the educational and industrial condition of their sex.

In March, 1868, Switzerland, in its turn, began to move. At that date I published a letter, *Etats-Unis d'Europe,* inviting the women of all nations to form a society, which might serve as a bond of union between them and promote their common interests. In 1867 I was present at the Peace Congress held in that year at Geneva and was struck with the advantages resulting from the meeting of all those superior men, come together from the four quarters of the globe to protest against war, and who, for the most part unknown to each other, now became acquainted, discussed the questions which interested them and finally separated, but not until they had created the International League of Peace and Liberty. Why should not women imitate this good example and also assemble to consider their rights and to found an international society? This simple and natural idea was the origin of the invitation sent forth in the spring of 1868. In July of this same year the Women's International Association was created, and I was elected its first president. The constitution of the new organization limited the membership of the central or executive committee to women, and this committee forthwith set to work. One of its first acts was to address a letter to the central committee of the International League of Peace and Liberty, which had announced its next meeting in September at Bern, asking that women be admitted to the congress. After a long discussion, the president of the committee, Gustave Vogt, of Bern, now a distinguished lawyer and journalist of Zurich, replied that not only would women be admitted to the congress, but that the last day—Saturday, September 26—would be given up to those women who wished to speak, adding that "it was not by gallantry, but by a sentiment of real justice, that the League afforded women an opportunity to make known their claims." This society, therefore, has the honor of being the first in Switzerland to admit women into its midst as equals.

[...]

It may be pointed out here, that, except in England, all the women's societies created in Europe had, up to the time of the organization of the [Women's] International Association, refrained from touching the question of the political rights of women. The Swiss association, on the contrary, always included this subject in its program. But, unfortunately, at the moment when our efforts were meeting with success, and the future was full of promise for the cause which we advocated, the terrible Franco-German war broke out, and, for various reasons unnecessary to go into here, I felt constrained to resign the presidency, and the association came to an end.

Translator unknown

Lida Gustava Heymann and Anita Augspurg

The Conservative and the Radical Women's Movement *(1941)*

In the political life of Germany in those years [from 1848 to the 1880s], little or nothing was first noticed of the cheerfully energetic struggle of women for their freedom. This changed towards the end of the 1880s; women began to stir noticeably. The struggle commenced, and not only with the social environment in the male state, but also with German female society itself, where now two tendencies opposed each other. In our view these can be characterized objectively and briefly as follows. One of them can be designated as the conservative, the other as the radical tendency. The conservative tendency, always stressing the different nature of the female sex, aimed at creating educational and professional opportunities for women, so that through social activity in the community they could gradually grow into a helpful and supportive role in the existing male state. The tactical approach toward this goal was, of course, always: "Careful! Do not give offense! One must not provoke men too much, because they rule the state; the sympathy of influential circles toward us has to be ensured, because we need them. In order to achieve partial successes, one always must be ready for compromises."

How different was the radical tendency! Pointing out unsatisfactory conditions in the state and society, it simply denied men's right to absolute power. For their purposes of winning equal economic, social, and political rights, there was no cause to see a sign of secondariness and inability in the difference of the female sex. For radical women, the norms and goals of the existing states, ruled one-sidedly by male spirit and male interests, were no *noli me tangere* to which they would have to assimilate and submit. On the contrary, for them these norms and goals were an often irrational, inadequate patchwork in need of new stimuli and initiatives, for which women, excluded thus far from all participation, felt themselves as much called upon and responsible as men. Moreover, as far as the political immaturity of German women was concerned, experience had taught that it was by no means greater than that of men when they came into their political rights in 1867 and 1870. Only those who jump into the water learn to swim.

Radical women pursued the tactic of expressing what they demanded forcefully, distinctly, and clearly, without any heed to male outrage and sensitivity. Men were to find out that there were women who were not ready for any compromises, but demanded absolutely what they had been deprived of for centuries, namely: to develop according to their own understanding and conviction, to shape their own lives, to earn their own living, and to build, together with men, a humane world in place of the hitherto existing vale of tears.

In view of this, it becomes understandable that since the end of the 1880s there has been constant friction and conflict between the two tendencies within the organized women's movement in Germany, be it about educational opportunities, morality, sexuality, and political rights of women, or about questions of national and international politics, war or peace.

When, after long years, successes were brought about through the actions of the radical women, it all too often happened that the conservative women not only reckoned these successes as a result of their caution and willingness to compromise, but claimed them unscrupulously for themselves and declared that they, after all, had always been striving for the fulfilled demands.

In Imperial Germany, the women's movement became a factor that political men began to take into account only after the middle of the 1890s. Neither existing books about the development of the German women's movement edited by conservative women nor the yearbooks of the Federation of German Women's Associations [Bund Deutscher Frauenvereine] mention that credit for this is due to the radical women. Thus, it remains an irreparable mistake that radical women, entirely devoted to their holy cause, put all their energy into vital initiatives, always using the moment for struggle and never taking the time to record, retrospectively and systematically for posterity, the work they performed and the stimuli they provided. Thus it came about that in Germany and abroad one encountered the view that all achievements of the German women's movement were due to the work of the Federation of German Women's Associations. However, the Federation hardly ever accepted or supported the propositions made by radical women for united action with regard to the political demands of women or international questions like war and peace. On the contrary, almost without exception such propositions were assured a more or less scornful funeral.

Translated by Jörg Esleben

Helene Lange

There Were No Social-Democratic
Women's Organizations *(1921)*

At the founding of the Federation[1] in spring of 1894, the question that caused the liveliest debates was our position toward women who were affiliated with the Social-Democratic Party. Some (such as Lily Braun in *Memoirs of a Social-Democratic Woman*) tried to portray this debate in a way that suggests that bourgeois narrow-mindedness within the founding groups promoted the exclusion of women who supported socialism. This was *not* the case. It was rather a purely formal problem that was connected to the existing law regulating organizations [*Vereinsgesetz*].[2] In most of the federal states, women were not allowed to be members of political organizations; and those that accepted women as members or consisted of women were dissolved. Therefore, there *were* basically no Social-Democratic women's organizations—by law they were *not allowed* to exist even if the usual way of interpreting this law at that time made it possible to declare some of the female workers' associations political organizations. The BDF could not admit such organizations without risking its own disbandment, especially since it was founded in Berlin. There were, however, some crypto-socialist female workers' organizations in existence at the time. Of course, the BDF was willing to admit them solely as female workers' organizations under the existing law. Responding to a somewhat provocative inquiry, Auguste Schmidt explained that the BDF would be happy to admit female workers' organizations but it could not admit Social-Democratic women's organizations, since that was against the law. This statement—which had perhaps not been formulated clearly enough—was the origin of the persistent legend that at its founding the BDF had excluded female workers' organizations. [. . .]

But this legend *persisted* deliberately, even though it finally amounted to little more than splitting hairs, since the socialist

---

1. Bund Deutscher Frauenvereine, BDF.—Eds.

2. *Vereinsgesetz*: Prussian anti-association laws of 1850, which prohibited participation in public meetings or political associations to persons who were minors, dependents, mentally defective, or female. Repealed in 1908.—Eds.

women had no *thought* of joining the BDF. The view of the Social-Democratic women—one that had been discussed a hundred times over—was that there was no need for a separate women's movement beyond the class struggle of the proletariat, in which women were fighting shoulder-to-shoulder with men. The liberation of the fourth estate included the emancipation of women. Therefore, the women's movement was by its very nature limited to the bourgeoisie, since it was only necessary there. For this reason, both at the time and later, the Social-Democratic women consistently refused to unite with the neutral women's movement, which had been branded "bourgeois." [. . .] But there were also factions within the BDF that repeatedly invoked this view [of us] in order to emphasize their own ideas. And so, I come to our "Leftists"—the "radicals." [. . .]

What did radicalism mean in the women's movement? On the one hand, it meant the carryings-on of a group of women who were younger, not in terms of years but in terms of their historical maturity. But it also meant a different way of looking at things.

Minna Cauer and Anita Augspurg were the leaders of this group. It became the Union of Progressive Women's Organizations [Verband fortschrittlicher Frauenvereine], which was founded in 1899 and had a rather noisy but not very creative existence until 1913.

The radical women felt superior to us since they considered themselves "politically more effective." Necessity, goal, and direction of the women's movement had been determined by the *inner* experiences of the older generation. On this basis, the movement was searching for new forms. Achieving public success mattered little unless these inner conditions were addressed. Organic growth from within was our first priority. The radicals, however, were propagandists for the women's movement, they wanted "political" success with political means, they wanted to have a broad impact, they measured the value of their demonstrations (literally!) by the weight of the newspaper clippings that dealt with them, and they were determined to make an impression in the political sense. Thus the change from an educational to a political movement came about.

Looking back, I understand a certain justification for such a change of tactics. Still, I remain convinced that this external agitation should *never* shape the character of the women's movement, that inner development should always remain its essence.

The "radicalism" of the "progressive" women was tied to such public activity. The older generation wanted that for which they seemed inwardly ready. The "progressives" wanted everything at once. They did not hesitate to rally the young around these goals—on the contrary, they *wanted* to arouse and to shock them. By and large, there were no great differences regarding the goals themselves. Louise Otto-Peters and Auguste Schmidt were true suffragettes. But they saw the way to their goal in a process of maturing and the surprise attacks of the [radical] women as well as the of the public went against their nature as responsible and serious educators.

There were also deep contrasts in temperament. This difference was all the more difficult to reconcile as the radicals criticized the older leadership ever more ruthlessly and objective differences later became more evident.

As I said before, these differences did *not* pertain in regard to the goals that were recognized by the public as "most radical": suffrage, equal rights for women in marriage and such. The differences lay in the rationale for these public demands. Abstract legal principles were much more strongly and at the same time individualistically foregrounded by the radicals. [Our] arguments for new and improved conditions for women which were derived from the fact of psychological gender *differences*—from the peculiar essence of woman— were surpassed by their stronger emphasis on *equality*. At the same time, they were less committed to historical development—for these women it was only important to fight for something, not to develop towards something. They operated much more with accusation and indignation, with strong words and gestures. For them, the *political* side of the movement with its political goals was foremost. With the greatest disdain, they condemned the more peaceful and milder approach of the earlier period—perhaps on the face of it a less effective approach—as being out-of-date, timid, and hesitant.

As I mentioned before, it is, by the way, false to relate in any sense the expression "younger generation"—which they attributed to themselves—to the age of its proponents. With regard to their members and their leadership, the radicals were certainly not younger.

Translated by Patricia A. Herminghouse
and Magda Mueller

Our Goals (Excerpt from *Die Frau)* *(1893)*

The time of *closed ranks* of opposition from German men against the women's movement is over. [. . .] For there is a growing recognition that the fate of the people shares a reciprocal fate with that of women; that the woman question is also a man question; that as the worth of women diminishes, as the ennobling influence of women declines, so goes the fate of all people. There is a growing recognition that a renewal and ennobling of family life, which our time so urgently needs, is indivisibly linked to a deepening of women's perspective on the world, a broadening of intellectual horizons for mothers: that inner independence and the acute feeling of a greater responsibility alone can be enough to get them through the difficult tasks that our time assigns them.

One thing remains unassailable even in the new age: the thought that the *ultimate* profession for women is that of *mother,* inasmuch as this profession comprises raising the upcoming generation. Only foolish or antagonistic opinions accuse the women's movement of wanting to alienate women from this highest occupation. But to address this particular criticism, and in reference to Goethe's claim that the most superior woman is she who if necessity demands it can also take the place of the *father* for her children, there should be a different, more thorough education for women, better intellectual training, a stricter inculcation of the idea of fulfilling one's duty in a profession, or in service to the community—until opportunity finds her, which she now all too often unworthily seeks. [. . .] And for this reason, we will hold one of our first and most important tasks to be to advocate in this journal for a change in the education of girls in the manner indicated.

If a thorough internal and external education is on the one hand necessary for future wives and mothers, it is on the other hand indispensable for the millions of women who stand alone in life and take up a profession for their own satisfaction, or their own livelihood. To assist them, to show them the way by means of practical advice, and in time to publish offers of employment, will be another important focus for us. Even if we would above all like to see the occupations of woman doctor and the educated woman teacher made accessible to German women, since these professions are linked to a far-reaching influence on the development of young people and the healthy constitution of women's lives, our concern and care will encompass all other lines of employment already open to women and at the same time will be devoted to opening new opportunities. As much as is possible, we will be devoted to directing those in need, and simultaneously encouraging independence of both thought and deed. [. . .]

We hope to make progress among German men with the idea that the focus in the women's movement is that of working toward progress in the development of all of humanity, and this in the way it has always been understood—where noble powers that have been contained are allowed to unfold. We hope to awaken the tepid and indolent among women to the knowledge that women who have acquired greater leisure through present-day circumstances have other things with which to fill their days than the latest trifles. We hope to induce them to gather up their energies, to become more mature, to develop from representing a type to becoming individuals, in order then, according to their strengths, to become active in their community. However one may judge our circumstances today, however much one may claim to run up against signs of social deterioration, for us women this is an important time. It is a time of growth and becoming for which we call out with Hutten,[1] "It is a pleasure to live, for the spirits have awakened." Let those awaken who yet slumber, let those try it who hold themselves aloof from a movement they misunderstand. We are not concerned with a dependent imitation of men, but with the full unfolding of the unique qualities of women through the free development of all of their abilities, in order to make them completely useful for the service of humanity. Only in *this* way will we have victory.

Translated by Lisa Roetzel

Käthe Schirmacher

The Modern Woman's Rights Movement in Germany *(1912)*

In no European country has the woman's rights movement been confronted with more unfavorable conditions; nowhere has it been more persistently opposed. In recent times the women of no other country have lived through conditions of war such as the German women underwent during the Thirty Years' War [1618–48] and from 1807

---

1. Ulrich von Hutten (1488–1523), humanist and supporter of Luther, popularly viewed as a warrior for freedom.—Eds.

to 1812. Such violence leaves a deep imprint on the character of a nation.

Moreover, it has been the fate of no other civilized nation to owe its political existence to a war trimphantly fought out in less than one generation. Every war, every accentuation and promotion of militarism is a weakening of the forces of civilization and of woman's influence. "German masculinity is still so young," I once heard somebody say.

A reinforcement of the woman's rights movement by a large Liberal majority in the national assemblies, such as we find in England, France, and Italy, is not to be thought of in Germany. The theories of the rights of man and of citizens were never applied by German Liberalism to woman in a broad sense, and the Socialist party is not yet in the majority. The political training of the German man has in many respects not yet been extended to include the principles of the American Declaration of Independence or the French Declaration of the Rights of Man; his respect for individual liberty has not yet been developed as in England; therefore he is much harder to win over to the cause of "woman's rights."

Hence the struggle against the official regulation of prostitution has been left chiefly to the German women; whereas in England and in France the physicians, lawyers, and members of Parliament have been the chief supporters of abolition. I am reminded also of the inexpressibly long and difficult struggle that we women had to carry on in order to secure the admission of women to the universities; the establishment of high schools for girls; and the improvement of the opportunities given to women teachers. In no other country were women teachers for girls wronged to such an extent as in Germany. The results of the last industrial census (1907) give to the demands of the woman's rights movement an invaluable support: *Germany has nine and a half million married women*, i.e., only one half of all adult women (over 18 years of age) are married. In Germany, too, marriage is not a lifelong "means of support" for woman, or a "means of support" for the whole number of women. Therefore the demands of woman for a complete professional and industrial training and freedom to choose her calling appear in the history of our time with a tremendous weight, a weight that the founders of the movement hardly anticipated.

[. . .]

About fifty women doctors are practicing in Germany; as yet there are no women preachers, but there are five women lawyers, one of whom in 1908 pleaded the case of an indicted youth before the Altona juvenile court. Although there are only a few women lawyers in Germany, women are now permitted to act as counsel for the defendant, there being sixty such women counselors in Bavaria. Recently (1908) even Bavaria has refused women admission to the civil service.

In the autumn there was appointed the first woman lecturer in a higher institution of learning,—this taking place in the Mannheim School of Commerce. Within the last five years many new callings have been opened to women: they are librarians (of municipal, club, and private libraries) and have organized themselves into the Association of Women Librarians; they are assistants in laboratories, clinics, and hospitals; they make scientific drawings, and some have specialized in microscopic drawing; during the season for the manufacture of beet sugar, women are employed as chemists in the sugar factories; there is a woman architect in Berlin, and a woman engineer in Hamburg. Women factory inspectors have performed satisfactory service in all the states of the Empire. But the future field of work for the German women is social work. State, municipal, and private aid is demanded by the prevailing destitution. At the present time women work in the sociological field without pay. In the future much of this work must be performed by *professional* social women workers. In about one hundred cities women are guardians of the poor. There are one hundred three women superintendents of orphan asylums; women are sought by the authorities as guardians. Women's cooperation as members of school committees and deputations promotes the organized woman's rights movement. The first woman inspector of dwellings has been appointed in Hessen. Nurses are demanding that state examinations be made requisite for those wishing to become nurses; some cities of Germany have appointed women as nurses for infant children. In Hessen and Ostmark [the eastern part of Prussia], women are district administrators. There is an especially great demand for women to care for dependent children and to work in the juvenile courts; this will lead to the appointment of paid probation officers. In southern Germany, women police matrons are employed; in Prussia there are women doctors employed in the police courts. There are also women school physicians. Since 1908, trained women have entered the midwives' profession.

When the Allgemeiner deutscher Frauenverein [German general women's association] was formed in 1865, there was no German Empire; Berlin had not yet become the capital of the Empire. But since Berlin has become the seat of the Imperial Parliament, Berlin very naturally has become the center of the woman's rights movement. This occurred through the establishment of the magazine *Frau-*

enwohl in 1888, by Mrs. [Minna] Cauer. In this manner, the younger
and more radical woman's rights movement was begun. The women
who organized the movement had interested themselves in the educational field. The radicals now entered the fields of social work and
politics. Women making radical demands allied themselves with
Mrs. Cauer; they befriended her, and cooperated with her. This is
an undisputed fact, though some of these women later left Mrs.
Cauer and allied themselves with either the "Conservatives" or the
"Socialists."

[. . .]

In 1894, the radical section of the Bund Deutscher Frauenvereine
[German federation of women's clubs] proposed that women's trade
unions be admitted to the Federation. This radical section had often
given offense to the "Conservatives"—in the Federation, for instance—by the proposal of this measure; but the radicals in this way
have stimulated the movement. As early as 1904, the Berlin Congress
of the International Council of Women had shown that the Federation, being composed chiefly of conservative elements, should adopt
in its program all the demands of the radicals, including woman's
suffrage. The differences between the radicals and the conservatives
are differences of personality rather than of principles. The radicals
move to the tempo of *allegro;* the conservatives to the tempo of *an-
dante.* In all public movements there is usually the same antagonism;
it occurred also in the English and the American woman's rights
movements.

In no other country (with the exception of Belgium and Hungary)
is the schism between the woman's rights movement of the middle
class and the woman's rights movement of the Socialists so marked
as in Germany. At the International Woman's Congress of 1896
(which was held through the influence of Mrs. Lina Morgenstern and
Mrs. Cauer) two Social Democrats, Lily Braun and Clara Zetkin,
declared that they never would cooperate with the middle-class
women. This attitude of the Social Democrats is the result of historical circumstances. The law against the German Socialists has increased their antagonism to the middle class. Nevertheless, this harsh
statement by Lily Braun and Clara Zetkin was unnecessary. It has
just been stated that the founders of the German woman's rights
movement had included the demands of the working women in their
program, and that the radicals (by whom the congress of 1896 had
been called, and who for years had been engaged in politics and in
the organization of trade unions) had in 1894 demanded the admission of women's labor organizations to the Federation of Women's

Clubs. Hence an alignment of the two movements would have been exceedingly fortunate. However, some of the Socialists, laying stress on ultimate aims, regard "class hatred" as their chief means of agitation, and are therefore on principle opposed to any peaceful cooperation with the middle class. Some of the women Socialist leaders are devoting themselves to the organization of working women—a task that is as difficult in Germany as elsewhere. Almost everywhere in Germany women laborers are paid less than men laborers. The average daily wage is two marks (fifty cents), but there are many working women who receive less. In the ready-made clothing industry there are weekly wages of six to nine marks ($1.50 to $2.25). At the last congress of home workers, held at Berlin, further evidence of starvation in the home industries was adduced. But for these wages the German woman's rights movement is not to be held responsible.

[. . .]

Peculiar to Germany is the denominational schism in the woman's rights movement. The precedent for this was established by the German Protestant Woman's League, founded in 1899, with Paula Müller, of Hanover, as president. The organization of the League was due to the feeling that "it is a sin to witness with indifference how women who wish to know nothing of Biblical Christianity represent all German women." The organization opposes equality of rights between man and woman; but in 1908 it joined the Federation of Women's Clubs. In 1903 a Catholic Woman's League was formed, but it has not joined the Federation. There has also been formed a Society of Jewish Women. We representatives of the interdenominational woman's rights movement deplore this denominational disunion. These organizations are important because they make accessible groups of people that otherwise could not be reached by us.

Another characteristic of the German woman's rights movement is its extensive and thorough organization. The smallest cities are today visited by women speakers. Our "unity of spirit"—praised so frequently, and now and then ridiculed,—is our chief power in the midst of the especially difficult conditions in which we must work. With tenacity and patience we have slowly overcome unusual difficulties—thus far without any help worth mentioning from the men.

[. . .]

The most significant recent event is the admission of women to political organizations and meetings by the Imperial Law of May 15, 1908.[2] Thereby the German women were admitted to political life.

---

2. This measure repealed the Prussian *Vereinsgesetz* (Anti-Association Laws) of 1850, which prohibited women's membership in "political" organizations.—Eds.

The Woman's Suffrage Society—founded in 1902, and in 1904 converted into a League—was able previous to 1908 to expand only in the South German states (excluding Bavaria). By this Imperial Law the northern states of the Empire were opened, and a National Woman's Suffrage Society was formed in Prussia, in Bavaria, and in Mecklenburg. As early as 1906, after the dissolution of the Reichstag, the women took an active part in the campaign, a right granted them by the *Vereinsrecht* (Law of Association). In Prussia, Saxony, and Oldenburg women worked for universal suffrage for women in Landtag [regional] elections. Since 1908 the political woman's rights movement has been of first importance in Germany. As the women taxpayers in a number of states can exercise municipal suffrage by proxy, and the women owners of large estates in Saxony and Prussia can exercise the suffrage in elections for the District Diet (*Kreistag*) by proxy, an effort is being made to attract these women to the cause of woman's suffrage.

Translated by Carl Conrad Eckhardt

Adelheid Popp

The New Woman *(1893)*

The change in social systems that is being sought by Social Democracy cannot be accomplished unless people also change themselves. One cannot build a socialist society with downtrodden, undernourished, fearful people who are doomed to subservience from childhood to old age. If indeed this transformation requires that people be different, then this is especially true for women. The female sex cannot remain enslaved, without rights, and held to be inferior if socialism is to triumph, for all people who believe in socialism expect it to release all fetters under which they are currently suffering. Who then should not hope more than those who are the most tightly chained, who are suffering the most? And who would not argue that these are women? Even under the most splendid exterior, a creature is often hidden who does not dare express her own will, and often does not even recognize that this is possible. As workers, women are more subservient than men; they are quick to compromise, make fewer demands, are easier to satisfy, and cannot imagine that it could be otherwise. In the family, the woman is also the more acquiescent; she is more likely to sacrifice her own well being, her own personality, even when nothing forces her to do so. As mothers, women are willing to sacrifice themselves to the final degree. Mothers are prepared to sacrifice their own happiness, their entire futures, not only for the actual happiness of their children, but also for an imagined one. Such is the nature of woman: willingness to sacrifice and subservience.

It is to be expected that the event that has now shaken the world for more than a year, the most terrible war that humanity has ever experienced, has not left women untouched. Wives and mothers in all social classes, who have until now been influenced by men's direction and will, have lost their support. They are suddenly standing alone in the world, laden with worry about their own and their children's existence. Women who have never left the domestic hearth are suddenly being forced out into the world where workers are needed.

Everything that makes life hard and burdensome becomes woman's lot. Tens of thousands, who only a few months ago were accustomed to going through life under the protection of men, now have to tread this path alone. Ten thousand other young female creatures, whose educational path had up until now led in the direction of marriage, are being thrown off this track, since as a result of the terrible deaths of men, marriage will now be unattainable for many. That which until this time appeared to be a desirable goal for the majority of the female sex—arriving safely in the harbor of marriage—will be barred to many for the foreseeable future.

It has therefore come to pass that the methods of educating women must change, because circumstances require it. Even though it can never be good to view marriage alone as giving content to life, changed circumstances now require a different approach, a different way of thinking for the female sex. People must be encouraged to recognize that women too should earn recognition and be valued for their own personalities, their knowledge and abilities. What until now has only been granted to a few exceptions must become common to all women.

The striving of women for economic independence should no longer be seen as feminist ravings, but as determined by necessity and the demands of the age. All people will have to learn to recognize things as they are, including what pertains to women. The economic independence of women will, however, give greater assuredness to her entire personality and will make changes unavoidable in many other areas.

It will not be possible to apply different legal standards to women who have arrived at a more meaningful place in society than those that are applied to male citizens. The law will have to open its doors to women even more rapidly, once women themselves recognize that the duties required of them allow them to demand these rights.

If war is to be the reason that women come closer to their goals, we nevertheless do not want to sing the praises of war; instead we want to keep present the knowledge of its horrors and its countless victims as a holy, never to be extinguished flame, in order that women who achieve greater social and political rights learn to see it as their most hallowed duty to use them to bring together all of humankind as brothers.

The new woman who will come, and must come, should be free of the pettiness and narrow-mindedness of the past. She should also be without prejudice toward her fellow women. She should not consider herself too lowly to seek influence in all places, and should seek such influence with all of her strength. The poet's words, "a person grows when greater things are demanded," will also become true for women. They should not only appear to the world as defenders of the rights of their own sex, but as fighters for a new human ideal that is revealed to us by socialism. May the new woman have the will and the strength to recognize these duties as her own; may she not lack for courage and energy also to fulfill them.

Translated by Lisa Roetzel

Rosa Luxemburg

Women's Suffrage
and Class Struggle *(1912)*

"Why are there no organizations for working women in Germany? Why do we hear so little about the working women's movement?" With these questions, Emma Ihrer, one of the founders of the proletarian women's movement of Germany, introduced her 1898 essay,

"Working Women in the Class Struggle." Hardly fourteen years have passed since, but they have seen a great expansion of the proletarian women's movement. More than a hundred fifty thousand women are organized in unions and are among the most active troops in the economic struggle of the proletariat. Many thousands of politically organized women have rallied to the banner of Social Democracy: the Social Democratic women's paper [*Die Gleichheit,* edited by Clara Zetkin] has more than one hundred thousand subscribers; women's suffrage is one of the vital issues on the platform of Social Democracy.

Exactly these facts might lead you to underrate the importance of the fight for women's suffrage. You might think: even without equal political rights for women we have made enormous progress in educating and organizing women. Hence, women's suffrage is not urgently necessary. But whoever thinks like this is deceived. The political awakening and unionization of the masses of the female proletariat during the last fifteen years has been magnificent. But it has been possible only because working women took a lively interest in the political and parliamentary struggles of their class in spite of being deprived of their rights. So far, proletarian women are sustained by male suffrage, which they indeed take part in, although only indirectly. Large masses of both men and women of the working class already consider the election campaigns a cause they share in common. At all Social Democratic election rallies, women make up a large segment, sometimes the majority of the public. They are always interested and passionately involved. In all districts where there is a firm Social Democratic organization, women help with the campaign. And it is women who have done invaluable work distributing leaflets and getting subscribers to the Social Democratic press, this most important weapon in the campaign.

The capitalist state has not been able to keep women from taking on all these duties and efforts of political life. Step by step, the state has indeed been forced to grant and guarantee them this possibility by allowing them union and assembly rights. Only the last political right is denied women: the right to vote, to decide directly on the people's representatives in legislature and administration, to be an elected member of these bodies. But here, as in all other areas of society, the motto is: "Don't let things get started!" But things have been started. The present state gave in to the women of the proletariat when it admitted them to public assemblies, to political associations. And the state did not grant this voluntarily, but out of bitter necessity, under the irresistible pressure of the rising working class. It was not least the passionate pushing ahead of the proletarian women themselves which forced the Prussian-German police state to give up the famous "women's section"[1] in gatherings of political associations and to open wide the doors of political organizations to women. This really set the ball rolling. The irresistible progress of the proletarian class struggle has swept working women right into the whirlpool of political life. Using their right of union and assembly, proletarian women have taken a most active part in parliamentary life and in election campaigns. It is only the inevitable consequence, only the logical result of the movement that today millions of proletarian women call defiantly and with self-confidence: *Let us have suffrage!*

Once upon a time, in the beautiful era of pre-1848 absolutism, the whole working class was said not to be "mature enough" to exercise political rights. This cannot be said about proletarian women today, because they have demonstrated their political maturity. Everybody knows that without them, without the enthusiastic help of proletarian women, the Social Democratic Party would not have won the glorious victory of January 12, [1912], would not have obtained four and a quarter million votes. At any rate, the working class has always had to prove its maturity for political freedom by a successful revolutionary uprising of the masses. Only when Divine Right on the throne and the best and noblest men of the nation actually felt the calloused fist of the proletariat on their eyes and its knee on their chests, only then did they feel confidence in the political "maturity" of the people, and felt it with the speed of lightning. Today, it is the proletarian women's turn to make the capitalist state conscious of her maturity. This is done through a constant, powerful mass movement which has to use all the means of proletarian struggle and pressure.

Women's suffrage is the goal. But the mass movement to bring it about is not a job for women alone, but is a common class concern for women and men of the proletariat. Germany's present lack of rights for women is only one link in the chain of the reaction that shackles the people's lives. And it is closely connected with the other pillar of the reaction: the monarchy. In advanced capitalist, highly industrialized, twentieth-century Germany, in the age of electricity and airplanes, the absence of women's political rights is as much a reactionary remnant of the dead past as the reign by Divine Right on

---

1. The "women's section" had been instituted in 1902 by the Prussian Minister von Hammerstein. According to this disposition, a special section of the room was reserved for women at political meetings.—Trans.

the throne. Both phenomena—the instrument of heaven as the leading political power, and woman, demure by the fireside, unconcerned with the storms of public life, with politics and class struggle—both phenomena have their roots in the rotten circumstances of the past, in the times of serfdom in the country and guilds in the towns. In those times, they were justifiable and necessary. But both monarchy and women's lack of rights have been uprooted by the development of modern capitalism, have become ridiculous caricatures. They continue to exist in our modern society, not just because people forgot to abolish them, not just because of the persistence and inertia of circumstances. No, they still exist because both—the monarchy as well as women's lack of rights—have become powerful tools of interests inimical to the people. The worst and most brutal advocates of the exploitation and enslavement of the proletariat are entrenched behind throne and altar as well as behind the political enslavement of women. Monarchy and women's lack of rights have become the most important tools of the ruling capitalist class.

In truth, our state is interested in keeping the vote from working women and from them alone. It rightly fears they will threaten the traditional institutions of class rule, for instance militarism (of which no thinking proletarian woman can help being a deadly enemy), monarchy, the systematic robbery through duties and taxes on groceries, etc. Women's suffrage is a horror and abomination for the present capitalist state because behind it stand millions of women who would strengthen the enemy within, i.e., revolutionary Social Democracy. If it were a matter of bourgeois ladies voting, the capitalist state could expect nothing but effective support for the reaction. Most of those bourgeois women who act like lionesses in the struggle against "male prerogatives" would trot like docile lambs into the camp of conservative and clerical reaction if they had suffrage. Indeed, they would certainly be a good deal more reactionary than the male part of their class. Aside from the few who have jobs or professions, the women of the bourgeoisie do not take part in social production. They are nothing but co-consumers of the surplus value their men extort from the proletariat. They are parasites of the parasites of the social body. And co-consumers are usually even more rabid and cruel in defending their "right" to a parasite's life than the direct agents of class rule and exploitation. The history of all great revolutionary struggles confirms this in a horrible way. Take the great French Revolution. After the fall of the Jacobins, when Robespierre was driven in chains to the place of execution, the naked whores of the victory-drunk bourgeoisie danced in the streets, danced a shameless dance of joy around the fallen hero of the Revolution. And in 1871, in Paris, when the heroic workers' Commune was defeated by machine guns, the raving bourgeois females surpassed even their bestial men in their bloody revenge against the suppressed proletariat. The women of the property-owning classes will always fanatically defend the exploitation and enslavement of the working people from which they indirectly receive the means for their socially useless existence.

Economically and socially, the women of the exploiting classes are not an independent segment of the population. Their only social function is to be tools of the natural propagation of the ruling classes. By contrast, the women of the proletariat are economically independent. They are productive for society like the men. By this I do not mean their bringing up children or their housework, which helps men support their families on scanty wages. This kind of work is not productive in the sense of the present capitalist economy, no matter how enormous an achievement the sacrifices and energy spent, the thousand little efforts add up to. This is but the private affair of the worker, his happiness and blessing, and for this reason nonexistent for our present society. As long as capitalism and the wage system rule, only that kind of work is considered productive which produces surplus value, which creates capitalist profit. From this point of view, the music-hall dancer whose legs sweep profit into her employer's pocket is a productive worker, whereas all the toil of the proletarian women and mothers in the four walls of their homes is considered unproductive. This sounds brutal and insane, but corresponds exactly to the brutality and insanity of our present capitalist economy. And seeing this brutal reality clearly and sharply is the proletarian woman's first task.

[. . .]

Considering all this, the proletarian woman's lack of political rights is a vile injustice, and the more so for being by now at least half a lie. After all, masses of women take an active part in political life. However, Social Democracy does not use the argument of "injustice." This is the basic difference between us and the earlier sentimental, utopian socialism. We do not depend on the justice of the ruling classes, but solely on the revolutionary power of the working masses and on the course of social development which prepares the ground for this power. Thus, injustice by itself is certainly not an argument with which to overthrow reactionary institutions. If, however, there is a feeling of injustice in large segments of society—says Friedrich Engels, the co-founder of scientific socialism—it is always a sure sign that the economic bases of the society have shifted considerably, that the present conditions contradict the march of development. The present forceful movement of millions of proletariat women who consider their lack of political rights a crying wrong is such an infallible sign, a sign that the social bases of the reigning system are rotten and that its days are numbered.

Translated by Rosmarie Waldrop

Clara Zetkin

Women of the Working People *(1915)*

Where are your husbands?

Where are your sons?

For eight months now, they have been at the front. They have been torn from their work and their homes. Adolescents, the support and hope of their parents, men at the prime of their lives, men with greying hair, the supporters of their families: All of them are wearing military uniforms, are vegetating in trenches and are ordered to destroy what diligent labor created.

Millions are already resting in mass graves, hundreds upon hundreds of thousands lie in military hospitals with torn-up bodies, smashed limbs, blinded eyes, destroyed brains—ravished by epidemics or cast down by exhaustion.

Burned villages and towns, wrecked bridges, devastated forests and ruined fields are the traces of their deeds.

Proletarian Women! One has told you that your husbands and sons left for the war in order to protect their weak women and children and to guard home and hearth.

But what is the reality?

The shoulders of the weak women now have to bear a double burden. Bereft of protection, you are exposed to grief and hardships. Your children are hungry and cold. One threatens to take away the roof over your head. Your hearth is cold and empty.

One has talked to you about a grand brother and sisterhood between the high and the low, of a cessation of strife between poor and rich. Well, the cessation of strife meant that the entrepreneur lowered your wages, the tradesman and unscrupulous speculator raised prices and the landlord threatens to evict you. The state claims impoverishment and the bourgeois welfare authorities cook a meager soup for you and urge you to be thrifty.

What is the purpose of this war which has caused you such terrible suffering?

One tells you, the well-being and the defense of the fatherland. Of what does the well-being of the fatherland consist?

Should it not mean the well-being of its millions, those millions who are being changed to corpses, cripples, unemployed beggars and orphans by this war?

Who endangers the well-being of the fatherland? Is it the men who, clad in other uniforms, stand beyond the frontier, men who did not want this war any more than your men did and who do not know why they should have to murder their brothers? No! The fatherland is endangered by all those who reap profit from the hardships of the broad masses and who want to build their domination upon suppression.

Who profits from this war?

Only a tiny minority in each nation.

The manufacturers of rifles and cannons, of armor plate and torpedo boats, the shipyard owners and the suppliers of the armed forces' needs. In the interest of their profits they have fanned hatred among people, thus contributing to the outbreak of the war. This war is beneficial for the capitalists in general. Did not the labor of the dispossessed and the exploited masses create piles of goods that those who created them are not allowed to use? They are too poor to pay for them! Labor's sweat has created these goods and labor's blood is supposed to fight for new foreign markets to dispose of them. Colonies are supposed to be conquered where the capitalists want to rob the natural resources and exploit the cheapest labor force.

Not the defense of the fatherland but its expansion is the purpose of this war. The capitalist system wants it that way, and without the exploitation and suppression of man by man, the system cannot exist.

The workers have nothing to gain from this war but they stand to lose everything that is dear to them.

Wives of Workers, Women Workers! The men of the belligerent countries have been silenced. The war has dimmed their conscience, paralyzed their will and disfigured their entire being.

But you women who besides your gnawing concern for your dear ones at the front have to bear deprivations and misery, what are you waiting for in expressing your desire for peace and your protest against this war?

What is holding you back?

Until now you have been patient for your loved ones. Now you must act for your husbands and sons.

Enough of murdering!

This call resounds in many tongues, millions of women raise it. It finds its echo in the trenches where the consciences of the sons of the nation are stirred up against this murder.

Working Women of the People! In these difficult days, Socialist women from Germany, England, France and Russia have gathered. Your hardships and sufferings have moved their hearts. For your own sake and the sake of your loved ones, they are asking you to work for peace. Just like their minds met across the battlefields, so you must get together from all countries in order to raise the cry: Peace! Peace!

The world war has demanded the greatest sacrifices from you. The sons that you bore in suffering and pain, the men who were your companions during difficult struggles, have been torn away from you. In comparison with these sacrifices, all other sacrifices must seem small and insignificant.

All humankind is looking upon you women proletarians of the belligerent countries. You are destined to be the heroines and redeemers!

Unify as one will and one deed!

What your husbands and sons cannot yet aver, announce with a million voices:

The laboring people of all countries are a people of brothers. Only the united will of this people can stop the killing.

Socialism alone will assure the future peace of humankind.

Down with capitalism which sacrifices hecatombs of people to the wealth and the power of the possessing class!

Down with War! Break through to Socialism!

Translated by Kai Schoenhals

Bertha von Suttner

Speech in San Francisco *(1912)*

. . . The strides you have made for peace and suffrage since I was over here eight years ago, in 1904, are unmeasurable. You are organizing the whole country and federating all the branch societies and your executive head is the chief apostle of the movement.

If I tell this to the European audience they not only disbelieve it, but laugh with derision. When people speak to me of the future. I tell them "Go to America and look at the future, for there it has already arrived. They are fifty years in advance of us ethically."
[. . .]
On my way to America through Europe, I was shocked to meet, everywhere, the cry of *war,* and great military maneuvering going on in every station and capital.

In Paris, the populace was celebrating a religious holiday with shouts of "Vive l'armée," "Down with the Prussian," and the papers were blazing with passionate editorials. English journalism too was recommending conscription and fanning afresh patriotic flames. Alarm is general everywhere and no one can give a rational cause.

In America, the reverse is the truth, you are busy with welfare missions, child-saving, the religious movement is reinstilling some of the puritanic ideal—a renaissance of the spirit as it were. Your religious denominations are redoubling their energies to counteract the present-day tendencies toward a lowering of standards. Your reformers and settlement workers are fighting slum evils and labor unrighteousness. In my city they are putting guns into the public schools and making the curriculum less and less liberal, more and more militant.

I am over in America to catch a new breath, to take a hold higher up, to see if I cannot enlist your rank and file to help us.

Hail to the Future! America is the Future embodied so far as my generation shall see it realized! The American people can well afford to glorify their founders and their leaders for what they have wrought for them. Our founders died in the battles for pillage, and our leaders, to our sorrow, are busy planning still other campaigns, while the people hopelessly ask "Who is our enemy; we know no cause for war!"

I have been asked to cross the water by the American women. They wrote me what can we do to help? I have taken them seriously. I have a definite plan to put before them. I must have their cooperation or yield reluctantly to the uphill struggle which antiwar ideal is bound to have in a military power. There is but one help and that is an unmuzzled press—a press in the hands of trained independent peace workers who can tell the truth to the enslaved masses, which today are not permitted by the ruling institutions to think but only to shoot, and to shoot each other to uphold their master's prestige.

Our State Church is not the avenue for free discussion. The press is the tool of the War Department. The school gives our boys rifles along with their books.

While the women in California are glorying in their suffrage[1] our men in Hungary are rioting for theirs. We need the enlightment of truth to know our rights before we can attain them, and we can only get that through an honest press. We have already a large body ready to blaze the response to such a voice.

The Peace Movement takes on three distinct aspects.

We consider it as a Religion, as a Science, and as Warfare.

As a Religion it deals with our duties toward God and Man, and appeals through our noblest feelings of Love and Mercy to all that is divine in our souls.

As a Science it bases its arguments on History, on Statistics, on Political Economy, on the natural laws of Harmony and Progress.

As Warfare it rouses in our hearts the energy for contest, the resolution for victory, the passion of contempt for the lies and the follies and the cruelties of the other side.

As a Religion we preach it; as a Science we teach it; as Warfare we fight for it.

Translator unknown

---

1. Individual states, especially in the American West, granted women suffrage before the Nineteenth Amendment to the Constitution was ratified in 1920.—Eds.

Lida Gustava Heymann

Female Pacifism *(1917/1922)*

The Past

In order to evaluate objectively the work for pacifism contributed by
women in the past, we have to understand that the modern civilized
states are male states. States of men in which everything—family,
schools, prisons, the legal system, politics, etc.—is based on and
geared toward the male principle, i.e., the principle of force, authority, the struggle of all against all, and fear of each other.

This male principle, which has completely dominated the life of
individuals and peoples for centuries, has in the end led again and
again to catastrophic eruptions of power and to rebellions: wars,
civil wars, revolutions. The World War has proven that the male
state, built and ruled by force, has failed utterly; the proof of its
uselessness has probably never been demonstrated more plainly. The
male principle is corrosive and will, if perpetuated, bring about the
complete annihilation of humankind.

This male, destructive principle is diametrically opposed by the
female, constructive principle of mutual aid, kindness, understanding, and cooperation. In the modern male states, women were not
only deprived of any chance to bring their very own nature into play,
but also had to submit to the male principle and forcibly acknowledge it: they were violated. Many women, just in order to be able to
live, to endure, adopted the male principle.

The mass of women became slaves of men not only externally, but
what was far worse, internally. For as long as the world has existed,
such enslavement—i.e., enslavement of one's very nature—as that of
the woman by the man has never before taken place. It was done by
the most cunning means and carried out for centuries systematically
and with never-failing consistency.

The few women who, despite all this, retained their natural characteristics, who did not submit to the idea of the male state, were
engaged in constant struggle to gain for their sex at least formal
equality with men. This struggle was based on the assumption that
removal of the external chains of slavery meant the first step toward
inner liberation of women, a return to their own selves.

Men are most to blame that in the past the nature and character of women did not come into play and was lost for pacifism. For female nature and instinct are identical with pacifism.

If, despite everything, individual women—I will only name Bertha von Suttner here—managed to perform constructive work for pacifism, even to blaze a trail for organizing pacifism, that only proves that female nature cannot be exterminated, in spite of its most extreme violation by men. One should never forget that the complexity of modern male states excludes the possibility that great catastrophic eruptions like wars can be prevented by a few people—in this case women—who are not in positions of authority, and that it borders on irresponsible ignorance of the facts to accuse women of having been able to prevent the World War and not having done so.

The Future

What was done by women during the World War inspires the fondest hopes for the future of pacifism.

What was done?

It is a singular occurrence in the history of modern wars, that, while their husbands were tearing each other apart on the battle fields, women of many countries came together without any hostility and bitterness and demanded an end to the war, as happened in The Hague in May 1915. From there, delegations of women were sent to the governments of all nations participating in the war in the attempt to persuade them of the compelling necessity of ending the war. That they did not succeed in no way diminishes their action. Moreover, it is well established that the theses for the realization of world peace which the International Women's League for Peace and Freedom set forth in The Hague formed the basis of the famous fourteen points of Wilson, which were acclaimed by the whole world. Since 1915, women have worked tirelessly for pacifism: together, they founded the International Women's League for Peace and Freedom. At present, women from thirty countries are in contact with each other.

So what differentiates this organization from the prewar international women's and men's associations? Surely, international organizations have effected more positive achievements in science, legislation, public life, social work, trade, industry, etc., but no international association has so far given more to the world in terms of the true spirit of international community and human solidarity, in terms of pacifism. This is the spirit—the female as opposed to the male principle—that governs everyone and that so far has overcome all conflicts in such a manner that not even the faintest trace of bitterness has remained. This small circle unites a world, elevated above any desire for power, above false nationalism, permeated by the truth that suffering, diseased humankind can only be helped in a nonviolent way, by mutual support and the attempt to understand. Here is the model for a genuine League of Nations.

In the International Women's League, it is not a question of theoretical pacifism, but of its practical application; pacifism is lived here.

Every human being, man or woman, who is truly a pacifist will not only condemn war in itself, but must also fight the currently all-destructive male principle, which wants to solve conflicts in the life of peoples and humans by force, and be willing to supplant it by the creative, constructive female principle of goodwill.

This female principle characterizes many, particularly eminent, men, but it is a basic instinct of women, although many have been weaned from it through the inner enslavement of their nature as result of their adoption of the male world view. Once liberated from this enslavement—and we are well on the way there in all countries—female character will be able to find fulfillment and be an inexhaustible source for the promotion of pacifism. No matter how frequently this source may be obstructed by external difficulties, it will always find its way again. Let us never forget, in judging the state of affairs, that fundamental changes in the life of peoples do not come about overnight, but in the course of time.

If pacifism is to prevail in the future, then it will only happen if the constructive female principle becomes the governing one in the intercourse of humans and in the coexistence of peoples.

Translated by Jörg Esleben

Gabriele Reuter

Love and the Right to Vote *(1914)*

As long as man, laboring under the delusion of his sexual love, perceives woman as his property, with which he has the right to do as he pleases, he will try to prevent any kind of development beyond those features that are to his advantage. As long as he loves woman as an object, to satisfy his aesthetic sensibilities, he will worry that in her struggle with life she will lose the sweet beauty and innocence that inspire his soul to such deeply poetic passion. As long as he sees her as an object whose sole purpose on earth is to relieve him, the man, of the barren agony of his intellect, he will want her to be a dull creature of nature. If, however, she is supposed to purify him of earthliness and vices, she has to be otherworldly, distant and holy. And if she is to give him the peace of domesticity, she has first of all to be a mother. As long as man loves woman with the kind of love that seeks an object for the strivings of his will, as long as he treats her as a child, educates her, leads her, and protects her, he will only hesitantly, due to social constraints and not his own convictions, grant her small freedoms; and he will always be prepared to take them away again as soon as they go beyond his own plans.

[. . .]

On the path that woman must take, even when so many obstacles are placed in her way, the right to vote is only one step. But it is a very important step. We women recognize that an active part in public life, which today only the right to vote can give us, is necessary to realize our full human potential. And only we ourselves can decide what is necessary for us. No one else can decide this for us. We want to learn—we want experience—we want to get to know ourselves, our nature, our strengths and possibilities. Perhaps they are tremendously broader and greater than we ourselves used to think they were. Perhaps they are more limited and constricted than we now hope they are. We will not know until we test ourselves. As long as we do not face situations that require courage, cold-bloodedness, power of judgment, and objectivity, we cannot possibly know if these qualities will be at our command in a given moment. Whether the participation of women in government, in politics, in parliament, in legislation will turn out to be a blessing for our people or not remains a controversial question.

[. . .]

We are not striving for a feminist era in place of a masculine one. The attainment of female suffrage is not at all about questions of power but about questions of mutual development. Working with woman will, after all, have to lead to changes in man's character and emotional life, as well as in ours. But those changes will not be of the same kind.

Translated by Gabriele Westphal and Thomas D. Colby

Alice Salomon

The German Woman and Her Tasks
in the New Republic *(1919)*

Women's Suffrage as Experience of the Idea of the State
Women who championed the demand for suffrage for a long time
had imagined the hour of its fulfillment, the mood it would trigger,
altogether differently. This is true not only in the external sense that
nobody could have imagined the deep misery and powerlessness of
the fatherland that we now experience and that only now turns us
women into citizens. It is not only true in the sense that this time of
humiliation from without and collapse from within makes us incapable of joy about new rights, which in the light of the moment can be
understood exclusively as duties and responsibilities.

It has always been clear to women that suffrage would not be a
goal, but a new point of departure in their endeavors. They knew
that it would only hand them the means to gain factual equality and
thus in this sense must lead to new duties.
[. . .]

The Social Idea as Pillar of the Republic
. . . The first political act of the German woman is participation in
the elections for the German National Assembly and the assemblies
of the individual federal states. Women have to express their opinions about vital questions regarding the nation, about the form of
the state, the constitution, unity of the Reich, and reconstruction on
a field of rubble. They had only a few weeks to adjust to this new
responsibility and to prepare for tasks that surely cannot be called
women's affairs.

As this is being written, it remains uncertain whether the mass of
women will become aware of the significance of the moment and of
the influence given to them. Only the result of the coming elections
will show whether they have been drawn into the current of political
life, whether the proportional participation of the entire population
in the vote has risen compared to the former turnout of eligible vot-
ers, and what share women have in this. As far as one can tell from

attending urban conventions, from the participation of women in the election work of all parties, and from the feverish enlightenment of women by women in town and country, this vast responsibility has stirred them and lifted them beyond their own horizons.

[. . .]

To what extent the special talents and strengths of women enable them to participate positively in shaping the [new] German republic can only be judged years from now. But we can already make some surmises and indicate guidelines that bring the task closer and make it visible for us.

[. . .]

There is one thing that women in particular contribute to the new state, and that is the sense for the whole of the popular organism, the social idea, which grows out of the maternal destiny of woman and gives her the special ability to feel and act beyond her own interests and those of her closest circle.

This idea must become the foundational pillar of the republic, without which the state can never gain form and strength, which must serve as the spine for all its regulations, laws, and organizations. There is no true democracy as long as the life of a people is split by class interests, and perturbed and torn by class movements and class struggle. The republic needs citizens who place the interests of the whole above their own interests. In its perfection, in its ideal form there would be no parties—but there would be occupational groups and guilds. These, however, would be aware of the mutuality of their interests and would know that in the long run one group cannot rise at the cost of the others, that no one rises or falls alone, and that all limbs of the body politic are connected inextricably with one another. (Menenius Agrippa!)

[. . .]

[The fact that women are less organized in interest groups] has its cause above all in the psychical characteristic of woman, which emanates from motherhood and from her destiny for this condition. Of course those whose natural, central, and highest task in life it is to take on and direct the care for and protection of tender and helpless life as well as the physical, intellectual, and psychical development of youth, go beyond representing their own interests. A mother who is unable to do this is an unnatural mother. A woman without any of this ability within herself, the ability to transcend one's own life and to embrace wider concerns, is not a true "woman."

Due to the nature of special female tasks, the woman is also less inclined to regard the economic factor as determining and ruling her relationship to others. Women will therefore be harder to win over for incorporation into interest groups.

Class Struggle and the Republic

... Without a doubt, proletarian women also have common interests with the women of other circles, and the endeavors of the women's movement to establish a link between them were quite justified and well founded. That socialist women did not acknowledge this up until the war, and that in their rejection they branded the women's movement as "bourgeois," can be explained by the situation of the working class up to this point, which allowed this class no full rights of participation in political life and no sufficient influence on the economic order. After all, the struggle for economist interests makes most sense for those who sorely feel their own misery and oppression on a daily basis. Furthermore, this struggle is also marked by a high degree of idealism, which is widely underestimated. During the first decades of the socialist movement, participation of individuals by no means meant improvement of their own situation. Rather, they knew that they could only sow a seed, so that the next generation might harvest.

However, even though the working class and thus proletarian women were able to disseminate their idealism in the class movement, the theory and practice of class struggle, through decades-long rejection of any shared interests with other movements, has caused serious harm to the attempt to shape the life of the German people and has had divisive and deleterious, even obstructive effects on the development into a republic.
[...]

The Women's Movement and the Social Idea

[The elements most capable of building community and least affected by class conflicts and economic struggles] are the women of the middle class. The development of the women's movement up to this point has clearly demonstrated what eminently social forces slumber in women, and how easily they can be awakened and made effective. The women's movement was also in danger of becoming an interest group like the workers' movement, because it also started from the demand of rights for an oppressed, held-back part of the population. But while fully retaining these demands, it nonetheless has become something altogether different. In the last decades, it has been much less a movement for rights than ˈ educational movement. All rights and freedoms had only hˈ ˈded as means to gain responsibilities, after all. All individualistic starting points were bridged by setting a larger social goal. This characteristic aspect of the movement found its classical expression in the program of the German General Women's Association [Allgemeiner deutscher Frauenverein], which states: The women's movement seeks to help woman's civilizing influence to develop freely and to reach its full social effectiveness.

Some of the social attitude of the women's movement may be credited to its leaders. Other aspects may be explained by the fact that some of the original demands—but only some—have been fulfilled. But the essential reason lies in the nature of women, which is expressed most strongly in the leaders. Likewise, the setting of a new goal after successes are achieved only proves that, once freed of fetters and impediments, women gain an ever deeper understanding of their own essence.

Translated by Jörg Esleben

Helke Sander (speaker)

Origins of the Contemporary Women's Movement *(1968)*

Speech of the "Action Council for the Liberation of Women" at the Twenty-third Conference of the Representatives of the Socialist German Students Association in Frankfurt, September, 1968

I speak on behalf of the Action Council for the Liberation of Women.[1] The Berlin SDS[2] gave me a seat here as a representative, although very few of us women are SDS members. We are speaking here because we know that we can only accomplish our work in connection with other progressive organizations and, in our opinion, only the SDS can be counted among the progressive ones at present.

---

1. The speaker was Helke Sander, at that time a student at the Berlin Academy of Film and Television, later a well-known feminist filmmaker.—Eds.

2. SDS: Sozialistischer Deutscher Studentenbund, the organization of Socialist German students, which initiated protest movements in the 1960s.—Eds.

Cooperation, however, presupposes that the SDS understands the specific issues that confront women. This implies that conflicts that have been suppressed in the SDS for years are finally being articulated. In so doing, we are extending the debate between the antiauthoritarian and the CP-faction[3] and simultaneously confronting both camps because we have both against us, in *practice* if not in theory. We will try to explain our position and we demand that the substantive content of these issues be discussed here. We will no longer be content with being occasionally permitted to also say a word, which is listened to by those who identify themselves as antiauthoritarian and then go back to the order of the day.

[. . .]

Because of the separation between her life in private and in society, the woman is drawn back into the individual conflict that she faces in her isolation. She is still being raised for private life, for the family, which in return depends on the very conditions of production that we are fighting against. This training for her role, this instilled inferiority complex, this contradiction between her own expectations and those of society generate a permanent bad conscience because she is not able to do justice to the demands of society or to choose between alternatives, which in any case entail giving up her own vital needs.

Women are searching for their identity. They cannot achieve it by participating in campaigns that do not directly touch upon their own concerns. That would be sham emancipation. Women can only achieve this identity when the social conflicts that have been displaced into private life are articulated, so that women can develop solidarity and become politically active. Most women are unpolitical because up until now, politics has always been defined unilaterally and their needs have not been considered. They therefore persisted in the authoritarian call for legislation because they did not see their demands as the contradiction that could blow up the entire system.

Women with children comprise the groups that can be most easily politicized. Among them, aggression is most strong and speechlessness most minimal. Women who are able to attend the university today do not have the bourgeois women's movement to thank as much as economic necessity. When these privileged women then have children, they are forced back into patterns of behavior that, thanks to their emancipation, they thought they had already overcome. Their studies are interrupted or delayed, their intellectual development comes to a halt or is severely diminished by the demands of

---

3. Communist Party.—Eds.

husband and child. In addition, there is the insecurity that derives from not having been able to choose between becoming a blue stocking or the lady of the house, between building a career at the price of foregoing happiness or finding her identity in consumer culture. In other words, these are privileged women who have learned that the bourgeois route to emancipation was a false one, who have recognized that they are unable to emancipate themselves by means of the competitive struggle, who recognized that the general performance principle has become the determining factor within relationships and that the route to emancipation is already inherent in the method with which one tries to achieve it.

At the very latest, when these women have children, they realize that all their privileges are of no help at all. At best, they are in a position to draw attention to all the garbage of social life, i.e., carrying the class struggle into their marriage and personal relationships. In this, the man assumes the objective role of exploiter or class enemy, which, of course, at a subjective level, he does not want to play, since this role is in turn forced upon him by a performance-oriented society that imposes certain role-specific behaviors.

From all this, the Action Council for the Liberation of Women drew the following conclusions:

We are unable to solve the societal oppression of women individually. We cannot postpone this until after the revolution, because a revolution that is merely economic and political will not eliminate the repression of private life, as has been proven in all socialist countries.

We seek conditions of life that eliminate the competitive relation between man and woman. The creation of a democratic society can only be achieved through the transformation of the relations of production and thus of the relations of power.

The potential for solidarity and politicization is greatest among women with children. Since they are the ones who feel the greatest pressure, we have thus far concentrated our political work on their issues. That does not mean that we do not regard the problems of childless women students as unimportant, nor that, despite the common features of oppression in all women, we have overlooked the class-specific mechanisms of oppression; it just means that we want to work as efficiently as possible and that we have to find a point of departure that allows us to approach the problems systematically and rationally.

[. . .]

The helplessness and arrogance with which we have to appear before you is not particularly enjoyable. We are helpless because we expect progressive men to comprehend the explosive nature of this conflict. Our arrogance derives from seeing how dense you must not be to recognize that the people to whom you never gave any thought are organizing, and indeed organizing in such numbers that you would consider it the dawn of a new day if they were workers.

Comrades, your meetings are intolerable. You are full of inhibitions, which you then release as aggression against comrades who say something stupid or something that you already know. These aggressions result only partly from political recognition of the stupidity of the other camp. Why don't you finally admit that you are exhausted after last year, that you don't know how you can continue to expend yourself physically and mentally in political action without getting any pleasure out of it? When you plan a new campaign, why don't you first discuss how you are going to carry it out? Why do you buy all the books of Reich?[4] Why do you all talk here about the class struggle and at home about problems in achieving an orgasm. Isn't that a topic for the SDS?

We refuse to continue to be complicit in this repression.

In our self-chosen isolation we did the following: we have focused our work on women with children, since their situation is worst. Women with children will not be in a position to think about themselves until presence of their children no longer constantly reminds them of the failures of society. Since political women are interested in not raising their children according to the principles of the performance-oriented society, we have followed through by taking seriously the demand of society that women should raise the children. We interpret that claim in such a way that we refuse to continue to raise them according to the tenets of the competitive struggle and the performance principle. We know that both these principles must be maintained as conditions for the preservation of the capitalist system.

Already within the existing society, we intend to develop models of a utopian society. In such an alternative society, however, our own needs must finally be accommodated. Thus our concentration on education is not an alibi for our own repressed emancipation, but rather the precondition for solving our own problems in a productive way. The main task consists not in forcing our children onto islands far removed from any social reality, but rather in providing the chil-

---

4. Wilhelm Reich (1897–1957), author of numerous books on mass and popular psychology. He was particularly fashionable among leftists in the sexual revolution of the late 1960s. See The German Library, vol. 62, *German Essays on Psychology.*—Eds.

dren with the power to resist by supporting their own efforts at emancipation, so that they can resolve their own conflicts with reality in a way that changes reality.

Translated by Patricia A. Herminghouse
and Magda Mueller

Ulrike Maria Meinhof

Women in the SDS; or, On Our Own Behalf *(1968)*

That tomatoes and eggs are well suited to producing a public sphere where otherwise the issue would have been completely silenced has been only too well known since the visit of the Shah of Iran. On several occasions they've already proven useful for reinforcing an argument. But the students who befouled the Shah did not act on their own behalf, but rather on behalf of the Persian peasants who are in no position to resist under present circumstances, and the tomatoes could only be symbols for better projectiles. Whether one approved of the students' actions or not was a question of hard-won knowledge, a personal decision, a self-chosen identification. The world of the CIA and the Shah is not going to be changed with tomatoes, which is something these people might still think about, despite having thought about it already.

The tomatoes thrown at the Frankfurt conference of SDS representatives did not have any such symbolic value.[1] The men whose suits were soiled (women would have to clean them again) were supposed to think about things that they had not yet given any thought to. The idea was not to stage a spectacle for the media, which preferred to hush up everything, but rather for the benefit of those who

---

1. In September 1968, the Berlin Aktionsrat zur Befreiung der Frau [Action council for the liberation of women] intervened at the Twenty-third Conference of Representatives of the SDS. Speaking on behalf of the Council, Helke Sander [see pages 156–60, the speech that precedes this selection] addressed the antiauthoritarian SDS authority figures with the reproach that within the organization women were just as oppressed as elsewhere in society. When the next speaker, Hans-Jürgen Krahl, did not respond to her speech, the women pelted him with tomatoes.—Eds.

got it in the head with those tomatoes. And the woman who threw the tomatoes, as well as the women who provided the rationale for this action, were not talking on the basis of vicarious experience; by speaking and acting on behalf of countless women, they were speaking and acting on their own behalf. And—because they would have suffocated if they had not exploded at this point—they did not give a fig if what they had to say was up to the very lofty theoretical niveau that is expected in the SDS or whether every term they used was exactly correct or whether *Der Spiegel*[2] would agree with them. Every day millions of women are suffocating on what they have to swallow and then they swallow pills—thalidomide when they're particularly unlucky—or beat their children or lob ladles at their husbands, scold and—if they are somewhat polite—shut the windows so that no one hears what everyone knows: that things can't go on as they are now.

The conflict that again began public in Frankfurt after who-knows-how-many decades—if it ever had been public in such an adamant way—was not just imagined, not something which can be seen this way that or picked up through reading. It is a conflict that everyone who has a family knows intimately; the difference is that here for the first time it has been made clear that this private matter is really not a private matter.

[. . .]

In Frankfurt the women from Berlin refused to play along any longer because they also have to bear the whole burden of raising their children, although they have no influence over the source, the goals, or the reasoning that determines these children's education. They will no longer allow themselves to be insulted just because, for the sake of their children, they have had a poor education, or none at all, or have not been able to practice their profession. All of this leaves its traces, for which they themselves are again made responsible. They have made it clear that the conflict between raising children and working outside the home is not their personal failure but the doing of society, which has brought about this incompatibility. Indeed they made a lot of things clear and when the men refused to respond, they got it in the head with tomatoes. The women didn't go around complaining and representing themselves as victims who were looking for sympathy and understanding and a dishwasher and equal rights and such nonsense.—They started to analyze the private sphere in which they live for the most part and whose burden they

---

2. *Der Spiegel,* German left-liberal weekly news magazine.—Eds.

bear; they came to the conclusion that, from an objective point of view, the men in this private sphere are functionaries of capitalist society in the oppression of women, even if, subjectively, they do not want it that way. When the men could not respond to this, they got it in the head with tomatoes.

The idea was not to promote permanent marital conflict, but conflict in the public sphere, where communication and rapprochement can be established between those who impulsively grab for projectiles, so that for once arguments and not just the superiority of the man on the basis of his socially superior position come into play.

If Frankfurt represented a success for the women, then it was just because a spade had been called a spade, because it had been accomplished without a lot of complaining and rancor, because a few women who took action in Frankfurt already had considerable organization experience behind them, including a few months (not years, as Bissinger[3] claims) of working for women, experiences that revealed both possibilities and problems.

At this point, it cannot possibly be in the interest of women to have SDS to take over the women's issue. It's fine if they want to support women, but no telling us what to do. The response of the men at the conference as well as that of the journalists, however well-meaning, shows that they won't begin to get the idea until entire freight trains of tomatoes have been hurled. The consequence of the events in Frankfurt can only be that more women begin to think about their problems, to organize, to work through and learn how to formulate their issues, and in the process demand of their male partners only that they leave them to deal with this matter by themselves and wash their tomato-stained shirts themselves, maybe because the women have to attend a meeting of the Action Council for the Liberation of Women. And the men should refrain from making stupid remarks about the strange name of the organization because its usefulness will be demonstrated in what it is able to achieve. Since Frankfurt there is no doubt at all that it faces mountains of necessary and difficult work.

Translated by Patricia A. Herminghouse
and Magda Mueller

---

3. Manfred Bissinger, then editor of the weekly illustrated magazine *Stern*.—Eds.

Christina Thürmer-Rohr

Cross-Thinking/Counter-Questioning/Protest *(1987)*

To research means to ask. What's "special," what's "different" about feminist research is the question itself: its origin, impetus, content, direction. What's important is *who* asks. For women what already exists is not normal; it is questionable from the ground up. What's "different" about feminist research thus lies primarily not in its specific methods or its "female-specific" content, but in the person doing the asking, and in her social status.

[. . .]

Feminist research [. . .] develops through questions—embittered, unabashed, agitated questions that arise from looking and listening. Its basic subject area is the world of male society—for there is no other—which imposes conditions on women's admission and station: reality, as seen from women's perspective. It includes the male constructs surrounding them as well as the male constructs imposed on them and female constructs imposed on themselves. Thus the material that fuels feminist research is shocking in nature.

The space which a woman takes up in this society, and the gaze she directs at what she finds there and at herself, reflect her attempts at admission and her orientation in a landscape where she is not at home but where she is nonetheless provided for. The effort to view the material of this life and its earlier history, to sort through it, to give it form, and to present it is a mental exertion that keeps running into external and internal hurdles. The view is not always pleasant, and so the gaze tends to welcome distraction. It is prompted by the same efforts at appeasement which otherwise support women's habit of making their life more acceptable. Subverting the images of femaleness and maleness has disturbing effects for all who do it. Thus even to think of possible subversion is already to be frightened, worried, and held back by its possible consequences.

[. . .]

Women, it is true, form an oppressed human group, but not one that has remained untouched by or immune to their circumstances. They are involved up to their ears in the very thing that weakens them, offends them, makes them sick. They are deeply infected. Neither their historical nor their present position is understandable if women insist on seeing it apart from men's placement of women at man's side and apart from women's assignment of themselves to man.

The locus of feminist research is not a clean and heart-warming place, not a noble, untainted position shared by those who come up short in society. It is rather a soiled and ice-cold place, steeped in and burdened by history, shame, and sorrow. It is not a place of affirmation and agreement, not even agreement among all women or unbroken agreement with oneself, but a place of negation and contradiction where women are not accepted, unwanted, rejected; for all that it's not easy to leave. Thus efforts at exposure and negation are directed not only to the deformations of the "outer world" of male society and its male representatives and perpetrators, but also to those deformations in women which make them co-promoters and co-perpetrators.

What this means for feminist research is that the impulse for solidarity, for "sisterly" commitment to women, as they are, does not become absorbed in social work for fellow victims of injury and oppression. Rather, it means radical questioning of our own sex and its secret understandings, subverting the construct of "femaleness" instead of upgrading it, elucidating those mechanisms by which women actively ensnare themselves in a net that forces or tempts them into invisibility and non-presence. It means confronting our own damaged and self-damaging history and present.

Thus feminist research does not restrict itself to "female-specific subjects." It does not just address what women do and think or did and thought, leaving the rest of the world untouched. Instead it asks fundamental questions about everything we take offense at, everything we want to get rid of, to subvert and expose, to drag into the light and make ridiculous, everything that we cannot believe and accept.

Feminist research cannot merely add to the answers of existing research, filling the gap and reducing the deficit by omitting and subsuming women. Feminist research does not fill any gaps; it is not a previously missing addendum to current subjects of research in the form of the un-cultivated or mis-cultivated female subject. It runs counter to these subjects. It is cross-thinking, counter-questioning, counter-seeing, contradiction, protest. It is thus also indifferent to the reproach of one-sidedness. As long as it does not reduce itself or allow itself to be reduced to what is "female-specific," it is not one-sided or half-true. It seeks to uncover the standardized systems, understandings, and lies of the androcentric worldview.

This approach is "special" not just because of the consciousness and rage of woman as *victim,* who recognizes her *exclusion* from patriarchal culture and from the "subject" of history, but just as much because of the consciousness of woman as *accomplice,* who recognizes her *inclusion* and *enclosure* in this culture. Her contribution as the man's housemate and lover, as participant and coworker, as cofunctionary and affirmer of male deeds, as protector of male advantages, muse of male development, caring supporter, approving co-thinker or silent partner, as both sufferer and upholder of male overvaluation and her own egolessness—all this makes her part of the subject of history, one who belongs and is excluded at the same time, a part whose questionable weight seems to disappear under the heavy weight of the male. This is evident not only in the male's ignorant, self-satisfied gaze, but also in the woman's tendency toward blurred vision of herself.

Feminine complicity in the cynical development of civilized male societies consists—beyond any given historical change in appearance—in the "normal features" of the female social character, which guarantees that absolute affirmation of man and his world, in the specifically female acceptance of the perpetrators. This is conveyed by the woman's active and complex dealings as she buys herself the advantage of a home base in male society by attempting to make herself unrecognizable as a negating subject. Woman's "complicity" means her active entanglement in the normal doings of male society.

Complicity is an analytic and moral-political category. To put it at the center of feminist questioning means, first of all, recognizing, challenging, and exposing patriarchal acts of force and men as past and present criminals. It means, second, analyzing woman's dealings with man and herself as actions oriented to the social criminal and his products, actions which may not be visible but are highly effective, indeed indispensable, contributions. Third, it means judging and negating woman's complicity, that is, taking a stand against it. When complicity is understood apart from the violent context of the crime and is no longer seen as the systematic functionalization of women for men's crimes, it turns into isolated female self-accusation and thus loses the character of protest. Women become perpetrators instead of collaborators; the view of power relations between the sexes as determined by patriarchal law is obscured. Insidiously, the woman makes herself the criminal. But complicity does not convey equal blame, and so it cannot serve to exonerate men. (As if now finally, with the consent of feminists, they had female criminals with equal rights beside them, instead of their own accusing victims at their feet.) Under the concept of complicity the man is the perpetrator of this devastating history, the woman the injured party. But her injuries do not simply diminish her and make her harmless. They are functionally contingent on what man needs from woman: her agreement, her loyalty toward his person and his crimes—her active need of him.

Understanding woman as an active subject and revoking our consent to the violent relations of the sexes is the challenge for research that calls itself feminist. Otherwise women's studies will also become an "accomplice to the crime."

Up to now I have thought that the concept of women's complicity should not pose the question of *guilt*. I have changed my mind. The analysis of complicity does not, like the legal concept, assume *consciousness* of the crime, knowledge of the goal, dedication to its intentions, the *will* to commit the "criminal act." Instead of asking for empirical evidence of guilt, it asks about the character of the involvement of the woman as a patriarchally constructed sex within the overall historical complex.

The question of women's collective complicity is thus primarily posed independent of their individual knowledge and the consciousness that was historically possible for them. Looking back we can try to recognize with what effects, in what capacity, and with what behaviors women have done, not done, or helped to do something, without blaming them. Rightly or not, in looking at the past we shy away from naming collaboration as collective guilt, for the question of guilt presupposes the possibility of determining one's own behavior. We are not entitled to judge this if we do not know from experience our own conditions of acting and nonacting, of knowledge and conscience.

But this does not apply to the present. We can see the result of the behavior of the sexes and can no longer spare ourselves the evaluation of its consequences. These are not remorse, repentance, punishment, or atonement, but the process of *separating* ourselves from the relations of agreement and affirmation, and revoking them. Feminist abstinence and discretion about the question of collective and personal guilt, which arise from protectiveness toward the victim, incapacitate women as coparticipants in history and acquit them of making decisions compelled by knowledge and responsibility for their own actions.

Translated by Lise Weil

Frigga Haug

The End of Socialism in Europe:
A New Challenge for Socialist Feminism? *(1992)*

Women's Issues as Paradoxes

Rethinking the breakdown of the socialist countries and especially the unification of the two Germanies as a socialist feminist from the West, I am first of all confronted with the experience that a number of the Left's convictions have become problematic. Concepts such as market, plan, and property have to be rethought by all branches of the Left. Are there also new uncertainties for socialist feminists? Thinking about women's issues in these times of rapid historical change, in which one entire world system is in collapse and the other winning a surprising victory, the first thing I noticed is a series of paradoxes.

The political paradox

The former socialist model did not eliminate women's oppression; in fact, the situation of women was not even relevant to the dominant theory, which saw feminism as a bourgeois deviation. Nevertheless, it is above all women in movements in the former socialist countries who appear to be ready to think about an improved model of socialism. The Independent Women's Union founded in December 1989 in East Germany was one of the groups which fought for a different socialism, rather than for incorporation by capitalism.

A paradox in theory

Socialist feminists all over the world have long sought to work out the correlation between capitalism and patriarchy. The question was not whether it was only capitalism which oppressed women or whether women's oppression would altogether disappear with the elimination of the capitalist mode of production. Rather, it was necessary to understand the specific usefulness or even the fundamental role that women's oppression plays in the capitalist mode of production. I have tried to outline this correlation as follows: the production of use-values in accordance with the profit motive is only possible given the precondition that a whole series of use-values—as well as the production of life itself and its direct nurture and preservation—operate beyond the laws of profit. Women provide this necessary pillar in capitalist relations of production, owing to their ability to give life to children, and as the outcome of struggles lasting throughout a long period of history. The rest is the work of culture and ideology. This system we understand as "capitalist patriarchy." But this confronts us with a theoretical paradox: as much as this analysis might satisfy those of us who live under capitalism, there remains the amazing discovery that women's emancipation made hardly any progress in those countries which did not function according to the profit motive. Indeed, in the various conferences of East and West German women in Berlin and elsewhere after the opening of the Wall, the one point of dispute was whether Western women were more liberated than those in the East who needed to be taught feminism by their *apparently* more advanced Western sisters. Hope for a strengthening of the women's movement by uniting forces with Eastern "feminism" was soon overthrown by a sort of Western despair that unification would not only fail to strengthen the movement but indeed weaken it, because of a gap in feminist consciousness in the East.

The cultural paradox

When we study the attitudes and behavior of women in East and West, we find other paradoxical results. After forty years of socialism, many women from the East are much more self-confident than most women in the West. Their stride seems more extended, they habitually walk erect, and above all they lack what I will provisionally term a passive sexism. By this I mean that they do not act as if they were constantly balancing the effort to please men in a provocative or even exciting way while at the same time maintaining the necessary distance and inaccessibility. The recent victory in East Germany of Beate Uhse (who owns the biggest chain of sex shops in the West), the invasion of Western peepshows by Eastern men, and the new "freedom" to obtain pornography all indicate that my impression of East German women is valid, and that East German men "suffered" from the freedom of their women. This relative absence of pornography, while the oppression of women continued, also serves to contradict recent feminist ideas about pornography being the original source and the basis of women's oppression. This desexualization of the bodies of East German women coexists with a lack of awareness, even an indifference, concerning quite obvious instances of discrimination against the female sex. Among other things, there has been no feminist revolution in language. Without any hesitation, women in the East refer to themselves in the masculine form (for example, as businessmen or craftsmen). This is a particular problem in German, for many occupational labels, including doctor, economist or historian, assume maleness; to refer to a woman the ending "-in" must be added. It was one of the victories of feminism in the West to bring this into public consciousness, but this has not taken place in East Germany.[1] To speak a male language prevents any clear perception of existing masculinist culture, which among other things determines access to specific jobs.

[. . .]

Economy of Time in the Former GDR

In the former socialist countries [. . .] there was little readiness to take up the task of overcoming the divisions of labor and their effects throughout society. Following Lenin, some effort was made to reduce the cultural gap between city and countryside, but the question of gender relations fell into oblivion. Or more correctly, there was a general assumption that including women in the social labor process was sufficient to overcome their oppression. Our Western media never grow tired of pointing out to us that things have been the same in East and West, as in both societies women bore responsibility for household and childcare and were therefore totally overworked, carrying the entire burden of labor-force participation. However, their mocking contempt of the socialist economy and its management points to inroads into the logic of profit-making that at least deserve mention.

East Germany was obviously more advanced in those very areas now blamed for being nonproductive and described as industrial junkyards. The fringe benefits offered by Eastern companies included some which contributed to women's liberation. They involved a partial suspension of the profit motive as the general basis of production. This made the companies appear particularly unproductive from the standpoint of the logic of profit. Childcare centers, meals, portions of health insurance were paid for by the companies, as were holiday centers. In regions of exceptional beauty, by the seashore, where we would expect grand hotels for the moneyed élites, we still find a variety of holiday camps run by different companies (these camps, by the way, offer a somewhat vulgar obstacle to proper capitalization).

---

1. In this connection, see the essay by Luise Pusch in this volume.—Eds.

It is true that the more "society" appropriates the work of women free of charge, the richer it gets, so long as only healthy male workers are considered to be temporarily used while they exert their labor power to the utmost solely for the advantage of the company. As one might expect, the numbers of women and youth among the East German unemployed were already remarkably higher than those for adult men just four months after the introduction of West German currency.

Although our conservative press does not report on the brutality of the West, but only on its freedom, wealth, and so forth, we can decipher out of the very details it does give just how great the dehumanization exported by West Germany really is. I shall give one small example; a few months ago there was a short report on the unparalleled lack of productivity at an East German chemical company. As a result, seven hundred employees, all of whom were well over sixty-five years old, were to be dismissed. Women as old as eighty-four regularly came to the factory and were paid, because they were lonely at home. The company will now switch its policy and dismiss all persons over fifty-seven. It will also get rid of eighty Vietnamese workers and send them back to Vietnam. The company had also had a health center staffed by thirty doctors that cared for the health of adults and children in the entire region. These institutions are to be separated from the company and only after all these improvements have been made will a Western chemical factory be so kind as to appropriate this factory.

Let us assume that women's oppression is grounded in the division of society into an area that is "productive" and one that is "nonproductive" and therefore superfluous in terms of the logic of profit. Their interrelation in the realm of political administration, which necessarily remains a male domain, decrees that women are responsible for the unproductive segment and ensures their non-development culturally and bureaucratically. In this respect we see in the former socialist countries a deliberate effort to establish a cost-benefit analysis that takes a segment of those unproductive tasks over into the productive account balance. On this basis female waged employment became ordinary and was culturally and politically realized.

The question remains of why this shift and rearrangement did not lead to a greater liberation and inclusion of women in the regulative structures of society. At present it appears as a problem of patriarchal bureaucracy. A burden was lifted for women so that they could enter the "productive" area; but the division between these two areas, and the fact that social progress only related to one of them, was not recognized as the problem. Those at the top decided which products, which free spaces, which activities were to be exempted from the general cost-benefit analysis. Freedom planned from above cannot be perceived as freedom. Agreement to a certain way of life can only be productive and creative if those concerned take the satisfaction and development of their needs into their own hands. But to carry out the planned economy and the subsidizing of particular areas in the East, the eternal patriarchy was once again required, emerging from past circumstances both morally and mentally (as Marx put it in his *Critique of the Gotha Program*). And this patriarchy believed it knew how best to foster human development and enacted laws, duties, and regulations to accomplish it.

What could the "miracle women" do but agree? A women's movement aiming at liberation could hardly grow under these circumstances. But, on the other hand, it becomes clearer why women from the former East German state are less inclined to turn their backs on a socialist project. The so-called return to a market economy definitely hits them the hardest.

The development of one area was not simply accomplished at the cost of the other, men did not develop solely at the cost of women, but by the centuries-old neglect of human development, except as a by-product of profit and utilitarianism. Time for human development would have required the direct subjective participation of all concerned in order to achieve liberation, rather than planning, commands, and administration. Such a step would have also shown that time is not only a dimension that is measured as productive in the sense of growth and competition in the world market, or unproductive in the sense of giving more scope to humanity and generally improving the standard of living, but that time is also a dimension that permits the development of human lives, and that it is necessary if people are to participate in the political regulation of the community as a civil society. Thus the women's question is a question of democracy and, concomitantly, there will be no democracy and no socialism without a solution to the women's question.

As far as the newly unified Germany is concerned, there is a social commitment to the currently existing freedom and democracy of the West. Any violation will be prosecuted. As long as this democracy and this freedom are understood in the old patriarchal way, women will remain outlaws and will be forced to fight for a new order.

Translated by Rodney Livingstone

ISSUES
OF GENDER

Sidonie Hedwig Zäunemann

Jungfern-Glück

Niemand schwatze mir vom Lieben und von Hochzeitsmachen vor,
Cypripors Gesang und Liedern weyh ich weder Mund noch Ohr.
Ich erwehl zu meiner Lust eine Cutt- und Nonnen-Mütze,
Da ich mich in Einsamkeit wieder manches lästern schütze.
Ich will lieber Sauer-Kraut und die ungeschmeltzten Rüben.
In dem Kloster vor das Fleisch in dem Ehstands-Hause lieben.
Mein Vergnügen sey das Chor, wo ich sing und beten tuhe,
Denn dasselbe wirkt und schafft mir die wahre Seelen-Ruhe.
Will mir den gefaßten Schluß weder Mann noch Jüngling glauben,
Immerhin, es wird die Zeit euch doch diesen Zweifel rauben.
Geht nur hin, und sucht mit Fleiß Amors Pfeile, Amors Waffen,
Und geberdet euch darbey als wie die verliebten Affen!
Dorten stund in einem Carmen auf den Herrn von Obernütz:
Kriegt das schöne Jungfern-Röckgen einen Flecken, Ritz und Schlitz,
So muß auch der Jungfern Glück und die edle Freyheit weichen,
Und dargegen sucht die Angst sich gar eilend einzuschleichen.
Dieser Vers hat recht gesagt, Jungfern können kühnlich lachen;
Dahingegen manches Weib sich muß Angst und Sorge machen.
Kriegt die Noth durch Gegen-Mittel eine Lindrung und ein Loch,
Ey, so währt es doch nicht lange, und man schauet immer noch
Eben so viel Bitterkeit als in Erfurt Mannes Krausen,
Leid und Trübsal, Gram und Pein will die armen Weiber zausen.
Kriegt ein Weib von ihrem Mann manchen Tag ein Dutzend Mäulgen,
Ey! so sagt, was folgt darauf? Über gar ein kleines Weilgen
Brennt des Mannes Zorn wie Feuer, und er schwöret beym Parnaß:
Frau! ich werde dich noch prügeln, oder stecke dich ins Faß.
Dieser Weiber Noth und Pein will ich mich bey Zeit entschlagen,
Denn so darf kein Herzens-Wurm jemahls meine Seele nagen.
Drum so sag ich noch einmahl; Gute Nacht, du Scherz und Küssen,
Ich will deine Eitelkeit bis in meine Gruft vermissen.

Sidonie Hedwig Zäunemann

A Maid's Fortune *(1739)*

Let no one speak to me of love and matrimony, please,
Neither my lips nor ears shall grace Cyprian melodies.
For my earthly pleasure a cowl and nun's veil I choose
Because in my chaste solitude I'll be spared from much abuse.
Sauerkraut and raw turnips, convent fare, I would rather eat
Than in a conjugal house be served the choicest meat.
The choir is my amusement, in which I pray and sing,
For that is soothing and gives me a sense of true well-being.
Should neither man nor youth believe in my conviction,
It doesn't matter! Time will convince you of my prediction.
Go ahead and search for Cupid's weapons, Cupid's darts,
And in the process, act like apes who've lost their hearts!
In a song of Herr von Obernütz these verses one can hear:
If a fair maid's skirt should show soil, slit, or smear,
Then her freedom and good fortune will abandon her apace
And before you know it, fear will try to take their place.
This verse tells it as it is: A maid can laugh in all propriety,
While many a good wife must live with troubles and anxiety.
And assuming her distress should be lessened by some remedy,
Oh, this can't last too long before again you'll see
Just as much bitterness as there are frills for Erfurt's men:
Grief and misery, pain and suffering are a wife's daily regimen.
If on some days a wife receives a dozen kisses from her spouse,
Oh! tell me what will come of that? Before the day is out
His anger'll flare up like fire and by heathen gods he'll swear:
Wife, I'll thrash you soundly or I'll lock you up somewhere!
Such conjugal grief and suffering I've chosen to forego
Because I won't allow my heart to suffer so much woe.
Therefore I shall say again: Adieu to kisses and to jest!
I don't need your vanity while life beats in my breast.

Translated by Susan L. Cocalis
and Gerlind M. Geiger

Fanny Lewald

A Marriage Proposal *(1862)*

I came into the dining room one morning[1] and saw my father sitting by the window over a glass of wine with two other men, whom I did not recognize. That was not very unusual, because Father often brought business acquaintances home when he needed to have longer discussions with them. I made a bow, therefore, and started heading into the next room, where I had something to attend to, when my father called me and introduced me to the gentlemen.

The older one was a merchant from a provincial town, the other, a man in his middle thirties, a lawyer elected as district magistrate, who lived in one of the most inhospitable regions of East Prussia, on Tuchler Heath. We exchanged a few words, I asked the usual question about how long the gentlemen were staying in Königsberg, and received the answer that the older one, the uncle, was leaving, but the nephew would stay for a while to become acquainted with our city. My father invited him to dinner the next day, a Sunday. That was all in order, but I suddenly had the idea that he could be the bridegroom picked for me, and I was not wrong. The following noon I became better acquainted with him.

None of our regular guests had been invited for Sunday dinner, presumably so that the claimant could assert himself better, and he proceeded to do this in his own way. He told us of the nice little gatherings of notables in his home town, described his house, spoke of his important relatives in Berlin and Breslau and of his hopes to be promoted and not always be magistrate in his present district. He threw in remarks about the beautiful species of hyacinths he was raising and lingered lovingly on the pleasures of catching crabs by torchlight. That did not help the situation between us; I disliked him intensely. His short, fat body and expression of smug, arrogant self-satisfaction, a certain assured and provincial manner of speaking, and the presumptuous confidence with which he acted toward me would have made him unpleasant and unsympathetic to me even if I had not the image of another man and a passionate love for him

---

1. The event Lewald describes here took place in 1837.—Eds.

in my heart. I constantly looked at my father, who usually was an uncompromising judge of such airs as my claimant had, to see if he did not find the man as obnoxious as I did. But my father and my mother, who usually saw the comical aspect of such matters, seemed completely blind this time. The magistrate returned several times in the course of the following days. My sisters made jokes about him, my parents praised him, while I was deeply offended and bitter that they could even think of choosing as my husband a man whom they would surely not have admitted to their social circle if he were not thinking of marrying me.

Finally, the chambermaid came to me one afternoon with the request that the master wanted me to come up to my brother's room. I knew what lay ahead of me. With my heart pounding wildly, but certain of what I had to do, I climbed the stairs. I found my father alone and very agitated. He said I undoubtedly knew why he had summoned me. The magistrate had asked for my hand, and Father hoped that I was prepared to accept his offer. This way of speaking, which was totally alien to my father's usual manner, revealed that he, too, was not really enraptured with my suitor; so I declared quite frankly that I was sorry not to be able to fulfill my father's wishes and hopes.

He was silent for a moment and then remarked, "Think of the situation, my child. You are no longer young. You are twenty-five. I am not in a position to give you a considerable dowry; you know I am not a wealthy man and I have five other daughters. Two of them are already grown, the others will be so in a few years, and six grown daughters will not get along well in one house. The magistrate wants you for yourself; that is something not even many wealthy girls get, and as the wife of a district magistrate, who will certainly advance in his career, you will have an honorable position and a certain income. Don't forget that a woman in a not quite happy marriage is still better off than a spinster."

I asked if my father had learned this from his youngest sister, whose unhappy marriage was a source of distress for all of us. He answered that the magistrate was an educated man who could not be compared with my aunt's husband, and added, "I don't know what wishes and expectations you cherish, but I think they have no basis, and you might later regret having turned down the offer of an honorable man. This magistrate is indeed an honorable man from everything I have heard and found out about him."

The conversation continued in this manner for a while. My father was very tender and calm. The various considerations went through my mind again and again. I wanted to be calm, too, but my heart was beating so fast I could hardly breathe and the blood was pounding in my temples. I felt I had to put an end to this kind of proposal once and for all. I therefore explained to my father that nothing in the world would force me to marry someone I did not want. If he wished to persuade me, if he had the intention of making a cipher of me, as one of the women who sells herself to a man for a comfortable life, he should not have given me the upbringing he had nor have made me so independent. To me, a prostitute who sold herself for money because she was poor and had no education was not half as despicable as a girl who had learned enough to support herself and sold herself for house and home.

My father interrupted me, because I had become very agitated. "Before you say anything else, I want to remind you of one thing. I know how much you love your Aunt Minna.[2] I did not want to make this decision myself. I wrote to her and asked her what she would do in such a case and if she would not feel justified in forcing her daughters into a marriage, if they rejected it without sufficient reason. Your aunt agreed that I should use all means necessary to exercise such pressure."

He handed me a copy of his letter to my aunt and her reply. I was supposed to read it, but I could hardly comprehend it because of the rage, shame, and insult I felt. I thought that they wanted to break off my relationship with Heinrich by these letters, to take away any hope for his love, and that they believed they would be able to force me. The idea that my father, whom I so adored, could pressure me, could force me into unhappiness (as I thought of it in my outrage) just to get rid of me, made me beside myself.

"You want to force me? How are you going to do that, dear Father?" I asked. "Do you plan to lock me in or let me starve to death? What can you do to make me lower myself so much? Am I a burden to you, dear Father? Just say so and I will go and earn my own living, since you have been generous enough to teach me the means to do so. It would perhaps be best for me and for us all if that happens!"

My poor father's eyes filled with tears. He was obviously not prepared for this and probably thought that I was no longer happy in his house or happy at all. He took me by the hand and spoke to me in that tone of voice I could never resist. "Fanny! Who's thinking of

---

2. Minna Simon, beloved older sister of Lewald's father and mother of her cousin Heinrich, for whom Fanny held an unrequited love.—Eds.

that? But I beg you, your father begs you, to enter this marriage; it would make me and your mother very happy."

I began to cry. To hear my father's request and not to be able to comply broke my heart. "Don't torture me, dear Father," I pleaded. "I can't; I can't marry him."

My father sat on the sofa, I stood before him. He had propped his head on his hand. All at once he stood up. "So this is your final word—no!"

"That is all I can say," I repeated.

"Good, then it's 'no,' and I hope you will not regret it later." He kissed me and started to leave; when I wanted to follow him, he gave me a signal to remain behind. "Calm yourself first and wash your face, so that the household cannot see you were crying," he said, and left me after embracing me again.

I remained there to cry out my despair with fervent bitter tears. I have never felt more miserable than I did at that moment. I had much grief and many hurt feelings in later years. These were very painful, but they did not hurt as much, because they did not come from a father whom I loved as a veritable god. I have been accused of many unwarranted or unreasonable things, but only by people who did not know me as well as I knew my father did. They could not measure how much they trespassed on my real nature by their demands. The rug had been pulled away from under my feet; I trusted no one any more, not my father, not my aunt. I kept telling myself, "How superfluous I must be in my own home, how little my father must know me, if he wants to drive me out, to force me to be unhappy, only so that he will not have to provide for me anymore!"

It was completely futile to tell myself that most parents would do the same thing, how certain of my acquaintances would have married the good magistrate with great joy, how most people would think that I had turned down a most suitable marriage. I told myself all kinds of generalities to find consolation for the personal element, but it did not work. I was not like everyone else. I cherished a great and strong belief in a noble love, in an ideal marriage, which was something holy to me; I had a feeling for the essential dignity of a human being, a dignity which is violated when a person acts against his own inner convictions. From that hour on, I never ceased feeling all the misery, all the insult, all the furious outrage that has evoked the outcry for emancipation in the hearts of thousands of women, until I achieved what I needed in order to insure myself against the demeaning assumption behind the phrase "What is to become of you?"

These words, which everyone feels justified in addressing to a woman without means, simply and obviously imply this: "What is to become of you if you don't throw yourself into the arms of some man, whether you love him or not, for the price of being supported for the rest of your life."

If you would ask this question of anyone who praises our social arrangements, our current mores, and our family life, as they are now constituted, it would be obvious he does not have much of a sense of true personal pride or feeling of shame, without which neither man nor woman can respect themselves or earn the respect of others.

Even now I cannot think, without shuddering, of what my lot would have been if I had been less certain of myself, less firm in character, and less idealistic in that hour. My otherwise clever and good father would, because of prejudice and shortsightedness, have driven me out to a misery which I could only estimate. When I am happy with myself, am on the heights of life, fully enjoying the sublime, the great, the beautiful aspects it has to offer, I still think of the Tuchler Heath and the unfortunate man my father selected for me. I would have perished in despair, without my strong sense of self-preservation.

Translated by Hanna Ballin Lewis

Louise Aston

Banishment *(1846)*

An eventful life lay behind me, as I took up residence in Berlin in August of the previous year. In my early youth, before I had an idea of what love was, I had been married to a man who was a stranger to my heart; possessing all external trappings of happiness, but alone and unhappy in the midst of the most auspicious circumstances, I learned early about modern life in all of its conflicts and contradictions. Soon I also came to know the greatest contradiction that destroys the hearts of women and threatens to upend the order of the world as she knows it: the opposition between love and marriage, inclination and duty, heart and conscience.

[. . .]

We divorced. From the general shipwreck of the things I held most near and dear, I saved nothing but the strong resolve to place myself above fate by keeping my eyes open and my will strong, and to steel my heart by educating my mind, and thus to keep restlessness at bay through the peace felt when thought is in itself satisfying. This was my intention as I moved to Berlin, inspired by the new, lively scholarship taking place there. Within the circles of those who represented these new movements, I was determined to forget the wounds inflicted by adversarial forces in life, to educate myself, and to gather my forces for literary activity.

[. . .]

Berlin, with its rich intellectual life, the city of thought and of intellectuals, seemed to be the most suited to my intentions, and to the attainment of my literary career. After registering with the police and meeting all of my legal obligations, I received a residency permit. On the twelfth of February 1846, this residency permit had expired, and I sent it on that day to the police with the request to renew it, but received no new card, but instead an order to appear at the police station *myself*. Since I was ill, I sent a doctor's excuse signed by my physician, Dr. Perle, which I sent again to police headquarters [*Präsidium*] with the plea to renew my card. My request was, however, ignored again. A few days later a police officer named Goldhorn appeared in the name of the superintendent of police [*Polizeirat*] Hofrichter, in order to ask me a few questions. At the same time, he told me that they did not want to extend my residency permit, because several *anonymous* letters had been sent to headquarters, indeed to His Majesty the King himself, in which I was accused of attending the most frivolous men's clubs, of founding a club for emancipated women, and furthermore of not believing in God. There were other things that spoke against my application, the dedication of Gottschall's *Madonna and Magdalena*,[1] in which similar tendencies were celebrated, and whose objectionable quality had been proved most conclusively by the reviewer in the *Blätter für literarische Unterhaltung*. I attempted to instruct this officer, as much as possible, in a better opinion of myself and of my life, and then wrote the president of the police von Putkammer himself. In this letter, I

---

1. Rudolf Gottschall (1823–1909) sang the praises of free love in this volume. —Eds.

explained how my *beliefs* and *thoughts* are my own property, and of no concern to anyone else, and how those anonymous letters could only come from my personal enemies. I asked for an extension of the residency permit, because my literary activities, especially the pending publication of my poems, *Wild Roses,* was keeping me tied to Berlin and made my residency in the same necessary.

I pointed out that one could only accuse me of a lack of morals inasmuch as it is immoral to smoke cigars and to interact with intellectual men; I closed with the plea to allow me to continue to be called a citizen of the *moral city of Berlin,* as well as to overlook any eventual irregularities in my writing.

As the result of this letter, at the end of February I was ordered to appear at police headquarters before deputy Stahlschmidt, who told me to wait in the anteroom until commissioner [*Regierungsrat*] Lüdemann, who was actually the person who would talk to me, had finished his other business, and had time for my affairs. In the mean time, Mr. Stahlschmidt chatted with me in a highly friendly and jovial manner, turned the conversation toward *religion* and *marriage,* and led me—by employing questions from a number of different angles, and seemingly in jest—to indeed reveal my most private opinions. I therefore did not hesitate to express myself freely because the manner in which the questioning was done led me to hold this conversation to be a purely *private* one. After our conversation had ended, Mr. Stahlschmidt led me into the office of commissioner Lüdemann, and handed him to my greatest surprise a transcript of it with the words, "This is the confession of Madame Aston!" These notes, which had been taken without my knowledge during the conversation with Mr. Stahlschmidt, were now read to me. I was frightened and confused—a confusion that would be ridiculous in a man, but can certainly be excused in a woman who could not investigate such things in depth, and was completely lacking in knowledge of the methods of the Prussian administration. Because of this confusion and fear, I refused to sign the testimony, and only relented following the friendly persuasion of the worthy Mr. Lüdemann, who assured me in the kindliest tone that it would do no harm to my case if I signed; he would give his word on it. The word of a commissioner seemed to me an adequate assurance of the truth, for I didn't know that *to keep one's word* belonged in the Old Testament of political science, and had been banned from greater and lesser politics since Machiavelli. In my naiveté, in good *faith,* I signed the testimony and disproved by the action the accusation of *faithlessness.*

In the mean time, a bored correspondent of the *Deutsche Allgemeine Zeitung,* for lack of material used my person and my opinions to debut me as a Socialist; he gave my innocent cigar smoking a meaning in world history, made from my casually expressed opinions bold plans to improve the world, and, without the intervention of the police, predicted an organized women's movement in Berlin. This correspondent seemed to be taking more pleasure in the genius of his productive fantasy, the daring of his fabrications, and in the fear they incited than in a proper denunciation, even though this would be a fitting name for his article.

On March 21, I received yet another injunction to appear at police headquarters where Mr. Kopin, an assessor, verbally gave me the order to *"Leave Berlin within eight days, because I expressed and wanted to bring ideas to life that are dangerous for the civil peace and order."*

In this way an importance was conferred upon me by the police, which I would have never had the courage to confer upon myself, for how bold must a woman be to dream herself up as an enemy of the state.

Translated by Lisa Roetzel

Mathilde Franziska Anneke

Woman in Conflict with Social Relations *(1847)*

Louise Aston has published a pamphlet[1] revealing aspects of her outer life to public knowledge. [. . .] The voice in this little book woke up many a drowsing woman who had not yet been lulled fast asleep by the bubbling of the kettle on her hearth. It roused many women who silently endure and struggle, bleeding under the yoke of social squalor that, unsuspected and unrecognized, weighs down the hearts of women; it roused them in their failing strength to awareness of their ultimate rights, that they may pull themselves up and dare at

---

1. The pamphlet was "My Emancipation, Explusion, and Justification" (1846), excerpts of which appear in the previous article in the present volume.—Eds.

least to protest their fate loudly. It replenished their timid souls with the courage to shake the walls of the whitewashed old temple, decorated with the myrtle wreaths of sacrificed brides and resplendent with the halos of a thousand inwardly broken marriages—even if only to loosen one stone from this decaying structure. [. . .]

You women who willingly learned to accept a "happiness" for which you truly never felt the glow of longing in a youthful bosom: understand that your illusory happiness has turned you into simpering slaves; you have become unfeeling toward others and toward yourself, for you did not even feel the scorpion that stings your very heart and cheats you of your best lifeblood. What you call happiness is not even a *shadow of happiness*. Do not scorn the woman who burst the fetters of the oaths that your idols sanctified, who left sumptuous halls behind and entered the chambers of quiet poverty to spend in chaste widowhood her year of mourning at the bier of the expired happiness of her youth. O, do not scorn her if she, instead of squandering the riches of life in voluptuously stupefying pleasures, chose to stride forward into life, serious life, to take risks and contend with it—if instead of continuing hypocritically to betray herself and love, she fled—fled from deception and its delusion. [. . .] Louise Aston was exposed to indescribable afflictions and fears. But worst of all was what could befall her in her public life, her expulsion from the capital city, hitherto her place of residence. [. . .]

We are spontaneously moved to take a closer look at the dreams of a woman which seemed so threatening to the security of the state and to which the capital of the mighty kingdom of Prussia ascribed such great importance. Therefore we ask: "What evil may Frau Aston's declaration have contained, such that by confirming it the authorities obtained sufficient articles of proof to justify carrying out their intentions?" Only from the dialogue reported to us in her little pamphlet, during the personal audience she was granted with Minister von Bodelschwingh, do we gather that Frau Aston's primary offense consists in having expressed her religious views freely and out loud. [. . .]

Why is such a declaration from the lips of a woman so harshly sanctioned? Why should the truth be obscured from women, the truth that is the legacy of our time and that is now becoming victorious in the battle with falsehood? Why do views that have been permitted to men for centuries seem *on the part of women* so dangerous to a state? Perhaps because they more so than men hold the power of circulating these views, which in wider circulation threaten to upset the world order and the state government of today?—Because they nourish with their lifeblood a better faith in a new human incarnation and can hand down to you in the next generation a healthier, freer race that will never again be sold into slavery?—*Is that why?*— Yes, that is why: because the truth that women bear will emerge victorious, toppling the thrones and altars of tyrants and despots. Because only the truth makes us free and releases us from the bonds of self-denial, from the fetters of slavery. Because the truth liberates us from the false delusion that we will be rewarded in heaven for our loving and sorrowing, for our enduring and serving; because it makes us recognize that we are as equally entitled to enjoyment of life as our oppressors; that they are the very ones who made these laws and gave them to us, not for our benefit, but for theirs, for their advantage. Because the truth shatters these tablets of the law, henceforth to stand victorious, nevermore the hunted fugitive who knocks at all doors and can find no place of shelter. Because as soon as the hearts of women are completely opened to it, the eternal refuge for this truth will be prepared and the legacy of humankind be won.

And the day has dawned when it comes knocking at your hearts. Open them wide, wide, and partake of your and your children's legacy. Cease to be betrayed! For you remain so, if you do not seize this inheritance with your own hands. Others try to cloud your senses with the fragrance of incense, to beguile you with bland words, to hand you fairy tales shrouded by perfumed blossoms instead of the simple truth. Gifted singers have cooed sweet-sounding lullabies to your waking and thinking, in melodious harmonies they have sung the praises of reverence on the countenances of women. And this reverence! I tell you—it is nothing but hypocrisy and deceit in the halo on which tears of sacrifice, of pain and unhappiness, indeed, tears of deprivation, grief, and affliction sparkle in quivering drops!

Reverence, this hypocrisy and deceit in the halo, has turned women into zealots, and they squander their passion on it—dream away the strength that is indispensable for a brisk, active life. In reverence, this indeterminate longing of the spirit, they have had to stop thinking—oh, woman was ever forbidden to think—, and have had to stop testing the good, seeking the best, and acting for themselves! In blind surrender they have entrusted themselves to chance. And this "chance" they call the "wise providence of the divine," this "blind accident" they call the "higher power" that shall lovingly reign over them!!! Oh, open your eyes and see how you have been toyed with, yes, open your eyes and you will see every hour upon the hour how you are betrayed, how that which you were taught and commanded is contradictory in every way. [. . .]

Become firmly convinced of the truth and through it, help vigorously to prepare the work for humankind.—Do not imagine, you mothers and wives, that I am placing too much emphasis on your presence! Do not imagine that I have been intoxicated by prevailing ideas of our age when I place the burden of care for that lofty work, the troubles and toil for it on your weak womanly shoulders and proclaim that the fate of the world will be resolved by *you!*—Oh mothers, see your infants lying in your arms! Do you want them henceforth to learn deceit with mother's milk? Do you not want to fortify them at your breast with the wholesome air of the new intellectual springtime and prepare them to solemnly receive the whole truth? It is *up to you* to make them receptive to the *truth* or—to deceit; it is up to you to lead your *free* son to his *free* father, that he may complete what you have begun, and in like manner!—It is *up to you* to educate daughters who will never gladden a slave with their smiles!

Translated by Jeanette Clausen

Louise Dittmar

The Rational Marriage *(1848)*

Reason proves itself by correctly grasping relations. To be a reasonable marriage is therefore the necessary condition for any marriage. However, the so-called rational marriages of convenience offer the most striking picture of the absurdity of our views on reason, since exactly that is called reason in which the pinnacle of all irrationality manifests itself. And yet, rational marriages should be deemed sensible and should be recommended. For if I have only the choice between throwing myself into the raging sea or being torn to pieces by a wild animal called chance, it is more sensible to surrender to the mercy of an irrational element than to fall prey to the *animal* power of irrationality, to the lawless power of animal drives.

"The lake, but not the governor, can show mercy."[1]

The governor ruling absolutely over the woman's happiness and honor is the licentiousness and barbarity to which the woman is subjected by legal servitude and by the reign of money over reason, honor, property, and life. Indeed, a rational marriage is the only harbor into which the storm-tossed ship of female nature must strive to enter under full sail, no matter whether the ship incurs an irreparable leak, no matter whether it and others are destroyed. The rational marriage is the artfully spread net into which the startled deer jumps, hunted and pursued from all sides, no matter whether it submits life and limb to the power of its rulers.

We have said that love is the sole, the true, and the highest condition of matrimony. Depending on the person, this love can manifest itself to a higher or lower degree, as enthusiastic rapture or as comfortable satisfaction; without fail, however, respect is the first condition for this love. Without respect, any love rests on a deception of spirit or of the senses. Thus, in a rational marriage, love is negated decisively and respect is called into question; it is not a condition but a matter of luck, a bonus. For in a rational marriage it is not the essence of matrimony that is the origin of the union, but an external motive: material advantage. What is thus missing is the spirit of the matter. Where the enlivening cause, spiritual communion, is absent, the spiritual effect—communication, exchange and reciprocity—must also be absent. Where self-esteem is lacking, where disrespect for one's own nature prevails, where the manifestation of that which one loves and respects does not occur, there one's own self must sink ever deeper due to the continued existence of such a relationship. And so it does. Woman and man sink, their drive for activity slackens, the vital impulse is missing, they are no longer driven by anything but external influences. They do not drive, they drift; they do not live, they just let life go on and let themselves be exploited by circumstances. Do we not see this in our contemporary marriages, which are almost without exception rational marriages of convenience, marriages which have been contracted by chance and the superior power of external circumstances?

Through a rational marriage I therefore confess my powerlessness to overcome external obstacles, I confess the subordination of my spirit to matter, I confess the rule of animal over human nature; thus

---

1. Friedrich Schiller, *Wilhelm Tell,* act I, scene 1 (1804). Tell is encouraging a fisherman to ferry a man fleeing the governor's forces across a stormy lake.—Eds.

I deprive myself of my human nature, which consists of struggling against and overcoming obstacles recognized as inhuman.

A rational marriage is a sign of helplessness. In it one seeks money, property, position, influence, honor, and prestige; in short, one endeavors to acquire something that one does not possess, but must or wants to possess for the activation of one's nature. Without the rule of money over humans, without the suppression of and encroachment upon their natural needs, without the subordination of human beings under those circumstances that are meant to raise them, in short, without the perversity of things, a rational marriage would be impossible. Rational marriage is therefore either an emergency anchor in life, or a means to secure a better life. It contradicts the essence of marriage, love, which is the absolute end in itself of the human being. It is a deceptive barter, in which the end is exchanged for the means to the end. It is a thoroughly immoral relationship, since material things may only be exchanged for material ones, and moral values only for equally moral ones, thus marriage only for love. Rational marriage corresponds neither to the nature of matrimony, nor to that of man and woman, nor to that of love, nor to that of freedom or liberation.

Translated by Jörg Esleben

Marie von Ebner-Eschenbach

Selected Aphorisms *(1880)*

Nothing alienates two people who have nothing in common more than living together.

There are women who love their husbands with an infatuation which is as blind, effusive, and enigmatic as that of nuns for their nunnery.

Whoever believes in the freedom of the human will has never loved or hated.

It is unfortunate that a good talent and a good man seldom come together.

Let us not demand honesty in women as long as they are brought up to believe that their primary purpose in life is to please.

Where would the power of woman lie, without the vanity of men?

The man is master of the house; but the woman alone should rule inside the house.

An intelligent woman has millions of born enemies . . . all the stupid men.

Contracting a marriage of convenience in most cases entails amassing all convenient reasons to justify committing the most foolhardy act a human being can commit.

To be young is beautiful, to be old is comfortable.

A man who feels contradicted in a conversation with his wife straightaway begins to shout her down. He wants it known, and is able to prove, that his is the first voice, even if he sings wrongly.

In her love for an excellent man the woman loses the consciousness of her own worth; the man comes to a consciousness of his only through the love of a noble woman.

There are more naive men than naive women.

It's bad enough when married people bore one another; but it's much worse when only one of them bores the other.

The greatest power over a man is that of the woman who actually refuses him but who knows how to make him think she's responding to his love.

Woe betide the woman who in time of need is unable to face up to adversity like a man.

The innocence of a man is called honor; the honor of a woman is called innocence.

When a woman learned to read, women's issues entered the world.

The woman who is not capable of influencing her husband is a silly goose; the woman who does not wish to influence him—a saint.

Many a man thinks he is a Don Juan but is really only a faun.

The only uncontested honors a woman is entitled to in the eyes of the world are those she enjoys as a reflection of the honors of her husband.

When a woman says "each" she means each person. When a man says "each" he means each man.

Men are the leaders in all areas, only on the way to heaven do they allow women to take the lead.

Translated by David Scrase
and Wolfgang Mieder

Irma von Troll-Borostyáni

Shame *(1896)*

There is nothing more contradictory in our shame-feigning era than our wedding customs.

While in "good" society—as a direct consequence of designating the "mortification of the flesh" the state of highest moral perfection—everything related to the needs and expression of sexual life is covered by a thick veil (under which however sexual depravities spread wildly despite all denial, or rather, are aided and abetted by it); while a false sense of shame treats the natural relation of the sexes to each other as an ugly secret that everybody knows but nobody is allowed to mention and that must be kept not only from children but also from young women, despite the fact that marriage and motherhood are incessantly preached to them as their natural vocation: this conventional modesty is suddenly pushed aside when it comes to the marriage ceremony. The fact, which concerns no one except those most intimately involved, that a man enters into an alliance with a woman for the purpose of procreation, is shouted from the rooftops, shamelessly made public, celebrated with feasting and dancing, spiced up with more or less oblique, delicate jokes and innu-endoes about the wedding night and the imminent arrival of the stork. One would never cease to be amazed by this striking contra-diction between the shame-free homage paid to the enactment of the human mating instinct during public celebration of marriage and the prudery that is otherwise put on display in all spheres of the civilized world, if one did not find the key to this contradiction in a strange combination of a remnant of ancient heathen veneration of nature and our Christian condemnation of nature.

Translated by Jeanette Clausen

Prostitution *(1896)*

Prostitution . . . as we have it today—an eyesore of civilization—is a product of the enslavement of women, of economic need in society, and of the brutal selfishness of men. It is the result of legal restric-tions on women's opportunities for education and gainful employ-ment, which force countless unfortunate and hungry women to offer their physical charms for sale; it is a result of the contempt and pro-found disgrace that modern society heaps upon these poor "lost souls." [. . .]

If we examine, without preconceived ideas, the nature, signifi-cance and effects of modern-day prostitution—for that alone con-cerns us here—and the position that society must take with regard to it, the facts are these:

Satisfaction of the sex drive, which is innate to all living beings, including humans, clearly cannot be either moral or immoral in and of itself, no more so than eating to still hunger, drinking to slake thirst, and sleeping when rest is needed are moral or immoral. Na-ture and her laws know nothing of morality.

But it is equally clear that the manner in which this natural instinct is satisfied must be regarded from the standpoint of morality—that is, from the standpoint of the common interest—as permissible or as prohibited, considering its relation to the population as a whole, considering its harmful or neutral effects on the welfare of others. Furthermore, it is clear that the individual, who as a member of soci-ety can no longer live in the unbridled freedom of primeval humans, is morally obligated and should be legally obligated to permit himself satisfaction of sexual desire only within the limits imposed to protect the common good. Likewise, society is entitled to require this self-restraint from its members, just as it requires them to honor the rights of ownership to protect the public interest, permitting no one to help himself to another person's property in order to still his hunger. [. . .]

Now one could, recognizing this position on determining permissible and impermissible sexual relations as valid, still feel tempted to define prostitution as permissible and say: If a man wants to purchase the satisfaction of his natural desire, and if a woman offers herself voluntarily to him in exchange for money, who has the right to interfere in this transaction, why should society care about such a business arrangement from which it incurs no harm? And one could not deny that this viewpoint had a certain validity, if the matter were that simple.

But on the one hand, society does in fact care very much about prostitution, even in those countries where it seemingly does not, i.e., where prostitution is unregulated, where there is no system of control by the police; and it does so by treating the man who makes use of prostitutes with all the respect due an honorable man while kicking the woman who prostitutes herself into the mud, making her an outcast from society, although it lacks the authority to do so based on the principle of neutral non-interference. On the other hand, society also has the responsibility of caring very seriously about prostitution (though not in this most outrageously unjust manner), first because of its social and ethical significance and second because of its unhealthy effects on the population as a whole. Society must not overlook the spread of horribly contagious and hereditary diseases that poison the health of whole generations through and through.

Concerning the first point, our Pharisee-like morality has, to be sure, always contented itself with sighing and piously rolling its eyes, declaring prostitution to be a lamentable cultural-historical fact, a necessary evil. On the other hand, recognition of the responsibility to give serious attention to its implications for public health has become almost universally accepted. Yet the measures that have been implemented to protect society from the devastating effects of prostitution on the health of the human race are so fundamentally wrong, so incongruous, so immoral—in the fullest sense of the word—and perpetrate such a shameless violation of justice and personal freedom, that they must be characterized as thoroughly reprehensible.

These measures consist of an abominable system of tolerance with a despicable, dehumanizing brothel mandate; registration and surveillance of streetwalkers by the police and hunting down of the unregistered; compulsory mass medical examinations, during which the girls are treated like a herd of cattle; denunciations that are often motivated purely by maliciousness and personal animosity, in the course of which perfectly respectable girls, indeed, even virgins are often subjected to persecution by the "brothel control" and to insulting sanctions.

And this entire system of refined tortures, this monster of an imagination wallowing in orgies of degrading atrocities—is useless and futile, because it is based on the enslavement of woman, on her complete dependence on a man, making her a helpless and disenfranchised instrument for the satisfaction of his passions!

Yes, useless and futile, for it is a statistically proven fact that sexually transmitted diseases with all their most horrible side effects are continually on the rise, despite all corrective measures enacted against prostitution.

Clearly, the lamentable disaster that the control system has suffered in its attempt to wipe out or even to diminish these diseases, the disaster that occurs again and again, must originate in a flaw that is basic to the system's structure. And this very flaw is also clear—to everyone who does not deliberately close his eyes to it.

It consists in the half-measures and one-sidedness of the regulations, which extend only to disease carriers of the female sex, not to those of the male sex.

One does not really know whether to call these half-measures foolish or criminal. Are we stupid enough to believe that the spread of devastating diseases can be checked by allowing one infected party—the male—to keep on carrying the infection without interference, or is it deliberate malice that the heavy hand of the laws created to protect half of society are imposed only on the female—the prostitute—and that simultaneously the whole female sex and the whole younger generation of humankind are sacrificed to poisoning by the male!

It is high time for us to realize that the only kind of moral and health control by the police that one can rationally and legitimately justify must be one that extends to both sexes, and that, if state supervision is to achieve its goal of preventing infection, the men who patronize prostitutes must be subjected to a compulsory medical examination just the same as the prostituted women. If every man has to submit to a medical examination before he is allowed to enter a brothel, then the internment of prostitution in public buildings can be recognized as purposeful and justified. But as long as no attempt is made to eliminate both sources of infection, female and male, one must continue to condemn the control system that extends to only one sex as legal rape of women, which is as useless as it is unjust.

But even if prostitution were free from the danger of contagious diseases, it would still be an evil in the social organism, although not a necessary one, and not only as a moral, physical, and social degradation for women but also as an encouragement and continual incentive for the male to engage in sexual excesses that physically debilitate and morally corrupt him.

But prostitution is not an evil that can be eliminated, as has so often been tried, by drastic legislative measures directed against it. It is a disease of the social organism that has its origin in our social order and that will disappear by itself in a restructured society built on a foundation of social justice, in which hereditary capitalism is abolished and equality of the sexes is established.

Translated by Jeanette Clausen

Lily Braun

A Manifesto to Germany's Women *(1908)*

German women: we turn to you in the name of your children, in the name of those yet to come. You must join together in a mighty league for protection and resistance—a league without bylaws, because its bylaws are what you learn from life; and without members' dues, because your energy will be your dues.

An insidious poison threatens to destroy the body of our nation and menaces our children's flourishing bodies and pure souls. Born in misery, often without knowing their father, surrounded by distress, spoiled by bad example, neglected at home and in school, paid starvation wages for heavy labor, young and yet excluded from the happiness of youth, hungry for life and yet cheated by life—in this fashion thousands and many more thousands of our sex turn into whores. Whenever an investigation has been made, it turned out that the overwhelming proportion of prostitutes originated in the proletariat, so that it was poverty that compelled them to sell their bodies. Nor has the force of this coercive whip abated. Just in Berlin in the last twenty years the number of prostitutes has increased at twice the rate of the total population. The confines of our Reich capital contain from 50,000 to 60,000 "joy girls," as lewd cynicism is wont to call them, and in all large industrial centers the proportion is similar. Sticking to the heels of these unfortunate women are parasites of the basest and most exploitative kind: procurers and procuresses, pimps, landlords, innkeepers and—to round up more "consumers"—the makers and peddlers of pictorial and literary filth.

As soldiers and students, as workers, businessmen, and public officials, young males come into the city. Their sex draws them to the woman, just as it draws the woman to the man, and nature tells us that new blooming life is to grow out of the love of young men and women bursting with strength. But misery has defeated even Mother Nature and has contorted her noble face into a grimace. They are not allowed to choose the woman they love as the mother of their children, because maintaining a family costs money; to live with her "in style" costs many people a fortune, and they will have that only when their youth begins to wane. But those who have the money are taught by custom and are often admonished by their own fathers: enjoy your freedom, don't tie yourself down. They get to know the mystery of love in the filth of the street. The goddess thus desecrated takes fearful vengeance on them: venereal disease takes hold of their bodies. The daily number of incidents of venereal disease in Prussia is estimated to be 100,000. At least 80 percent of men in big cities have been ill with gonorrhea at one time or other in their lives, at least 20 percent with syphilis. The prematurely broken strength, the intellectual and physical feebleness of their sons, for the cause of which so many mothers search in vain—it is to be found right here. And here too is the cause of the life of suffering of countless of their daughters. They enter marriage, the hoped-for child does not come— almost half of all cases of barrenness are to be explained by venereal disease transferred from the man to the woman. The host of female ailments that destroy zest, energy, and family happiness is its consequence. With dreadful force, Jehovah's monstrous curse, which promises vengence for the fathers' sins into the third and fourth generation, is fulfilled: idiotic, blind, crippled, with a body that willingly grants entry to all sorts of disease germs—thus countless children of such marriages come into the world; those incapable of survival are still the luckiest among them.

In the face of this misery, it seems to us to be all women's most sacred duty as mothers to declare once again a crusade to liberate our children from it. But let us not act in the manner of lazy and short-sighted people who cover the filth and then tell themselves it is no longer there—no, we want to hunt it into its most hidden sources, even when in the end they lead us where the discovery hurts the most: to our own selves. Our children are well bred, well behaved, and obedient we tell ourselves for our own excuse. Was it not our up-bringing which broke their will, so that it would submit to ours, instead of steeling it so that it would remain stronger in the fight with evil? We have kept everything that is unclean from them, we argue once again. But would it not have been better to show it to them as it is, so that it might not later overwhelm them dressed up in the deceptive garb of enjoyment? And is it not our fault if our sons look for love in the gutter? Have we, after all, ever proclaimed to them the greatness and magnificence of love? Have we not ourselves dese-crated the wondrous growth of new life by offering our children lies and old wives' tales instead of the pure truth? But our guilt grows to even more menacing proportions when not only our own children's misery accuses us but also we become conscious of our responsibility in the face of all earthly wretchedness.

It is us the outlaws of our sex accuse. Why do we not fight for their right to life? Why do we not see to it that full wages for honest work be guaranteed to women as to men without abridgement? It is us the "fallen" men accuse. Why do we not, all of us, come to their side? Why do we all too frequently hinder them in that great struggle for better work conditions, which would make it possible for them to create and maintain the children of their love? It is us the children marked by disease and death and the vast number of those unborn accuse.

Not from the palaces of the princes, not from the green tables of the cabinet ministers do we expect and beg for help: from ourselves, and from you, mothers of the nation, we demand it. If you are united and if you are without fear—and when was a mother ever fearful where the life of her child was at stake?—then the words of princes and the wisdom of ministers will be blown away before your power as chaff before the wind. Come, the time is ripe, humanity is waiting for you.

Translated by Alfred G. Meyer

Hedwig Dohm

Three Doctors as Knights of the *Mater Dolorosa (1902)*

There is a group of physicians who oppose women's liberation on the basis of physiology. Knights of the sad countenance who cling to conditions of the past and still mistake the kitchen maid for a Dulcinea—for the flower of womanhood. The fact that it is primarily doctors who arm themselves for a crusade against the women's movement, who deliver its funeral oration in advance, is understandable. Hannibal *ante portas*. The practice of medicine is the first area of conquest upon which women has set foot.

The physicians surpass themselves in presenting an argument that rivals the dictum of the medieval church fathers. They declare point-blank: the one and only vocation of woman is the reproductive process.

That we women do not agree, that we resist with every fiber of our beings—though these fibers are sick through and through, according to the physicians—should not be held against us.

Let me interject here that attacking the medical profession as such is the farthest thing from my mind. There is no profession that I hold higher, that I find nobler than that of the physician, and I know not a few doctors who meet the most ideal standards. I am rebelling against only that category of doctors who see woman as nothing but an instrument to serve—the masters' purposes.

[. . .]

"The gynecologist," it says [in a pamphlet by the director of a women's clinic], "has the maximum opportunity to study the inner life of women."

I disagree. The gynecologist is consulted only for births and for diseases of the female sexual organs. He is thus, in contrast to the family doctor, a stranger to his female patients. I know any number of women who have had to consult a gynecologist and I can swear that not one of them has offered this stranger any information about her inner life, not has the gynecologist shown any inclination to be informed about it. Indeed, I denouce the gynecologists for giving far too much attention to the local—and only the local—disease, often omitting thereby the patient's overall health from consideration.

Obviously, there are exceptions. Even a gynecologist may have a gift for plumbing souls. It is possible that this gentleman [a famous Leipzig physician] is one of those exceptions. But let him ask his specialist colleagues about their female patients' inner lives. They will have something to say about the women's physical charms or lack thereof, but their psyches—let him ask them!

I knew an excellent gynecologist—he was also a handsome and imposing man—who, whether instinctively or by intellectual calculation, never looked his patients in the eye during a consultation; a practice that seems to me appropriate to the situation and that lends the interaction an impersonal tone. A woman has an instinctive need to remain distant from the gynecologist. Only when it absolutely cannot be avoided does she confide in one whom she knows or is closely related to.

[Another doctor], the director of the women's clinic admits that psychological studies of women encounter difficulties. First there is the "sexual instinct," which hampers neutral judgment, and second: "We men, if we have been well brought up, are used to judging women through the mask of gallantry."

A gallant gynecologist! dreadful! unthinkable! impossible!

In another passage, however, he states "that men, along with and in the guise of gallantry, are also brutal toward women. . . . To keep this brutality in check, society has, as we know, created a codex of sexual morality and imposed certain limitations of intercourse upon the female sex as a means of assuring female virtue, . . . I repeat, solely in woman's interest and for her protection."

A naive conclusion that he draws from male brutality! Because men are brutal, let us lock women up, so that men cannot hurt them! And on page twenty-four he repeats: "From what do we provide protection?" The answer is: "from the brutality of men."

Well, we would need no protection at all if men were not brutal. Would it not be possible to do away with male brutality?

The neuropathist takes the floor: "During puberty, the most important period for the female sex, a period when every harmful factor must be carefully eliminated, harsh reality must not inflict incurable injuries upon the sensitive organism. During this time the female should acquire an abstract secondary education." [. . .]

But, but, puberty for girls falls—as the doctors surely know—between the twelfth and sixteenth years of life. And during this time the girls sit in the often so poorly ventilated and shabby rooms of private girls' schools, while high school boys enjoy themselves in their spacious, well-ventilated rooms.

To tour a building, I once entered the low-ceilinged schoolrooms of one of the most elegant girls' schools in Berlin just as the children had left the room and the windows were not yet open. A gust of dreadful air greeted me. I thought back with real dismay on the fact that my daughters had to breathe air like that for so many years. But since this air exudes its noxious gases in girls' schools, does it inflict no incurable injuries on the sensitive organs? In my girlhood, I was taught in a seminar room that was so dark that the gas light had to burn all morning.

And would the air in secondary schools also be musty—does it have to be? A law of nature? Then it should be the responsiblity of physicians to work with architects, on improving the quality of air.

But what about that "abstract secondary education"!

It seems almost ludicrous to speak seriously about it. The knowledge that does not burst the brain of the most simple-minded boy will not cause a girl's brain to come apart at the seams either.

Good heavens, how miserable their own educations must have seemed to these doctors!

Because of their physical constitution, because of menstruation, pregnancy, birth and its consequences, women can and must not study medicine!

The two doctors' statements on menstruation agree almost word for word. They believe this process to be not only a local one, but ascribe to it a psychic influence on women, which they call nervous weakness. They claim that women's productivity is reduced during these days, their energy for tasks that lie outside their sexual sphere is diminished; in addition they are supposedly prone to local illnesses during menstruation.

Possibly there are illnesses that are caused by menstruation. I know of no single case.

I grew up with eight sisters, have four daughters, and have spent my life almost exclusively in the company of women.

My sisters and I had no idea, when we were young, that menstruation was a noteworthy event. No one told us that, no one asked about it. We went dancing during "those days" (which was surely not right), we took the longest walks. I do not remember any of us suffering from notable psychic or physical depression in so doing. Possibly there were minor deviations from normal well-being. But if those directly affected do not notice it themselves, or if in other cases only a slight measure of self-control is needed to overcome the depression, why make such a fuss about it!

Of course I know that there are numerous female individuals who suffer more or less during menstruation. Women with anemia are the largest contingent among these sufferers. However, we cannot base a social order on anemia or other physical abnormalities! Only the most nearly normal constitutions can be relevant here.

In their pamphlets, both doctors return repeatedly, and most energetically, to the protection of women.

Well, if they absolutely must be protected, why are they not protected now?

"Women are sick for six days each month," says the neuropathist, and in another passage: "Women are healthy only at intervals during a continual state of illness."

And the director of the women's clinic: "Shame forces women to secrecy about their sexual processes. In particular, the monthly menstrual period is concealed as carefully as possible, and all sorts of tricks are devised to eliminate the presence of this process altogether from their surroundings, that is to say, from the world of men."

But if shame forces her to conceal the process, nobody will know about it and who will protect her then, if nobody knows when protection is needed?

Is not this concealment very convenient to those responsible for protecting?

The menstruation argument is absolutely insupportable as long as all working women are not suspended from work while menstruating. Would the doctors be content with cold meals during their cooks' menstrual periods, or with a cuisine debased by depression? Would they not much rather exchange the cook who divulges the secret of her menstruation every month for a more discreet one?

[...]

Women's productivity is reduced, according to the doctors, to a much great extent during pregnancies, births, and their consequences than during menstruation.

For women who are fairly normal, the reproductive processes do not usually produce secondary illnesses. In addition, a great many of these illnesses can be traced to neglect of some kind and, among the proletariat, to lack of care and to the fact that women, with their aversion to being examined by male doctors, often seek medical advice too late.

The doctors refuse once and for all to believe in this aversion, which arises from shame. How do the gynecologists know that women are not filled with shame and anger when forced to consult a male doctor about sexual disorders? No woman is stupid and tactless enough to proclaim such feelings to the doctor. Indeed, shame itself forbids her to let shame show. They ascribe feelings of shame to women when it suits them, for example, in order to exclude them from medical science. They deny or condemn women's feeling of shame when it is inconvenient to them or contrary to their interests. [. . .]

The more intellectually developed, intelligent, and knowledgeable a woman is, the better she will understand how to protect herself and, especially, be able to protect herself. The problems of life deny the working-class woman this protection. Can it really be that fewer women of the proletariat come to the medical clinics with gynecological problems than do the women of the upper classes? Women who have given birth must leave the maternity hospitals nine days after the birth, often still too weak to nourish themselves and, in most cases, their child as well. Here is the source of so many infanticides!

Why do these doctors think the women of the upper classes are such fanatics for work that they will do their utmost to work themselves to death? And if these women really do want to work themselves to death, they must have the right to do so, and whether they do it in the dissecting room and the clinic or at the wash tub and in the factories amounts to the same thing.

No, it is not the same thing if a female physician *wants* to work herself to death or the working-class woman *must* work herself to death.

If even a female physician does not know how and when she must protect herself, well, self-murder cannot be done away with, but murder by society can.

This is an immense field where true welfare for women must be implemented. Why this petty grumbling that a few hundred German women should be prevented from studying medicine, while hundreds of thousands perish in the factories!

You physicians: help strengthen women's wretched physical nature! Discover, invent new ways and means, methods, preventive measures to reduce female sexual disorders, to strengthen the resistance of the poor invalids and infirm women, and to drive the woeful *mater dolorosa* more and more out of reality and into literature. But hurry! Women are close on your heels.

Much, much more than to doctors with their millions of iron pills that—in my experience—never yet cured a girl of anemia—the state of women's health is indebted to the stimuli (I mean stimuli) of a

Pastor Kneipp[1] and certain natural healing sanatoria, whose ideas and methods have made the doctors rich.

Women have prescribed the healthful blessing of the bicycle for themselves. The demise of the corset and the introduction of reform fashions (probably the clothing of the future) are the work of women who belong to the woman's movement.

The gynecologist does not want his explanations (that the sexual sphere is the true and only vocation of women) to be misunderstood to mean—oh no, not that!

For he writes: "The instinct for sexual union is by no means the focus of sexual experience in women; rather, it is the prelude to a whole series of sexual activities, among which the primary instinct is the desire for children."

Will we forever have our eyes fixed on this idealistically soulful desire for children as the focus of women's sexual experience? Has this manner of thinking permeated the flesh and blood of our society?

"Women cannot sin against nature without being punished," so says the gynecologist. But should she—through no fault of her own—find no legitimate partner to fulfill her desire for children and give nature her due illegitimately, then the punishment is meted out to her in reverse, for not sinning against nature. Society damns her, while not a hair of her male partner's head is harmed—the desire for children is not part of his vocation, not on your life!—although the door to the justice of the peace is always open to him, and he, bearing the opposite of a desire for children in his secret or perhaps not secret heart during those kinds of irregular unions, is only following sensory urges. Is that not extraordinary? Even highly extraordinary? [. . .]

When the antifeminists deny that women are capable of higher cultural achievements, they unanimously attribute it to female nature. They assume that the Lord God created woman with very specific vocational qualities, unalterable for all eternity. And the good Lord has contrived it so splendidly: all that she should and is allowed to do, that is her happiness, her one and only; and that which she should and must not do would be her undoing, were she to do it anyway. And if she fails to grasp this fact, it is simply—bad luck for her.

Every high school pupil today knows that, according to the law of adaptation through constant, continuing practice of certain activi-

---

1. Sebastian Kneipp (1821–79), a pastor who developed a holistic health treatment based on natural foods, exercise in the fresh air, and cold baths.—Trans.

ties, one acquires qualities corresponding to these activities, while abilities that are not exercised remain rudimentary.

It is a scientific fact that little animals that by some accident end up in dark caves and remain there through many generations lose their eyes. They lose them because they no longer need them.

One denies intellectual work to women, takes away their opportunity to exercise strength of will and action, and if the weaker specimens then—in the course of adapting—approach the ideal of a sheep, one cries triumphantly: "Behold—female nature!"

Translated by Jeanette Clausen

The Old Woman *(1903)*

I have often fought for women's rights, for the rights of girls, married women, and mothers. However, I have hardly ever mentioned the old woman. Now I want to talk about her. Like a shadow cast by creation, the poor old woman evokes displeasure in mankind. If, generally speaking, woman—at least until recently—is or has been the pariah of the human race, the old woman has been triply so, and still is today. [. . .]

For a long time now, it has often been said and deplored that the woman is only valued for her sex. But I want to emphasize this, because the contempt that is projected onto the old woman is grounded in this valuation. When a woman became unfit for giving birth, caring for children, and being a lover, her existence lost its justification. Whatever demands she might still want to make of society appeared more or less ridiculous; at best they were ignored by kinder and more gracious souls.

So the measure of a woman's value is her sexual attractiveness and usefulness! This is a bestial and naively shameless conception of her essence. It may have been appropriate in former times, but such a view mocks the development and refinement of present-day culture because it dehumanizes woman. Obviously, condemning this view need not mean rejecting the sensual and aesthetic pleasure we find in youth and beauty nor the joys of love.

Some states of being are tombs for the living: infirmity and incurable grief, for example. The extreme old age of a woman is also such a tomb; in her lifetime she is already laid to rest.

Poor old woman! Gradually, you are left completely alone. At first, your longing gaze follows those who abandon you: children, friends, society, all withdraw further and further—until they vanish. Loneliness surrounds you like a shroud, oblivion is the inscription above your house, hopelessness the lament of the raven above your bed. Silence surrounds you; and you are silent too, because no one wants to hear you. Poor old woman! You feel as if you ought to be ashamed because you, now grown so useless and already so old, are still alive. Old age weighs heavily on you like guilt, as if you were usurping a place that is others' just due. You sense around you a way of thinking that is hustling you out of life.

A famous artist once said (while I was posing for a painting and was already over forty years old) that women who have passed their fortieth year of life are a burden for society and would do best to join their forebears. The old barbarian custom of immediately getting rid of surplus female children right after their birth seems kinder to me, since newborns do not yet know the beauty of being alive and may thus be less sensitive to being expedited into the hereafter than those who are fully adult.

I have heard good and kind people say that old women are "hideous." I even heard this remark from the mouth of a young woman, who herself had a mother.

[. . .]

Old age destroys the beauty of one's figure and features. The effects of this destruction can be alleviated—and in most cases eliminated. Old women tend to neglect their appearance since they believe it does not matter how they look. They no longer matter. Who pays attention to them? That at least is the way they come to terms with the situation.

They are wrong.

I think old women should dress in white. I believe they have earned the right to this color, which is related to light. I would like to see them wearing something sacerdotal, sublime, and luminous. But not only an older symbolism but also aesthetic reasons speak for the white garb. Nobody should observe the rules of aesthetics more than the old woman. Meticulous cleanliness and care in personal hygiene and dress ought to be her rule. Personal hygiene includes all forms of preventive care, everything that preserves strength and flexibility and helps to avoid clumsiness and obesity.

One might object that an old woman holds herself up to ridicule when she does things that are not commensurate with her age. Things that *are* not commensurate or are not *considered* commensurate? This difference is important. That which is considered inappropriate is mostly based on custom and contemporary prejudice. The proof for this is that the very thing that is considered ridiculous for an old woman earns applause, often most lively applause, for a man of the same age. An old woman on ice-skates, on a bicycle, or on a horse: ridiculous; yet the eighty-year-old Moltke[1] on a horse was admired as a phenomenon; a white-bearded ice-skater is regarded only with benevolent looks.

[. . .]

Listen, old woman, to the word of another old woman: Resist! Have courage for life! Never think about your age for even a minute. So you are sixty years old. You can become seventy, eighty, or even ninety years old. Much younger people may go to the grave before you. To anticipate and have presentiments of death means to deny the present its due. Even if you live only one more day, you have a future before you. Life is a struggle, as everyone says. One fights against enemies and age is an enemy. Keep on fighting!

Do whatever brings you joy for as long as you have sufficient strength of mind and body. Especially since you do not have much time left, enjoy every minute to the full.

[. . .]

If you enjoy it and are strong enough, go biking, riding, swimming, traveling to discover new beauty and new worlds. A famous seventy-six-year-old English physician tells of taking long camel rides through the desert. Perhaps you can become as strong as this doctor and ride through the desert like him. Let your white hair—in case you have some and are comfortable with it—flow freely about your head. Mingle with those who study and learn. It seems almost ridiculous to me that you should be ashamed of longing for knowledge, as if dying were a delightfully serious business, and to hinder it indecent. A tree continues to live even after it has yielded all its fruit; it lives on, resplendent in the new beauty of its autumn foliage until it dies in the winter's frost.

I know a seventy-three-year-old woman who has started to learn Latin; of course, she takes the lessons in a remote pavilion of her park so that no eavesdropper may spot this outrage. And I know another woman who, when she recognized that she had begun to forget words and expressions for what she wanted to say, did not tolerate such weakening of her brain power. Just as a child practices

---

1. Helmuth von Moltke (1800–1891), chief of the Prussian and later of the German General Staff, who retired at the age of eighty-eight.—Eds.

learning to speak, she practiced not unlearning the language. She addressed herself in monologues and lectures; cleverly she tightened her grip on her slipping memory and partially replaced it by an exemplary routine. She kept a diary to account for her state of mind. And she was astonishingly successful.

Do you complain, old woman, that people no longer want anything to do with you? And if mortal—all-too-mortal—beings are no longer interested: there are higher things. Bathe your soul in the moonlight of the spirits. Are the living the only ones who bring joy? Don't forget fair and wild nature with her secrets and revelations. And the animals. They are not concerned about age and ugliness. They love you for your own sake, for what you are to them. Above all, there are the dead. With them one can often converse better than with the living. They live for us via their works, which hold inexhaustible mental and spiritual treasures. So, do not talk about loneliness. Constant activity, whether mental or physical, keeps body and mind functioning, just like oil in a machine. It assures mental longevity far beyond the years when these powers have customarily taken their leave. Inactivity is the soporific that they offer you, old woman. Do not take it! Be something. Creative activity is joy. And joy is close to youth. [. . .]

Translated by Patricia A. Herminghouse
and Magda Mueller

Anna Rueling

What Interest Does the Women's Movement Have in the Homosexual Question? *(1904)*

(Speech given at the annual conference of the Scientific Humanitarian Committee, October 8, 1904, Prinz Albrecht Hotel, Berlin)

The women's movement is necessary to the history of civilization. Homosexuality is a necessity in terms of natural history, representing the bridge, the natural and obvious link between men and women. This, now, is a scientific fact against which ignorance and intolerance struggle in vain. Nevertheless, some will ask why I mention the history of civilization and natural history in one breath, two fields which upon cursory examination seem to be diametrically opposed. There is a basis for this broader view.

In general, when homosexuality is discussed, one thinks only of the Uranian[1] men and overlooks the many homosexual women who exist and about whom much less is said because—I would almost like to say "unfortunately"—they don't have to fight an unjust penal code which resulted from false moral views. Women are not threatened with painful trials and imprisonment when they follow their inborn drive for love. But the mental stress that Uranian women endure is just as great, or greater, than the burden under which Uranian men suffer. To the world which bases its judgment on outward appearances, these women are much more obvious than even the most effeminate man. Only too often, misdirected morality exposes them to scorn and mockery.

[. . .]

Thanks to the poor education we provide for young girls, Uranian women often stumble blindly into marriage, without clear views and concepts of sexuality and sex life. As long as so-called "society" views spinsterhood as something unpleasant, even inferior, Uranian women will all too often allow outer circumstances to drive them into marriages in which they will neither give nor receive happiness. Aren't such marriages far more immoral than the love pact of two people who are drawn to each other by a powerful force?

The women's movement wants to reform marriage. It wants to bring about legal changes so that present conditions will cease to exist, so that discord and injustice, arbitrariness and slavish subjection will disappear from the family, so that future generations will be healthier and stronger.

In connection with these attempts to reform, the women's movement must not forget the degree to which absurd attitudes toward homosexual women are responsible for tragic marriages. I specifically say "the degree to which" because naturally I do not attribute total blame to those absurd attitudes. But because even part of the blame lies there, the women's movement cannot dismiss its responsibility for informing society by spoken and written word how pernicious it is to force homosexual women into marriage.

---

1. The term *Uranian* was first introduced in reference to male homosexuals by Karl Heinrich Ulrichs (1825–95) in his book *Mennon* (1867). It refers to Aphrodite Urania, patron goddess of men who love other men.—Eds.

[. . .]

Now, I personally want to reiterate a point frequently made by Dr. Hirschfeld,[2] and that is that homosexuals do not belong exclusively to any particular social class; that is, homosexuality does not occur more frequently in the upper class than the lower class, or vice versa. No father or mother—not even those among you—can safely assume that there is no Uranian child among his or her offspring. There is a strange belief prevalent in the middle class that homosexuality does not exist in their circles, and from this group comes the greatest opposition to Uranian liberation. I myself remember that once in my parents' home, when homosexuality became a topic of conversation, my father declared with conviction: "This sort of thing can't happen in my family!" The facts prove the opposite! Nothing else need be said!

To return to the marriage question, I would like to note that a homosexual woman almost never becomes what can be described as a "spinster." And this remarkable fact makes Uranian women more easily recognized, especially in their later years. If one looks at an unmarried homosexual woman between the age of thirty and fifty, none of the ridiculed characteristics attributed to the average single heterosexual woman can be found. This is interesting because it proves that sensible and moderate satisfaction of the sex drive also keeps women full of life, fresh and active, while absolute sexual abstinence easily causes those unpleasant qualities we find in the spinster, such as meanness, hysteria, irritability, etc.

In order to obtain for homosexuals and all women generally the opportunity to live according to their natures, it is necessary to actively aid the women's movement's efforts to expand educational opportunities and new professions for women. But what about the ancient argument of sexual superiority? I believe that with a little good will the dispute can be settled after examination of nature's intent in creating man and woman and the transitions between the two. One must conclude that it is wrong to value one sex more highly than the other—to speak of a first-class sex, man, a second-class sex, woman, and a third-class sex, the Uranian. The sexes are not of different value, they are merely of different kind. Because of this, it is clear that men, women, and Uranians are not equally suited for all professions. This is a fact the women's movement cannot change, nor does it want to.

---

2. Magnus Hirschfeld (1868–1933), founder of the Scientific-Humanitarian Committee in Berlin, which represented the interests of, and supported research on, homosexuals.—Eds.

[. . .]

Contrary to the belief of the anti-feminists that women are inferior and that only persons with strong masculine characteristics are to be valued, I believe that women in general are equal to men. I am convinced, however, that the homosexual woman is particularly capable of playing a leading role in the international women's rights movement for equality. And indeed, from the beginning of the women's movement until the present day, a significant number of homosexual women assumed the leadership in the numerous struggles and, through their energy, awakened the naturally indifferent and submissive average women to an awareness of their human dignity and rights. I am unable and unwilling to name names because as long as many consider homosexuality criminal and unnatural, at best sick, ladies I could call homosexual might feel insulted. Above all, decency and duty forbid indiscretion, and neither the noble love of a Uranian suffragette nor the feelings of a heterosexual need be aired in a public forum. But anyone with the slightest bit of familiarity with homosexual traits who has been following the women's movement at all or who knows any of its leading women personally or by pictures, will find the Uranians among the suffragettes and recognize that Uranians are often noble and fine.

Considering the contributions made to the women's movement by homosexual women for decades, it is amazing that the large and influential organizations of the movement have never lifted a finger to improve the civil rights and social standing of their numerous Uranian members. It is amazing that they have done nothing, absolutely nothing, to protect many of their best-known and most deserving leaders from ridicule and scorn by enlightening the general public about the true nature of Uranianism.

[. . .]

An important fact that has been completely ignored by the women's movement's struggle against the increase of prostitution and its destructive companion, venereal disease, is that 20 percent of all prostitutes are homosexual. At first this may seem odd because of the contradiction between homosexuality and constant sexual intercourse with the male. This situation has been explained to me more than once by a "girl of the streets" who told me that she considered her sad trade as business—completely divorced from her sexual drive, which was satisfied by her woman lover. Adverse domestic and economic conditions had driven these girls into the street.

When the women's movement succeeds in creating a situation in which occupations are open equally to all people according to their individual talents and capabilities, homosexual prostitutes would disappear, and a large percentage of the heterosexual girls who now turn to prostitution because of bad social conditions could support themselves better and with more human dignity.

[. . .]

Just as woman is battling to win back the ancient human right which was taken from her by raw force, the Uranians have an innate, natural right to their love, which is as noble and pure as heterosexual love when the persons involved are good. There are good people among homosexuals just as there are among the so-called "normals."

I want most of all to avoid the appearance of having overestimated the Uranians. I can assure you, ladies and gentlemen, that I have not. I recognize the faults and weaknesses of homosexuals too well, but I also know their good points and therefore can say: The Uranians are neither better nor worse than heterosexuals—they are not of different value, only of different kind.

In summary, I want to emphasize once more that the Uranian woman has played an important part in all aspects of our great women's movement. With her androgynous characteristics, she was often the one who initiated action because she felt most strongly the many, many injustices and hardships with which laws, society, and archaic customs treat women. Without the active support of the Uranian women, the women's movement would not be where it is today—this is an undisputable fact.

Translator unknown

Adele Schreiber

Unwed Mothers *(1912)*

Many great creative artists have transformed the profound cult of motherhood into works of art; religions have enshrined motherhood and its symbol as an object of worship; and fairy tales and legends tell of motherly love that conquers all and sacrifices everything. In present-day cultures, however, all this glorification contrasts with the reality of shameful neglect and disrespect for motherly love. Like so many party decorations and festive ornaments that are not needed on a daily basis, panegyrics for motherhood are stored up for special occasions, for impressive public speeches, and for the evocation of emotion and popularity. In everyday life, we see the mothers of the nation succumb to the triple burden of overexertion in work, indigence, and motherhood; we see pregnant women on the brink of poverty doing heavy work until the last possible minute and that same inseparable, cruel companion of the proletariat[1] dragging the woman in childbed from her bed and pushing her back out into the struggle to earn a living, regardless of her health and that of the newborn child. In our mind's eye, an endless line of coffins passes by, in which all too soon the victims of motherhood have found eternal rest, a rest which they were otherwise never granted. When the tired and work-worn hands of the mothers who bore children without complaint grow stiff[2]—hands that suffered so much in order to secure the bare minimum existence for husband and children—only then will the breakdown of the home and the desperate fate of the orphans show how important this wretched mother was.

But still all these who suffer so much at least have a home and are able to mother their children, so that in midst of all this impoverishment joy does blossom, like pathetic flowers that grow on barren, sandy earth, but flowers nonetheless! Besides these there is in Germany another group of mothers, not few in number and increasing in each decade by almost two million. The unjust and harsh morals of society mark them with an invisible stigma that sets them apart and forces them to lead a shadowy existence; humiliated and degraded they are supposed, contrary to all laws of nature, to be ashamed of their motherhood and to deny it.

Women who through narrow-minded pride in their virtue do not know this life and men, who know this life quite well and have no reason to be proud of their virtue, all feel entitled to call these mothers "fallen women" and to equate them with people who have committed a shameful deed.

Only in recent times has a drastic change begun to occur. In the endeavor to shed light upon the question of illegitimacy and its causes, social work, as well as psychological and sociological studies, have completely undermined the foundation for such obsolete points of view. Its imminent collapse will also mean the end of the errone-

---

1. Poverty.—Eds.
2. In death.—Eds.

ous idea that unwed mothers comprise a homogeneous group of despicable characters, who may be judged, or rather condemned, on the basis of their lack of legal standing. In place of such a comfortable generalization, which salves the conscience of society with the alleged guilt of the illegitimate mother, there is rather a duty to trace what has befallen all of them to its deepest roots. These traces will lead to a frank exposure of guilt in our society, to the recognition that the present-day manifestation of unwed motherhood as a mass phenomenon is merely a symptom of the economic and sexual hardship that is grounded in the flaws of a double moral standard, of the laws and organization of society.

There are no unitary explanations for the phenomenon of illegitimacy. It is determined by a multiplicity of elements that interact with one another in unique ways. [. . .]

Unwed mothers are as different as the conditions under which their motherhood came about. Those institutions that under the rubric "endangered and fallen women" admit a motley assortment of mothers from each category, such as degenerate women, criminal offenders, prostitutes, abandoned but morally sound unwed mothers, thereby offend against the highest principle of effective welfare services—individualization—and put many a young woman whose entire "guilt" consists of her motherhood into a dangerous as well as shameful position. Insofar as we are dealing with typical unwed mothers, it is not at all a matter of changing these women but of rectifying the conditions and the institutions that make their motherhood legally ambiguous and socially disadvantageous.

There exists no social class, no profession, and hardly any mental and psychological trait that I have not observed among unwed mothers in more than ten years of dealing with the problem on both a theoretical and a practical level. Besides the numerous cases that I personally followed over a shorter or longer period, I have also studied several thousand questionnaires; my conclusions are thus derived from a fairly large number of observations of the activities of private welfare associations.

[. . .]

Based on the social situation and educational level of those who seek help, about ten percent belong to the educated class: young women who have at least attended the *Höhere Töchterschule*[3] and have sometimes had further education. This can be traced to the economic shift that is bringing more and more daughters of the middle classes

---

3. Upper-level school for girls.—Eds.

into professions. Since such bourgeois jobs often require the woman to remain single, the female teacher, the female civil servant, often also the female private white collar worker, the female nurse, and so forth, are all not allowed to marry. At the same time, however, since marriage with an impoverished woman is only possible for most men if the woman works as well, a sexual crisis arises that results in numerous carefully concealed extramarital relationships. Every impediment to marriage promotes extramarital relationships; even officials should be able to understand something so obvious.

The obstacle to marriage presented by a woman's profession is also partly responsible for the fact that domestic servants have the highest percentage of unwed mothers. Many other circumstances also play a role. Domestic servants enter their jobs at a very young age and as unskilled workers. For the most part, they are torn away from their families and familiar surroundings; many come to the city from the country or from small towns. Their constant and close encounter with an affluent societal stratum that enjoys more pleasures in life prepares favorable grounds for the first seduction. Often, without guilt on the part of any one person, the ongoing reduction of the entire servant class casts its shadow, producing general dissatisfaction, mutual mistrust, and rapid changes of places of employment. No warmer relationship between employee and employer develops; the young women remain, partly with and partly without justification, permanent outsiders in the employer's household. In their free time they therefore look for companionship; in the cities, however, this very often proves to be their undoing. Inexperienced, gullible, and uprooted, these women comprise a not small proportion of the form of unwed motherhood that is least desirable, both in terms of the nature of the relationship that led to it and of its consequences for the mother. But especially in the situation of the domestic servants one can see how little the threat of their economic vulnerability is able to contain the strong sexual drive. Even though these women surely understand before they enter such relationships that they will almost always be dismissed if they become pregnant (often on the spot and with unjustifiable harshness), even though until now there has not been the least protection for them via legalized access to health insurance, and even though they know that, without a home, they face months of the greatest hardship, domestic servants—the largest cohort of unmarried women in the work force—always constitute the largest contingent of unwed mothers.

While in many cases female workers find support and help from members of their own class, the domestic servant is usually abandoned at the beginning of her visible pregnancy. It is therefore no wonder that among this class one can find the dark aspects of motherhood at their saddest: abortion with all its danger and serious consequences for the woman's health, the attempt to conceal her pregnancy until the last moment, a secret, lonely delivery, suicide, and infanticide. A mother in the servant class can rarely keep her child: the child's fate is to be put out to board, without a home to call its own, and very often without love. The mother, who is forced to separate as quickly as possible from her child, can often feel no motherly love for the little stranger who, rather than a bundle of joy is only a heavy burden for her. This is especially true when the father does not pay support and she has to use almost all her earnings for her child's boarding expenses. This unbearably heavy burden practically forces the mother to turn her back on honorable work altogether since, despite all of her efforts, she is unable to provide for both the child and herself. The situation becomes completely desperate if she is about to become a mother for a second time; most financial resources that were available the first time are now closed to her, and the woman thus basically faces the alternatives of ruin or dishonesty. [. . .]

There are also many more unwed mothers within the bourgeoisie than one usually suspects. For these unwed mothers, unlawful motherhood [sic] results in a complete upheaval of the life they had known. It produces intense conflicts that easily lead to deep depression and can result in suicide if the father of the child abandons the mother. This is the area where understanding personal intervention is most successful because the more educated women turn exclusively to organizations where they can expect the highest discretion and fullest human consideration and avoid all official institutions, including municipal or other authorities that offer help or information. They therefore do not show up in the statistics of such institutions, although they play a large role in the experience of private organizations that work autonomously and do not smack of religion. These women account for about one tenth of all unwed mothers. They shy away from any encounter with representatives of bureaucratic pettiness and moral indignation and avoid every request for inquiries and certificates, official letters, and so on, which could jeopardize their reputation. Even in the case of nonjudgmental organizations in midsized and even in larger cities, they are concerned that, due to the intricacies of private connections, their secret might not be secure; they therefore seek out the largest cities, most preferably Berlin. [. . .]

Thus, all these mothers are as different from one another as the circumstances and the psychological factors that have shaped them: intellectual impoverishment, emotional and intellectual deficiencies, lack of experience, gullibility, youthful hot-bloodedness, loneliness and lack of a home to call their own, longing for human comfort, loss of faith, a passionate self-surrendering love deceived or wounded by the insurmountable adversity of fate, profound motherly longing that deliberately sought and found fulfillment—all of these factors play a role and need to be understood. Then we would no longer have to fight constantly against parental severity, the indignation of the virtuous employer, and the pharisaic, self-righteous lack of compassion in society. Then at last the wandering about without a home to call one's own, the flight to the city in order to disappear in the masses, fear of the child to come, the worry that suffocates every emotion of motherhood—all of these would end, and the voices that in dark hours give desperate women the idea of killing themselves and the germs of a new life within them would cease. We of a newly enlightened age must make reparation for so much unexpiated human guilt. Walls of prejudice, of unkindness, and of spitefulness have to be torn down. Who will help us?

Translated by Patricia A. Herminghouse
and Magda Mueller

Helene Stöcker

Marriage and Sexual Reform *(1916)*

[. . .] Our modern movement has created two positive concepts and introduced them into public consciousness: "The New Ethics" signifies adherence to a morality of personal responsibility and the refinement of individualization in the area of sexuality. "Protection of motherhood" encompasses the essence of all work and care for mother and child, for improvement of the race, for the coming generation, as a consequence of our new recognition of responsibility.

The responsible personality, man or woman, is the focal point of our new ethics; this personality should also become the focal point of modern law. Even if this principle of self-responsibility is acknowledged in other areas today, this acknowledgment is still missing in the area of sexual morality. It is particularly difficult to create a new sexual ethic, because here, even more so than in other areas, darkness and superstition, hunger for power, and tradition reign.

Professor Freud, to whose demands with regard to the destruction of superstition in sexual questions we owe so much, declares that we do not yet know nearly enough about the biological processes of which sexual life consists: our individual insights are not sufficient to propose a theory that would explain both the normal and the pathological. The fateful dualism of our sexual life, which was perhaps necessary in a certain phase of human development, should now gradually yield to a purified monism, a unity of body and soul.

Our entire modern development is nothing but the struggle against this old dualism, which even Luther's fearlessness in sexual questions could not overcome. Not until the end of the eighteenth and beginning of the nineteenth century did modern art and philosophy bring about the refinement of sexual life. Above all Goethe, the Romantics, and Nietzsche should be mentioned here. The main ideas that modern love owes to Romanticism are those regarding the unity of spiritual and physical aspects in love, the equality of man and woman, the significance of personality in love, as well as the recognition of the consequent possibility to err.

In the great history of love's evolution from naked physical desire to wonderfully harmonious union of all physical and spiritual human powers, the Romantic era a hundred years ago is the period in which we became conscious of love as the highest blossoming of culture. Thus love begins to turn into that power of individual choice and thus the personality of lover and beloved first comes fully into its own.

[. . .]

While similar cultural revolutions then took place in all European countries, we in Germany were blessed with the continuation and fulfillment of Romantic longing in Friedrich Nietzsche. His grave demand is to understand, as far as possible, sexual life as holy; to him the institution of marriage in its contemporary form seems *not at all to further* his supreme goal: refinement and improvement of the race. Next to the commandment "Thou shalt not kill" there stands, in his opinion, the far graver prohibition of decadence: *"You shall not procreate."* Again and again, he stressed responsibility as the most genuine mark of morality.

Our current work for protection of motherhood and for sexual reform is embedded in this cultural context. For one thing, our modern ideal of the harmoniously developed personality demands a completely different attitude towards life and love. Like work, love plays a greater role for modern human beings than ever before, precisely because we see the goal of our striving in the cultivation of personality, no longer in the state, as in antiquity, no longer in the hereafter, as in Christian religion. We no longer see our highest good in "God," but in the *human being,* whom we want to move closer to his own highest ideals, his "gods." Thus love, as the complementary relation between equal personalities, has become the crown of life. This new understanding of sexuality and of love in its highest sense has now also completely changed our attitude toward marriage as a legal institution. In our moral judgments, we place realities of the soul over merely formal-legal realities. So if we assign less value to the *forms* of marriage today, it is because the inner obligations that arise from shared life seem so deeply rooted and indestructible to us, that in contrast to this *inner duty,* external compulsion seems relatively unimportant to us. We modern sexual reformers also believe in the "eternalness" of marriage—not because external laws have forced it on people, but because marriage has sprung from the innermost need of human nature, the need of the individual as well as the need of the community. On the basis of our principles, we will not deny our cooperation to any initiatives—whatever their origin—to reform existing marriage legislation and to improve social and economic conditions. But in other quarters people should also no longer close their minds to the insight that with maternity protection, we do not want to bring licentiousness, but personal as well as legal responsibility *into* relationships that today are outside of the laws.

A new factor has emerged today, one which had not yet existed in earlier times and which to a high degree carries within it the possibility of realizing our ideas, as even the more discerning of our opponents recognize: today, the intellectual emancipation of women is joined by economic, legal, and finally also political emancipation. The recognition is also dawning that society as such has the right and the duty to provide for the thriving of the new generation. Thus in regard to influencing legislation we strive to make the economic burden of providing for a new generation more and more into a concern of the generality, through protection of expectant and new mothers, protection of growing children and benefits for children, through general access to education and so forth. We also strive to give women a share in the processes of production, as is already the case for almost ten million women today. On this basis, our demands are internally consistent—even our opponents admit that. When it comes to marriage, it is necessary, as Friedrich Naumann[1] once stressed very correctly, to differentiate between the essential, "eternal" elements and transitory forms. Even an economically free woman will not want to do without the essential, eternal tasks of marriage. An "abolition" of marriage, i.e., of the life companionship of father, mother, and children, as some opponents still insinuate is our goal, could only be "decreed" by a Don Quixote. It is a little hard on any historically and psychologically semi-educated person to even be expected to defend oneself against such nonsense.

Translated by Jörg Esleben

---

1. Friedrich Naumann (1860–1919), leading left-liberal politician in Wilhelminian Germany.—Eds.

Käthe Kollwitz

Against Paragraph 218 *(1924)*

Käthe Kollwitz: Poster against Paragraph 218 [Law criminalizing abortion], Lithograph, 1924. © VG Bild-Kunst, Bonn. Courtesy of Käthe Kollwitz Museum Köln, sponsored by Kreissparkasse Köln.

Alice Schwarzer

How It All Began:
"I Have Had an Abortion"[1] *(1981)*

"Historically, privileged people have never freely given up their rights. That's why we demand: Women must become a power factor in the battle to be waged! Women must organize, because they must recognize their most basic problems and learn to represent their interests." Applause from the majority. Boos from some. It was late afternoon already when these now-historic utterances resounded over the microphone. Sentences with which—fifty years after the death of the first German Women's Movement—the second German Women's Movement was born. Location: the Youth Hostel in Frankfurt on the banks of the Main River. Midwives [to this development]: about 450 women from forty groups from the entire Federal Republic gathered here for the first Federal Women's Congress.

There were stormy months preceding these statements. And had someone prophesied to these 450 women a year previously that they would be participating in the rebirth of feminism—most among them would have shaken their heads in disbelief. For at that time the concept of feminism was a pejorative term—especially among the ranks of politicized women. After the first protest in the wake of the 1968 Protest Movement, the beginning of the 1970s seemed to have a deadly calm in terms of women.

In search of a photogenic Women's Lib at home, the magazine *Brigitte* complained coquettishly as late as Spring of 1971: "German women do not burn bras and wedding dresses, do not storm any beauty contests and anti-emancipation editorial boards, do not advocate getting rid of marriage, and do not compose manifestos for eradicating men. There are no witches, daughters of Lilith, like in the United States not even Dolle Minnas with a sense of humor like in Holland, there are no aggressive magazines. No anger."

Well, there was anger. More than *Brigitte* and company liked. It was quickly directed toward the abortion law and the dictates of

---

1. This retrospective account of the famous events of 1971 appeared in the German feminist magazine *Emma,* edited by Alice Schwarzer, who is presumably the author of this piece.—Eds.

femininity. The catalyst was the antiabortion law (Paragraph 218). The background for it was the increasing infamy and schizophrenia of women's new role. At that time, the much-propagated double burden was beginning to peak: Hold down a job on the side and at the same time be the perfect housewife, good mother, smooth lover—that was the new ideal that we were to attain. Only the spark was missing from the powder keg—but who was going to ignite it?

[. . .]

In April of 1971, 343 French women declared openly: "We have had an abortion and we demand the right to free abortions for every woman." The action was initiated by the Paris Women's Movement, the MLF. The Left Newspaper *Le nouvel Observateur* had published their appeal. It was by chance that the movement spread so rapidly to neighboring Germany. Alice Schwarzer, at that time correspondent in Paris and herself active in the MLF, transported the idea to her German sisters. Determined to keep the feminist impetus of the action, she looked for comparable Women's groups and, on the other hand, for an avenue for publication.

Stern,[2] which had recognized the dramatic aspect of the action, agreed. Thus we had the ticklish, but ultimately successful short mésalliance between the Hamburg men's magazine and the women's project. The women had their forum and the *Stern* its scandal. If *Stern* had actually known whom it was helping, it would surely have kept its hands off the whole thing.

The next step was to find women who would participate. Since it soon became clear that there was no women's group like the Parisian one, which could carry the project centrally, Alice pounded on a lot of doors—including those of SPD, DKP[3] and trade union women, but all refused. Argument: "Such a project would only harm us—it doesn't sound serious." Or, "It would only shock the grass roots." However, from the total of four women's groups remaining, three were prepared to go along with it: (1) the "Frauenaktion 70" in Frankfurt—it had arisen out of the Humanistic Union, consisted of largely middle class working women, and had already taken to the streets with the slogan "My belly belongs to me." (2) The Socialist Women's Federation in Berlin, and (3) The "Red Women" of Munich. Piqued, the student-dominated "Weiberrat" [Women's council] of Frankfurt rejected the project, finding it unpolitical and reformist. On that Friday in May, on which Alice submitted the plan to the

---

2. *Stern*, liberal German weekly illustrated.—Eds.
3. SPD and DKP, German Socialist and German Communist Parties.—Eds.

"Red Women," the group split spontaneously. One part stuck to its doctrine; the others jumped at the chance: "We were delighted to be able to do something for once."

Feverish activities began. The three women's groups gathered about half of the 374 signatures in less than a month, and the rest snowballed in. One woman told another, friends, colleagues, neighbors decided together. The courage of these women was enormous. No one can imagine today what it meant to admit to an abortion at all, much less to make a public confession. Thanks to this campaign, the topic of abortion has, to be sure, not yet been solved, but has largely lost its taboo. At that time it was simply a monstrosity, which you didn't admit even to your best friend. . . . Contrary to later propaganda, most of the 374 women were anything but of the privileged class. Among the first 374 only nine were actresses. The rest were secretaries, housewives (a *lot* of housewives), students, workers, white-collar women. The oldest was seventy-seven, the youngest twenty-one.

The campaign was daring on all levels: daring in its collaboration with *Stern* and in the personal risk for each woman. But precisely this risk, the resoluteness of the women not to follow the rules which weren't theirs, and the demonstration of their solidarity constituted the action's immense effect. On July 6, 1971, the open confession of the 374 broke the plot of silence. Millions of copies of *Stern* were at the newsstands, with names and faces of well-known and unknown women who declared in common: "We've had an abortion. We don't demand alms from lawmakers and reform in portions! We demand the cancellation of Paragraph 218 and no substitute laws!"

[. . .]

But really revolutionary was the demand to abolish Paragraph 218 via the demand attached to it that the woman determine her own destiny! These first weeks and months after June 6 were exciting and radicalizing for all who took part. Ute Geissler: "When I signed the document I was very afraid. And then, when this police raid took place a few months later, it became clear that we wouldn't allow ourselves to be intimidated any more." The police actions "by night and fog," like those in Munich where a raid took place, no longer weakened the campaign, but rather strengthened it, brought a wave of sympathy to it, and—a further wave of women seeking help. Thus the women of Project 218 were initially alone—with the thousands of women who needed counselling and abortions. The only way out was to break the law in their own country or travel abroad. The first contacts with foreign countries were made. In November 1971, women took to the street in almost all Western countries for the right to abortion and self-determination of women. In Paris alone, over 4,000 demonstrated.

Translated by Naomi Stephan

The Function of Sexuality in the Oppression of Women *(1975)*

Almost always (in these past years) when I have tried to speak with men about emancipation—quite apart from whether they were friends or colleagues, on the left or the right—these talks would end up with that one "slight difference." Emancipation was all well and good, but that slight difference—we didn't want to get rid of that, too, did we?

Oh no! We would never dare. Most definitely not! There would always be the eternal *petite difference,* of course. Right? And the more progressive the circles in which it was debated, the smaller the difference was—except the consequences remained equally great.

It is time, therefore, to ask ourselves finally what this oft-quoted slight difference consists of and whether it justifies making "people" into "men" and "women" instead of just letting them be "people." You don't have to look far in this potency-crazed society for said difference.

Actually, it's not very big. In a state of rest, the experts assure us, it's three to three and one-half inches; aroused, another two to three inches.

And in this nubbin resides manhood, the magical power to make women lustful and to rule the world? The nubbin-wearers, at least, seem to be convinced of it. I think it's nothing more than a pretext. Not this *biological* difference, but its *ideological* consequences must be categorically eliminated. Biology is not destiny. Masculinity and femininity are not nature but culture. In every generation they represent a renewed, forced identification with dominance and subjection. Penises and vaginas don't make us men and women, but power and powerlessness do.

The ideology of the two halves that supposedly complement each other so well has crippled us and created a rift which is seemingly impossible to overcome. Men and women feel differently, think differently, move differently, live differently. Everyone knows only too well how the stigma of masculinity or of femininity branded on our foreheads confines and defines us. Nothing, neither race nor class, determines human life to the extent that gender does. Here women and men are both victims of their roles—but women are still victims of victims.

The fear, dependence, distrust, and powerlessness experienced by women are enormous. [. . .] The closer we look, the deeper the rift between the sexes. Only those who dare to bridge this gap will—one distant day—be able to overcome it. Only those who admit existing conditions will be able to make changes. In the long run, both sexes stand to gain; in the short run, women stand to lose their chains and men their privileges.

All who speak of equality—in the face of the inequality between the sexes—are compounding their guilt daily. They are not interested in humanizing men and women but rather in maintaining prevailing conditions, from which they themselves profit. The exploitation of women has not diminished in recent decades but has rather become more acute. Women work more than ever before. Only the forms of this exploitation have sometimes become more subtle, more difficult to detect. What is officially understood by the word *emancipation* often means nothing more than that women who were slaves have now become free slaves.

[. . .]

Vaginal Orgasm and Sex Monopoly

What can we say in favor of penetration? Nothing for women, a lot for men. Coitus, which damns women to passivity, is for men the most uncomplicated and comfortable way of practicing sex: They don't have to communicate with women, don't have to stimulate them mentally or physically—passive compliance is enough.

You really can't underestimate the psychological implications for men of this violent act of invasion. *Screwing,* as it is so aptly called in everyday language, is the highest demonstration of male potency! Besides, for many men power is pleasure and that's why penetration is perhaps the most erotic stimulation for them today. (That women, on the other hand, have become largely unable to experience sex as satisfying because of their oppression and the perversion of relations between the sexes, seems to me to be an indication of their physical integrity. They are evidently not prepared for the perverse separation of physical and mental communication which male society openly practices.)

But that alone does not entirely explain the absolute compulsion for sexual norms which are contrary to the needs of one half of humanity (the female half) and which bring with them the enormous burden of contraception. Imagine: The horror of unwanted pregnancies and abortions, the attendant side effects of the pill, and inflammations caused by the diaphragm—all of this—would become superfluous with one blow if women were allowed to experience their sexuality in accordance with their natural needs. Heterosexual penetration would no longer be a form of making love but would be reserved for procreation. Unwanted pregnancies would no longer be possible.

But neither the misery of abortion nor female frigidity was able to shake the dogma of the vaginal orgasm. The reasons for this have to be momentous. My theory: Only the myth of the vaginal orgasm (and of the importance of penetration) insures sexual monopoly of men over women, which, in turn, is the foundation of the public monopoly of male society over women.

In other words: in this society, people are lonely without a love relationship in which they must buy affection and tenderness with sex; thus, women, like men, must resort to sexual relationships. If this sexuality is only possible under the guise of that certain "difference," if heterosexuality is given absolute priority, then women and men must turn to each other. The monopoly is therefore reversible, it would seem. But only apparently. A man without a woman in our society is still a man, but a woman without a man is not a woman. [. . .]

A woman has no existence as an autonomous being—only in relation to a man. Her definition is that of a sexual being. Every attempt at emancipation must come to a dead end sooner or later, as long as every woman is individually subject to a man on a private level. And as long as she has no alternative, she cannot choose her relationships freely.

That's the important point: the sexual monopoly of men over women ensures their emotional monopoly (women fall in love only with men, of course), their social monopoly (for social recognition women must depend on marriage or a relationship with a man), and their economic monopoly (women accept gratis work in the home and "additional income" jobs out of love for men).

Thus only the destruction of the male sexual monopoly from the foundation up will cause gender roles to collapse.

Why Compulsory Heterosexuality Is So Political

Categories like heterosexuality and homosexuality are cultural in nature and cannot be justified on a biological basis. The prevailing heterosexuality is a culturally induced, forced heterosexuality. Just how insupportable the concept of a "natural" heterosexuality is was illustrated by [Alfred] Kinsey in his report on *Sexual Behavior of Women*. [. . .]

In a culture in which procreation is not the primary impulse for human sexuality, homosexuality as well as heterosexuality and a sexuality with one's self would have to be taken for granted as part of the free development of the individual.

There are political reasons for why things are not that way. The only way the male sexual monopoly can be ensured is through a heterosexuality that is elevated to the status of dogma. Its pretext is that "little difference."

[. . .]

In her militant book, *The Dialectic of Sex,* Shulamith Firestone places the question of sexuality in relation to the question of class:

> Just as the end goal of socialist revolution was not only the elimination of the economic class *privilege* but of the economic class *distinction* itself, so the end goal of feminist revolution must be . . . not just the elimination of male *privilege* but of the sex *distinction* itself. (11)

Because this way of thinking regularly elicits fears of castration and hysterical reactions in males and because it is not a common perspective, I want to explain it in my own words once again:

What this means is that people are first and foremost people and only secondarily female and male. Gender would no longer be destiny. Women and men would not be forced into role behavior, and the masculine mystique would be as superfluous as the femininity complex. Sex-specific divisions of labor and exploitation would be suspended. Only biological motherhood would be woman's affair; social motherhood [the rearing of children] would be men's affair just as much as women's. [. . .] People would communicate with one another in unlimited ways, sexually and otherwise, according to their individual needs at any given time and regardless of age, race, and gender. (There would be no class system in this liberated society.) A utopia for tomorrow, but also goals and perspectives which we cannot lose sight of today. From now on, these things must determine what we do.

Translated by Naomi Stephan

Marielouise Janssen-Jurreit

The Future of Feminism *(1976)*

Those who want to reform society in small steps proceed on the utopian assumption that women have only to build their own organizations in order to dissolve them at some future time, when the policy of small steps has led to equality. Most of the women's organizations that have been formed within political parties, unions, and other associations regard it as their goal to make themselves superfluous. Their declared end is to integrate women into the main organization, which—for now, as they claim—is dominated by men. Under the illusion of this idea of integration they perpetuate themselves as organizations of female vassals without influence, which do not come closer to the goal they strive for. These women's organizations are mistaken in two respects. They fail to recognize the immanent character of our institutions as male clubs. State, economy, political parties, the press, and universities are not gender-neutral institutions, but instead one of their essential functions lies in incessantly producing male identity and enabling it to prove itself.

In primitive societies, the man protects his sphere of identity by setting up taboos. Should a woman learn the cultic secrets of the men's house, she would be threatened by the death penalty.

In our systems institutions are somewhat more flexible. Some women are integrated. This gives their rulers an alibi. The remark by the president of the Bavarian parliament, Michael Horlacher, that a single woman in parliament has the effect of a flower, but masses of women that of weeds, is a good illustration of this point. Headlines like "Poppies in the Wheat-Field," "Specks of Color in the Parliamentary Grey" signify the nature of this form of integration. Statistically, there is no evidence of a trend that women are advancing into the centers of decision-making in greater numbers. In the eighteenth century there were more ruling women than today. Women who are integrated into the system can, frequently enough, only survive in the institutions through acts of mimicry. Rarely can they be representatives of women's interests. In a study of female employees, Helge

Pross found some years ago that most women on the job feel like guest workers in a man's world.[1]

A further factor in favor of independent women's organizations consists of the obvious point that in political parties and other large organizations, the sexes in principle remain separate. In the political parties women do the same thing as they do in autonomous women's groups: they associate according to gender, but submit to male supervision and control. Nowhere has integration really taken place; instead, groups are formed within the parties and organizations corresponding to the same anthropological characteristics that structure communal life in primitive societies, namely the association of males (the umbrella party), youth, and women. Moreover, most of the youth organizations are young men's associations that decorate themselves with a few women.

The admission of women into parties and unions was agreed to gradually by the male members at the beginning of this century, when it became clear that they would not disturb the male sphere of identity by their membership, but rather built female caucuses everywhere. This behavior can be observed around the world. Independence movements, national unified parties, socialist and bourgeois parties, unions, churches—they all have their own female ghettos by now. Most of these are organizationally, financially, and ideologically dependent on the male-dominated "umbrella organization" controlling them and have to get all of their own initiatives authorized by it.

Anyone who wants to integrate women into parties, unions, and associations always makes them into objects of integration. Acceptance into the existing social institutions that exercise power and make decisions always takes place under conditions that the object of integration cannot determine herself.

Feminist self-organization demands separation or at least distancing from the institutions that base themselves on similar political positions, like unions and socialist parties in the Western countries. Since feminism strives for fundamentally different psychological, sexual, and economic relations between men and women, in which there are no more privileges whatsoever, the precondition for this struggle is a separate organization of women, or at least one that is able to act on its own initiative. (Only when the women's organiza-

---

1. Helge Pross (1927–), a German sociologist, published many studies of the work lives of housewives and employees, including a 1973 empirical study of 7,000 European working women.—Eds.

tions of the established parties, unions, and large associations manage to create their own spaces for organizing and setting political goals can they play an important role in the women's struggle.) Feminism is directed against the patriarchal character of all existing institutions, without exceptions. Feminist and socialist organizations can build coalitions in order to achieve common goals, but on the basis of reciprocity, not of the one-sided co-optation of women for goals that profit them little or not at all. Women—as the oppressed of the oppressed—are not fighting a minor contradiction of capitalism, but a general social contradiction, patriarchy.

An essential task for autonomous women's groups consists in taking stock of the female situation, of the dependence, fears, and desires of women, in order to enable and form a self-confident own identity. One essential consciousness-building goal of feminism is to integrate the history of women into their self-image and their identity. Only through historical comparisons can women arrive at an understanding of their situation today. It is not a question of glorifying the individual deeds of women in history or evaluating women uncritically. The goal of eliminating their historical deficit is not to add a history of great women to the history of great men, but to correct historical research in terms of the questions it asks and in its conceptions of importance and rank.

Translated by Jörg Esleben

Silvia Bovenschen

The Contemporary Witch, the Historical Witch, and the Witch Myth: The Witch, Subject of the Appropriation of Nature and Object of the Domination of Nature *(1978)*

The topic of "witches" has become fashionable, has indeed already acquired a fatal glamour. It has even achieved scholarly legitimacy.

The fact that researchers are once again concerned with the historical phenomenon of witch persecution is by no means the origin of the lively interest in the subject today: that would be the vain assumption of ivory tower scholars, researchers who, imagining their scholarship to be autonomous, have failed to notice that they are merely the rear guard of a movement.

In a demonstration against the Italian abortion laws in Rome, 100,000 women shouted, "La Gioia, la gioia, la si inventa, donne si nasce, le streghe si diventa!"[1] and "Tremate, tremate, le streghe son tornate!"[2]

Is the image of the witch a wish projection resulting from unrealized female potential? Are witches for feminism what Spartacus, the rebellious peasants, the French revolutionaries and the Bolsheviks are for the Socialists? During the protest against a trial in Itzehoe, Germany, which was sensationally blown up by the press because the accused women were having a lesbian relationship—and the sentence was an unusually severe one—women called the proceedings a witch hunt. In many feminist demonstrations the participants dress up as witches. Women's bars have names such as *Blocksberg*,[3] books have titles such as *Hexengeflüster* (Witches' Whispering), a women's rock band proclaims the return of the witch . . . the rumor spreads and an image crystallizes. But apparently without the explicit intention of constructing, *a posteriori,* the revolutionary, historical continuity of feminism. The assimilation of the witch into feminist visual and linguistic parlance happened spontaneously, not as the result of a plan. The revival of the word, the image, the motif doubtless has something to do with the new women's movement (although in the old movement it hardly played a role), but not in the sense that learned women turned thoughtfully and scientifically to feminist historical archaeology, dug through several layers of history and finally discovered in the witch pogroms of the late Middle Ages proof of the oppression of women (there is, after all, enough oppression in the present). It was not the flood of theoretical historical works which initiated the frequent and exemplary use of the word and image and brought about the astonishing renaissance of the witch.

The empirical witches of today—those women who apply this term to themselves—have, at first glance, little in common with the historical witches who were burned at the stake. Until recently they did not even have a clear picture of witches' existence in the past (there was usually nothing about them mentioned in school). Since it

---

1. "Joy, joy, joy, is invented, born as a woman, made into a witch!"—Trans.
2. "Tremble, tremble, the witches have returned!"—Trans.
3. Site of witches' rites.—Trans.

cannot be assumed that those 100,000 women in Rome who threateningly shouted the word "witch" had appropriated that almost inaccessible historical knowledge, there must be a more direct preconceptual relationship—possibly in connection with a diffuse historical idea—between the word on the one hand and the personal experiences of today's women on the other.

[. . .]

Up until recently the word witch did not have a pleasant ring to it. It evoked childhood fears—we often called old teachers whom we could not stand and whom we feared by that name. The word "witch" experienced the same transformation as the word "queer" or "proletarian": it was adopted by the person affected and used against the enemy who had introduced it. At this point, if not before, it became apparent to women that, by labelling other women "witches" (the term "bluestocking" has a similar function), they were doing the same thing as the assimilated homosexual who fingers a "pansy" in the hope that the pressure would be on the other rather than on himself. Thus, we wanted to use the expression to turn attention away from ourselves, towards others. Sartre tells a story about the young Genet who once stole something. People said, "He is a thief," and he then became a thief. In the case of Genet it was an individual act. But to the extent that women have appropriated the frightening apparition and collectively taken over the myth, the individual is freed from it.

The fact that women are dressing up as witches for their demonstrations and festivals also points to this mimetic approach to their own personal history through the medium of mythological suggestion. They are, to a certain extent, practicing witchcraft. The antifeminist metaphysics of sex kept conjuring up the magical demonic potential of femininity until this potential finally turned against it. Magic approaches reality via images, visions; "Like science, magic pursues aims, but seeks to achieve them by mimesis—not by progressively distancing itself from the object."[4] The mimetic moment in the demonstrations exemplifies on the one hand a critique of and ironic approach to the male mystification of the female, and on the other, a relationship to history and nature which actually is unique. *In the image of the witch, elements of the past and of myth oscillate, but along with them, elements of a real and present dilemma as well. In the surviving myth, nature and fleeting history are preserved.* In turn-

---

4. M. Horkheimer and T. W. Adorno, *Dialectic of Enlightenment.* New York: Continuum, 1972, 11.—Trans.

ing to an historical image, women do not address the historical phenomenon but rather its symbolic potential:

> Thus utopian function very often has a double profundity, that of submersion in the midst of that of hope. Which can only mean that the groundwork for hope is partly done in the archaic frame here. More precisely, in those archetypes which still arouse consternation and which have possibly been left over from the age of a mythical consciousness as categories of the imagination, consequently with a non-mythical surplus that has not been worked up.[5]

The fantastic qualities of imagination go far beyond what theoretical discourse, hostile towards images as it is, can transmit.

> Fantasy is cognitive . . . in so far as it protects, against all reason, the aspirations for the integral fulfillment of man and nature which are repressed by reason. In the realm of fantasy, the unresonable archetypal images of freedom became rational.[6]

To elevate the historical witch *post festum* to an archetypical image of female freedom and vigor would be cynical, considering the magnitude of her unimaginable suffering. On the other hand, the revival of the witch's image today makes possible a resistance which was denied to historical witches.

This moment of resistance is, however, contemporary and political. It is not based in mythology even though it occasionally makes use of mythological imagery. However, I find the reference to myth dangerous when it is used as proof of the eternal recurrence of the same, thereby obscuring the difference between myth, history, and reality. [. . .]

Translated by Jeannine Blackwell,
Johanna Moore, and Beth Weckmueller

---

5. Ernst Bloch. *The Principle of Hope.* I, Oxford, 1986, 159.—Trans.
6. Herbert Marcuse, *Eros and Civilization.* Boston, 1955, 145.—Trans.

Karola Bloch

For the Dignity of Woman[1] *(1981)*

I regard acts of abuse against women not as random occurrences, but as profoundly socio-political developments. It is said that women are beaten when men are under the influence of alcohol, or when they are upset because of job stress. Then the woman becomes the object of their accumulated aggression. That might be true, but the deeper reason for this lies in the fact that in human history, women have always been oppressed. Abuse of women thus becomes a symbolic act that reflects how women are thought of in society. They are treated as outsiders and, despite the progress of women's emancipation, it is still difficult for them to achieve equality with men, to play, for instance, a decisive role in politics. In politics, God knows, men have not exactly covered themselves with glory, especially when one thinks of all the wars they have been involved in.

In the opinion of some, abused women should find their way back to their partners. I regard it as disgraceful that a woman who has been treated in such a despicable way should be expected to try to return to a brute in boots who may have been kicking her pregnant body. Houses for battered women are meant not only to help women escape mistreatment, but also to help them develop self-confidence through communicating with other women and with people in the know about their situation. Especially since some women feel guilty about their own miserable situation, they need to learn to understand the deeper social and political context that leads to such extreme circumstances. Their stay in a house for battered women can therefore not be limited to just a few days, since it takes a long time to establish new patterns of thinking. Reorienting oneself to a different, self-determined life also takes time. And above all: the woman needs to enter the world of employment. Of course, many women do return to their partners. But they usually do it on account of their children, or because of financial need; they do it out of desperation. Let

---

1. Speech given February 19, 1981, in Tübingen at the demonstration for an autonomous house for battered women, sponsored by the organization *Frauen helfen Frauen,* which had been cofounded by Karola Bloch.—Eds.

us work to prevent this unbearable situation. Let us be sure that external factors rather than personal motives do not lead women to choose to be abused rather than remaining lonely and unsheltered.

Translated by Patricia A. Herminghouse
and Magda Mueller

Monika Treut

The Ceremony of the Bleeding Rose: Preliminary Reflections on a Film Project *(1984)*

The debate over sexuality, eroticism, sensuality, and love has now picked up steam among women as well. Women write and talk about their erotic wishes and experiences; they produce images and films and reflect about the social and private meaning of pleasure.

But the women's movement has also contributed its share to veil all of this with maternal love and the gospel of sentimentalities. Especially transgressions—sensual excesses, violent pleasures, cruel love-making—are still taboo for the most part. No, we women do not want to have anything to do with that.

One of these possible transgressions is called "sadomasochism." At its center stands a figure full of old and modern mysteries: the cruel woman. An ancient and still vivid projection of the enigmatically feminine, which seems all the more threatening the more the woman is defined as wife, daughter, and motherly woman. The cruel woman: as conceived and imagined, she is a reason for fear, hostility, and rejection.

Sadistic behavior is judged as aggression of one body against another and, because it is identified as patriarchal violence and destruction, it is rejected and negated. Masochistic behavior, by contrast, is rashly equated with the old status of women as victims, which, after all, we are supposed to overcome. No, we do not want anything more to do with these "male" forms of power.

This misunderstanding extends from the sexual science of the last century to current everyday consciousness: that sadomasochistic practices are dead-serious events, manifestations of one human being's rule over another, born of a "perverse" predisposition.

Not the slightest trace remains of the pleasure, the art, and the original thoughts of the sadomasochistic universe. A renewed reading of the texts of de Sade[1] and Sacher-Masoch[2] could help clear up these misunderstandings.

I am not interested here in the real brutality, the social imbalances of power that produce a sexualization of domination. That is the "perversion" that we find as hidden violence in all kinds of groups of institutions: in marriages and families, in nursing homes and schools, in hospitals and prisons. . . . I am interested in the liberating possibility of a game that appropriates the images and projections of cruel women in order to draw from these its pleasure and its sovereignty.

De Sade's Juliette talks about thoughts; Sacher-Masoch's Wanda about art; Freud's Mama and Papa about repression; and Carol talks about pleasure.

The nineteenth century is not only the site of a struggle of the sexes that manifests itself in the masochistic fantasy of being bound and beaten. It also gives rise to the disciplinary power that asserts itself in a heterogeneous grid of surveillance and controls, regulation and standardization: a manifold, differentiated system of disciplinary acts, which are directed particularly toward bodies and what they are allowed to do.

In the area of erotic passions, this disciplinary power is also beginning to play a crucial role. However, it does not appear openly, but prefers mostly to hide under the guise of a scientific study. In place of a (sadistic) fantasy of transgression and libertinage, and of a (masochistic) fantasy of pleasurable submission, the science of sexuality, *scienta sexualis*, appears.

It pronounces sadistic and masochistic conceptions to be psychopathologically interesting facts, which are to be described, collected, catalogued, classified, and evaluated. What is "good" is the form of normal heterosexuality that fulfills itself in the coital act with a person of the opposite sex, for which marriage supplies the socially

---

1. Marquis de Sade (1740–1814), French author of erotic texts with sexual fantasies that gave rise to the term "sadism."—Eds.

2. Leopold von Sacher-Masoch (1836–95), Austrian writer whose texts depicting the sexual pleasure derived from being subjected to cruelty gave rise to the term "masochism."—Eds.

sanctified context. What is "bad," by contrast, is everything accompanying "atypical" forms of achieving sexual pleasure. Now at last "perversion" is discovered. It figures as psychopathological failure, contradicts disciplined normality, and finds its particularly horrible form in sadistic and masochistic fantasies and stagings.

In our century, psychoanalysis has carried on this tradition of sexual disciplinary power. Despite its enlightening-therapeutic character, it remains caught up in the prejudices of the *scientia sexualis* and focuses its gaze on the cruel woman as a sadistically perverse or masochistically perverted authority figure. Sado-masochism appears as a combined form of two basic perversions, which have to be recognized if one is to be healed from them. To be sure, it is not without irony that despite this turn to "psychic reality," the cruel woman exists entirely as a fantasy figure, more a surface for projections than a real being. Although she no longer personifies a philosophical enlightenment that has ceased to accept taboos and irrational authority, and is also not a literary character who plays a confusing and seductive role in the masochistic imagination, she now has all the characteristics of a dream figure, whose meaning is hidden as in a rebus. For psychoanalysis, the woman in the S/M-scene is not a manifest figure who is what she appears to be. She is wearing a mask, is a coded figure. But who is behind the mask?

The psychoanalytic interpretation shows how much everything here is still seen from the perspective of a man, a man who is not willing to give up his social power. For in analytical terms, the cruel dream figure is only the apparition of a paternal power that is active behind the scenes and appears disguised as domina in the masochistic fantasy. In playing with the phantasms of power and powerlessness, domination and submission, the man is still supposed to take the primary role which is inscribed in him as paternal head of the family. Psychoanalysis continues to speak in the name of the father, against which the cruel Juliette already waged her deadly struggle, even if she could not win it in cultural-historical terms and, in the form of the pseudo-domina Wanda, was subordinated to the direction of the masochistic male. Now the only thing left is the nameless instance of a paternal position that appears in ever different disguises as always the same.

Translated by Jörg Esleben

Margarete Mitscherlich

Aggression and Gender *(1985)*

Are there such things as male and female forms of aggression, or
even male and female death drives? Most women and men—
colleagues and noncolleagues—whom I have asked about gender-
specific forms of aggression have replied in the affirmative. They
found it harder to describe in greater detail what they regarded as
typical female and male forms of aggression.

[...]

Most people still regard women who take part in revolutionary activities as perverse. There was widespread disbelief when it turned out
that some European terrorist groups were made up of at least as
many women as men. Women were criticized even more strongly
than their male comrades for their deviant behavior and inhumanity.
Most of them came from well-to-do middle-class families, a milieu in
which one would expect women to conform. The women terrorists
transgressed all boundaries of what had always been regarded as pre-
dictable female conduct; and this "misconduct" engendered general
incredulity and anger. Some had left their husbands and children;
others eschewed heterosexual relationships.

The middle class is likewise perplexed by the fact that lesbian relationships are becoming increasingly common. The search for scape-
goats begins once again. What else than the women's movement,
usually scorned by the middle class anyway, could be responsible for
these awful, shocking developments?

Most psychoanalysts, too, regard feminists as unnatural or ridiculous and, if possible, will have nothing to do with them. They are in
the habit of labeling them "phallic women." Whatever women can
muster in the way of self-assertion, envy, or even creativity is frequently designated "phallic" by psychoanalysts. This cliché is supposed to prove to women that they are living in a world of illusions;
they are obviously unable to free themselves from the fantasy of having a penis.

Psychoanalytic pronouncements about femininity often become
muddled in stereotypes about the "nature of women." A woman
who refuses to accept her "deficiency" is defending herself against

reality by wishful thinking. She has not reached, it is said, the stage of "mature femininity," the genital stage.

If one has already classified feminists according to a psychoanalytic system, taking them seriously becomes unnecessary, for their conduct, their achievements, their revolt against a society ruled by men, is, of course, based on a fantasy. Only the actual possession of a phallus would legitimize such conduct, only then would it be "natural" for a woman to rebel against the injustice she encounters daily. According to this view, women are realistic only when they direct their aggressiveness and belligerence inward, make the family the locus of their activities, and sacrifice themselves to their husband and children, or when they sublimate their cravings for love in service professions.

In numerous books, women have attempted to show that Freud's ideas and theories stand in the way of women's efforts to achieve emancipation and equality. It is true that to a large extent Freud accepted his society's notions about the role and nature of women. [. . .]

Many analysts seem to regard Freud's hypotheses about female sexuality as a proven theory. This attitude may be regarded as a form of defense. Those in power do not like to question themselves. In theory, psychoanalysts may well know that something approaching reality can only become apparent through constantly renewed efforts to critically examine one's own conduct and theories, and that one can liberate oneself from thought prohibitions and compulsions only by making unconscious motives conscious. But in practice, this knowledge does not prevent them from clinging to theories that they are comfortable with and that spare them from having to revise their attitudes.

[. . .]

Issues of the *International Journal of Psychoanalysis* or *Imago* from the 1930s astound one with the liveliness and clinical immediacy of the discussion surrounding issues related specifically to women. In the volumes for 1933–1934 alone, there were some fourteen articles concerned with the psychosexual development of women or with phallic defensive mechanisms in men. Lilian Rotter (1934) attempted to explain male fears of women and of their sexual power over men; they provoke erections beyond a man's control, often through their mere visible presence. Even a little girl, Rotter said, is aware of her sexual power over men and builds her sense of self around being able to seduce men. When during sexual childplay a little girl discovers that she can cause erections, it awakens the feeling in her that the penis is subject to her control and is thus also a part of her own body. Thus penis envy would only appear, according to Rotter, when a woman has the feeling that her influence over men has disappeared. In accordance with this female experience, some men regard woman as the "true owner of the penis." Rotter's paper does not take into account what it means for both the man and the woman when the man is incapable of having an erection, and the woman thus cannot "manipulate" him. The hatred that this triggers in both, which is perhaps not merely the consequence but also the source of the man's impotence, should not be underestimated. Freud established early on that the frustration of sexual desires can call forth considerable aggression in both sexes. The basis of homosexuality is occasionally that a man, instead of a woman, has the power to excite other men or confront them with their impotence. But if a woman's sense of self-esteem depends on her ability to seduce men, this does not exactly promote her autonomy and creativity.

[...]

Freud recognized that the first great problem with which a child concerns itself is not the question of the difference between the sexes but that of where children come from. Not until a boy discovers that he is incapable of bearing children does he begin to attach particular importance to being different from his mother, a task in which he is supported by society. This suggests that the discovery of penis envy itself might be an expression of male wishes to make women as jealous of male anatomy, and the abilities that go along with it, as men are of women. Perhaps Freud had to emphasize over and over again that jealousy and envy are primarily female characteristics in order to repress his own feelings of jealousy and envy.

Translated by Craig Tomlinson

Elisabeth Moltmann-Wendel

Feminist Theology *(1985)*

The Model of Liberation Theology

In the 1960s, minorities throughout the world—blacks, Latin American farm workers, Indians—became aware of how little their social and personal situation was affected by the traditional theology and praxis of the church. At the beginning of the 1970s the first models of liberation theology emerged in which the disadvantaged groups sought to understand their oppression and their expectations of liberation afresh in the light of the gospel. Once they had begun to fight for their independence they recognized that the God who was proclaimed to them by white men was not an expression of their feelings, their longing for liberation and redemption. The Jesus who was to be their brother had the face of their colonial master. Where was their God? Was the God of the white oppressor not the God who was the cause of their dependency, who guaranteed their oppression? Where was the God who stood by their side in the battle against unjust conditions, who freed them, who broke open their prison, as Jesus had said in the messianic promise in Luke 4.18.

In parallel to this, women, who from the end of the 1960s had been engaged in the feminist movement against sexism, the oppression of one sex by the other, began to develop a feminist theology. Where and how could theology support and accompany them in their fight against male rule? Where was theology itself so male dominated that it was of no use for women's liberation? How could a religious and political spirituality develop which helped women in the search for their identity?

American women who saw how minority theologies developed in their own country and who, unlike their European sisters, were more practised and socially versed in theology, led the way and still are providing the decisive stimuli. In the middle of the 1970s this spark spread over to Europe and meanwhile it has produced a growing grass-roots movement of feminist theology, which flourishes above all in places of work and autonomous groups.

However, in German society there has long been mistrust of the term *feminism*. In contrast to the United States, for us the word feminism is fraught with a fear of aggression, anarchy, misandrism. Hitherto it was almost completely unknown, and in our first women's movement it played only a marginal role, whereas for example in Anglo-Saxon countries, thanks to their older democratic tradition, minority programs like feminism were more easily accepted. All attempts to replace this word, which is so fraught with aggression and which seems so "frivolous" alongside the "serious" word theology, have so far failed. "Theology of women for women" or "feminine theology" does not convey anything about the social situation without which feminist theology is unthinkable.

[. . .]

Theology is praxis. Action and reflection affect each other reciprocally. Theology takes place in just action and in the struggle for a new society. If we have been reared in the traditional scheme we distinguish between theology and praxis: theology is thought, praxis is action. Anglo-Saxon and Third World theologies were already oriented to praxis. In pietism we had the *praxis pietatis,* which seemed more important than the abstract speculation cherished and cultivated by theologians. Women in our history have also preferred commitment to reflective theologizing. So far what the church has done specifically for women is often more important than any theological thinking. Church structures often seem to be impenetrable, repressive, and highly superfluous. Women—having attained positions of responsibility in the church—have often survived with a minimal theology, but in so doing have also surrendered something of themselves. If we do not reflect at the same time, our action becomes no more than menial work. If we separate the spheres of action and reflection we sin against the whole, violate our rational capacities and resign ourselves to being women who sacrifice themselves and disintegrate as real persons.

Feminist theology, which is practical theology, is fascinating for women because *women* are reflecting their situation, acting as women who are aware of themselves, and becoming clear about themselves and experiencing their own liberation in liberating action toward others. Their action is constantly bound up with reflection; just as something of life is suppressed in women, so too it is suppressed in others, and should come to life again. Work in shelters for women and with the underprivileged, consciousness-raising groups with women, banana campaigns on behalf of the Third World, boycotting of fruit from South Africa are endorsed, justified, and given theological significance.

At the same time this implies more perception of responsibility for the world. Just as I am made the good, whole creation of God, so society has a goal and a promise: the liberation of the oppressed. Anyone who is at the margin, in a position without responsibility, now becomes someone who acts with responsibility; the oppressed is not a passive object of the compassion of others but an agent who can encounter depression and resignation and who has a vision which gives a future to her and to others.

This makes obsolete the old formula which derives from Reformation theology about the relationship between justification and sanctification, a formula which has been discussed *ad nauseam*. In ourselves, in the totality of our experience, knowledge, and action can become one and we can be clear about what is "right" and where it is leading. Since we "understand with the body" (Christa Wolf), we set new standards for thought and action.

If liberation theologies have helped us to see divided human experience as one more consequence of wrong social developments and to recognize the human being in his dignity as a person on God's side, something new arises with feminist theology:

(1) There is a reawakening of sensitivity to the forgotten dimensions, to the spheres of the senses, the psyche, the body, the imagination, which hardly had any status in an abstract intellectual theology. Feminist theology continues the humanizing of theology in an unprecedented way.

(2) The substance of theology, which had hardly been criticized by liberation theologies, can now be investigated critically with respect to its masculine imagery, its masculine torso (the Bible), and its hierarchical structures (the church). Feminist theology thus inaugurates a real renewal of theology.

Translated by John Bowden

Luise F. Pusch

Language Is Publicity for Men—
but Enough Is Enough! *(1995)*

The process of language change set in motion by women during the last twenty years is the most significant and far-reaching linguistic innovation of the century. Not just in German-speaking areas, but worldwide. Far-reaching, because women did not stop with the lexicon (the usual arena of language change), but went straight to the core, to patriarchal grammar itself. There used to be almost no space for woman in this *manor* house, but she has meanwhile spread out comfortably and settled in. This makes it somewhat narrower and less comfortable for the master, who no longer has the entire terrain to himself. We women have long known that the feminization of language brings the human race a step closer to humanity. Woman is glad that this has now been acknowledged by some men as well, including such a highly regarded institution as the Wiesbaden Gesellschaft für deutsche Sprache [German Language Society]. For it is not so long ago that professors at German universities used to advise enthusiastic women students wishing to write their M.A. theses (then called Master's theses) on sexism in the German language that they had better not because the topic was only a passing fad.

Magazine editors occasionally ask me if I can produce an article on women's language. "Possibly," I usually reply, "and what did you have in mind?"—"Perhaps something like 'Is women's language passé?' After all, one does not hear anything about it these days, don't you agree?" Well, maybe "one" does not, but women certainly do. Specifically, women hear a lot of ignorant griping from the masculine side of the house. Good, we say to ourselves, the guys are taking the subject more seriously now, because things are starting to get serious. Even in Mexico, one of the stubbornest bastions of machismo, there has reportedly been a legislative decision to abolish linguistic machismo in schoolbooks. The new *Oxford Bible* was cleansed of all sexist usages and other forms of linguistic discrimination. Many political bodies, from city governments and provincial legislatures on up to the German Bundestag, have yielded to pressure from women, resolving that the section in the German Basic Law guaranteeing men and women equal rights should be implemented with respect to language too. Some like to play dumb, arguing: "The right way is 'He's an *Ingenieur* [engineer], she's an *Ingenieur,* and they're both *Ingenieure* [engineers]'—you can't get any more equal than that! So, who needs this idiotic feminine suffix *-in?*"[1] Well, women think equality could also be achieved by saying "She's an *Ingenieurin,* he's an *Ingenieurin,* they're both *Ingenieurinnen.*" This idea finds scant support among men in our master culture, where feminization means becoming declassed, pure and simple, because the feminine is in second place. If not last—it appears that the typical male is much fonder of his car or his livestock than his wife. In California, you can get up to a year in jail and a $1,000 fine for abusing your wife, but abuse of animals is punished by up to a year in jail and $20,000 in fines.

Women's language is not passé but alive and getting better all the time. It has gained wide acceptance, so that in many areas following its guidelines has become simply a matter of politeness and good style. In fact, at a hearing in the provincial court of Lower Saxony seven years ago, a German professor remonstrated with me: What was our problem? After all, using double forms of nouns (i.e., *Leserinnen und Leser,* female readers and male readers) was long since totally taken for granted—we women were simply beating down doors that are already open. The fact that the doors have been open a very short time and that what is "taken for granted" was only recently dismissed by his colleagues as a "passing fad" is something he forgot to mention. This is a favorite tactic: When women have struggled to gain ground, essentially having wrested something away from men, they are regularly met with the explanation that they have had it all along anyway. In this view, it is not the men who have suffered a defeat, but the women who are hysterically fighting the wrong battle, running like chickens with their heads cut off to beat down doors held open by men, generous cavaliers that they are.

So, we and the German Language Society maintain: Women's language is not passé by any means; indeed, it is making excellent progress. Now that this has been officially recorded, I would like to

---

1. In German, a great many feminine nouns are formed by adding the suffix *-in* to the masculine noun; each noun has its own plural form: *der Ingenieur* [engineer, masc.; plural *Ingenieure*]; *die Ingenieurin* [engineer, fem.; plural *Ingenieurinnen*]. Not unlike English, standard German grammar specifies the masculine noun as the generic or (supposedly) gender-neutral form.—Trans.

summarize, for those who have slept through the debate up to now, why women's language is inescapable. The language we inherited from our fathers is a language that eliminates women. Concepts and images are overwhelmingly and most persistently generated by words. Every woman who is acquainted with talk therapies knows that words become realities via our imaginations. The best-known example is probably autogenous training. You tell yourself "My right arm is warm" and in a short time your temperature rises measurably. The most horrifying example is the murder of the European Jews. First they were defined as vermin by a perfidious discourse, by words, and then they were treated like vermin—exterminated. And us women? We are and were literally not worth talking about, which is exactly how we are treated. What do you think of when you hear or read words like "actor," "poet," "street sweeper," "reader," "passerby," "Swiss citizen"? These words, patriarchal grammar assures us, are gender-neutral. But can you picture a gender-neutral Swiss citizen? Just try it. See, it does not work. You are picturing men. And because this is true, women have all but disappeared from the human imagination. It is especially difficult for women to think about themselves. The man of course thinks this is fine—woman is supposed to think about him, after all, and possibly also "his" children. As we know, the female Swiss citizen was denied the right to vote until 1971. A favorite argument was: "The law says that every *schweizer Bürger* [Swiss citizen] is eligible to vote; it says nothing about *Bürgerinnen* [female citizens]." So much for the gender neutrality of masculine nouns. The concepts are interpreted according to the master's pleasure. If we are talking about rights, woman is excluded; when it is a question of responsibilities or punishment, naturally she is included.

The goal of all advertising is to anchor the product for which a suitable match is sought (see what I mean?)[2] firmly in the head of the consumer (are you visualizing a female consumer? If so, you are not normal). Commercial and service industries pay enormous amounts of money to the various media for this. But the medium of the German language is organized grammatically in such a way that the image "male person" is generated by almost every sentence that men-

---

2. The phrase glossed as "a suitable match" contains in German an untranslatable wordplay involving the word *Mann* [man or husband]. The expression *an den Mann bringen* means both "to find a buyer for" and "to find a husband for"—thus, "das . . . 'an den Mann' zu bringende Produkt" can be read with both meanings—"the product for which a buyer/husband must be found."—Trans.

tions people. German grammars prescribe that any group of women, no matter how large, symbolically becomes a masculine group the moment that one single man joins it. Thus, ninety-nine *Sängerinnen* [female singers] and one *Sänger* [male singer] become in German one hundred *Sänger* [male singers]. It is up to the *Sängerinnen* to figure out what happened to them; the main thing is for the male to be linguistically present and accounted for.

Language is the medium of all media. Without language the other media would not exist—there would be no newspapers, no radio, no television, no Internet, no E-mail, no multimedia. And this medium, the basis for all the others, is arranged such that women hardly appear at all. Men's language is a grandiose, ingeniously constructed publicity machine for men that operates totally free of charge. The women competitors have been crowded out to the margins. This propaganda works at a largely unconscious level, for most people are unaware of linguistic mechanisms and indeed must remain so in order for communication to work. As Hitler's propaganda minister Goebbels so clearly recognized: "Propaganda becomes ineffective the moment it is recognized. But at the moment when it hovers as a current in the background, it is effective in every respect." That most people are not aware of the propaganda for men known as language can be discerned from the deeply irritated sighs of many men and some women wondering if we don't have anything more important to do than make the German language unwieldy to the point of uselessness by adding feminine forms.

The publicity machine's success in maneuvering women to the sidelines can be seen in the circumstances of women worldwide, which were spelled out once again, and rightly so, at the International Women's Conference in China in 1995. Women do two thirds of the work in this world, for which they receive one tenth of the pay. And we possess one one-hundredth of the world's wealth. Ninety-nine percent of all the goods in this world are in the possession of men. In order that it not remain so, we interrupt the vicious cycle of power. We women have—as yet—little access to power, but we have access to language and we are using it. Language produces concepts, concepts influence our actions, actions influence our political and economic situation (our so-called reality), and this in turn influences language. If we change language, there is no doubt that we will change concepts too and thus, everything else. It is urgently necessary.

Translated by Jeanette Clausen

Chong-Sook Kang

Forty Years of Migrant Women in Germany *(1996)*

Variety of Living Situations

"The migrant woman," "the female foreigner" as such does not exist, just as "the" German woman cannot be defined solely by her nationality. Migrant women must not be reduced only to their national origin. They are much more than that. They have diverse ways of structuring their lives and lifestyles, which have to be seen against the various backdrops of their immigration status, their experience with migration, and their different lifestyles and cultures.

A Turkish girl of the third generation perceives Germany as her home country, whereas her mother is still longing for Turkey. The women of a family of *Aussiedler* [ethnic Germans from outside Germany] came here as if they were coming to a foreign country and had to leave their familiar surroundings, for instance, a village in the former Soviet Union. A Brazilian woman married a German whom she had met through a marriage broker. Women from former Yugoslavia came here in order to protect their lives. Iranian women had to seek refuge from political persecution, which they often suffered simply for being women. Each of these women has her own problems to cope with and her own plans to realize.

[. . .]

Stopgap Workers in the Labor Market

Many women of the first and even the second generation have had few opportunities, if any, to receive professional training of any kind. Thus, they fail to meet the minimum requirements for even a modestly remunerative job here in the Federal Republic. Most foreign women are therefore forced into either low-wage jobs or unemployment. Even in the area of part-time jobs (typically done by women), it is the foreign women who occupy the lower levels. They are discriminated against more than German women are, and often get those jobs that are not attractive enough for women from Germany or from other EU countries. Foreign women work mainly in the processing industries or in the service sector as cleaning personnel. 13.3 percent of foreign women work in cleaning jobs (5.7 percent of German women), whereas only 10.5 percent have administrative or office positions (30.8 percent of German women). Those kinds of jobs are usually monotonous and go hand in hand with repetitive motion syndrome, shift- or piecework. Thus, their capacity for work is seriously strained and their health jeopardized. In addition, they have to deal with racist harassment by their fellow workers. During downsizing, foreign women are the first to be laid off. The older ones and those who have never received sufficient professional training often have no chance to find another job. All they can get is menial work like cleaning. The most common career for a foreign woman is a cleaning job in the health services or in a restaurant.

Foreign Girls in Search of New Identities

The tragedy of the situation of foreign families and foreign women is that social inequality and discrimination are for the most part not temporary or short-term phenomena in the initial phase of immigration, but essentially constant. This applies not only to the first generation of immigrants, but presumably to the subsequent generations as well. Inequality and discrimination dominate the daily life of young girls in their schooling, training, and profession. Their subjective dissatisfaction with their lot in life is reinforced by their objectively provable disadvantages. Even forty years after the first migrations, young people of ethnic minorities still do not get the same chances when it comes to education and job openings. More and more young foreigners of both sexes fail in the constantly intensifying competition for "work and bread."

In 1991/1992, nineteen percent of all foreign women who left school left without a diploma. Of all students leaving school without a diploma, foreign students made up forty-six percent that year. Eighty percent of the students at the vocational schools for young workers in Munich are foreigners. Their number in "special" schools is also disproportionately high. School curicula usually make no reference to the real lives of foreign girls and their families. The girls do not see their life experiences reflected in their lessons, and have little chance to come to terms with them in the school setting.

The gender-specific labor market makes access to certain professions difficult for German and foreign girls alike. In addition, foreign girls have to struggle against structural discrimination. Although they are generally more successful in school (in terms of choosing the type of school and earning a diploma) than boys of the same nation-

ality, foreign girls are less likely to continue in a job training than foreign boys or German girls. While the total number of female apprentices has increased to forty-two percent, the number of girls among foreign apprentices remains at a constant thirty-three percent.

Parents of foreign girls cannot give their daughters enough support in choosing a profession because they are not sufficiently familiar with the choices or have different expectations regarding their daughters' futures. Parents often choose a profession for their daughter which, in case of her return to the home country, will guarantee her a high standing (and a good income) or make her marriageable. Such a choice, however, makes less sense in the context of the German labor market or the specific situation of the girl in Germany. The girls' interests focus on only a few trades, mainly in the service sector, such as hairdresser, sales person, clerical worker, or doctor's or pharmacist's assistant. Generally, they focus on the same kind of professions that German girls prefer but in a different order of priority and on a smaller number of professions.

In addition to their particular financial-social situation, many young foreign women have to cope with their own psychological-emotional state: it is difficult for their self-esteem to develop freely and positively.

Their socialization has been shaped by the experience of migration—multiple painful separations and many confrontations with foreignness. These young women feel different both from their parents and compatriots and from their German peers and their German environment, and in their search for an identity they must deal with the resulting conflicts. They are less ready than their parents to accept being underprivileged because they compare themselves to their German peers and seek recognition in the German environment much more than their parents do. Their search for identity enters a state of crisis not only because of the cultural conflicts within their families but also, and predominantly, because of the pressure to assimilate to German society on one hand and the rejection by that same society on the other.

In the eyes of the young people, parents lose more and more authority. The lifestyles and habits of the parents—their focus on the home country, self-deprecation, religiosity, gender roles and relationship—are less and less accepted. Social trends in Germany, including increasing emphasis on individuality, influence their family structures. "Family ties" gradually loosen. For foreign girls, family means protection. On the other hand, they feel restricted in their efforts to become autonomous. Within the family, they often have to live up

to values and expectations that have no meaning in German society and may even be ridiculed. Thus, they frequently find themselves under great psychological pressure, which leads to numerous conflicts between the girls and their parents.

Translated by Gabriele Westphal and Thomas D. Colby

WOMEN
IN ART AND
LITERATURE

Annette von Droste-Hülshoff

Am Turme

Ich steh auf hohem Balkone am Turm,
Umstrichen vom schreienden Stare,
Und laß gleich einer Mänade den Sturm
Mir wühlen im flatternden Haare;
O wilder Geselle, o toller Fant,
Ich möchte dich kräftig umschlingen,
Und, Sehne an Sehne, zwei Schritte vom Rand
Auf Tod und Leben dann ringen!

Und drunten seh ich am Strand, so frisch
Wie spielende Doggen, die Wellen
Sich tummeln rings mit Geklaff und Gezisch
Und glänzende Flocken schnellen.
O, springen möcht ich hinein alsbald,
Recht in die tobende Meute,
Und jagen durch den korallenen Wald
Das Walroß, die lustige Beute!

Und drüben seh ich ein Wimpel wehn
So keck wie eine Standarte,
Seh auf und nieder den Kiel sich drehn
Von meiner luftigen Warte;
O, sitzen möcht ich im kämpfenden Schiff,
Das Steuerruder ergreifen
Und zischend über das brandende Riff
Wie eine Seemöwe streifen.

Annette von Droste-Hülshoff

On the Tower *(1842)*

I stand on the tower's high balcony,
The shrieking starling streaks by.
And like a maenad I let the storm
Rumple and tear at my hair.
Oh my wild comrade and crazy boy,
I long to embrace you and match
My strength against yours, two steps from the edge
And wrestle with you to the death.

And as I look down at the beach, the waves
Are like hunting dogs at play,
Foaming and bellowing they rave,
And up leaps the glistening spray.
How gladly I'd jump to be among
That raging pack of hounds
And follow through the coral woods
The walrus with merry sound.

And further I see a pennant blow
Bold as a battle banner.
And the prow of the ship goes up and down,
As I watch from my airy rampart.
Oh, I want to stand in that fighting ship
And grasp the steering wheel
And over the spitting, hissing deep
Glide as the seagull will.

Wär ich ein Jäger auf freier Flur,
Ein Stück nur von einem Soldaten,
Wär ich ein Mann doch mindestens nur,
So würde der Himmel mir raten;
Nun muß ich sitzen so fein und klar,
Gleich einem artigen Kinde,
Und darf nur heimlich lösen mein Haar
Und lassen es flattern im Winde!

If I were a hunter, out in the wild,
If I were a bit of a soldier,
If I were at least and simply a man,
Then Heaven would counsel and hold me.
But now I must sit like a good little girl,
Sweet, delicate and fair.
And I have to hide to let the wind
Blow freely through my hair.

Translated by Ruth Angress (Ruth K. Klüger)

Sophie von La Roche

The Daily Routine of an
Eighteenth-Century Woman Writer *(ca. 1783)*

I arise at six A.M. and dress immediately, then engage in writing and
reading for my own benefit until 7:30, when La Roche and Baron
von Hohenfeld come to breakfast, and stay until nine. Then, since I
myself am versed in the culinary arts, I go into my kitchen and set
things up, supervise all the tasks in the house, and take care of the
household budget. Then I work on *Pomona*[1] and write letters until
noon. At 12:30 we have dinner, where Baron Hohenfeld, La Roche
and my two sons, and the daughter of my husband's step-brother—
whom we have regarded as our own child for twenty-three years—
and I are all together until two o'clock. Up to six entrees are
offered—because, for one thing, I have to provide for an entire
household, and, for another, because since his youth my good La
Roche has been accustomed to a good meal.
[. . .]
Therefore, the round of six dishes includes soup and beef, vegetables
and a side-dish, today perhaps a ragout and baked goods, tomorrow
a roast and baked goods. From two o'clock, when we have coffee,
until three, when the mail arrives, we remain together in conversation about a variety of topics. If visitors come, or for as long as the
men remain in my parlor talking and reading their learned journals,
I devote myself industriously to my needlework. After that, I return
to my kitchen at five o'clock to take care of supper. At seven o'clock,
my sons come to me to pursue French, geography, and history. These
are precious hours because we chat amiably with one another and
moral precepts flow easily into their souls. At table, with visitors, at
breakfast and coffee, we converse about things both pleasant and
practical. My husband goes calling, but I do not. [. . .] Thus are my
hours filled for me and thus I also fill them.

Translated by Patricia A. Herminghouse
and Magda Mueller

---

1. The first "moral weekly" for women in Germany, *Pomona* was published by
La Roche in 1783–84.—Eds.

Fanny Lewald

Women Writers *(1862)*

As long as I have been capable of thinking, it has annoyed me to hear how this or that achievement was considered good enough, if one took into account that it originated from a woman. For this reason, when I sent my first literary works to my cousin [August] Lewald, I signed them with a man's name. I wanted to be treated fairly. Nothing more. Nothing less. My father agreed to this intention of mine, but Lewald didn't want to hear of it. Thus, my first novel, *Clementine* (1842), was published without any name and the second one, *Jenny* (1843), was designated "a novel by the author of *Clementine.*" After the appearance of *Jenny,* I had the fun of seeing that this pseudonym, strangely enough, was perceived as a cover for a male writer. But the satisfaction this gave me became very ambivalent when, after my name had become known in connection with *Jenny,* Dr. Heinrich Laube admitted in his journal that he was now pleased to acknowledge that he had underestimated the capability of women. Likewise, I derived only mixed satisfaction from the fact that the authorities allowed a statement that would otherwise not have been allowed to pass censorship, because it was made by a woman.

If one takes a sense of responsibility away from someone, one also takes away his [sic!] sense of importance. And if a person is told right from the beginning, as too often happens when critics are dealing with women writers, that he [sic] is granted only a very relative and limited capacity, he is then deprived of all the true pleasure of earnest striving. His attention is directed to all the trivial things, for which he is then reproached. What I ask on behalf of the woman writer is that she be treated without forbearance, but also without prejudice; that one refrain from discussing the person and stick to the literary achievement—in a word, that the woman writer be assigned a place equal to the man's, with the equal responsibilities and the same equal rights, something which certainly does not happen often enough in our society. And thus I return again and again to the demand for women's emancipation that I have often expressed in these pages: emancipation that lets us earnestly fulfill our duties, assume serious responsibility and thus attain the equal rights that serious work among serious workers must earn for the individual.

*Translated by Patricia A. Herminghouse
and Magda Mueller*

Rosa Mayreder

Family Literature *(1905)*

Never before have the ordinary conceptions of femininity, of the imaginary "ideal woman," been so simple-minded as in the nineteenth century. In order to understand the full extent of this oversimplification we must contemplate the picture of femininity which is afforded by literature that is written especially for women. For the present age has the questionable distinction of possessing a literature especially for women.

In ancient civilisations previous to the decline of Rome, there was no feminine "literary public" whatever; women were not admitted to the theater; and their lack of education, their inability to read, as well as their circumscribed life within the house, prevented them from having any access to poetical productions, whether written or recited. Yet ancient literature presents us with a richly individualized picture of woman, especially in the form of feminine deities.

On the other hand, in the Middle Ages it was precisely the women who, together with the clergy, were the bearers of culture. As arbiters of manners and refinement, they far excelled the priesthood. Women were also the chief patrons of secular poetry, but this did not exert any inhibiting influence either on its subjects or on its modes of expression, even though it was written especially for them. In this literature, too, we encounter woman in a multitude of personalities, many of whom, such as Kriemhilde or Isolde, or the women of the Charlemagne epic, are far removed from "the pattern of ideal womanhood" which we are now accustomed to admire.

This "pattern," and the literary precautions which are taken to protect it, are creations peculiar to the present age. Goethe, to be sure, complained to Eckermann of the effect on dramatic art of the presence of young girls in the theatre, but since then this influence has increased enormously.

For now there are two distinct provinces of literature. One is the province of free and personal creation wherein the individuality of the author, his own experience of the world and of life, reign supreme. But to this province the greater part of the output of our printing presses from year to year does not belong. Circulations in the hundreds of thousands, which bring so much employment and so much profit to authors, and are an unfortunate feature of modern German literature, are the privilege of a far different province—that of so-called family literature.

Everyone is aware that the phrase "family literature" is not an honorific title. It is not based on the literary quality of the work, for artistic excellence is not the focus of its critics. No honesty of observation, no creative invention, nor new problems which indicate literary development are expected here. Whether the works be literary or scientific, novels or poems, treatises or anecdotes, they must all be produced according to a fixed pattern, must have a certain sort of moral foundation, and a certain conventional relation to reality, or they will never pass the censorship of the family journal. This procedure is, of course, most fatal for the purely literary production, since the chief object of this system is to provide mental food for the family table. The world which must be here represented is enclosed within a sort of Chinese wall, and the plot must proceed according to fixed rules. It is a puppet show in which a number of stereotyped figures and thoughts relate with constantly repeated variations a *fable convenue* which is supposed to represent the ways and works of human beings.

[. . .]

If we examine the feminine types which dominate this kind of literature, we find them to be stuffed dolls arbitrarily fashioned to conform to the established pattern. They depict woman as she should be and as she should not be, which is at once their limitation and their purpose.

This family literature has an especial mission to fulfil which cannot be combined with an artistic presentation of reality. Who, then, are these "younger members of the family" who exercise such decisive influence? Certainly not those sons who are in the process of growing up. All this reticence about political, religious, and erotic questions is not maintained on their account. Not for them is the romantic tale produced, the pleasant ending, rose-coloured, sentimental and unreal. Indeed, why should it be? Already at school there has been opportunity enough for them to learn in some degree the stern realities of life. One has but to look through the leaves of any popular journal written for the "family" to see who plays the leading part. Never is the youth of eighteen the hero or the central figure of the story. His joys and sorrows do not form the themes for writers of this literature; if he appears at all it is merely to play a comic part. No! This despotic influence is exercised by no one but the young girl! And she it is for whose mental innocence the family is always trembling, and for whose eighteen-year-old intelligence all literary food must be adapted ere it can find a place upon the family table. Yes, for the girl of eighteen years, for at that age the well-bred young ladies of middle-class society are supposed to have done with their intellectual development.

[. . .]

The relations of men and women to one another form the most important theme in family literature, as is quite natural when the readers are mostly women. But it is not marriage, that difficult and complicated relationship, so full of conflict, and so decisive in its influence upon a woman's life, that constitutes the chief theme, but only love and betrothal. It is inevitably a pair of lovers who are brought through "exciting complications" and the most varied impediments to the "happy ending" of marriage. As soon as the affair has reached that point, the author takes leave of his readers with the comforting assurance that the wedding day is the crowning glory of life and the joyful ending of all troubles and disappointments. Only when he is very thorough in his work does he once more at the conclusion raise the curtain for a moment, to show us the young wife wallowing in ecstasy and bliss with a six-weeks-old infant on her lap.

"The education of well-bred women," says Nietzsche, "is wonderful and monstrous; all the world has agreed to bring them up as ignorant as possible '*in eroticis.*' " The most wonderful feature of this system, however, is that the female imagination is continually stimulated with erotic matters, and the most monstrous that these erotic subjects should always be treated in a false and deceitful manner when offered as food for the female imagination. In this way the most painful wounds and disappointments are prepared for the credulous and innocent. Considering the overwhelming importance of marriage to a young woman of the middle class, her education ought to furnish her with at least sufficient knowledge and the requisite capability necessary for forming a reasonable judgment about it. But our customs have now come to such a point that they are absolutely absurd. They prescribe for a girl an ignorance and unfamiliar-ity with the world which were, perhaps, important conditions in days when the parents still chose the husband, and when the relations between married people were settled by social rather than by personal considerations. But now in the eyes of civilized nations it has become almost a moral postulate that personal attraction between those who are to be married should be taken into account. Even royal marriages, which are notoriously arranged for reasons of state, are publicly represented as being marriages of affection. Complete ignorance of life is incompatible with the ability to form a personal decision respecting a bond which is to last a lifetime. It would be no exaggeration to ascribe to family literature a chief part of the responsibility for unhappy marriages, although divorce, to be sure, never comes within its range of vision. But a literature which is essentially false and deceitful, which is subservient to unwholesome and unpractical prudery, cannot fail to lead astray the imaginations of those for whom it is the only permissible mental food. By continually occupying the minds of its readers with "enthralling" romances, that is to say, with novels in which the natural course of life is twisted arbitrarily in order to produce striking effects, it has in itself a corrupting influence, weakening their power of judging ordinary people and commonplace events. The exclusively romantic depiction of love also stimulates extravagantly those high-flown expectations of happiness in married life which are so great a danger and source of weakness for all young women.

[. . .]

Why should we laugh at those silly illusions of the girlish mind which lead her to believe that love will change every suitable candidate for her hand into a romantic hero and a fairy-tale prince? Is it possible that anyone except a maiden of seventeen would believe in sober earnest that an "ordinary citizen's son" will, after his marriage, be anything else than—the son of an ordinary citizen?

Why should young girls be thus intentionally deceived? Why should they be filled with such miserable illusions for the sake of preserving their "innocence" and their "poetic nature"?

We have not far to go when seeking the reason for this apparently benevolent deception, which is, in truth, so inexcusable. A certain type is supposed to be cultivated, and to this type the individual is sacrificed. Her own personal interests in life are not regarded; they are subordinated to a higher aim. She must be fitted for the marriage market, in which the traditional "ideal womanhood" has the best chances. And family literature affords the most effective means for suggesting and producing this sort of womanhood.

It has been whispered that many of these well-guarded maidens do not restrict themselves to these official precepts, but secretly extend their knowledge of the world by reading forbidden books. That may be. It is certainly not easy for any single individual to break that iron band which the notions of good breeding have welded about the female intellect. Can anyone imagine that there could be any beneficent educational influence in such indiscriminate reading of forbidden books, even if none of them should happen to be bad?

Thus, the young girl would seem to be a hindrance and a danger for the mental life of the nation, at least so far as real literature is concerned. In what way? Is she more responsible for this than for the other rules and regulations of good breeding? Are there not other social powers desirous that she should be shaped as she is by this false literature?—Other powers which admire this type of woman and decree which are to be thus disciplined?

As a mental factor in a nation's life the female sex is not so unimportant and ineffective as these powers appear to imagine. Those who look upon the struggle of women for a masculine education as the mere hobby of a few, or as a part of the general women's movement, forget the intimate connection of every cultural movement with the whole domain of culture. They are, among other things, blind to the importance of women as consumers of literary works. The history of the development of family literature shows plainly that just in the measure in which women's training has lagged behind the training of the men, that division in literature has arisen, producing that monstrous excresence in the intellectual life of the nineteenth century. This symptom of profound organic disturbance will be removed only when the underlying evils have been cured.

Translated by Herman Scheffauer;
revised by Patricia A. Herminghouse

Lou Andreas-Salomé

A Fable *(1906)*

Once there was an attic.

Low and slanted walls reached down toward wooden floor boards, and the daylight had to find its way laboriously through cob-webbed dormer windows and cracks. But over those boards, hay was spread carefully and a water-filled barrel was placed there. For here, people held all kinds of animals captive and weaned them from the life of nature through domestication and care. Fowls of every sort cackled, goitered doves cooed on the metal rim of the barrel, and tumbler pigeons fluttered from their nests under the rafters. Far down, however, in the straw, frightened rabbits crawled under the brittle conifer needles of several Christmas trees that were to repre-sent a forest, although the leftover colorful tinsel of the previous Christmas still clung to their branches.

In a half-darkened corner stood a newly-woven basket which was upholstered comfortably and with special care. For it sheltered the noblest of all creatures deprived of their freedom, namely, a wild duck and therefore "a truly wild" bird.[1] It seemed not only to be the noblest but also the most pitiable among them all. Though its fellow creatures willingly adapted themselves to an artificial idyll, isn't it surely and necessarily a tragedy for a bird of the wild to be confined to an attic?

For that question, we have six answers and six stories.

Nora

Perhaps, as a small helpless bird, she was taken from a maternal nest and put among domestic animals. Brought up without any knowl-edge of her true nature and original home, and surrounded with con-stant pampering and preferential treatment, she enjoys herself innocently in her attic, which is like a large, gay playroom. What she discovers there through the eyes of a wild bird does not give the

---

1. All of the "wild ducks" of Andreas-Salomé's fable bear the name of female protagonists of some of Henrik Ibsen's most famous plays: *A Doll's House,* 1879 (Nora); *Ghosts,* 1882 (Mrs. Alving); and Hedda Gabler, 1891.—Eds.

impression of a real world, but shows an artificial imitation of such a world, which serves as a welcome playground with colorful toys for her childlike strength. So, she slowly becomes adjusted. Yet there is woe when the season has approached whose storms rattle the dormer windows and eventually tear them open with a gust of abrupt force, suddenly revealing to the small wild duck a view of heaven and earth. With the first flood of light that unhaltingly sweeps over her, there comes also remembrance and recognition. With the first full stream of air that breaks into the damp room of wooden boards, there also intrudes what seems like a greeting waving from an intuited distance; it is like the fragrant breath from an original home that lies far beyond all the rooftops of the city with their chimney smoke, high and away over all antics and prisons. She does not know as yet where her home is, only that it cannot be here; and so, her undeniable instinct and a deep, mighty longing command her to spread her wings. And soon it is no longer a question of whether the unpracticed wings can carry the wild duck and whether there is a path ahead through the beckoning distance, for there is no longer a question of what remains behind—the ill-will and sorrow, the anger or tameness of the others. The duck silently spreads her wings and floats out into the measureless unknown, exchanging the large playroom for the All.

[. . .]

Mrs. Alving

Perhaps the little wild duck is not destined for such a fortunate fate. No storm comes to tear open the gates of her prison, nor any gust of wind blows them in with sudden force. So she grows up, lives, ages, and finally passes away—ever in the same attic. Through careful training, she had been taught that the worm-pocked wooden walls were unscaleable barriers and that the discipline and order of the domestic animal world was to be regarded as nature's law. She was taught to regard everything that surrounded it like a stage set, as the big and only reality, beside which no other any longer exists. Slowly accommodating and subordinating herself to the surroundings, the poor little duck strove hard to emulate the obedience and contentment of the tame animals; she wanted to control the strong and eager wings that suddenly spread in the wondrous dreams of night and impatiently beat against the moldly walls. But all patient efforts fail. For the knowledge of her homeland, of the wilds and freedom, penetrates the attic. Even if freedom cannot come loudly and suddenly with the releasing force of a storm, still it sneaks in softly as an ever-returning, quiet messenger. The sun's rays bring that knowledge. They are awaited daily and eagerly, even by the domestic animals, if not as messengers from some distant and more beautiful land, then as a welcome transfiguration of their attic world. The rays cast an hallucinatory shimmer over the old rubbish; they tease luminous reflections from the clouded water of the barrel; and they cause the cobwebs and dust clouds to flash brightly and glimmer like clear strands of gold; their warm glow over the dried-up Christmas trees is like the reflections of spring.

But an entirely different message reaches the wild duck. The sun's rays do not beautify the duck's surroundings; on the contrary, they reveal with sharp glare the whole stage-world of illusion, casting a merciless light that relentlessly and vividly glides over the naked poverty of the attic room, revealing every last sad aspect, down to the most hidden crevices hitherto protected by the veil woven by twilight. The wild duck follows the light rays with deep horror and longing, for they have brought recognition and disillusionment; she understands slowly that her own sharp, undeceivable eyes—a wild bird's eyes that look about angrily and painfully—were meant to view the sun and the heights with integrity. She realizes that she lives in a world full of illusions, and that the true world lies far distant behind the blind windows through which the sun's light comes.

Dreamlike, in unclear quivering outlines, there rises before her a picture of that reality, like a murmuring and whispering from distant waters and forests, like hovering flight under a wide, silent sky. And gradually that picture gains luster and color and fragrance and light, conjured up through the wild energy of desperation and yearning, until it stands there, almost graspable, so warmly and strongly lifted into a living and breathing world that the surrounding theatrical world seems to evaporate into a disembodied ghostly being. In the midst of the cackling and chattering of domestic companions, in the midst of the dust and the shabby confines of the wooden partitions, the wild duck dreams herself inwardly into being united with thousands of blissful, free-born swarms that wing their way unencumbered over the earth and toward the light of the sun.

Who would say that in this dream perception there does not truly lie release for the wild bird, a liberation that lifts her over restrictive barriers, while at the same time she dies, her thirsting eyes searchingly directed toward the sun, and with drooping wings crouching lonely among the sorrowing ghosts amid the withered Christmas trees?

[. . .]

Hedda

Perhaps if people can shamefacedly and happily experience this [freedom found in love], they would never again close their attic dormers; they would break apart walls and install large windows so that air and light would surge in unrestrictedly and permit birds to exit and enter at will. With that, the attic room would slowly unfold from a prison into an asylum of freedom, a sanctuary for everything which wanders homelessly under the wide sky and which cannot find its way home: a sanctuary for the reconciliation and merging of the tame and the wild. It would be comparable to a great, warm nest which lies in sunshine on the roof—as if it were on a high watchtower visible and open to all, related to all the countless small wild nests that are created in nature through diligence and freedom. For there is one place where even the most unquiet urge for wandering and journeying into the distant is calmed, voluntarily limited, and relieved from its striving restlessness—and that is the nest-building springtime of love—a home.

What kind of creature might there be which remains excluded from such a community? It must be a bird who is damned to homelessness among its peers. A bird without a real drive for wandering or journeying into distances because it lacks the courage of those born free in the wild, but also because it is full of hatred against protection and peace among companions—she, no less, lacks the sensitivity and gentle disposition of the tame inhabitants. Neither capable of fighting against convention nor of bringing opposite demands into accord, she must forever stew in powerless unrest, without seeing the wide world of freedom outside because, despite all her brightness and beauty, she can only perceive a threatening and empty distance. Yet she is also unable to see the small world around her—even in the warmest of nests, she sees only confinement. The nesting instinct that drives both the wild and the tame to create a home is repugnant to her, and so she lacks the drive for life itself. For that reason there was for her no possible form of existence in the world of the living and, above all, the creative; she could not even escape anymore from her own existence. It may be that by falling into other people's hands she relieves life of the superfluous: a quick death in front of the hunter's gun barrel.

Translated by Siegfried Mandel

Lily Braun

Backstage *(1894)*

The child who for the first time sees the colorful curtain rise and then watches with breathless wonder the fairy tale being played on the stage believes that the wondrous world behind the scenery could not be any different from that in front of it. As the human being grows into adulthood, he will gradually lose some of his illusions, but none-theless he may often think with concealed envy of the "free and jolly artists' life" of the men and women who are not forced to stand behind the lectern or the store counter. The experienced roué does not share these ideas; for him the theater is a place of entertainment, and every female who enters the stage appears to him to be indicating thereby that she is in a mood to lend a willing ear to his wishes. Not dissimilar is the judgment of the virtuous bourgeois housewife who, however, not only holds the "princess of the stage" in contempt but also harbors an irrepressible feeling of envy when she sees the ac-tresses wearing costly modern gowns on stage and when she attri-butes to them a carefree life commensurate with such luxurious clothes.

Who has ever looked behind the scenes except with prying or lascivious eyes?

Who has tried to judge fairly whatever he saw?

Not many people; and whatever they said has gone without echo. The majority of women wrap themselves in the mantle of their vir-tue, close their eyes and ears, and pay no attention to those not walk-ing on their own straight and narrow path. The actresses themselves, however, are groaning under the yoke of the worst kind of slavery without being able to shake it off by their own effort alone; every single attempt to do so results in its becoming ever more oppressive. I am here appealing to the hearts and the reason of fair-minded men and women by reporting facts about the life of artists; as soon as such people come together in order to help those who are being sacri-ficed to penury or to shame for the sake of their enjoyment and de-light, then—I hope—the actresses' feeling of solidarity will stir also and will give them the strength to shake off the yoke of slavery by *joint effort.*

The theaters in which the female personnel occupies the best position are the small court theaters. Provincial theaters usually pay very low wages, on the average, so that the only actresses finding employment there are very young, very old, or mediocre. Every ambitious talent who wants to have a future must have worked, at least for a few years, at one of the larger Berlin theaters and cannot afford to be deterred by the deplorably low moral climate of the Berlin stage, which is generally known in artists' circles. The general public does not know much about the vast extent of this corruption. Only once in a while a particularly tragic case lifts the veil with which the producers, in alliance with agents and unscrupulous representatives of the *jeunesse dorée,* cleverly manage to cover up all this misery. Let me just recall the suicide of one of our most charming comedy actresses; she had been unable to face the destruction of her bridal happiness by slander of the most wicked kind. Rumor had it that the director had demanded to see her in the nude before signing her contract; that she had consented; that he had allowed other people to watch, hidden behind the scenery; and that years later these people told about what they had allegedly seen. Only after her voluntary death did the hapless woman receive that justice which she had demanded as the most beautiful decoration for her grave.

[...]

A poor decent girl will only in the rarest cases be able to get ahead, given the situation on our stages today. To begin with, the expenses of an education at a theater school are considerable. Most students there take a one-year course for which they have to pay a fee of 75 to 100 marks a month. Besides that, the student will have to have sufficient cash to pay for adequate food and good clothing, for in the competition with her colleagues what ultimately counts most of the time is her external appearance. Once the training is finished, the actresses pour out of the schools, and since their number increases from year to year, they bid against each other more and more fiercely. Like beasts of prey, the agents stalk these novices of the theater. To be sure, the young actresses often are told that it is their own fault if they allow themselves to be exploited by their agents; after all, they could get in touch with the directors directly. But that is possible only if the actress has excellent connections and is financially independent enough to spend a long time fighting against the intrigues of the agents who use all their resources to keep theaters from hiring a girl who does not put herself into their clutches. Most of the time, moreover, directors have a regular business arrangement with certain agents so that they procure their "merchandise" only through these middlemen. The actress is obliged to pay three-to-five percent of her wages to the agent who got her the engagement. In the case of guest appearances, the cut is 10 percent. The poorer a girl is, the more urgently she wants to find a position; in her anxiety, she often will turn not to one but to two agents. If the two get together and obtain one and the same engagement for her, she must pay the agreed upon percentage to both of them.

[. . .]

At many of our private theaters we will find ladies employed who are distinguished by great elegance and who are given the best roles to play and who nonetheless receive no wages or a very low wage. They are the "girlfriends" of rich men. Their "patrons" not only support them but also quite frequently pay the directors for hiring them, in order to give them public status. Most of the time the directors have no reason to be unhappy about such an acquisition: The lady in question lures the most affluent men into the theater and lends it a certain glamour—and she costs nothing. The task therefore is to keep her with the theater as long as possible. Should the director ever wish to place a budding talent with unblemished reputation in front of the footlights, it may very well happen that one of the ladies discussed above will prevent him from doing this by threatening to quit. Frequently a gifted actress is assigned a role which doubtless suits her competence. But then it will be taken away from her and given to a colleague who compensates for lack of talent with glamorous clothing. Let us place ourselves in the situation of a girl who enters into a stage career with a lofty conception of art, uses all her energies to make something of herself, and then has to realize on repeated occasions that prudence wins out over purity, toiletry over talent! If under such conditions she does not lose her enthusiasm for her calling and preserves her purity, she is worthy of our admiration. But if she falls, we must not throw stones at her because it is we ourselves, by tolerating such conditions, who are responsible for her fall.

[. . .]

Schiller,[1] as we all know, talked about the stage as a moral institution. He believed that a profoundly moral movement might result from the works which the stage presents to the public. Our contemporary literature is not poor in works of this kind; but I cannot put great stock in the moral effect it may have as long as it consists in

---

1. Friedrich Schiller (1759–1805): "Die Schaubühne als moralische Anstalt betrachtet" (1785).—Eds.

momentary compassion or indignation and nobody asks how those people live who stir those feelings in us. I would rather see all our theaters closed down than have our delight and our uplift purchased at the price of misery and shame. And even if our greatest writers produce the best works, the stage will not be a moral institution as long as immorality is promoted backstage.

Translated by Alfred G. Meyer

Marieluise Fleißer

Women's Dramatic Sensibility *(1930)*

The other day, a bookseller remarked that fifty percent of the best-selling books today are written by women. If we take this figure as a symptom of awakening female talents, we are prompted to ask: why does woman's vigorous presence in the literary market contrast so starkly with her near absence from dramatic production?

We know of a number of plays by women, to be sure, yet none of them have attained fame or importance. The plays tend to have an air of singularity, of nerves strained to the utmost; usually they represent a one-time effort and then the author returns to the epic form which is more congenial to her. To put it bluntly, play writing is not something one can do on the side, as an occasional piece, but is rather a fundamental talent. For the dramatically gifted the so-called first attempt will always be the beginning of a certain grand arc that he[1] must follow laboriously and out of an inner necessity. The one who gives up after the first attempt reveals that he lacks the highly charged tension of a special inclination, the fierce drive to innovate and explore, which is indispensable for the mastery of this difficult form of expression.

I have been asked what I have to say about women's dramatic sensibility. Insofar as this question presupposes the existence of a specifically female talent for drama, it is premature. Just as the drama

---

1. The gender of pronouns used in the original has been retained throughout this translation.—Trans.

only appears among nations that have reached an advanced level of culture, women as a rule are not yet capable of this achievement. Not until we have whole series of women-authored dramas in which the further development of their talents allows us to recognize with increasing clarity what they are trying to do will we be able to say something conclusive about women's plays.

In the meantime we must limit ourselves to sketching woman's particular disposition for this branch of production, to convey her proximity to the goal much in the way the athlete in training assesses his accomplishments by measuring how far he is from the intended goal. What does woman notice about someone else's play, what conclusions for her own work does she draw from it? Most certainly these include those details within a play that the mere technician tends to underrate, such as certain outbreaks of emotion that worked well on stage, a special atmospheric tension, the psychological antagonisms that clearly differentiate the protagonists from each other. If mere conflict were drama, many a woman would have written plays already. But she lacks an inner affinity to what is called well-balanced construction. She faintly senses the demand that every play build toward a single climax, but she does not see the one, clearly defined line. That is the charge brought against women's plays time and time again: they're not constructed. If a woman envisions the play she wants to write, she sees separate scenes in her mind's eye, masterful in the poetic compression of short sentences, effective because the things said in them are of general interest and engaging in their lively presentation; but the unification of the scenes, that ultimate accomplishment, is not within her reach, for her it only occurs subconsciously through the rising pressure of the atmosphere. This is where she still has much to learn, everything else is there. We have the language, we have the scenes, we have especially characters, that special female gift, because the woman observes closely and with great attention to details, she walks around the whole human being, so to speak, with a fine sensitivity for human idiosyncrasies far superior to the man's, until she finds the key to a personality. We must now strive for our next accomplishment—the play.

Translated by Katrin Sieg

Irmtraud Morgner

Making Use of Sexuality as a Productive Force: Karin Huffzky in Conversation with the East German Writer Irmtraud Morgner (1975)

Karin Huffzky: Since the publication of your novel The Life and Adventures of Trobadora Beatrice *you are seen by male and female readers in West Germany, and especially in West German literary circles, as "the feminist of the GDR." What do you think about this assessment?*

Irmtraud Morgner: I don't like the word "feminist," because to me it has a faddish, non-political ring and because it implies that the task of making women into human beings is entirely up to women. But it's a problem that affects humankind. Emancipation for women is unattainable without emancipation for men and vice versa. *Trobadora Beatrice* was written by a Communist.

The goal is a problem for humankind, but don't women have to fight for the path that leads there?

Yes, women together with the working class and as part of it. Whoever wants something must get involved. It's not a question of continuing the war between the sexes that's gone on for who knows how long; it's a question of finally ending this war. And what might look like an intensification of this war can, I believe, be the prelude [*Vorspiel*] to peace.

But doesn't this prelude have to take the offensive? And isn't it somewhat "unemancipated" to use the word "Vorspiel" ["foreplay"]?

It's impossible to speak of this process in either an "emancipated" or an "unemancipated" way; one can only speak of it in political terms. By using the word "*Vorspiel*," I am suggesting that solving this problem will take a lot of time. Customs that have evolved over thousands of years cannot be changed in decades. This is an unpleasant realization, because our lives are short. Impatience is understandable, but unfortunately not appropriate to great historic moments. Great historic moments last a long time. Anyone who fosters illusions about time is, consciously or unconsciously, contributing to the nostalgic setback that necessarily follows disappointed hopes.

What you're saying here sounds comparatively harmless. But when I think of your "Trobadora" novel, I recall that you sometimes expressed tremendous hatred toward men. You speak, for example, of men's "grotesque chauvinism" toward women, of "humiliations," and "fantasies of subjugation." You call the penis an "apparatus" and a "scepter of domination." Isn't this the voice of a woman who is full of hatred?

If you have looked at my book carefully, you will notice that I have described two sides of a phenomenon, sometimes seriously, sometimes amusingly, but never "harmlessly." On the one hand, there is man as a social phenomenon, the way he has developed historically and exploits woman, which is not to be blamed on individual men. On the other hand, there are men as non-historical phenomena, the way they could become, a sort of utopia that we occasionally encounter in real men, at least from time to time. And here I believe I sing the praises of the beauty of the male body, just as men sing the praises of women's beauty. I couldn't do that if I were a man-hater. However, I do hate the customs that often keep men from behaving humanely toward women.

[. . .]

Let's come back to feminism. If you regard this term, which has its origins in the West, as faddish, do you then regard the movement that stands behind it as a fad, too?

Historical movements are grounded in social conditions, not in fads. I welcome the rebellious energy of this movement. But of course I also see that in your country [West Germany—Trans.] and other capitalist countries, this movement has been rather successfully marketed as a fad, in order to trivialize it, just as the refusal to follow fashion has been marketed as a fashionable refusal. The emancipation movement is articulated in many diverse ways, it's subject to the pressure of a mechanism that is enormously manipulative. Only the orientation that sees itself as political do I regard as effective.

So you believe that it's wrong to consider the sort of feminism that sees itself in opposition to men as a political movement. Isn't all activity political?

Political, certainly, but with what effect? I believe that the process of social change that makes women into human beings can't really begin until after the socialist revolution. And this process is not automatic. Getting rid of the exploitation of man by man does not automatically mean getting rid of the exploitation of woman by "man." For this reason socialism starts by liberating women through laws, to the extent that is possible. The GDR is, of course, still a man's state—the leading positions in the state, the economy, and cultural institutions are still overwhelmingly occupied by men. This is hardly surprising. . . . After all, equal rights are of no use to women if they still have double duties. These laws thus do not simply guarantee rights; they also stir up dissatisfaction on the part of women and, in fact, encourage it.

How do you think that women in capitalism should fight for social equality with men, for their right to be human beings? Should they wait for the revolution and for the pro-woman legislation that it will bring about?

If you are convinced that the socialist revolution is the only way of abolishing a despicable state of affairs, then you don't just wait for it. You do something to change the economic conditions in order later to change the moral order. You do one thing and keep the other in mind. It's good to know in advance what your goal is.

To put it another way: Do you think that women in capitalism should first get involved in the class struggle instead of focusing on their gender-specific problems?

They should do both at the same time, in the awareness that economic change is the first goal.

And what can and should women in the GDR do to raise customs and morality to the level of its pro-woman legislation?

In the GDR, eighty-three percent of the female population of working age goes out to work and, in most cases, not just for financial reasons. A man with some self-respect will, of course, have a wife with a job—this is practically a matter of honor. Wives who are simply housewives may make life more comfortable, but they are not held in particularly high regard by men. At any rate, under socialist conditions in the GDR, women have been able to do quite a bit, both for themselves and for a new climate between the sexes. As a writer, I contributed by writing this book, and now I am writing a play. You can only change customs and morality by making people conscious of the fact that they are odd and inappropriate; in the literary realm, for example, this can be done by encouraging readers to take part in a creative process of thinking about things and becoming surprised at themselves. A change in customs and morality is a creative process both for society and for each individual, a process that leads to discoveries. Literature, for instance, can stimulate people to make such discoveries and especially, of course, to discover themselves.

So what should a secretary or woman worker do? Read your book . . . ?

I'd like that, of course. But just reading is not enough. To be effective in society, to have a voice, you have to join together with people who think like you do, in the workplace, in organizations.

Let's talk about equal rights. One of the women in your "Troba-dora" novel says that she's fed up with the kind of equal rights that permits women to work like men and then on top of it all like women. Isn't this a realistic description of how emancipation functions in the GDR today?

This is an angry outburst based on the conviction that, unfortunately, there is no road to emancipation that can avoid, at least for the time being, the double burden. Statistics show, for instance, that in the GDR a working woman with two children still has to work over fifty hours a week in the household. On the other hand, a woman living alone, with or without children, is no longer regarded as an incomplete person here; she can live "normally," be thought highly of and respected.

But isn't the crucial question here in the GDR how the attitude of men toward women and how the consciousness of women themselves can be changed? Literature is only one way.

The best way for women to change their consciousness, and that of men, is through the self-confidence that comes from self-realization, mainly in their work. In addition, propaganda is good. In the mass media. . . .

There again, dominated by men. . . .

But you'll find, for instance, differences in the way things are advertised in your country and ours. Advertising that flatters people by saying what they want to hear always states things very directly. Here advertising for laundry detergent shows men doing the laundry, and in store ads, there are men doing the shopping. It's not something we even notice, except in contrast to advertising in your country, where women are expected to have a guilty conscience if their laundry isn't fluffy enough.

In the emancipatory literature of the GDR, in literary writing about the problem of emancipation, it becomes increasingly obvious that the body, eroticism, and sexuality are being written about, sometimes still shyly—by Sarah Kirsch, for example—but already at times quite without inhibitions, for example in your "Trobadora" novel. Is it fair to conclude that, with the help of its emancipatory literature, the GDR is in the process of gradually emancipating itself from its prudery?

It's been generally observed that revolutionary movements often have something ascetic about them. And we're no exception. On the other hand, the wave of pornography merely suggests a crisis and has nothing to do with emancipation from prudery. On the contrary: you can't enjoy pornography without the feeling that you're seeing something forbidden. A feeling of sinfulness, which does not have to be directly religious, is what produces the pornographic effect. Many pornographic films depend for their effect on the tradition of objectification of the woman, who is normally expected to say "No." Those who do not respond prudishly in this case are often simply inhibited, unable to own up freely to their own sexuality, and in need of outlets.

In your novel, you say that women still need to learn to use the productive force of sexuality freely. What do you mean by that?

A well-known philosopher [Schopenhauer] once said that one could not expect any productive achievements from women because they have nothing to sublimate. This theory implies that women have no sexuality. Here traditional morality is confused with biology. The philosopher describes a moral commandment as a condition of nature. A respectable woman is not supposed to have any sexuality. Meanwhile, science has long since proven that separate sexual organisms form an organic whole, and that the sexual responses that are part of their physical makeup can only be achieved through mutual interaction. Mating as a physical experience of success (independent of procreation) is an important humanizing factor in life, mating with orgasm for both partners. Women, who for centuries have been required by tradition to suppress their sexuality, necessarily become stunted, and you can't expect original accomplishments from someone who is deformed in this way.

Then what does "making free use of sexuality as a productive force" mean?

Sexuality is a precious state of unrest that makes erotic relations possible, not only toward people, but also toward landscapes, sounds,
colors, smells—phenomena of this world in general. Without sexuality, there would be no enthusiasm, no intellectual passion, no *esprit*.
No thinker, no politician, no scientist, no poet, no composer works
only with his head. He works as a whole person: the head is part of
the body, not its adversary. In harmony and tension with oneself the
world is created, inside us and outside us. That's true for women as
well as for men.

*Your "Trobadora" novel is first and foremost an innovative achieve-
ment. It is emancipatory literature that sees itself as an "experimental montage novel." The novel has an unusual structure and even
contains a ten-page long outline of its construction at the end. So*
Trobadora Beatrice *is not only a book about emancipation, it is by
its very form an act of emancipation within literature. Am I right in
assuming that women who in their writing approach their own process of becoming human, who experience themselves as subjects in
their writing, also develop new literary forms? In fact, must develop
them—in contrast to women whose writing is mostly a matter of
hard work and competence?*

There is an enormous social difference between the lives of men and
women—the biological difference is comparatively minor. And different ways of living necessarily lead to different literary outcomes.
Style is the person, and style cannot be created. It evolves. The literary forms that men have developed over the centuries are forms that
have evolved. Women can admire these forms, but they cannot adopt
them as models. They must develop their own forms. This is not
something you can force; it demands the effort of generations. The
beginning cannot bring forth a strict closed form; it demands the
strict open form. The beginning is necessarily experimental. The form
must be able to demonstrate the process of arriving at the truth. A
closed form presumes that one already has command of one's material at the outset—a result of the preliminary work of others. No one
has done this preliminary work for women. They have to find their
own truth and their own form, simultaneously. All this may take
several centuries, but then, someday when there is hardly any social
difference in the lives of men and women, it should be possible for a
cultural tradition developed by both sexes to come into existence.

*Translated by Patricia A. Herminghouse
with Jeanette Clausen*

Silvia Bovenschen

Is There a Feminine Aesthetic? *(1976)*

Old and New Appraisals of Women's Artistic Production

The time has come for a campaign against all the weeping and wailing. Even the media have got the hang of it—with their usual inconsequence. Women are oppressed, exploited, degraded. . . . Although this state of affairs has hardly changed since it was first articulated, to continue to proclaim it, now in the artistic realm, seems almost pointless. But this need not necessarily be the case. As can be seen upon closer examination, it is the tone and the platitudinous character of the lament that make it seem inadequate. The form the lament takes still acknowledges its addressee. Traditionally it was women—professional mourners—who rendered grief public, be it in regard to death, to suffering, or to the victims of massacres; this was one of their rare opportunities to assume a public function. But precisely for this reason it was not at all startling, indeed, no one particularly noticed, when women began publicizing and decrying their own lot, that of their sisters, their female ancestors and, should women's fate not improve, the lot of future women. Clearly, Cassandra was not a false prophet. She was simply not heard. No one paid attention to her.

Lately though, the pitch has become more shrill, and lamentation has turned into accusation. Since there is no reliable authority guaranteeing justice, women are leaving the wailing wall.

For this reason I thought it tedious to enumerate once again the entire battery of obstacles constructed to frighten off and exclude women from the artistic realm. Yet, the handicaps and the absences are also part of women's history, and perhaps even the greater part, since women did not clomp through history in combat boots, and their traces are fleeting and obscured. To be sure, we do not complain as much today because we have a movement making demands that will change the future. Nevertheless, in respect to the question of a "feminine aesthetic," we need to reexamine its traditional assessments once again, if only for the reason that we lack a viable conceptual basis to work from.

[. . .]

Repeatedly and rightfully women have bemoaned the "deformations of even their own cultural taste": "I would . . . far sooner have been caught dead with Hemingway than with Virginia Woolf in my hands," says Shulamith Firestone about her development.[1] The pursuit of art, often based on the search for a realm of sensitivity in hopes of thereby escaping the confines of the home, may become a trap for women just as easily as other pursuits. When discussing that which we associate with patriarchal structures in the cultural realm, we immediately take note of a scandalous situation which, along with many others, was uncovered long ago but still prevails. Just to refresh our memory, Simone de Beauvoir established long ago that men mistake their descriptive perspective for absolute truth. The scandalous situation, then, is: the equation of truth with the masculine perspective, that is, with everything observed, examined and portrayed from a male point of view, which we were made to adopt very early in life. This false equation did not only predominate in the production and reception of art. It also guaranteed that, despite our fervent endeavor, this sphere remained external, foreign, and remote. This was but one reason for our exclusion among the many overt and lucid strategies employed by men to repress us when they found that our perceptive powers had not been sufficiently blunted.

[. . .]

Critics have always regarded the female producers of literature, art and music, few and far between as they are, as exotic aberrations. From a purely quantitative point of view, this indeed was and still is the case, although we have yet to rediscover the many women artists who were consciously forgotten.

[. . .]

To be sure, women's representation in the arts is a rarity. And even this rarity is always measured in terms of production norms within the established framework defining the division of artistic labor, a framework which does not encompass forms of social creativity. And when a few works do manage to find their way to the public despite all obstacles placed in their path, they tend to be viewed in the following manner: Though women may have accomplished some rather nice and enjoyable things now and then, all the major innovative achievements have nonetheless remained the exclusive territory of the great *masters* of the pen, the brush or the keyboard. (Thus any mounting anxiety can be quickly and easily quelled.)

The pitiful little chapter that the cultural historian devotes to the handful of women writers and painters, not to mention women com-

---

1. Shulamith Firestone, *The Dialectic of Sex.* New York, 1970, 161.—Eds.

posers, alongside his exaggerated obeisances to the reigning men in art, serves as argument enough for conservatives. This ratio is all the evidence they need, for art cannot be women's metier if they are hardly ever represented. An argument based on such evidence is sheer infamy; it points an accusing finger at the just barely kindled spark of feminine artistic effort by means of a tautological reasoning process: Women's absence from the hallowed chambers to which they were denied entry is now presented as evidence of their extraordinary lack of ability. The recourse to nature for the substantiation of uniquely "sexual" characteristics postulated *a priori* certitude and guaranteed agreement.

[. . .]

In the meantime the picture has changed. Today the line of argument emphasizing equality belongs to the repertoire of men in "progressive" circles. Cultural historians readily sacrifice the statistical aspect of frequency or rarity in favor of a well-intentioned reappraisal. Scientific thinking suddenly springs into action. The limitations of and impediments to women's opportunities can now be explained sociologically. Such cultural and historical investigations are indeed essential, there is no doubt of that. But the sudden change of course is suspicious. To return to the threat mentioned above: cooptation, the desire to ignore and obscure differences—these are inherent in the claim that there are no longer men and women, but just thousands of human beings. Every woman has had countless experiences which render such contentions absurd. This kind of different-ness is not something which can simply be conjured up or made to disappear depending on one's momentary mood or situation. . . . But what if we no longer view the difference as deficiency, loss, self-effacement and deprivation, but rather as opportunity? We shall come back to that later.

[. . .]

The Aesthetic and the Feminist Public Spheres

A feminine approach to art must include both aspects mentioned above. It cannot ignore the problems of what is aesthetically possible, the difficulties involved in working with artistic material, the matter of technique and of the intrinsic dynamics of various media, but neither can it ignore the question of the relationship between art and feminism.

Once before, it seemed as though a new age were dawning. Virginia Woolf: "But here, too, women are coming to be more independent of opinion. They are beginning to respect their own sense of values. And for this reason the subject matter of their novels begins to show certain changes. They are less interested, it would seem, in themselves; on the other hand, they are more interested in other women. . . . Women are beginning to explore their own sex, to write of women as women have never been written of before; for, of course, until very lately, women in literature were the creation of men."[2] . . . and once before, these literary expectations were dashed, bound up as they were with the development of a new feminine self-consciousness and the hopes engendered by the women's movement. Once before, female artists were thrown back upon themselves and forced to rely upon a male dominated public in order to get their works published or shown, in order to obtain even the slightest degree of recognition.

Thus far, I have found tangible instances of what might be termed female sensitivity towards writing (or towards painting, etc.) only in certain moments of female subversion, female imagination or formal constructs within various works. And I find these only when the specifics of feminine experience and perception determine the form that the work takes, not when some "feminine concern" has merely been tacked onto a traditional form. The question directed at a painter of why she did not portray women's demonstrations or activities in her paintings, is an objectively cynical and insulting one. Such a question reduces her work to the level of photo-journalism in weekly news magazines, something any man could do just the same. The feminine quality of a work ought not be determined solely by its subject matter.

The Pre-Aesthetic Realms

Even in the past, I contend, the exclusion of women from the artistic realm could not extinguish all their aesthetic needs. These creative impulses, however, were shunted off into the "pre-aesthetic" realms, where they evaporated under the strain of women's daily routine. Women furnished the living quarters, set the tables, arranged, decorated and adorned their clothing and above all themselves.

That was allowed, as long as it was being done to please the man. These activities quickly corrupted women. They set the table for the man, they dressed and adorned themselves for the man—not for themselves or for each other, but rather in competition with each other. They busied themselves weaving and knitting, but such functional artworks, handicrafts and decorations have always been con-

---

2. Woolf, "Women and Fiction," *Collected Essays,* vol. 2. New York, 1967, 146.

sidered inferior, commonplace. This verdict is of course not entirely unfair, especially in those cases where even these most timid efforts were channeled into subservient obsequiousness and excessive affection-seeking.

Here the ambivalence once again: on the one hand we see aesthetic activity deformed, atrophied, but on the other we find, even within this restricted scope, socially creative impulses which, however, have no outlet for aesthetic development, no opportunities for growth. These impulses could not be concretely realized, nor could they lead to an artificial desire to experiment.

It is true that these activities never had to become static, unchanging artistic norms. They never became obsolete products, they remained bound to everyday life, feeble attempts to make this sphere more aesthetically pleasing. But the price for this was narrowmindedness. The object could never leave the realm in which it came into being, it remained tied to the household, it could never break loose and initiate communication. . . .

But what would happen if someday we cleared out this realm and opened it only to ourselves and other women? What if we alternated painting our faces with painting on canvas? What if we turned recipes into poetry? What if all these activities were to shed their utilitarian rationale of male approval?

Perhaps that is all too simple, too superficial. Attempting to knit the gap between the artistic realm and social reality is problematic in that this gap is not simply the result of foolish blunder but is rather the result of particular preconditions.

However, it can be proven that women succeeded in entering the artistic realm when they gained access to it via the adjoining "pre-aesthetic" realms. In the eighteenth century women were able to enter the realm of literature by means of letters (the epistolary novel), since this was an age in which letters and novels were gaining dignity and the dissolution of rigid formal rules allowed greater flexibility. Experience could be gained in writing private letters. Since letters and diaries have no clearly defined literary niche, it was all right for women to practice on them. Only the Romantics considered conversation—another feminine domain in literature—to be aesthetic activity. The letters of Caroline Schlegel are true masterpieces of mixed aesthetic form: wardrobe descriptions alternate with philosophical discourses, gossip with literary quotations, allusions and criticism. Men were amazed by the new tenor, the new tone, the irreverence and more sensual descriptions unique to women's letters, and on occasion they even showed open admiration. It did not take long for this medium to be included in the literary canon.

However, it is difficult simply to go back, optimistically to take up again these "feminine" media—letters, weaving. It is, in fact, almost more difficult to do this than to work with the "unfeminine" technical media such as film, since these need not contend with being traditionally relegated to the domain of the housewife. We should not foster the false assumption that our sewing teachers indeed pointed us in the right direction. There is no direct path from the decorative potholder to the tapestries of Abakanovicz. Besides, I am still horrified by the whole ruffles-and-sewing basket business we were subjected to as young girls.

I believe that feminine artistic production takes place by means of a complicated process involving conquering and reclaiming, appropriating and formulating, as well as forgetting and subverting. In the works of those female artists who are concerned with the women's movement, one finds artistic tradition as well as the break with it. It is good—in two respects—that no formal criteria for "feminist art" can be definitively laid down. It enables us to reject categorically the notion of artistic norms, and it prevents renewal of the calcified aesthetics debate, this time under the guise of the feminist "approach."

If, however, women have different assumptions with regard to their sensory approach, their relationship to matter and material, their perception, their experience, their means of processing tactile, visual, and acoustic stimuli, their spatial orientation and temporal rhythm—and all these things are what aesthetics meant at one time, according to its original definition as a theory of sensory perception—then one could logically expect to find these things expressed in special forms of mimetic transformation. Put emphatically, this would mean that within the framework of a female cosmology there would be a changed relationship between the subjective artistic appropriation of reality on the one hand, and formal suggestiveness and receptive perception on the other. But it will be nearly impossible to find categorical evidence for this changed relationship: reality is not that logical, and there is no female cosmology either.

[. . .]

Is there a feminine aesthetic? Certainly there is, if one is talking about *aesthetic awareness* and *modes of sensory perception*. Certainly not, if one is talking about an unusual variant of artistic production or about a painstakingly constructed theory of art. Women's break with the formal, intrinsic laws of a given medium, the release of their imagination—these are unpredictable for an art with feminist intentions. There is, thank heavens, no premeditated strategy which can predict what happens when female sensuality is freed. Because it is a process and historically tentative, we cannot verbally anticipate this freeing of feminine sensuality either at its traditional erotic center (even though there's a lot going on there every month) or in the context of individual choice. We can do it only on the basis of a movement by women for women. Art should become feminized, and women's participation (limited by men to their sensuality alone) would do it a lot of good. Perhaps then our male colleagues would not need to proclaim the death of art one year and recant the next. But that is only peripheral here.

It is also premature to revel in women's spontaneous activities, such as their parties, as if they represented a new, "vital" aesthetic, totally different from the aesthetic of objectified art products. (This would be analogous to the slogan of the student movement that art would henceforth take place in the streets.) Women will know how to resist the imprisonment of their imagination in the artistic ghetto, not because this fits into their "aesthetic program," but rather because, whereas terminology may fail, this imagination constitutes the movement itself.

The predisposition to feminine/sensual cognition and perception becomes most apparent in women's collective actions, which in their appearance rise above the ordinary. Let us be wary of models, however. These actions would be quickly coopted as manifestations of living or body art, or body language. Feminist art is not a stylistic trend. Women's actions or demonstrations are not artistic events. The relationship between political actions and art—as well as the reflecting upon this relationship—cannot operate on the level of traditional leftist animosity to art. Nor can it exist on the level of apolitical esoteric views of the type which allowed a demonstration for legalized abortion to be interpreted as a rebirth of the "happening" scene. The point here is neither to rescue the notion of the "beautiful illusion," nor to overextend the concept of aestheties, a term which by definition already encompasses all activity and hence has become totally meaningless. The important thing is that women artists will not let themselves be kept back anymore. They work on canvas, they make films and videotapes, they write and sculpt, they work with metal and with fabric, they are on stage. . . . So let us take a look at what they are doing.

Translated by Beth Weckmueller

Angelika Mechtel

The White Raven Has Learned to Fly:
Some Ironic, Some Sarcastic, Some Serious Remarks,
Plus a Polemic on a Pressing Problem *(1977)*

The first troubadours were male, or so it has been passed down to us. So were the court fools, whom we still consider kindred souls. The "Nation of Poets and Thinkers" aligns itself with the male prototype. Whoever gives it an honest thought will make a remarkable discovery: that he associates German contemporary literature with Böll rather than with Bachmann. Male authors seem to have more weight; their names come to mind faster. We have not yet overcome the traditions in which we were raised.

According to the "Author Report," twenty-one out of every one hundred authors are female. Of every one hundred members of PEN, only eleven are women: as everywhere else, a man is in good company. Be it at conventions, in anthologies, in associations or literary groups: the writing woman is never represented as she should be according to the figure, twenty-one in one hundred.

Woman remains an exception. Woman is the white raven in the flock.

[. . .]

Only after giving it quite a bit of thought do we come upon the names of female authors, who, like Ingeborg Drewitz[1] for example, have supported and decisively influenced the building of organizations for authors through years of personal commitment and painstaking attention to detail. Drewitz's work is highly thought of by her male colleagues. They admire the dogged and energetic industry with which she fulfills her quota of work. They respect the modesty with which after one or two years of work she receives the applause given by those assembled at a general meeting and a few kind words by the chairman. And they elect one of their own as the new chairman.

[. . .]

Along the same line, the program planning of publishing houses generally caters to male authors. A young male author who hands in his

---

1. Ingeborg Drewitz (1923–86), politically engaged Berlin author of fiction, drama, and essays.—Eds.

first manuscript has only to survive textual criticism. A young female author, however, not only has to submit herself to quality control but in addition has to overcome the "quota obstacle." A tacit rule of which possibly even editors might not be aware says: It is sufficient to support one or two female beginners per publisher's list. The door remains shut for a third female candidate. Close examination of publishers' lists confirms this assumption. The woman who writes as supplement to a male program?

The Suhrkamp publishing house, for instance, returned the manuscript of *Such Sad Tidings* [*Mitteilung an den Adel*] to Elisabeth Plessen on the grounds that "such a subject can only be approached by an eighty-year-old." Those who are familiar both with the literary landscape and Elisabeth Plessen's book ask themselves: What kind of an eighty-year-old would have written such a book and at the same time would have had a chance to publish it? Couldn't Karin Struck,[2] who was still struggling with the success of her literary debut, have been the real cause for the decision not to include another novice in the list?

Snobbishness in the trade? The white raven in a limited edition, hand signed and numbered? For those who call the shots in the trade, the white raven will remain an exception.

More alarming: The place value of a female author is, despite all intellectualism, that of a woman in a male-dominated society.

A sarcastic example: It may happen that a female author with serious intentions and a radio play script goes to a radio station and encounters a nice editor and gets a good response. Of course she is happy about the acceptance of her manuscript and the lavish care of the editor. The latter grows increasingly intimate. For whatever reasons, she rejects this rather politely—and that may put an end to her case. If bad luck is with her, she has hit a sensitive nerve in the editor and he continues to feel offended by her as long as he is in that job. In practice, this means: He will no longer accept any of her work. She will have to find another radio station.

[. . .]

A personal example: when my first publication in a so-called renowned publishing house was about to come out nine years ago, textual criticism was not actually much of an issue. The editor baffled me with a different kind of criterion for quality. "Your asset," he said, "is that you are young and a woman." With this, he thought, both the publishing house and I were bound to succeed. "When Ingeborg Bachmann started with us," he added, "she wore her hair much

---

2. Karin Struck (1947–   ) gained fame and notoriety for *Klassenliebe* [Class love], her first, autobiographical, novel, published by Suhrkamp in 1973.—Eds.

like you do." I consoled myself with the fact that in addition to her hair, Bachmann also had talent. A female editor would presumably not have reduced the distance between work and author to a minimum.

Ten years ago, when a female colleague who put her text up for discussion at the International Forum for Literature in Frankfurt and then rejected any critique violently (and emotionally), the attacks that initially were only aimed at the text eventually escalated into attacks on her makeup and her appearance. A strange incident that has not recurred in such a shocking way since.

Incidentally, it has been made clear to us time and again that we have an easier time rising high from down below simply because a woman who writes holds a special position within a male-oriented sector: the position of the white raven who has to keep her distance from the flock due to her peculiarity.

Once in a while, hidden allusions point to the fact that one was catapulted up to success. A healthy defense mechanism?

Of course, there are advantages, which the female author perceives from her position as an outsider. Advantages which no doubt give the female beginner a head start over the male beginner. Some of them are rather dubious.

The main feature of these advantages is this: the author as a person is being closely tied to her work, not only in the editor's office. Sometimes it seems as though the female author is more important than her book.

People prefer to build up a personality cult around female authors rather than around male authors.

It gets dubious when this personality cult starts to mix up private life and written word. I remember certain newspaper reports: Gisela Elsner had just published *The Giant Dwarfs* and appeared together with Günter Grass before the Berlin Academy of the Arts. In minute detail, the articles describe her black eyeliner and make conjectures about her relationship with Grass. She was successful from the start. To this day, I have not read anything about the streaked temples or the beard of a male colleague, much less read about his love life, marriage, or drug habits in a review of his latest book. For these kinds of details, Gabriele Wohmann and her *Ernste Absichten* (Serious Intentions) seemed to be much more fruitful to a critic of the weekly *Der Spiegel*. You think, this is all long ago?

The *Spiegel* issue of April 25, 1977, reviews Brigitte Schwaiger's novel *Why Is There Salt in the Sea*: "First works, especially those by women, are mostly concentrated autobiographies. Brigitte Schwaiger, too, packs her life into a book, with a first person narrator, slightly edited and nicely distanced." What follows is a portrayal of the failed Schwaiger marriage, linked to an analysis of her characters.

Looking at literary criticism in West Germany, it seems that critics and scholars of literature have always had enormous difficulties judging female authors according to rational criteria. Very often, one encounters emotional generalizations, ridiculous superlatives, or alienated underappraisals. Some of these statements deserve a place in a collection of curiosities.

And besides the traditional male literary critic a new variety has now come into existence: the female critic.

The prerequisites for the rise of the female critic should be pretty similar to those for a female author. A female critic does not have to hear that she was giving away private details in her book, but she has to confront the mechanisms of the literary business much more directly. Her bosses like to assign her to skirmishes with the Amazons, both small and large. Since she knows she is considered biased and since society has taught her early on that she has to perform twice as well for equal acknowledgment, she tends to wield her scalpel overzealously. Where a male critic would gallantly separate the meat from the tendons, she produces fine ground meat—ready to use for a meatball.

The melancholic-ironic conclusion is this: by publicity-enhancing measures, the cult of personality and subjective critiques, more freedom is created for the female author than for the male author.

Can it really be called freedom? Or is it rather a beautiful preserve for lovingly tended exceptions?

With the image of the white raven in mind: carefully looked after we remain what we are—marginal figures on the literary scene.

Marginal figures on the literary scene—also marginal figures in literature? In 1967, after the literary forum in Frankfurt, Robert Neumann wrote in *Die Zeit*: "Women are writing men to the wall." He was expressing what had begun to emerge then: the German *Fräulein*-Wonder in literature. He and others had observed in young female writers talents that were considered astonishing.

[. . .]

Female authors who had gained recognition for their writings from the late 1950s to the mid-1960s remained within the staked-out area of male standards. I didn't behave any differently.

We wrote about women because as women we thought we could deal with female characters best. But we choose to close our eyes to the actual situation and to our own. The so-called *Frauenroman*[3] had

---

3. A novel written for consumption by female readers.—Eds.

been the business of male authors for a long time. A woman who wrote a *Frauenroman* ran the risk of being categorized as kin to Courths-Mahler.[4]

The ground for a distinct literature by women was actually prepared at the grass-roots level. Young female authors, often committed to women's groups, wrote books about women for women but without receiving the necessary broad literary recognition, which is essentially bourgeois. Renowned publishing houses were careful in dealing with those kinds of writers and their manuscripts. A sad (?) example: Verena Stefan's *Shedding [Häutungen]* was not published by one of the "big" publishers but by the small publisher Frauenoffensive in 1975.

[. . .]

During the last three years, more female than male authors have caused sensations with their debuts. Books have been written that very consciously debate the situation of women. It looks like a time of new departures. A(nother!) new literary dimension.

The female author has become aware of her scope of action.

Has the white raven learned to fly? It is surprising that this literature, coming from women, has been included in the circle of men of letters and their literature without resistance and by acclamation. Or are awards and applause nothing but another form of affectionate pacifying gestures?

[. . .]

The situation of the woman who writes is very similar to that of the professional woman—with one difference: Our trade does not know *Leichtlohngruppen.*[5] In practice, however, there is a fine difference, based on everyday adversities. A female author tends to be defeated earlier by the trench warfare of the literary business. Handicapped by the dual burden of writing and taking care of a household and by the constant disruption of her concentration—if she has to take care of children—the female author often gets stuck in midfield with regard to her degree of fame, and is rewarded accordingly.

The conclusion for better or worse: She who renounces one part of her life has a better chance of success as an author. A disclaimer for the sake of literature? A sad chapter in the history of female development.

Translated by Gabriele Westphal and Thomas D. Colby

---

4. Hedwig Courths-Mahler (1867–1950), author of more than two hundred popular romances.—Eds.

5. Group of (usually female) workers paid less than workers in comparable jobs.—Eds.

Gabriele Dietze

Overcoming Speechlessness *(1980)*

> *Try it, 'tis beautiful to travel*
> *In forests by night*
> —Hedwig Sidonia Zäunemann

Will there be something like an end of patriarchy, as there was an end of the Stone Age? Do we live in the era of late patriarchy, as suggested by a comparison with the euphemistic concept of late capitalism? This is almost unthinkable, as brazen—protean but always the same—as patriarchal rule seems to be. That the colossus rests on clay feet is a hopeful but unproven claim. Still, if it has become possible to think the end of something, then the beginning of something new can also be brought into view. So far, the male gender has claimed time and the future for itself again and again, in an unending succession of generations. Industrial Revolution, Age of Imperialism, the great wars, technological revolution: each epoch bears and has born a male stamp. Products, productive forces, weapons arsenals, designed by men, controlled by men—let us here recall the share of female work in this—give shape to each respective era and necessarily, as it seems, also to the future. It seems "about time" to make a breach in all this naturalness. But is "equality of weapons" desirable, in order to struggle for power with the same knowledge, the same structures, and the same arsenals? Do we even want to take over power and rule from patriarchy?

Anyone fighting for power with the same means as those who rule, and be it under the banner of a revolution, submits to the logic of the given power structure and will use it if victorious.

So this cannot be what women feel and think if a beginning is to be made in bringing about the end of patriarchy. Truly critical theories have always refrained from formulating utopias, because they included the consciousness that present thinking is always full of the old, and that a new society also needs new human beings. So let us *not* imagine "an association of free human beings for a change," but let us state a utopian lack.

Should *feminism* develop into *the* critical theory and praxis against the patriarchal system, it can only aspire to and formulate the demand for a sweeping cultural revolution. No revolution in a single sector—least of all an economic revolution alone—can explode the complicated system of psychic, social, and economic conditioning for oppression. Everything needs to be changed: how we think—the dominant discourse; how we live—the family; how we work—the technological-industrial complex; even how we laugh, love, cry, and dream has to change. The gender that is only beginning to recognize itself as gagged, to stretch its limbs, and to practice speaking can still barely say by what means and point of view such change can be brought about. The only thing clear as day, immediately enlightening, so to speak, is that there has to be a revolution, if the gender under an alien law wants to enforce its own law.

[. . .]

If female speechlessness has evolved historically, it can also be replaced historically. It is not an anthropological quality.

By female silence thus far is not meant, by the way, that there have not been outstanding achievements by women in many epochs—there are, in great numbers and often suppressed by patriarchal historiography. The only claim is that there were hardly any autonomous female utterances that could have circulated outside the cultural consensus of an ostensibly human, but actually patriarchal society. Autonomous means: according to its own law. How can a group assert its own laws when it cannot even determine that which is its defining characteristic—to be "female"—according to its own law? A group that always only encounters the alien law, the Law of the Father, in what is said about it. A group that lives heteronomously, under an alien law, i.e., in a family-based patriarchal society, which is so universal that there is no place within this society free of its rule, from where one could speak. Only a movement that attacks this patriarchal totality, the women's movement, makes possible autonomous female speech that can escape heteronomy.

[. . .]

Female thought not only faces extraneous dangers, but also its own impediments. In women's groups, special structures of communication have developed, which have in common their polemical position with regard to the patriarchal world outside. The rejection of hierarchically run discussions, in which it is usually men who speak, leads to compulsive harmony, a prohibition of criticism in women's discussions.

[. . .]

The aversion to or absence of criticism within a movement is striking, but not gender-specific at first glance. Only a second look reveals feminine specificity. Another fear is anterior to the fear of criticism, and that is fear of the beginning. [. . .] If woman has been raised to love husband and children and *therefore* to work for them, then criticism amounts to something like cancellation of the love consensus. To criticize someone means—at least for a moment—to cut an emotional tie. Criticism is perceived as absence of love, and that cannot be tolerated. For if love were missing as lubricant in the mechanism of the bourgeois nuclear family, if the legitimation for working for others were to disappear, then the exploitative character of female family work would be obvious. It is quite possible that in the aversion to criticism, a form of the most archaic female conditioning for slavery has found its secret continuation.

Intellectual initiative and artistic creativity are closely linked. The gravitational force binding woman to her object status makes the question of female creativity decisive. For where there is creativity, there is a subject expressing itself. An autonomous female creativity, if it could be discerned, would tell us something about a female subject that once existed or that will exist one day. [. . .] The answers to the question of female creativity, if this creativity exists as a specific phenomenon at all, will also determine how a "femininity" that means more than slave virtues might appear as autonomous self-expression.

The wish to say at least something "positive" and worthy of identification about "femininity" is so overwhelming that it is hard to avoid. But the need for secure, idyllic little places shielded from the storm seduces one to premature rest on doubtful terrain and to intellectual laziness. All too lightly, "positive" feminine qualities are postulated, which are then never questioned as to the part played by male wishful projection. A more intimate female relationship with nature is asserted—an ancient attribution: man is culture/woman is nature. Furthermore, we are supposed to enjoy a more intact emotionality—to wit: woman is feeling/man is reason—or to have a more holistic, non-instrumental sensuality: woman is body/man is spirit. All these "qualities" seem made just to form a contrast to male achievements of civilization and domination. However, what should elicit distrust is that these "positive" characteristics were not polemically developed by women themselves, but are long-familiar strategies employed by male-dominated bourgeois society to put one in one's place, a place that particularly qualifies one for second-class standing in this same society. On the other hand, it is worth considering that despite the doubtful function of these "qualities" in the male discourse of domination, emotionality, closeness to nature, and holistic sensuality are also desirable, sought-after characteristics (just as, moreover, a sharp intellect can also be desired simultaneously). But all of a sudden wishes become attributions. "If that is what you want, then kindly stay out of everything else, because you *are* emotional, sensual, close to nature, and thus *not* rational and capable of abstraction and culture." The danger does not lie in wanting qualities of greater immediacy, but in slipping into the obligingly offered shoe of confinement to these qualities.

[. . .]

Some things have been identified that promote the overcoming of speechlessness and many that hinder it, but this does not achieve a true approximation of the place from which speech is possible. Perhaps the seeming lack is also an opportunity. Maybe there are no places, systems, or identities where an individual woman can stand phallically erected in order to survey the world. Maybe it is not the place but the journey, not the system but the aphorism, not the identity but the multiplicity from which one speaks. It could be playing with theory fragments, juggling with standpoints on a trial basis, just an unabashed eclecticism, that women put to their service. The only consensus lies in criticism of realities and theories in which women are acted upon and thought about without their involvement as subjects, criticism wherever women exist as objects, as secondary contradictions in Marxism, as representatives of lack in psychoanalysis and of headless beauty in art, or as merely implicit presences in philosophy, history, and politics.

Translated by Jörg Esleben

Jutta Brückner

The Spot of Blood in the Eye of the Camera *(1981)*

According to their own testimonies, women seldom attribute the same importance to seeing that men do. They have not attached their pleasure to the visible: it is easier for them to avoid doing this because their genitals are not visible. Their pleasure consists in being seen. Through cultural blinding their own gaze is not up to the standards of exact measurement, accurate observation, and precise registration of the masculine gaze. This proved profitable for the men. Not for nothing were women as receptive as men to the invisible erotics of power as to the aesthetic appeal of physical features, if not more so. Woman's gaze wandered, often skimming over the surface of things and not really attaching itself to them. The visual impressions of imagination and fantasy with their flowing borders, their lack of any real place (*Ortlosigkeit*), and their state of floating between nearness and distance all played a large role in the organization of woman's perception.[1] This gaze was distracted because it looked to the inside as well as to the outside and had to constantly harmonize both interior and exterior reality, constantly crossing the border between the inside of the body and the outside world. The imagined picture and the impression of reality were materialized as well as deprived of their substance in equal measure: which means that reality became transparent. This must be one of the roots of women's preference for flowing things. The indifference of perceptions, the merging of images, which Eisenstein explained as an inheritance from the feudal tradition in Japan (using the tradition of Kabuki theater), is found on a different level in women.[2]

This way of "seeing" is also seeing and not simply a lack of sight. Since Freud there has no longer been any doubt about that. And it can also be surmised that men also used to organize their perception in a similar way, before they trained their eye to conquer things. Perhaps dreams, as an archaic form of consciousness, may have preserved a historically more archaic way of seeing. The gaze of women that sees accurately only because it does not look too closely, because it also turns inward and opens itself up to fantasy images, allowing them to merge with the more concrete film images, is the basis for the identification that women in particular seek in the cinema. This identification happens at two moments: for one thing, precisely those films that have especially appealed to women have a peculiarly forceful system of leading the audience's gaze to identify with the male gaze that organizes the filmic space. Even where the content and the star seemed to promise a narcissistic glorification of the female identity, the woman was at the mercy of the guiding male gaze, which

---

1. Gisela Schneider and Klaus Laermann, "Augenblicke," *Kursbuch*, 49.
2. Sergej Eisenstein, "Ein unverhofftes Zusammentreffen," *Schriften*, vol. 4, ed. Hans-Joachim Schlegel. Munich, 1982.

absorbed hers.[3] The woman was not conscious of this because the cinematic mechanism did everything within its power to conceal it from her. And this was actually in agreement with her way of organizing perception, for the flowing camera movements, the invisible editing that was Hollywood's stock in trade at the time, when series of films were made for women, allowing them to forget the borders between the individual pictures and offering them their way of flowing, borderless sensual perception *(Abtasten)*. This identification was thus doubled and self-contradictory: with the male gaze identified on the woman, the editing and rhythm identified with her way of viewing reality. This produced a closed circle. Evidently, the rhythm played an important role here because it received and translated the unconscious movement of the body. All of these elements combined to produce a sensuality that gripped the woman in her whole body and gave her the impression of a "richer seeing," a seeing that was not only registering and recognizing but also experiencing.

The woman looks in vain for this cunning skillfulness in the porno movie. The editing is done when the "subject matter" requires it; there is no editing rhythm, the framing attempts nothing but the clearest possible demonstration, so that the porno film has at its core more in common with the scientific documentary or the industrial training film. Here there are no metaphors or symbols that conceal the thing in the way to which women have become accustomed. The sign is replaced by the thing itself, the representation is replaced by the presentation. The penis and the vagina are body parts and not the bearers of happiness or sorrow, life or death, fulfillment or failure. The expulsion of all psychology, all "sentimentality," all love and passion, the reduction to an assumption that the function alone means and guarantees pleasure, shows that the porno film has a mechanistic worldview. The wandering, identity-seeking perception of the woman is confronted with distance, borders, matter, function, and causality. The jump from the de-materialized image that she had of her sexuality up to this point to the concretizing gaze of the camera is the immediate confrontation between infinity and matter. The collision between the staging of her sexuality in the woman's own thoughts and the concrete masculine staging on celluloid involves the collision of two centuries as well.

If the women lets herself be entirely circumscribed by the porno film, then she aborts a dream. If she forces her gaze to the distance

---

3. Laura Mulvey, "Visual Pleasure and Narrative Cinema" (1975), in *Film Theory and Criticism,* ed. Gerald Mast and Marshal Cohen, 3rd ed. New York, 1985, pp. 803–16.

that the porno movie advertises and observes the male gaze trained on the woman, she will see the mechanism at work in these films, showing how she loves secretly, often nostalgically, and with a bad ideological conscience. The ruling male gaze of the cinema is robbed of its cultural disguises in the porno film; no skillfulness is used in covering it up, because it is precisely in this exposure that the pleasure lies. The male gaze is what it appears to be, the gaze at the woman's genitals. Women—who, like men, cannot resist letting their gaze be directed by the dominating gaze of the film—become the voyeurs of themselves. This corresponds perfectly to the perspective that they had had until now. The pornographic cinema is the most obvious consequence of a culture in which the women had delegated their gaze to the men. In that sense the gaze that they directed towards themselves was always a pornographic one.

The film that shows not only nakedness, but also shows itself as naked, is in the first place an apotheosis of naturalism; in addition, it wears a monstrous superstructure of illusion. Its claim that pleasure·is universal, available at any time, and heightened infinitely, is perhaps only the lonely singing of the (male) child in the dark forest. For in these films pleasure is an unequivocal (and perhaps a last) means of discipline, with which the man can prove to himself his indispensability to the woman. Just like this belief, the means of his cinema also capitulate before the moment of the silent flesh and the moaning mouth, because naturalism can no longer see anything if the mechanical connection between cause and effect is taken out of commission. If they want to, women could simply get up and walk out of the porno film at this point. But if they believe that they have thereby settled the relationship between themselves and their portrayal, they lose sight of themselves, even if they do not reject their own flesh along with the male gaze. Then everything will be the way it was. We would be better off proceeding from a new and different perspective.

[. . .]

The porno film image no longer offers space for that which we all know or think we know but can no longer find in it. Radically cut off from any possible idea that will not let itself be visualized, this picture shows the vagina and penis as automatic mechanisms that operate within a Pavlovian system of stimulation. The porno film makes a promise to the body that it does not keep, even with all its flesh. It does not interpret the body in terms of penis and vagina, but instead reduces it to those two elements. Sexuality becomes anonymous in front of the camera, even if the camera focuses on the face, which only groans and screams, and is not even capable of individualizing speech. This anonymity is characteristic of the whole porno film, and not only in front of the camera. Porno films have not (yet) had directors or producers whose identities were noteworthy. The main roles in these films are played by *The Penis* and *The Vagina*. That is hard to swallow for the women of today, who are so violently wrestling with their identities. And perhaps the deepest reason why women reject porno films is found here: our secret, on which we have tried in so many various ways to base our identity, is anonymous. But maybe this is also precisely the reason that our search for identity has so far been unsuccessful.

If this fear results in a fierce aversion to the porno film, then there is a great danger that we will quickly revert to being creatures who are beautiful, clever, lovable, and holy simply because we are women. This, then, is our way of singing sorrowfully and wandering in a forest that seems to be equally dark and life-threatening no matter where we turn. Therefore all this well-lit flesh can have a liberating function: it releases our sex from the mystery in which it had to dissolve itself. Perhaps the fun for women who like to go to porno films is a result of finally being free of a secret that the man had attached to them and that they did not even want. Full of curiosity, they can now begin to see an unveiled secret in the only meaning that it still has. For those who are not able to accomplish this so quickly, it is important to expose them to this anonymous sexuality in close-up, and not let them avoid it. Rather, we should present it to them, because every lively narcissistic identification that wants to base a new women's identity on the love of the vagina and the experience of self-examination sees here that it falls right back into an anonymity of the kind that the porno film claims and only reiterates this attitude. The materialization into the image can liberate us (if we do not evade it) from the fears that rule us and that we do not understand because they are so near to us. The cinematic image supplies, where it is most needed, the distance that the feminine gaze (often to its credit) lacks. The camera produces a meeting place in which we can confront our fears, a space that makes possible the vital confrontation between what I am and what I am not. Women's ability to negate borders has led to a lack of an image of her own body and its borders. The pornographic image forces her at last to perceive the border; it ends the borderless, narcissistic relation to sight (*Sehgefühl*). On the screen, the infinitely formable body of the woman consists of discrete pieces of flesh.

The woman as voyeur of herself is not someone who "sees" because she has no other choice or because real pleasure or experience is not possible for her. Rather, she is a voyeur because she has understood that she is searching for her image and that the *via regia* to herself travels through this image. The woman's narcissism is jerked out of its contemplative attitude and pulled into the creation of an image in which it wants to see itself reflected. Its assignment is to make the flesh into a body. This portrayal of the body is not allowed to be cleansed of a materially seen sexuality. So the pornographic gaze can be seen as a sort of birth canal for a gaze that enables women to have an identity based on a real, circumscribed picture of the space, character, and measurement of their bodies—an identity that is not built upon the chimera of a mystery, and that does not believe that a head that is searching for a body can create itself according to its own desires. In pornography there is a chance for us to come to a self-awareness that is not derived from the scientific, cerebral self-awareness of Cartesian culture. In the love story between us and the pornographic picture we can bring into the world the bodies that we want to be.

Translated by Joan Barrios and Kristie Foell

Elisabeth Lenk

Indiscretions of the Literary Beast: Pariah Consciousness of Women Writers since Romanticism *(1981)*

I would like to discuss a sociological and literary category which has not existed until now, but which I nevertheless consider relevant: namely, "pariah consciousness." This category is relevant for the description of a certain continuity in the consciousness of women, particularly women who have expressed themselves in writing about their situation, i.e., women writers. I hasten to add that I discovered this category through texts by women authors.

Class consciousness, of course, exists even though it appears to have fallen into obscurity in recent times. But "*pariah* consciousness"—what could that mean? Certainly it cannot be denied that excluded groups like the Sinti and the East Indians have just recently asked to be recognized. And the mere fact that they have spoken up has irritated society, whose consensus consists precisely in its exclusion of and disregard for such groups. What irritates society even more is the dim knowledge that they have committed an injustice against the excluded group. The hate of one group for another is frequently an additional legitimization for senseless force: we hate someone—a group or a whole people—because we have done them an injustice. That is the paradoxical structure of prejudice in our society. But can we apply what is true for Jews, East Indians, and Gypsies to the status of women?

[. . .]

In Ingeborg Bachmann's *Death Types,* the female protagonists—who do not live in the "dark ages" of the nineteenth century, but in the twentieth century and, what is more, in post-fascist times—utter such sentences as: "I am of a lower race." "My body is abused, at every turn abused." "The whites are coming." "Why have I been so despised? No, not I, but the other in me." "I am a Papua."

Since I discovered this problem through such reading experiences and, I admit it freely, through life experiences as well (I am, therefore, not totally unbiased), I began to examine anthologies by famous as well as unknown Germanists. I established that the problem of women's pariah consciousness does not appear in these essays. But could not this omission itself be a form of primary and indirect confirmation of the persistence of the problem? It is probably for this reason that women authors—and particularly those with a highly developed pariah consciousness—are treated like pariahs by that small society within society, i.e., the in-group of humanists, literary scholars and, in particular, Germanists.

The first point that can be made concerning the concept of the pariah is that "a ritual guarantee of social segregation takes place" such that every physical and, by extension, every psychic-intellectual contact with the member of the pariah caste "is a ritually contaminating blemish which must be atoned for" (Max Weber). This fear of contact goes so far "that the individual castes have, in part, developed completely separate cults and gods."[1] At least one thing became clear to me in my search: not a single goddess, not a single female genius has ever appeared in the cultic activity of German literary

---

1. Max Weber, *Politische Gemeinschaften,* vol. 8, *Wirtschaft und Gesellschaft,* Tübingen, 1922.

scholarship. Women are mentioned only indirectly and only insofar as they have been mothers, lovers, daughters, or sisters of male geniuses or insofar as they have been "immortalized" in literature.

Of course, there have been several women authors recognized in German literature—even according to the presentations of the higher caste—but they are discussed with the same precautionary measures described by Weber, i.e., with obvious disdain. For a long time, the highest form of praise that could be bestowed upon a woman writer was to omit even mentioning her sex. This highest praise from the lips of a man—which, so to speak, completely cancels the pariah past—has not as yet, to my knowledge, been bestowed upon a German woman writer.

[. . .]

I am not trying to single out individuals and suggest that misogyny is their natural characteristic. I am more interested in describing rituals and reflexes which are characteristic of one caste (in this case, the caste of literary men and, unfortunately, their accomplices, female assistants)—rituals which are directed solely toward averting contamination through encroachments of intruders. Women earn praise as long as they remain silently in their ghetto, or—since their urge to write can no longer be restrained—as long as they adapt themselves to the prevailing cultural establishment, in short, as long as they respect the caste rules which exclude them. The polemics are not directed against women *per se,* but against the few women who do not accept "their natural femaleness" and overstep the boundaries drawn for them as women.

[. . .]

Pariahs, like all people compelled to become members of a community, have no other choice but to share the values of the society which despises them, which considers them unclean and thereby excludes them from the in-group. Here are the origins of their self-contempt, their self-hatred. A process which takes place among everyone in homogeneous society is particularly apparent among pariahs: in order to gain approval everyone must hate the heterogeneous *per se,* or at least renounce it vigorously. This process leaves scars for all people, especially for the pariah.

[. . .]

For the pariah, there are only two possibilities: either a radical self-renunciation—the impure ones must permanently subject themselves to purification rituals; only then can they succeed in rising fairly high within the homogeneous social hierarchy—or a return to disavowed heterogeneousness, a rebirth of the (disavowed) convictions—the development of pariah consciousness. As a result of the latter choice, the pariah either begins a radical questioning of the values of the society which has devalued the pariah's "otherness," or the values are inverted in a manner distinctly characteristic of the pariah. To the degree to which pariahs have developed religions, Weber maintained, they are inclined to regard themselves and those like them as an elite class and to ascribe a nobler origin to themselves. A good example of this is the "elite consciousness" of the Gnostics, who characterized themselves as sons and daughters of the king of an invisible realm, who have fallen into the world as the chosen people of another, unknown god.

Pariah consciousness can only remain intact—or even come into being, for that matter—when a pariah has achieved some measure of individual upward mobility within homogeneous society. Clinging to their pariah status seems to be the only means available for protecting the personality in the contradictory situation in which pariahs, who have risen in a hostile society, find themselves. Hannah Arendt analyzed this phenomenon very perceptively using Rahel Varnhagen as an example.[2] One chapter of her Varnhagen book is entitled "Between Pariah and Parvenu" and concerns Rahel's connection with Varnhagen, which enabled Rahel to get out of a desperate situation—Rahel was neither beautiful nor wealthy, and was, moreover, a Jew and a woman. According to Arendt, "Rahel was a pariah and finally discovered that one finds a place in society only by paying the price of a lie." Precisely because she had been "nothing" before ("and that was a lot," Rahel says proudly), she cannot admit to being satisfied with the small reward society offers the pariah for self-renunciation.

[. . .]

In conclusion, I would like to address a characteristic feature of women's writing style, which, in my opinion, is connected with the pariah consciousness of women, namely their uncontrollable propensity for caricature. I believe that the misfortune which has befallen and continues to befall so many women writers—that they are scorned, devalued or simply silenced by critics—is connected with this propensity for caricature. Women have drawn aside the veil at the very spot most sensitive for men: men's image of women.

[. . .]

Much has been written about the process of exclusion and the problematics of the outsider. Nonetheless, in my opinion, this new knowl-

---

2. Hannah Arendt, *Rahel Varnhagen. Lebensgeschichte einer deutschen Jüdin aus der Romantik.* Frankfurt, 1959.

edge has not been used to create a new theory of cognition. The caste of the insiders continues to perform its scientific rituals, and its members continue to declare in chorus that the truth about socialization processes and cultural phenomena can be recognized only by those who have a place in society. The counterthesis to this hasty presupposition must finally be stated: effective reflection about societal matters necessitates a vantage point removed from society.

Besides the known God who created the world—the God of realizations—the God of the victor—the Gnostics postulated another unknown god who had nothing to do with the creation of the world, but endures it just as women endure the world created by men. This unknown god stands outside the world, and his eye penetrates everything with the unerring gaze of the stranger. Every human is both an acting being and a suffering creature in one. The truth about social processes is experienced only by that part of the person that suffers, i.e., that part which suffers the effects of these processes just as, according to Nietzsche, all concepts are generally born of pain. The "socialized" part of the person, in contrast, is trained to function according to the respective caste rules, i.e., to conceal "false perceptions." Where contradictions and inconsistencies are detectable, the homogenizing consciousness comes immediately into play: the fragmentary is converted into an orderly system, the crooked is made straight, the insufficient is transformed into the sufficient.

The propensity for caricature, for the grotesque is, therefore, not distortion but "rectification." And this feature is found in every literature that is more than an artistic rendering of the social facade. The point about which I spoke, however, concerns vital being, i.e., the heterogeneous which was excluded and transformed into nonbeing. Thus, pariah consciousness is consciousness of the heterogeneous and is—because of its outside vantage point—the quintessential mirror of society.

Ingeborg Bachmann was one of the few who—after a long, painful process—attained the vantage point from which the inhumanity of our post-fascist society becomes visible. What else should her novel cycle *Death Types* have been but a description of the imperceptible, unbloody annihilation of the "other" in the person, of the feminine ego, which is no longer allowed to say "I"—the destruction of an "it" over which men haggle.

In the opinion of the guardians of our culture, this "it" must learn to be totally absorbed into a new homogeneous "I." The eternal source of societal disorder would thus be totally eliminated. At the conclusion of Ingeborg Bachmann's novel *Malina*, the feminine "I" disappears—a normal process, this process of feminine socialization. But what appears to society to be successful "normalization" is, for Bachmann—i.e., from the pariah's perspective—an indictment of society: "I have no sex, none at all anymore; it has been taken from me." Feminine socialization is portrayed by Bachmann as a crime against women, as a process of annihilation. "It was murder" reads the last sentence of *Malina.*

The honorable deeds of history and culture—or so we are taught—demand victims. Since the time of Theseus and Heracles, the first club-swinging, cultural heroes of the West, it is obvious who is singled out as the victims: the descendants of Lilith, or—if you will—the Gorgons (women who have not been diminished through the socialization process). The bloody as well as the unbloody annihilation of women, their exclusion from society, their reduction to beasts of burden upon whom society rests was all made possible by the classical ideal, the balance of the homogeneous.

Countless men have laid countless wreaths on the grave of the Unknown Soldier. But before Ingeborg Bachmann, who had ever even noticed the "Graveyard of the Murdered Daughters?"

Translated by Maureen Krause

Sigrid Weigel

Double Focus:[1] On the History of Women's Writing *(1983)*

The History of the "Second Sex"[2] *in the Male World Order*
Feminist literary criticism investigates the consequences of the patriarchal order for the aesthetic representation of women in literature written by men (that is, *images of women*) as well as for the possible

---

1. The chapter title is full of ambiguities. "Der schielende Blick" can mean "the cross-eyed gaze," "the surreptitious gaze out of the corner of the eye" or "the gaze directed in two divergent directions."—Trans.

2. In the German this is "das andere Geschlecht" which means literally both "the other sex" and "the different sex." It is clear that Weigel is referring to Simone de Beauvoir's book *La Deuxième Sexe (The Second Sex).* Paris, 1949.—Trans.

existence and actual examples of literature written by women (that is, *women's literature*). This division into images of women and women's literature is merely a conceptual aid; it should not lead to a schematic confrontation between "masculine" and "feminine" culture. Instead, it should allow a detailed investigation into the relations between the two and prompt the questions: How far do the images of women in male discourse and male poetics take women's social and individual reality into account? Does women's literature reproduce these images or does it liberate itself from them, and if so, how?

The attempts (which have become much more vigorous over the last few years) to reconstruct the *cultural history* of women should no longer be content with just examining the gaps in the literary canon and filling in the blanks on the map of literary texts wherever a woman's name was "forgotten." They should not build a *museum* of earlier exemplary women and heroines (or victims) with the aim of proving the falsehood of women's supposed lack of culture and history, a museum in which all the "sisters of yesterday" are exhibited, who—in spite of all that men say—*did* manage to write, think, work, celebrate, or even be politically active.

[. . .]

The *partisanship* of feminist literary criticism must not be allowed to take the form of voluntarily sorting the sheep from the goats, that is, taking care of the "goodies" and leaving the "baddies" to the mercies of male criticism. This partisanship is far more productive if the texts and biographies of real women—their contradictions, problems, their mistakes, and even their failures—are read and examined as material women can learn from. A text which we discover in some dusty archive is not good and interesting just because a woman wrote it. It is good and interesting because it enables us to come to new conclusions about women's literary tradition; to come to new insights about how a woman copes in a literary form with her social position, the expectations attached to her role as woman, her fears, desires and fantasies, and which strategies she developed in order to express herself publicly in spite of the confinement in the personal and the private.

Women are not without a history, they do not stand outside history. "They are within history in a special position of exclusion in which they have developed their own mode of experiencing, their way of seeing things, their culture."[3] A new (feminist) analytical and

---

3. Rossana Rossanda, *Einmischung*. Frankfurt a.M., 1983.—Eds.

interpretational effort is needed if these are to be reconstructed. The theoretical and methodological steps towards this must start with the historical phenomenon that women are seen as the "second sex" and that they see themselves to be such. Here, second is not meant in the sense of comparison or otherness but in the sense of inferiority: men are the first, the authentic sex. Women are always defined according to male criteria as regards their characteristics, behavior, etc. Women in the male order have learned to see themselves as inferior, inauthentic and incomplete. As the cultural order is ruled by men but women still belong to it, women also use the norms of which they themselves are the object. That is, woman in the male order is at once *involved and excluded.* This means for woman's self-awareness that she sees herself by seeing *that* and *how* she is seen. She sees the world through male spectacles. (The metaphor "spectacles" implies the utopia of a liberated, unhindered gaze.) She is fixated on self-observation refracted in the critical gaze of man, having left observation of the external world to his wide-ranging gaze. Thus her self-portrait originates in the distorting patriarchal mirror. In order to find her own image she must liberate the mirror from the *images of woman* painted on it by a male hand.

The metaphor of the "mirror"—its reverse side and edges, its splintering and "doubling" effect—is now commonly used to describe female self-awareness controlled by the male gaze. However, the "search for evidence within individual concrete texts (pictures, films, etc.)" which Silvia Bovenschen in her article "Is There a Feminine Aesthetic?" postulated in 1976 has been undertaken only hesitatingly and sparingly.[4] There are still very few precedents for an investigation of this mirror relationship in the *actual* writing by women—that "complicated process involving conquering and reclaiming, appropriating and reappraising, as well as forgetting and subverting." In the following pages I would therefore like to consider a few actual examples of women's writing—necessarily rather disparate—looking at the writers' relation to the dominant image of woman, the strategies they developed within the context of the mirror-image and how they related to their existence as the "second sex" in the male order. But before that I shall look at the methodological basis of such an investigation.

[. . .]

The ambiguities in the emancipatory message of many women's novels are usually recorded only with helplessness or denigration by lit-

---

4. See excerpts of Bovenschen's essay in this volume, pp. 229–32.—Eds.

erary critics. In my opinion the contradiction between the female characters' protest and the affirmative stance presented in the text rests on a specific epic tension which corresponds to an ambivalent stance on the part of the author. Within the fictional space of the plot, escape is imagined, resistance is tested, indignation formulated. Without denying herself the pleasure of fantasizing, the author can, because she is responsible for the thoughts and actions of her heroine, remain conformist either by punishing her heroine or by letting her (understandingly) renounce. And so, perhaps, the message will still get through to women readers, but in a subversive way. I suspect that contemporary readers read the novels of Luise Mühlbach,[5] Fanny Lewald[6] and others between the lines, for how else could such literature have gained the disreputable reputation of being in the tradition of George Sand whose name was synonymous with the emancipated woman?

The Feminist Resource:[7] *Looking out of the Corner of One's Eye*
The argument so far may seen restricted in theme and concept. It revolves around *the Other,* the development of a female culture and utopia, and above all around the relation between images of women and female self-awareness. Women should allow themselves to look out of the corner of just one eye in this narrow concentrated way so that they can be free to roam over the length and breadth of the social dimension with the other. In order to be able to see through their specific role as women in all spheres and on all levels they need at least half their field of vision to concentrate this rigid gaze on the so-called "woman problem." They will only be able to correct this *sideways look* when the woman theme is redundant—when the living and writing woman has overcome her *double life* of living by the pattern set by the dominant images *and* in the anticipation of the emancipated woman.

[...]

There have been many attempts to formulate theoretically the connection between the analysis of political issues and the relationship

---

5. Luise Mühlbach (1814–73) produced almost three hundred volumes of novels and travelogues. The emancipatory tendency of her early works (1838–49) disappeared after 1850.—Eds.

6. Fanny Lewald, another prolific writer who was particularly concerned with the situation of women. See selections by her in this volume, pp. 25–27, 71–82, 116–18, 176–80, and 257–58.—Eds.

7. In German this is *Vermögen,* which means both "ability" and "wealth." —Trans.

between the sexes. The primary/secondary contradiction is one of the most tenacious and also one of the most unprofitable variants of these efforts. The slogan which has recently become popular, that "the personal is political," attempts to reconcile the opposition rhetorically. This is provocative because it offends the taboo surrounding what has been declared merely personal and publicizes the power relations within the home. It thus verbalizes the refusal of many women to tolerate the existing divisions any longer.

However, "the personal is political" is deceptive too if it promises a political solution to personal suffering. There can, thank goodness, be no political—that is, organized, formal—solution to the really personal, for that would mean the suspension of individual self-determination. Love, pain and happiness, the desire to overcome personal boundaries, and self-assertion cannot be distributed according to rules; that would result in the collapse of human relationships. This is shown by the literary utopias which attempt to reconcile the conflict between a desire to submit and a striving for autonomy, which in turn exterminates the roots of this conflict, that is, desire. Programs like these rest on a fundamental misunderstanding. They confuse the painful coupling of love and submission, the submerging of relationships by the patriarchal relations of power in which individuals confront each other as the carriers of gender roles, with the vibrant contradiction between freedom and identity which arises in every deep heterosexual relationship and which is also experienced in homosexual and lesbian ones. . . . Women will have to come to terms with experiencing the "personal" on their own for a long time to come. Wherever women are isolated they experience a hiatus, whether in connection with their jobs or in social, cultural or political life. The thread connecting what is otherwise experienced and lived in the company of and in conversation with women seems to be broken off. They become backsliders. Learning how to look out of the corner of one's eye as a feminist tactic includes seeing this not as a personal failure but instead as necessary, as a *double existence* which cannot be harmonized here and now, during this period of transition.

Let us return to the mirror image. If the projections, the images, are wiped off the mirror, then at first it is blank. The mirror can be painted with new concepts but these are equally images; even the shattering of the mirror leads to nothing. What the liberated woman will look like cannot be imagined with any certainty or in any detail at the moment, let alone how she will be experienced. In order to live through this transitional space between the *no longer* and the *not yet* without going mad, it is necessary for woman to learn to look in two diverging directions simultaneously. She must learn to voice the contradictions, to see them, to comprehend them, to live in and with them, and also learn to gain strength from the rebellion against yesterday and from the anticipation of tomorrow.

Both the hysterical woman who abandons her role and the mad woman who assails the male order use their bodies to articulate the contradiction. "Madness and hysteria are the two sides of female insanity as it has been defined (and incidentally also caused) by men."[8] By reading between the lines of the male definition, the rebellious element of hysteria has recently moved into the (feminist) field of vision. Yet even in this reading the ambivalence remains because the hysterical and the mad, by using their bodies, also abuse them and so harm themselves.

It is certainly some achievement not to become *de-ranged*[9] considering the present state of affairs. Elisabeth Lenk in her metaphor of the "self-reflecting woman" who can "develop the new relationship to herself only through relationships to other women" has shown the healing element in this madness:

> Woman often believes when she enters into this relationship to herself for the first time, when she for the first time reflects herself, that she has turned mad. But this apparent madness is no madness; it is the first step towards sanity.

This relation in which "woman will become the living mirror of woman by losing herself and then finding herself again"[10] can, in my opinion, only become a healing process if the woman does not see the other woman as a model[11] to be copied, only if she is prepared to discover and to accept the "no longer" and the "not yet," that is, her present double life. Rahel had an inkling of this double life. "[I have] the tremendous strength of being able to double myself with-

---

8. Claudine Herrmann, *Sprachdiebinnen*. Munich, 1977, 65.—Trans.

9. In the German this is *ver-rückt*. By hyphenating the word in this way, Weigel gives it another connotation to its usual meaning of "mad." It now also implies "displaced."—Trans.

10. Elisabeth Lenk, "The Self-Reflecting Woman." *Feminist Aesthetics*, ed. Gisela Ecker. London, 1985, 57.—Eds.

11. In the German this is *Vor-bild*. Again, by splitting the word, Weigel gives it another meaning. In common usage it means "exemplary model." But here it also implies an image which is placed in front of someone and also an image which chronologically precedes another.—Trans.

out confusing myself,"[12] by which she meant the irreconcilability of her inner and outer life. In her doubling of the self she retains what would have been destroyed if publicly exposed. It is this conscious renunciation of reconciling models and utopias which Julia Kristeva means when she says that "a feminine praxis must be negative if it is to say that this is and this is not yet" that is, "to say the not-being."[13]

The language we have learned is unsuitable for such a *negative praxis* as the speechlessness (the unwritten literature of women) and the volubility (the reams of trivial literature produced by women) show. Our language has been learned from our fathers—and mothers. The institution of "father" and the reproduction of "mother" in the forms which have been discussed/conjured up in an endless discourse over the last two hundred years from the days of the early Enlightenment to the ideologists of a bourgeois family politics are, however, the foundations of patriarchy. What holds true for appearance also applies to language. Female language (which does not mean a new vocabulary as is often thought) "does no longer" and "does not yet" exist; it is "no longer" pleasing and virtuous and "not yet" liberated and authentic. Therefore, we shall have to practice carefully using the newly acquired language accurately, aware of both its visible and hidden constraints, paying attention above all to the meaning of language patterns, rhetorical devices and genres.

If writing/literature is to be a space where the double life can be expressed, opinions exchanged in order to break down the concept of life as the mirror-image of male projections, where freedom can be tried out in order to find a language for our own desires and wishes, then the existing concepts (above all those of the dominant genres) are not adequate, or only at a pinch if their patterns are used in a refracted, paradoxical way.

Translated by Harriet Anderson

12. Rahel Varnhagen, *Buch des Andenkens an ihre Freunde,* 3 vols. Berlin, 1934. 2: 83.—Eds.

13. "Kein weibliches Schreiben? Fragen an Julia Kristeva." *Freibeuter* 2 (1979): 81–82.—Eds.

Ginka Steinwachs

the palatheater of the mouth *(1989)*

I. we declare that the theater has ceased to exist for some and almost everyone.

II. but here one continues to graze complacently.
salvador dali et alii, yellow manifesto, barcelona 1928.

programmatically:

we live at a time and in a century when the theater
—I intentionally disregard its rival, the motion picture—
has developed a so-called b o d y l a n g u a g e.
its historical beginnings were antonin artaud and his
t h e a t e r o f c r u e l t y.
that body language, stressing movement in d a n c e,
or compounding music and image and movement in
p e r f o r m a n c e,
using slides and film segments,
which personally is to my heart's content,
makes us forget t h a t the language of the mouth or mouthlanguage
is n o t m e r e l y o n e a m o n g m a n y gestural
languages, but the supreme one, ranking above
h a n d a n d f o o t, u p p e r a n d l o w e r b o d y.

I f o u n d that which I have i n v e n t e d.
the found object I invented is rather old and common.
rarely do we find human beings that were not born with it.
just as their parents and ancestors possessed it.

if I see Y O U, *my dear ladies and gentlemen,*[1] mesdames
messieurs, señors i señoras, Y O U, meine verehrten Damen
und Herren of the audience, in the light of the spotlight,
which blinds = blends me into Y O U, if I see and understand
Y O U right, you will not only permit me, but implore me, as
it were, to boost this f o u n d i n v e n t i o n like a
barker, llllll.oudly and llllll.ustily.

---

1. The italicized passages mark words that appear in English in the original.
—Trans.

ladies and gentlemen of the audience, dear *friends* = freunde,
sustaining friends, supporting friends, sponsors and benefactors,
here I have a model of the smallest and at the same time
oldest portable theater of the world (ddd DDD). it is an
e n l a r g e d model in relation to its o r i g i n k a l,
the mouth, and a m i n i a t u r e model compared to the theater.
(((((think for example
of the burgundypurplesnailred tonguerugs with which
the palatheater of the mouth of the M E T is lined))))).
if you please, I'd like to ask for. . . . . .
the goldenred wrapping around the theater begins to tremble;
it rises haltingly
. . . . . a hand for
t h e p a l a t h e a t e r o f t h e m o u t h.

as Y O U can see, the palatheater of the mouth
(((((vestibulum oris becomes vestibulum amoris))))), this
little anatomo-architectonic miraculous contraption, appears
in this model as under a magnifying-glass,
and when will they finally build a theater which will
resemble in every instance an ordinary mouth, with the
jaw = = = = = pointing = = = = = as auditorium and the
gorge = = = = = pointing = = = = = as an ensemble of stage floor
and fly space, with the lips
((((snow on the lips, says heiner müller)))))
and front teeth as curtain,
the front teeth are made of colored stones and glitter
from *canal surplus or industrial plastics supply on canal street,*
unnaturally black.
I re.peat the re.spit. as Y O U can see, the palatheater
of the mouth is unnaturally black. the lips
((((snow on the lips, says heiner müller))))
are closed. the lips ((((snow on the lips, says heiner müller))))
are closed tight.
they do not speak, but b r e a t h e through me
((((the M E D I U M M E))))
the words of the lesbian lover and beloved
marie dorval of my stage play:
g e o r g e s a n d, a w o m a n i n m o t i o n, a
w o m a n o f s t a n d i n g,
ullstein pocketbook no. 30 152, frankfurt, berlin, wien, 1983.
welt = ur = aufführung/première mondiale/opening 11/20/88 in bonn
addressed to her lover in male drag george sand.

by the way: marie dorval was a famous actor in her time
at the comédie humaine, ah pardon francaise, and the two of them
had,
long long ago,
long long EGO, a lll.ong lll.iaison with each other.

origin (k) alquotation marie dorval of the comédie
(of the *living theater*/of la mama/of the *performance garage*):

I C H never play more than I a m.
the whole holy family of I's.
rather than the I bérénice (BÉRÉNICE)
and the I phaedra (PHAEDRA) and and and
I would of course choose the I lélia (LÉLIA) and
indiana (INDIANA). . . .
to explore you, beloved monsieur george, "hermaphrodite
child of sun and moon" to the bottom of the root
of the palatheater of the mouth, to the depths of modern
inspiration in general. . . .
the closure of the lips
and my whispering through closed lips with marie's voice,
is compensated for by the burgundypurplesnailred venetian curtain.

the burgundypurplesnailred venetian curtain rises.
one can see. . . .
one can see. . . .
one can see. . . .
a hand in a white glove, this formerly mine right righteous
hand, as it strokes longingly in the manner of a sculptor
who wants to put the finishing touches on a work begun long ago.
the sculptor's name is alexandre manceau, and is, he is,
the thirtyfourth (34th) thirtyfourth youngest and last lover
in the ranks and rows of the pretendants to the affections of the
adorable
a m a n t i n e (AMANTINE)
l u c i l e (LUCILE)
a u r o r e (AURORE) d u p i n, baroness d u d e v a n t, alias george
sand.

e motu contrario::::::

by lending manceau a lyrical male voice, ICH myself benefit
from the state of grace of the "this as well as that" or
"adam kadmon" or "hermaphrodite child of sun and moon."

a tremor (earth worth quake) runs through the curtain like a
f-o-r-e-s-t.

originkalquotation manceau, hatedbeloved:

a garden of desire, these breasts I admire.
here, in this place, I could file away
the trace of a grain of sand.
llllakes that milllk and honey spilllll.
jugs with white and red wine filllled.

below, finely-tuned, the klavichord of the ribcage.
for this, chopin wrote his etude for black keys.
below: the equatorial belt-line.
swirling, whirling pearls divine.
the white of the loins will blind the blind.
hammer chisels at the mount, fount, source, remorse.
gestures.

I interrupt for a moment and express my outrage.
someone I suspect mistakes the p a r t of the mouth for
the w h o l e of the female body and, in his passionate
infatuation, which makes language melt like sugar on a
f o r k e d   t o n g u e, gropes far too low.
I re.peat the re.spit. below.

m-phatic & ex = tatic moans:::::
lower. . . .
lower. . . .
the clitoral crest, vaginal recess.
mist in mossy folds. Tell me, anatomists, doesn't this
streamlet trickle directly into women's heavenly harnessed sex?
lower. . . .
lower. . . .
below: as ancient pillars high, the thigh.
below: calves, spheric halves.
beneath ankles that drive me crankles,
at last, sehr gut, the naked foot.
white-clad hand plays = = = = = shoe.
no more wordy wit, let's get down to it.

pause. long pause. musically, a long time passes.
the white hand draws a treble clef in the air and dots
imaginary staff lines.

manceau sings in time to the studio of waltz dreams.
"these are still the golden days.
still the days of roses."

at this point, I read "wait till the applause has ceased."
wait.

wait.
ladies and gentlemen, mesdames messieurs, señors i señoras,
meine damen und herren, dear friends of the palatheater, i n
t h e o r a l t h e a t e r, that found object of olden times
= = = = =the theater is wrapped again in its goldenred cover = = = =
the words, I am sure YOU sensed, which fell, I am sure YOU
sensed, and which are chewed véritablement like chunks, I am
sure YOU sensed, and which taste of crust, I am sure YOU
sensed, the tongue, remember, fulfills a d o u b l e
function in the mouth: it articulates a n d tastes,
with emphasis on the a n d, are first and foremost, I am
sure YOU sensed, first and foremost expressions of body
language, or: in no other words: present in the flesh.

this////this////this
shows the very in = essence of my personal poetics: the utopia of the
    fleshy word,
of the full-bodied word, of the word that seduces you to
handle and smell and touch it, of the sensual word which has
a weight and exudes perfume, of the word that enlightens and
of the word that lives and delivers emotions.
for this word,
I commit myself, in the age of
teevee, micro = electronics and multiple over = kill
(lip service in black-and-white)
to dramatic writing.

frankfurt/barcelona/new york 1983–1988 gst.≡

Translated by Katrin Sieg

Libuše Moníková

Some Theses Regarding Women's Writing *(1997)*

What has changed since the emergence of "women's writing" in the 1970s?

A lot, I hope. Women no longer have to reveal and validate their body for literature, or to thematize the social and physical injuries that have been done to it. The first phase of women's writing was marked by these experiences; the impulse to communicate and to write usually started with them. For the taboo zone of one's own sexuality there was no language; for its literary treatment, no traditional form.

The first attempts to touch our own bodies led to naming, to comparisons and images that were no less uncertain and awkward, but that were recognized by an entire generation as "authentic" in their emphasis.

The "pumpkin-breasts and -bellies" *(Kürbisbrüste und -bäuche)* phase,[1] this aggressive declaration of physicality, ought to have given way in the meantime to the recognition that women also have a head. Sensations and sensitivities are no longer primarily dealt with (I hope) on the level of physical suffering and insult, but instead reflected on and dealt with intellectually.

Some things I am able to understand through my own writing: For my first book *Eine Schädigung* (Injury, 1981), I garnered approval from the women's movement primarily because the protagonist—a young woman who is raped by a police officer and then kills him in the heat of the moment—was above all a victim with whom most readers (women as well as men) could feel solidarity and with whom many could also identify. They could get emotionally involved, because this role was familiar to them.

The second book, *Pavane für eine verstorbene Infantin* (Pavane for a Dead Princess, 1983) bewildered my original supporters and scared off many of them. This time the woman was an intellectual who does not put up with the everyday, unreasonable expectations of her environment, who also thoroughly and rationally analyzes

---

1. This is an allusion to Verena Stefan's attempt to find a language to express women's experience of their own bodies in *Häutungen (Shedding)*, 1975. See the article that follows in this volume.—Eds.

them and finally "strikes back" in her own way. (She sits, although "healthy," in a wheelchair, blows off literature seminars and instead writes a continuation to the story of the Barnabas family in Kafka's *The Castle* in which she searches for a social solution for them.) This book was formally more advanced and more complicated than the first. New readers appeared, among them supporters who paid more attention to the construction of the text, but on the whole, the "comfortable pit of our misfortune," where it is so easy to complain, was missing—an intellectual woman was not a welcome theme in 1983.

Since then I have also been writing about men. As a rule they turn out more convincing and realistic than my female figures, who are usually too dominant and therefore appear less credible. My feelings for them betray wishful thinking. It is an authorial weakness.

I place demands on myself and my fellow writers: in this day and age I not only want women to see (and represent) themselves more clearly and convincingly as intellectuals rather than as weak, manipulated victims, but above all to fulfill expectations of form when doing so. A private history does not interest me if it is not of high literary quality. Then the woman represented can even be weak. The main thing is that the writing is strong.

What I still miss for the most part is literature by women that is funny, humorous, biting, satirical. Self-pity has diminished, but self-irony is still rare.

Women lack a certain ease and, furthermore, tenacity and economy of effort when dealing with larger thematic areas and quantities of material: beyond the horizon of the personal.

More humor.

More subversiveness in material and form. Why not write about men, make them the object of our literary desire? They used us for their creative fantasies for thousands of years (and those were not the worst ones).

More desire to experiment, incursive forms: cabaret, carnivalia—masks, "red noses"—*femmes fatales* as comrades, and comrades as intellectuals. I am not satisfied when women work off their feelings through writing (experiences from my seminars); that is self-therapy at best, but as a rule it is mush: diarists write diaries, rarely literature.

Self-criticism, based on a sound ability to make comparisons. Men might serve as a basis for comparison and competition—they have been developing the form for a longer time; art has its own rules and is dependent neither on ideologies nor bellies.

More professionalism. The constant complaints about women's "double role" have no place in art. It always comes down to "exceptions" when one deals with "women's literature," "minority literature": Women just write, and that's all there is to it.

I claim for women, for their writing as a social practice, full earnestness and full commitment; I do not want to have to take children into consideration, not in my own writing and not when judging others' texts. I can respect in addition that a woman is working under the more difficult conditions that a family means for her. This is not my primary interest, however. When judging art there are no extenuating circumstances.

We are not victims, and if we do not make progress, it is because of us, and because we are not able to get past the persistent stereotypes that we find confirmed in history and in our own childhood. I do not want any pity for women, especially self-pity.

There once was a woman, mother of several children, who died from hunger and mental fatigue at the age of forty-two. First, however, through her prose she advanced Czech as a literary language. Božena Němcová. Such achievements are unique. Still, I would have preferred if she had suffered less and written a few more books.

Misery is not a criterion for truth, pity not a basis for judging quality. Women who write must free themselves from misery, from their own, and also from the misery of an amateurish form; only then can they contribute with their work to reducing misery in the real world as well.

We ought to discuss the conditions of our literary production, as well as its weaknesses, without looking for excuses.

Translated by Lynn E. Ries

Verena Stefan

Cacophony *(1994)*

As a veteran of the new women's movement, I'm regarded as a symbol of the outbreak because I wrote *Shedding* and because *Shedding* was the first literary text to come out of the contemporary movement in Germany. With it we mark the history of a book that was also an event.[1] The market didn't make it, protect it, or launch it. Readers'

---

1. Stefan's 1975 book *Häutungen (Shedding)*, an experimental collage of prose and poetic forms, gained fame as a radical attempt to employ a new nonpatriarchal language to express female sexuality, including lesbian love.—Eds.

hunger for such a text pushed the printings skyward, which in turn insured the survival of the publisher, Frauenoffensive. The history of *Shedding* is an inverted one.

For me it is above all the history of the author I have since become. In 1977, I wrote in the afterword to the second edition of *Shedding*: "[This] is not the first installment in a literary career. Writing a book seemed at that time to be the most effective form of feminist activism. It doesn't mean that a second will necessarily follow."

After the shedding comes the identity crisis. As the number of *Sheddings* continually climbs, together with the euphoric and wrathful reactions to the ever increasing printings, an identity crisis ensues. Inner paralysis takes over, although at the time I'm not yet aware that later I will so name this epoch. Time seems to have fallen into a vacuum, as nonverbalizable and indescribable as in the era before *Shedding*. What cannot be said hurts now in another way because in the meantime I've learned that I *can* write pieces of it. What I have written has been heatedly discussed. This sensational success triggered envy, competition, avarice, intrigues, corruption, betrayal, and blockades. Fear snatched my tongue. This new speechlessness causes chronic pain, anesthetizing all my creative impulses. A part of my consciousness is only too readily occupied by wishing the pain would cease. The pain goes on. It kindly ossifies. My newly born knowledge freezes within me, my experience of whole nights spent feverishly writing, of haunted, inexorable writing, of the feeling of wanting to and being able to write. Self-doubt that had periodically tormented me and the momentary fear of publication couldn't stop the writing. Ossification now seems to be erasing me. I kick and punch but can't break out. Years of despair can't soften it. I'm too impatient and inexperienced a writer to understand that this paralysis is needed to protect my writing from destruction from without and thoughtless, hasty wear and tear. Paralysis eats my days. My emotions, pruned to cope with the new situation, need time to grow back. In 1976, an experienced journalist wrote me a letter with a passage that saved my life: "And just one more thing: don't let yourself be put under pressure of deadlines, not by anyone at any price. Write?—yes, try out a lot of things. But publish little. Be able to wait. Wait until what you write has sufficient 'bulk' so that it can't be ravaged. The capitalist market is a slaughterhouse. And just leave 'misunderstandings' to lie fallow, don't pick them up. You can't win. You'll only go under, and they'll have their harvest."

The pain has receded. Eighteen years have passed. For the last three days I've been pushing scraps of papers full of notes across my desk, reading old letters, reviews, and diaries, ripping up and burning a pile of paper ballast. I want to report on that era in simple sentences, but paralysis again sets in, keeping me from writing the first line. The moment I try, nausea overcomes me. Nausea spreads throughout my body. There's only one way to deal with the nausea: write the first sentence, and after the first the second, and after the second the third, without stopping, and after the first page I'll know how to go on.

It goes on in the hallway of a house on flat land. A friend calls. How are you? she asks. I don't know, I answer truthfully, I guess I'm depressed. That must have been the end of 1976. In the spring of 1976, the first meeting of women writers took place in Munich. Christa Reinig, Gisela V. Wysocki, Ursula Krechel, Monika Sperr, Luisa Francia, among others, participated. We were all seated together at one table. Today such a thing can't even be imagined. *Shedding* had already sold forty-four thousand copies. I can't remember ever having applied the word *depression* to describe my state of mind.

[. . .]

For years I would answer letters personally and send polite regrets to newspapers and bookstores. Many critics—sociologists, women in German studies, feminists—pronounced *Shedding* the bible of the women's movement, a book with which all women can identify, a symbol, a cult manual. All concepts having to do with collective action, collective beliefs. *Shedding* is in fact the offspring of a collective political process. My first published words appeared under a group signature. Like everyone else, we too were saying back then: "The personal is political." The oppressed were no longer exclusively other people, the exploited working class and inhabitants of the so-called Third World, but also us women. Books came out of the left and women's movements in which a single voice at last said "I." It was politically legitimate, and even a text consigned to the world of belles lettres appeared within the framework of the permitted. But who permitted? And who forbade? In that transitional situation many of us, with decreasing frequency, engaged in bitter verbal battle with our comrades, insisting that women were not a secondary contradiction but, rather, the salt of the earth. We gave ourselves permission to analyze from our own point of view the state of the female nation and to define it anew. Big Brother did not stop superintending us, from outside and inside our heads. Is it good enough, compared to the Great Tradition, Great Literature, Fine Art? The criteria and hurdles remained.

[. . .]

In 1974, as I was writing *Shedding,* I traveled for three months in the United States and Mexico. I stood in a Berkeley women's bookstore and, with my head slung low, swept along each and every shelf. Three thousand titles by women authors were standing there. In Germany at that time we had not a single women's bookstore and not a single feminist press. From the loudspeaker twirled "Lavender Jane Loves Women," and *Rubyfruit Jungle* and *Riverfinger Women* were that summer's hits. Judy Grahn showed me her long poem *A Woman Is Talking to Death.* She passed her hand along the book's spine and said with pride, "This time we not only did the text by ourselves but also the jacket and illustrations!"

Did the book already exist, the one I wanted to write? It didn't. Did I already know then what I wanted to write? Repeatedly over several months I read the same three books: *To the Lighthouse, The Bell Jar,* and *Flying.* I couldn't put a name to my own writing. I was concerned with THE truth, of that I'm sure. I was obsessed with stating THE truth. That made me frank, willing to take risks. Couples on the Left seemed thoroughly hypocritical to me, their behavior in stark contrast to revolutionary ideals. In my own voice I wrote a book to analyze in razor-sharp detail the incongruities in these relationships; I was liberal with prescriptions for action. Slowing things down, I dissected what seemed a hypocritical relationship into minute acts, separating them into individual movements and parts of a movement, into gestures and mannerisms. Close-ups, meetings in slow motion. What did this process reveal? The details contained as much mendacity as the broad lines of the relationship.

At the same time my intoxication with the truth allowed me to be effusive and inexact in my descriptions of the possible, of lesbian love. Looking back, I can wish I had had an editor who might have told me, "Wait with your descriptions of nature or of lesbian love and lesbian bodies until you know more about the one and the other and have become more experienced as a writer." But I was frightfully impatient. I was so completely preoccupied with the desire to say everything I had to say that I was totally in the grip of that feeling— let it all out. No one could have put the brakes on me, really. Inspiration and support came to me twice, from my female lover at that time and a male employee in a major publishing house. There was no editor for this book. It was zero hour. Each woman was discovering herself as an author, a publisher, a producer.

For the length of one stretched instant we could still think we were all equal. Wanting our own feminist press proved to be a binding political interest. *Shedding* created factions, infighting, pigeonholing. The women's movement put in a claim for *its* product, *its* author. Readers, friends, enemies, publishers' readers, academics, colleagues, other artists, organizers of cultural events, reviewers, bookstore owners, journalists, and publishers[2] took notice, considering precisely how the author represented the movement. Which feminist faction, which literary direction did she support? The women's movement split into various camps: Are you for or against its status as literature? its lesbianism? All my relationships became hostage to this. *Oh, so that's Verena? What! You know Verena Stefan?* Success corrupted all associations: *Why her and not me?*

Germany is a small country, and in the women's movement everybody knows everybody else. We all watched one another. Just as on the bourgeois literary scene, so in feminist literary circles, a point system of judgment declared *right* or *wrong, better* or *worse,* as it served one's literary career to call the shots.

[. . .]

After *Shedding* I wrote a second, third, and fourth book and am presently working on the fifth. I translated three books. My book of poems, *With Feet with Wings,* sold eight thousand copies and was never critiqued nor reissued because *poetry doesn't sell.* The remainders of the German translations of *Dream of a Common Language* and *Lesbian Peoples* are going for practically nothing because *they don't sell.* Where are the readers of these books? Twenty years ago we stood behind the Dream of a Common Language—we, the feminist publishers who today remainder these books, along with the authors who fought for such books.

During the Fifth International Feminist Book Fair in Amsterdam in 1992, I took part in two workshops, the first called "Censorship and Lesbian Writing." Censorship has many faces. I spoke about internal censorship. Success breeds it. So do expectations and disappointments. If a writer wants to go on writing, she's got to forget all the interpretations, everything that's been said or written about her style, literary talents and deficits, her appearance, her sexual preferences, her themes, her public appearances, and her politics. She's got to forget what other eyes see as correct or incorrect. She mustn't think that with the next book, too, reactions will be either "I'm so enthusiastic / so frustrated" or that literary criticism means above all finding fault. Only when she no longer hears these voices inside her can she find her own way to that unruly place from which her unique

---

2. All nouns are in the feminine in the original German.—Trans.

voice can proceed. If she's often been interpreted, if she's raised great expectations and provoked major disappointment with her first book, it means she's going to have to try even harder to forget, if she wants to write another book.

Translated by Tobe Levin

Anna Mitgutsch

What Is "Women's Literature"? *(1996)*

The concept of women's literature as it is used today—although perhaps in a less unreflected way than fifteen years ago—is contemporaneous with the beginnings of feminist theory in the 1970s. Feminist literary scholars employed it, on the one hand, to illustrate and solidify feminist theory within literary praxis and, on the other, to reintroduce forgotten or neglected literature by women into the canon and to point out a suppressed tradition of works by women. Without this pioneer work, the broad reception of women authors of the Romantic period and the rereading of authors who had been ignored by the always already normative literary canon would have not been possible, especially since feminine consciousness had no role in the establishment of this canon. The term *women's literature,* created by engaged women scholars in order to give women a voice and a space within male-dominated culture, was taken up in the literary market place and in literary criticism much more eagerly than is normally the case for theoretical concepts in the humanities. However, the term did not land on neutral ground, where it could be popularized in the meaning intended by its originators. It had already been taken up in another sense and would gain further negative connotations as the increasing numbers of women writing in the 1970s and 1980s were perceived as a threat by male authors. [. . .]

What are the typical features of treatments of women's literature?

Women's literature is defined by its content. It is said to be literature by women about women and for women or, put more eloquently, a conscious examination of the situation of women. Do men not write about men, or for men? Do they not examine their societal situation? Certainly, but language, narrative perspective, and structure are more important. Literature by women must often contend with an arrogant perception of its narrative perspective: here more than in language a specifically feminine aesthetic is revealed. What may most distinguish literature by women from the male way of seeing things is the subjective feminine definition of reality and approach to processes of perception and cognition, their relation to the real as well as to the imaginary, to the body and to everything that is simply—and erroneously—taken for granted in the male view. Does that mean that only a woman reader, a woman critic can appreciate the feminine narrative perspective? Why are male readers and critics often so negative, so malicious, so irritated by texts with a recognizably feminine narrative perspective? Apparently because they have not learned, and do not intend to learn, what women readers of male texts do as a matter of course: to read sensitively and not normatively, to adopt the narrative perspective of the text, i.e., to read it from within and not from without. Men do not recognize that they do read the classics, old and new, this way. But when they read women's texts, they apparently assume that there is nothing there to reward such sensitivity. The more closely a text written by a woman corresponds to the way readers have learned to read the canon—which has nothing to do with avant-garde and traditional narration—the more readily they will read it in the usual way. But it may also be that the woman author who subjugates herself in this manner to the male way of seeing and experiencing will so identify with the male subject that she relinquishes her own subjectivity in the shaping of her subject matter.

If women's literature is now defined by its content, i.e., if the reader's expectation is the same as for popular literature, then it is not surprising if the resistance that the text offers to the reader—resistance that is otherwise interpreted as a sign of high literature—provokes irritation. Content is what is sought after, female experience. If the narration is not straightforward, it can only be attributed to the incompetence of the author.

Women's literature is expected to follow a feminist program. It's as if women authors owe their women readers something, as if they had to fulfill a moral responsibility. Since literature by women that has been devalued as "women's literature" is normally ignored by men anyhow, feminists often review it according to the precepts of feminist ideology. That would be fine if the authors accept the label "women's literature" as appropriate for their texts. But the classification is handed down like a verdict, objections go unheard, and the term "women's literature" turns out to be what it was from the beginning: a form of trivialization and marginalization.

Women's literature is equated with literature of experience, whereby the accent is on self-experience, imitation of a distorted reality perceived through the filter of female experience, not serious because it is not universal, with no relation whatsoever to the *conditio humana,* a silly slice of distorted reality, embarrassingly exhibitionistic, presented in an unsublimated way. If literature makes a claim for unveiling a universal truth in a valid linguistic form, then what is regarded as "women's literature" is just the opposite of literature.

The question of a feminine aesthetic has often been raised. Perhaps it cannot be answered in a general or theoretical way, but only by example. But there is a danger that it will fall victim to the circular logic of all theorizing, that only those works are analyzed from which a theory can be distilled, and then only those that support the theory are incorporated into the canon.

The question of whether there is a women's literature that is not a sub-literature of doubtful aesthetic status but a serious literature with specific traits of feminine creativity can only be answered positively when feminine experience, feminine narrative perspective, and feminine perception are considered equal to that of men, when the opposite of the feminine experience is not common human experience but masculine experience, and when women have an equal claim to represent this common human experience. Then of course, the concept "women's literature" would also become obsolete.

Literature both by women and by men derives from subject matter, ideas, and experiences that are directly connected to the author. But it is only in the struggle with language, the process of writing, i.e., the creative process, that chance raw material—life—is translated into art. No author can avoid inscribing her/himself into the text. Therefore, literature by women cannot avoid bearing the mark of feminine experience. That need not be considered bad or unliterary if feminine experience is recognized as common human experience. The conflict between the generations, for instance, is an ancient literary topos. But only after daughters started dealing with the conflict between the generations did the topos, now labeled as the "mother-daughter problem," lose its canonical status and thereby its universality.

The demand of feminist literary theory that literature give voice to the other, the marginalized, the silenced means little for literary praxis, unless by that is merely meant the feminine perception of reality. That, of course, cannot be experienced by a woman writer as the other, as the Lacanian non-being, but as something uniquely her own, which may deviate from familiar forms of expression. The courage of a woman writer ought not consist of searching desperately for her own form as a lacuna in the male discourse but of inscribing her own specifically feminine voice into the text without even a sidelong glance to the canon and the *zeitgeist*. It should neither be necessary to create new myths of femininity, nor to demythologize femininity by adopting male subjectivity.

There is no feminine language in the sense that has been propagated as a utopia by French and Italian feminists. But language as a system of signs is also not androgynous. Men use the language available to them differently than do women, at least in the metaphorical, symbolic realm. As long as it is perceived as a compliment when one assures a woman that she writes like a man, then texts with a more pronounced feminine linguistic gesture will be dismissed as "women's literature."

Luce Irigaray and Hélène Cixous locate the feminine linguistic gesture in the fluid transition between outside and inside, in the stronger emphasis on the interior perspective. But perhaps a greater skepticism toward subjectivity that poses as objectivity is inherent in feminine language, a knowledge of the unretrievable elusiveness of experience and the non-narratability of experience. [. . .] Feminine narrative praxis could be a praxis that takes into account that which cannot be narrated and refuses unambiguous solutions, for how else should that which cannot be expressed become visible.

Translated by Patricia A. Herminghouse
and Magda Mueller

Acknowledgments

Every reasonable effort has been made to locate the owners of rights to previously published works and translations printed here. We gratefully acknowledge permission to reprint the following material:

Orlanda Frauenverlag for permission to use selections from *Daheim unterwegs. Ein deutsches Leben,* by Ika Hügel-Marshall; and portions from "Vagabonding: Feminist Thinking Cut Loose," by Christina Thürmer-Rohr. "Vagabonding" also published by Beacon Press.

"Vagabonding" by Christina Thürmer-Rohr Copyright © 1987 by Orlanda Frauenverlag. English translation Copyright © 1991 by Beacon Press. Reprinted by permission of Beacon Press, Boston.

Peter Lang Publishing, Inc., for permission to reprint "Instruction for Women" (chapter 9) from *Women and Their Vocation: A Nineteenth-Century View of Luise Büchner,* translated by Susan L. Piepke.

Lily Braun, edited and translated by Alfred G. Meyer, *Selected Writings on Feminism and Socialism,* by permission Indiana University Press.

Berg Publishers for permission to reprint Bertha von Suttner, "Speech in San Francisco in June 1912," from Kemp, Beatrix, *Suffragette for Peace: The Life of Bertha von Suttner.* London: Oswald Wolf, 1972.

Verlag J. H. W. Dietz Nachf. GmbH for Adelheid Popp, "Die neue Frau," in *Jugend einer Arbeiterin,* edited by Hans J. Schütz, Berlin/Bad Godesberg: J. H. W. Dietz, 1980.

International Publishers for permission to reprint from Clara Zetkin, "Women of the Working People" (1915), from *Clara Zetkin: Selected Writings,* edited by Philip S. Foner, translated by K. Schoenhals, New York: International Publishers, 1984.

Ariadne Press for permission to reprint from Marie von Ebner-Eschenbach, *Aphorisms,* translated by David Scrase and Wolfgang Mieder, Riverside, California: Ariadne, 1994.

Anna Rueling. Reprinted from *Lesbian Feminism in Turn-of-the-Century Germany.* Ed. Lillian Faderman and Brigitte Eriksson, Naiad Press, 1980 with the permission of the publisher.

Marielouise Janssen-Jurreit, "Die Zukunft des Feminismus" in *Sexismus: Über die Abtreibung der Frauenfrage.* © 1976 Carl Hanser Verlag München Wien.

Talheimer Verlag for permission for Karola Bloch, "Würde der Frau," in *Die Sehnsucht des Menschen, ein wirklicher Mensch zu werden. Reden und Schriften aus ihrer Tübinger Zeit,* vol. 1, eds. Anne Fromman and Welf Schröter, 1989.

Stroemfeld Verlag for portions of Monika Treut, *Frauen und Film 36.*

Fromm International for permission to reprint Margarete Mitscherlich, "Aggression and Gender" and "Female Aggression—A Model?" from *The Peaceable Sex,* New York: Fromm International, 1985.

Margarete Mitscherlich—*Die friedfertige Frau* ©1985 S. Fischer Verlag GmbH, Frankfurt am Main. Alice Schwarzer—*Der "Kleine Unterschied" und seine grossen Folgen* © 1975 S. Fischer Verlag GmbH, Frankfurt am Main.

Berghahn Books for permission to reprint Luise F. Pusch, "Language Is Publicity for Men—but Enough Is Enough!" translated by Jeanette Clausen in *Gender and Germanness: Cultural Productions of Nation,* Patricia A. Herminghouse and Magda Mueller, eds., Providence: Berghahn Books, 1997.

Annette von Droste Hülshoff (1797–1848), "On the Tower" (Am Turme). English translation by Ruth Angress. Reprinted, by permission of The Feminist Press at The City University of New York, from *The Defiant Muse: German Feminist Poems from the Middle Ages to the Present, A Bilingual Anthology,* edited by Susan L. Cocalis. Translation copyright © 1986 by Ruth Angress. Compliation copyright © 1986 by Susan L. Cocalis.

Christiana Mariana von Ziegler (1695–1760), "In Praise of the Male Sex, as Seen by Certain Females" (Das männliche Geschlecht, im Namen einiger Frauenzimmer besungen). English translation by S. L. Cocalis and G. M. Geiger, Reprinted, by permission of The Feminist Press at The City University of New York, from *The Defiant Muse: German Feminist Poems from the Middle Ages to the Present, A Bilingual Anthology,* edited by Susan L. Cocalis. Translation copyright © 1986 by S. L. Cocalis and G. M. Geiger. Compilation copyright © 1986 by Susan L. Cocalis.

Frigga Haug, "The End of Socialism in Europe: A New Challenge for Socialist Feminism?" from *Beyond Female Masochism: Memory, Work, and Politics,* translated by Rodney Livingston, London: Verso, 1992, from pages 255–68.

Sidonie Hedwig Zäunemann (1714–40), "A Maid's Fortune" (Jungfern-Glück). English translation by S. L. Cocalis and G. M. Geiger. Reprinted, by permission of The Feminist Press at The City University of New York, from *The Defiant Muse: German Feminist Poems from the Middle Ages to the Present, A Bilingual Anthology*, edited by Susan L. Cocalis. Translation copyright © 1986 by S. L. Cocalis and G. M. Geiger. Compilation copyright © 1986 by Susan L. Cocalis.

Verena Stefan, "Cacophony." Translated from the German by Tobe Levin. Reprinted, by permission of The Feminist Press at The City University of New York, from Verena Stefan, *Shedding and Literally Dreaming* (1998). English-language translation copyright © 1994 by Tobe Levin.

The Women's Press, Ltd., for permission to reprint "Double Focus: On the History of Women's Writing," translated by Harriet Anderson, in *Feminist Aesthetics,* edited by Gisela Ecker, London: The Women's Press, 1985.

Libuše Moníková, "Some Theses Regarding Women's Writing," translated by Lynn E. Ries. Reprinted from *Women in German Yearbook 13: Feminist Studies in German Literature and Culture* edited by Sara Friedrichsmeyer and Patricia A. Herminghouse by permission of the University of Nebraska Press. © 1997 by the University of Nebraska Press.

State University of New York Press, "How It All Began: 'I Have Had an Abortion' " and "The Function of Sexuality in the Oppression of Women," by Alice Schwarzer, pp. 102–9. Reprinted by permission of the State University of New York Press © 1984, State University of New York. All rights reserved.

State University of New York Press, "A Marriage Proposal," from *The Education of Fanny Lewald: An Autobiography,* Hanna Ballin Lewis (Trans.), pp. 176–81. Reprinted by permission of the State University of New York Press © 1992, State University of New York. All rights reserved.